GARDNER'S
ART
through the
AGES

THE WESTERN PERSPECTIVE

THIRTEENTH EDITION

BACKPACK EDITION
Renaissance and Baroque

FRED S. KLEINER

WADSWORTH
CENGAGE Learning™

Australia • Brazil • Japan • Korea • Mexico • Singapore • Spain • United Kingdom • United States

WADSWORTH
CENGAGE Learning

Gardner's Art through the Ages: The Western Perspective, Thirteenth Edition, Renaissance and Baroque, Book C
Fred S. Kleiner

Publisher: Clark Baxter

Senior Development Editor: Sharon Adams Poore

Assistant Editor: Kimberly Apfelbaum

Editorial Assistant: Nell Pepper

Senior Media Editor: Wendy Constantine

Senior Marketing Manager: Diane Wenckebach

Marketing Communications Manager: Heather Baxley

Senior Project Manager, Editorial Production: Lianne Ames

Senior Art Director: Cate Rickard Barr

Senior Print Buyer: Judy Inouye

Production Service/Layout: Joan Keyes,
    Dovetail Publishing Services

Text Designer: tani hasegawa

Photo Researchers: Sarah Evertson, Stephen Forsling

Cover Designer: tani hasegawa

Cover Image: ARTEMISIA GENTILESCHI, *Self-Portrait as the Allegory of Painting,* ca. 1630. Oil on canvas, $3' 2\frac{7}{8}'' \times 2' 5\frac{5}{8}''$. Kensington Palace, London. The Royal Collection © 2008, Her Majesty Queen Elizabeth II.

Compositor: Thompson Type

For product information and technology assistance, contact us at
**Cengage Learning Academic Resource Center,
1-800-423-0563**
For permission to use material from this text or product, submit all requests online at **www.cengage.com/permissions.**
Further permissions questions can be emailed to
permissionrequest@cengage.com

Library of Congress Control Number: 2008938883

ISBN-13: 978-0-495-79456-1
ISBN-10: 0-495-79456-2

Wadsworth
25 Thomson Place
Boston, MA 02210-1202
USA

Cengage Learning products are represented in Canada by Nelson Education, Ltd.

For your course and learning solutions, visit **academic.cengage.com**

Purchase any of our products at your local college store or at our preferred online store **www.ichapters.com**

About the Cover Art

ARTEMISIA GENTILESCHI, *Self-Portrait as the Allegory of Painting*, ca.1638–1639. Oil on canvas, 3′ 2⅞″ × 2′ 5⅝″. Royal Collection, Kensington Palace, London.

Until 1593, when Cesare Ripa (d. 1622) published a handbook for artists called *Iconologia*, Painting, unlike Poetry and Music, did not have an established form of representation. The inclusion of Painting in Ripa's handbook reflected the newly elevated status of painters during the Italian Renaissance. Ripa's personification of *La Pittura* is a beautiful woman with disheveled hair painting with her brush in one hand and holding her palette in the other. She wears a gold chain with a pendant in the form of a mask, because masks imitate faces and painting is the art of imitation. The chain symbolizes the continuous linkage of master to pupil from generation to generation.

Artemisia Gentileschi (ca. 1593–1653), one of the first women artists in history to achieve international renown, followed Ripa's prescription closely in her *Self-Portrait as the Allegory of Painting*, but instead of representing *La Pittura* as a frontal, emblematic figure, she portrayed her as actively engaged in her craft, seen from her left side. The viewer's eyes follow the line of her left arm and shoulders through the curve of her shoulders and right arm to her right hand, the instrument of artistic genius. It is noteworthy that the canvas in this painting is blank. This is not a self-portrait of the artist at work on a specific painting but a portrait of Gentileschi as Painting herself. To create this self-portrait, Gentileschi had to set up two mirrors in order to record her features from an angle, a highly original break from tradition and an assertion of her supreme skill in a field dominated by men.

Similar celebrations of the artist as an inspired genius are common since the Renaissance, but before the 14th century most artists, both male and female, toiled in anonymity in the services of their patrons, whether Egyptian pharaohs, Roman emperors, or medieval bishops. *Art through the Ages* surveys the art of all periods from prehistory to the present and examines how artworks of all kinds, anonymous or signed, have always reflected the historical contexts in which they were created.

CONTENTS

PREFACE

When Helen Gardner published the first edition of *Art through the Ages* in 1926, she could not have imagined that more than 80 years later instructors all over the world would still be using her textbook in their classrooms. Indeed, if she were alive today, she would not recognize the book that long ago became—and remains—the most widely read introduction to the history of art and architecture in the English language. During the past half century, successive authors have constantly reinvented Helen Gardner's groundbreaking survey, always keeping it fresh and current, and setting an ever-higher standard in both content and publication quality with each new edition. I hope both professors and students will agree that this 13th edition lives up to that venerable tradition.

Certainly, this latest edition offers much that is fresh and new (enumerated below), but some things have not changed, including the fundamental belief that guided Helen Gardner—namely, that the primary goal of an introductory art history textbook should be to foster an appreciation and understanding of historically significant works of art of all kinds from all periods. Because of the longevity and diversity of the history of art, it is tempting to assign responsibility for telling its story to a large team of specialists. The Gardner publishers themselves took this approach for the first edition they produced after Helen Gardner's death, and it has now become the norm for introductory art history surveys. But students overwhelmingly say that the very complexity of the history of art makes it all the more important for the story to be told with a consistent voice if they are to master so much diverse material. I think Helen Gardner would be pleased to know that this new edition of *Art through the Ages* once again has a single storyteller.

Along with the late Richard Tansey and my more recent collaborator, Christin Mamiya, with whom I had the honor and pleasure of working on the 10th, 11th, and 12th editions, I continue to believe that the most effective way to tell the story of art through the ages, especially to someone studying art history for the first time, is to organize the vast array of artistic monuments according to the civilizations that produced them and to consider each work in roughly chronological order. This approach has not merely stood the test of time. It is the most appropriate way to narrate the *history* of art. The principle that underlies my approach to every period of art history is that the enormous variation in the form and meaning of the paintings, sculptures, buildings, and other artworks men and women have produced over the past 30,000 years is largely the result of the constantly changing contexts in which artists and architects worked. A historically based narrative is therefore best suited for a comprehensive history of art because it permits the author to situate each work discussed in its historical, social, economic, religious, and cultural context. That is, after all, what distinguishes art history from art appreciation.

In the first (1926) edition of *Art through the Ages,* Helen Gardner discussed Henri Matisse and Pablo Picasso in a chapter entitled "Contemporary Art in Europe and America." Since then many other artists have emerged on the international scene, and the story of art through the ages has grown longer and even more complex. More important, perhaps, the discipline of art history has changed markedly in recent decades, and so too has Helen Gardner's book. The 13th edition fully reflects the latest art historical research emphases while maintaining the traditional strengths that have made previous editions of *Art through the Ages* so popular. While sustaining attention to style, chronology, iconography, and technique, I also ensure that issues of patronage, function, and context loom large in every chapter. I treat artworks not as isolated objects in sterile 21st-century museum settings but with a view toward their purpose and meaning in the society that produced them at the time they were produced. I examine not only the role of the artist or architect in the creation of a work of art or a building, but also the role of the individuals or groups who paid the artists and influenced the shape the monuments took. Further, I devote more space than previously to the role of women and women artists in diverse societies over time. In every chapter, I have tried to choose artworks and buildings that reflect the increasingly wide range of interests of scholars today, while not rejecting the traditional list of "great" works or the very notion of a "canon." Consequently, the selection of works in this edition encompasses every artistic medium and almost every era and culture in the Western world, and includes many works that until recently art historians would not have considered to be "art" at all.

The 12th edition of *Art through the Ages* was the number-one choice for art history survey courses and the best-selling version of the book in its long history, and for this 13th edition I have retained all of the features that made its predecessor so successful. Once again, this edition, which contains 25 chapters on the Western tradition and its roots in the ancient Near East and Egypt, plus a chapter on Islamic art and architecture, boasts roughly 1,100 photographs, plans, and drawings, virtually all in color and reproduced according to the highest standards of clarity and color fidelity. The 13th edition, however, also features hundreds of new or upgraded photos by a host of new photographers as well as redesigned maps and plans and an extraordinary new set of architectural drawings prepared exclusively for *Art through the Ages* by John Burge.

The captions to the illustrations in this edition of *Art through the Ages*, as before, contain a wealth of information, including the name of the artist or architect, if known; the formal title (printed in italics), if assigned, description of the work, or name of the building; the provenance or place of production of the object or location of the building; the date; the material(s) used; the size; and the current location if the work is in a museum or private collection. As in previous editions, scales accompany all plans, but for the first time scales now also appear next to each photograph of a painting, statue, or other artwork. The works illustrated vary enormously in size, from colossal sculptures carved into mountain cliffs and paintings that cover entire walls or ceilings to tiny figurines, coins, and jewelry that one can hold in the hand. Although the captions contain the pertinent dimensions, it is hard for students who have never seen the paintings or statues in person to translate those dimensions into an appreciation of the real size of the objects. The new scales provide an effective and direct way to visualize how big or how small a given artwork is and its relative size compared with other objects in the same chapter and throughout the book.

Also new to this edition are the Quick-Review Captions that students found so useful when these were introduced in 2006 in the first edition of *Art through the Ages: A Concise History.* These brief synopses of the most significant aspects of each artwork or building illustrated accompany the captions to all images in the book. They have proved invaluable to students preparing for examinations in one-semester art history survey courses, and I am confident they will be equally useful to students enrolled in yearlong courses. In the 13th edition, however, I have provided two additional tools to aid students in reviewing and mastering the material. Each chapter now ends with a full-page feature called The Big Picture, which sets forth in bullet-point format the most important characteristics of each period or artistic movement discussed in the chapter. Small illustrations of characteristic works discussed accompany the summary of major points. Finally, I have attempted to tie all of the chapters together by providing with each copy of *Art through the Ages* a poster-size Global Timeline. This too features illustrations of key monuments of each age and geographical area as well as a brief enumeration of the most important art historical developments during that period. The timeline is global in scope to permit students in Western art courses to place developments in Europe and America in a worldwide context. The poster has four major horizontal bands corresponding to Europe, the Americas, Asia, and Africa, and 34 vertical columns for the successive chronological periods from 30,000 BCE to the present.

Another pedagogical tool not found in any other introductory art history textbook is the *Before 1300* section that appears at the beginning of Books C and D. Because many students taking the second half of a yearlong survey course will not have access to Books A and B, I have provided a special set of concise primers on religion and mythology and on architectural terminology and construction methods in the ancient and medieval worlds—information that is essential for understanding the history of Western art after 1300. The subjects of these special boxes are The Gods and Goddesses of Mount Olympus; The Life of Jesus in Art; Greco-Roman Temple Design and the Classical Orders; Arches and Vaults; and Medieval Church Design.

Boxed essays once again appear throughout the book as well. This popular feature first appeared in the 11th edition of *Art through the Ages*, which won both the Texty and McGuffey Prizes of the Text and Academic Authors Association for the best college textbook of 2001 in the humanities and social sciences. In this edition the essays are more closely tied to the main text than ever before. Consistent with that greater integration, most boxes now incorporate photographs of important artworks discussed in the text proper that also illustrate the theme treated in the boxed essays. These essays fall under six broad categories, one of which is new to the 13th edition.

Architectural Basics boxes provide students with a sound foundation for the understanding of architecture. These discussions are concise explanations, with drawings and diagrams, of the major aspects of design and construction. The information included is essential to an understanding of architectural technology and terminology. The boxes address questions of how and why various forms developed, the problems architects confronted, and the solutions they used to resolve them. Topics discussed include how the Egyptians built the pyramids, the orders of classical architecture, Roman concrete construction, and the design and terminology of mosques and Gothic cathedrals.

Materials and Techniques essays explain the various media artists employed from prehistoric to modern times. Since materials and techniques often influence the character of artworks, these discussions contain essential information on why many monuments appear as they do. Hollow-casting bronze statues; fresco painting; Islamic tile work; embroidery and tapestry; perspective; engraving, etching, and lithography; and daguerreotype and calotype photography are among the many subjects treated.

Religion and Mythology boxes introduce students to the principal elements of great religions, past and present, and to the representation of religious and mythological themes in painting and sculpture of all periods and places. These discussions of belief systems and iconography give readers a richer understanding of some of the greatest artworks ever created. The topics include the gods and goddesses of Egypt, Mesopotamia, Greece, and Rome; the life of Jesus in art; and Muhammad and Islam.

Art and Society essays treat the historical, social, political, cultural, and religious context of art and architecture. In some instances, specific monuments are the basis for a discussion of broader themes, as when the Hegeso stele serves as the springboard for an exploration of the role of women in ancient Greek society. Another essay discusses how people's evaluation today of artworks can differ from those of the society that produced them by examining the problems created by the contemporary market for undocumented archaeological finds. Other subjects include Egyptian mummification, Etruscan women, Byzantine icons and iconoclasm, artistic training in Renaissance Italy, 19th-century academic salons and independent art exhibitions, and public funding of controversial art.

Written Sources present and discuss key historical documents illuminating important monuments of art and architecture throughout the Western world. The passages quoted permit voices from the past to speak directly to the reader, providing vivid and unique insights into the creation of artworks in all media. Examples include Bernard of Clairvaux's treatise on sculpture in medieval churches, Giovanni Pietro Bellori's biographies of Annibale Carracci and Caravaggio, Jean François Marmontel's account of 18th-century salon culture, as well as texts that bring the past to life, such as eyewitness accounts of the volcanic eruption that buried Roman Pompeii and of the fire that destroyed Canterbury Cathedral in medieval England.

A new category is *Artists on Art* in which artists and architects throughout history discuss both their theories and individual works. Examples include Sinan the Great discussing the mosque he designed for Selim II, Leonardo da Vinci and Michelangelo debating the relative merits of painting and sculpture, Artemisia Gentileschi talking about the special problems she confronted as a woman artist, Jacques-Louis David on Neoclassicism, Gustave Courbet on Realism, Henri

Matisse on color, Pablo Picasso on Cubism, Diego Rivera on art for the people, and Judy Chicago on her seminal work *The Dinner Party.*

Instructors familiar with previous editions of *Art through the Ages* will also find that many of the chapters in the 13th edition have been reorganized, especially in volume two. For example, the treatment of European 17th-century art now appears in two discrete chapters, one devoted to Baroque Italy and Spain, the other to Northern Europe. A single chapter is devoted to the 18th century, another to the period from 1800 to 1870, and a third to 1870 to 1900. In addition, in recognition that different instructors at different colleges and universities end the first semester and begin the second semester at different points, for the first time *two* volumes of *Art through the Ages* include Chapter 14 on Italian art from 1200 to 1400. And *The Western Perspective* is now also available in this special backpack edition consisting of four, rather than the traditional two, paperback volumes: Book A (Antiquity: Chapters 1–7), Book B (The Middle Ages: Chapters 8–14), Book C (Renaissance and Baroque: Chapters 14–20), and Book D (Modern Europe and America: Chapters 21–25). These books can also be purchased separately.

Rounding out the features in the book itself is a Glossary containing definitions of all terms introduced in the text in italics and a Bibliography of books in English, including both general works and a chapter-by-chapter list of more focused studies. In this edition I have also taken care to italicize and define in the text all Glossary terms that appear in Books C and D even if they have been used and defined in Books A and B, because many students enrolled in the second semester of a yearlong course will not have taken the first semester and will not be familiar with those terms.

The 13th edition of *Art through the Ages* is not, however, a stand-alone text, but one element of a complete package of learning tools. In addition to the Global Timeline, every new copy of the book comes with a password to *ArtStudy Online,* a web site with access to a host of multimedia resources that students can employ throughout the entire course, including image flashcards, tutorial quizzes, podcasts, vocabulary, and more. Instructors have access to a host of teaching materials, including digital images with zoom capabilities, video, and Google™ Earth coordinates.

A work as extensive as this history of art could not be undertaken or completed without the counsel of experts in all areas of Western art. As with previous editions, the publisher has enlisted more than a hundred art historians to review every chapter in order to ensure that the text lived up to the Gardner reputation for accuracy as well as readability. I take great pleasure in acknowledging here the invaluable contributions to the 13th edition of *Art through the Ages: The Western Perspective* made by the following for their critiques of various chapters: Charles M. Adelman, University of Northern Iowa; Kirk Ambrose, University of Colorado–Boulder; Susan Ashbrook, Art Institute of Boston; Zainab Bahrani, Columbia University; Susan Bakewell, University of Texas–Austin; James J. Bloom, Florida State University; Suzaan Boettger, Bergen Community College; Colleen Bolton, Mohawk Valley Community College; Angi Elsea Bourgeois, Mississippi State University; Kimberly Bowes, Fordham University; Elizabeth Bredrup, St. Christopher's School; Lawrence E. Butler, George Mason University; Alexandra Carpino, Northern Arizona University; Jane Carroll, Dartmouth College; Hipolito Rafael Chacon, The University of Montana; Catherine M. Chastain, North Georgia College & State University; Violaine Chauvet, Johns Hopkins University; Daniel Connolly, Augustana College; Michael A. Coronel, University of Northern Colorado; Nicole Cox, Rochester Institute of Technology; Jodi Cranston, Boston University; Giovanna De Appolonia, Boston University; Marion de Koning, Grossmont College; John J. Dobbins, University of Virginia; Erika Doss, University of Colorado–Boulder;

B. Underwood DuRette, Thomas Nelson Community College; Lisa Farber, Pace University; James Farmer, Virginia Commonwealth University; Sheila ffolliott, George Mason University; Ferdinanda Florence, Solano Community College; William B. Folkestad, Central Washington University; Jeffery Fontana, Austin College; Mitchell Frank, Carleton University; Sara L. French, Wells College; Norman P. Gambill, South Dakota State University; Elise Goodman, University of Cincinnati; Kim T. Grant, University of Southern Maine; Elizabeth ten Grotenhuis, Silk Road Project; Sandra C. Haynes, Pasadena City College; Valerie Hedquist, The University of Montana; Susan Hellman, Northern Virginia Community College; Marian J. Hollinger, Fairmont State University; Cheryl Hughes, Alta High School; Heidrun Hultgren, Kent State University; Joseph M. Hutchinson, Texas A&M University; Julie M. Johnson, Utah State University; Sandra L. Johnson, Citrus College; Deborah Kahn, Boston University; Fusae Kanda, Harvard University; Catherine Karkov, Miami University; Wendy Katz, University of Nebraska–Lincoln; Nita Kehoe-Gadway, Central Wyoming College; Nancy L. Kelker, Middle Tennessee State University; Cathie Kelly, University of Nevada–Las Vegas; Katie Kempton, Ohio University; John F. Kenfield, Rutgers University; Herbert L. Kessler, Johns Hopkins University; Monica Kjellman-Chapin, Emporia State University; Ellen Konowitz, State University of New York–New Paltz; Kathryn E. Kramer, State University of New York–Cortland; Carol Krinsky, New York University; Lydia Lehr, Atlantic Cape Community College; Krist Lien, Shelton State Community College; Ellen Longsworth, Merrimack College; David A. Ludley, Clayton State University; Henry Luttikhuizen, Calvin College; Christina Maranci, University of Wisconsin–Milwaukee; Dominic Marner, University of Guelph; Jack Brent Maxwell, Blinn College; Anne McClanan, Portland State University; Brian McConnell, Florida Atlantic University; Heather McPherson, University of Alabama–Birmingham; Cynthia Millis, Houston Community College–Southwest; Cynthia Taylor Mills, Brookhaven College; Keith N. Morgan, Boston University; Johanna D. Movassat, San Jose State University; Helen Nagy, University of Puget Sound; Heidi Nickisher, Rochester Institute of Technology; Bonnie Noble, University of North Carolina–Charlotte; Abigail Noonan, Rochester Institute of Technology; Marjorie Och, University of Mary Washington; Karen Michelle O'Day, University of Wisconsin–Eau Claire; Edward J. Olszewski, Case Western Reserve University; Allison Lee Palmer, University of Oklahoma; Martin Patrick, Illinois State University; Glenn Peers, University of Texas–Austin; Jane Peters, University of Kentucky; Julie Anne Plax, University of Arizona; Frances Pohl, Pomona College; Virginia C. Raguin, College of the Holy Cross; Donna Karen Reid, Chemeketa Community College; Albert W. Reischuch, Kent State University; Jonathan Ribner, Boston University; Cynthea Riesenberg, Washington Latin School; James G. Rogers Jr., Florida Southern College; Carey Rote, Texas A&M University–Corpus Christi; David J. Roxburgh, Harvard University; Conrad Rudolph, University of California–Riverside; Catherine B. Scallen, Case Western Reserve University; Denise Schmandt-Besserat, University of Texas–Austin; Natasha Seaman, Berklee College of Music; Malia E. Serrano, Grossmont College; Laura Sommer, Daemen College; Natasha Staller, Amherst College; Nancy Steele-Hamme, Midwestern State University; Andrew Stewart, University of California–Berkeley; Francesca Tronchin, Ohio State University; Frances Van Keuren, University of Georgia; Kelly Wacker, University of Montevallo; Carolynne Whitefeather, Utica College; Nancy L. Wicker, University of Mississippi; Alastair Wright, Princeton University; John G. Younger, University of Kansas; Michael Zell, Boston University.

I am also happy to have this opportunity to express my gratitude to the extraordinary group of people at Wadsworth involved with the editing, production, and distribution of *Art through the Ages.* Some of them I have now worked with on various projects for more than a decade and feel privileged to count among my friends. The success of the Gardner series in all of its various permutations depends in no small part on the expertise and unflagging commitment of these dedicated professionals: Sean Wakely, executive vice president, Cengage Arts and Sciences; P. J. Boardman, vice president, editor-in-chief of Cengage Learning Arts and Sciences; Clark Baxter, publisher; Sharon Adams Poore, senior development editor; Helen Triller-Yambert, development editor; Lianne Ames, senior content project manager; Wendy Constantine, senior media editor; Kimberly Apfelbaum, assistant editor; Nell Pepper, editorial assistant; Cate Rikard Barr, senior art director; Scott Stewart, vice president managing director sales; Diane Wenckebach, senior marketing manager; as well as Kim Adams, Heather Baxley, William Christy, Doug Easton, tani hasegawa, Cara Murphy, Ellen Pettengell, Kathryn Stewart, and Joy Westberg.

I am also deeply grateful to the following for their significant contributions to the 13th edition of *Art through the Ages:* Joan Keyes, Dovetail Publishing Services; Ida May Norton, copy editor; Sarah Evertson and Stephen Forsling, photo researchers; Pete Shanks and Jon Peck, accuracy readers; Pat Lewis, proofreader; John Pierce, Thompson Type; Rick Stanley, Digital Media Inc., U.S.A; Don Larson, Mapping Specialists; Anne Draus, Scratchgravel; Cindy Geiss, Graphic World; and, of course, John Burge, for his superb architectural drawings. I also wish to acknowledge my debt to Edward Tufte for an illuminating afternoon spent discussing publication design and production issues and for his invaluable contribution to the creation of the scales that accompany all reproductions of paintings, sculptures, and other artworks in this edition.

Finally, I owe thanks to my colleagues at Boston University and to the thousands of students and the scores of teaching fellows in my art history courses during the past three decades. From them I have learned much that has helped determine the form and content of *Art through the Ages* and made it a much better book than it otherwise might have been.

Fred S. Kleiner

About the Author

FRED S. KLEINER (Ph.D., Columbia University) is the co-author of the 10th, 11th, and 12th editions of *Art through the Ages* and more than a hundred publications on Greek and Roman art and architecture, including *A History of Roman Art,* also published by Wadsworth. He has taught the art history survey course for more than three decades, first at the University of Virginia and, since 1978, at Boston University, where he is currently Professor of Art History and Archaeology and Chair of the Art History Department. Long recognized for his inspiring lectures and devotion to students, Professor Kleiner won Boston University's Metcalf Award for Excellence in Teaching as well as the College Prize for Undergraduate Advising in the Humanities in 2002 and is a two-time winner of the Distinguished Teaching Prize in the College of Arts and Sciences Honors Program. He was Editor-in-Chief of the *American Journal of Archaeology* from 1985 to 1998.

A History of Roman Art (Wadsworth 2007; ISBN 0534638465)

Gardner's Art through the Ages: Non-Western Perspectives, Thirteenth Edition (Wadsworth 2010; ISBN 0495573671)

RESOURCES

FOR FACULTY

PowerLecture with Digital Image Library and JoinIn™ on Turning Point®
ISBN 0495792888

Bring digital images into the classroom with this one-stop lecture and class presentation tool that makes it easy to assemble, edit, and present customized lectures for your course using Microsoft Power-Point™. Available on the PowerLecture DVD, the Digital Image Library provides high-resolution images (maps, illustrations, and fine art images from the text) for lecture presentations, either in an easy-to-use PowerPoint presentation format, or in individual file formats compatible with other image-viewing software. The zoom feature allows you to magnify selected portions of an image for more detailed display, and another setting enables you to show images side by side for purposes of comparison. You can readily customize your classroom presentation by adding your personal visuals to those from the text. The PowerLecture also includes **Google™Earth** coordinates that allow you to zoom in on an entire city, as well as key monuments and buildings within it. Also included are panoramic video clips of architectural landmarks in New York City discussed in the text. Using a navigation bar on the video, you can move around the structure and zoom in/out, and right/left, to add a three-dimensional experience to your presentation.

This PowerLecture DVD also includes a Resource Integration Guide, an electronic Instructor's Manual, and a Test Bank with multiple-choice, matching, short-answer, and essay questions in ExamView® computerized format.

Text-specific Microsoft PowerPoint slides have been created for use with JoinIn™ software for classroom personal response systems ("clickers").

WebTutor on Blackboard or WebCT
WebCT ISBN: 0495792608
BlackBoard ISBN: 0495792586

This package allows you to assign preformatted, text-specific content that is available as soon as you log on, or customize the learning environment in any way you choose—from uploading images and other resources, to adding Web links to create your own practice materials.

Contact your Wadsworth representative.

FOR STUDENTS

ArtStudy Online

This tool gives access to a host of multimedia resources, including **flashcards** of works in the text, and a compare-and-contrast feature, where two works are displayed side by side for more in-depth analysis. Other features include critical-thinking questions, interactive maps, architectural basics materials, big picture overviews, multimedia mini-lectures, video clips of select architectural monuments, museum guide with links, **Google™Earth** coordinates, Student Test Packet, audio study tools, vocabulary of art history, a guide to researching art history online, tips on becoming a successful student and links to beneficial Web sites on art, artists, architecture and more, and tips on becoming a successful student of art and art history.

Slide Guide *Contact your Wadsworth representative.*

This lecture companion allows students to take notes alongside representations of the art images shown in class. New to this edition's slide guide are two features—the use of **Google™Earth** coordinates to link satellite images of historic sites and images to textual references, and end-of-chapter questions.

Web Site

Instructors and students have access to a comprehensive array of teaching and learning resources, including chapter-by-chapter online tutorial quizzes, a final exam, chapter reviews, chapter-by-chapter Web links, glossary flashcards, and more.

If you are interested in bundling any of the preceding student resources with the text, contact your Wadsworth sales representative.

To order student editions packaged with the Timeline and ArtStudy Online at no extra cost to students, use the following ISBNs:

Gardner's Art through the Ages: The Western Perspective, 13e
ISBN: 0495573558

Gardner's Art through the Ages: The Western Perspective, 13e
Volume I
ISBN: 0495573604

Gardner's Art through the Ages: The Western Perspective, 13e
Volume II
ISBN: 0495573647

Gardner's Art through the Ages: The Western Perspective, 13e
Backpack edition
ISBN: 049579442

To order the Backpack edition (Books A, B, C, and D):

Gardner's Art through the Ages: The Western Perspective, 13e
Book A *Antiquity*
ISBN: 0495794481

Gardner's Art through the Ages: The Western Perspective, 13e
Book B *The Middle Ages*
ISBN: 049579452X

Gardner's Art through the Ages: The Western Perspective, 13e
Book C *Renaissance and Baroque*
ISBN: 0495794562

Gardner's Art through the Ages: The Western Perspective, 13e
Book D *Modern Europe and America*
ISBN: 0495794627

BEFORE 1300

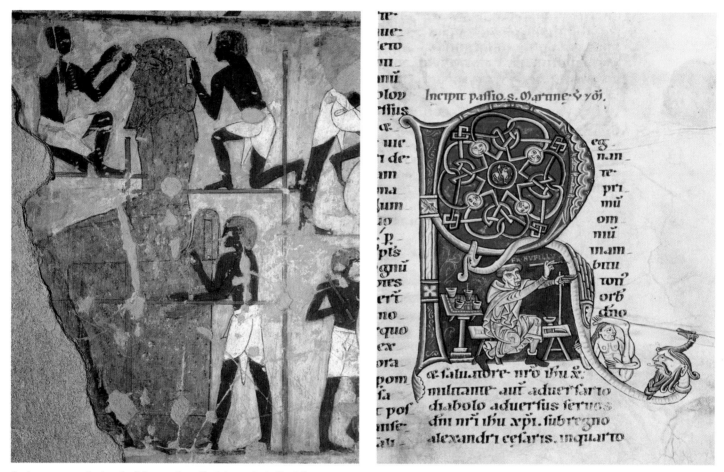

Sculptors at work, detail of the south wall of the main hall of the funerary chapel of Rekhmire, Thebes, Egypt, 18th Dynasty, ca. 1425 BCE.

RUFILLUS, Initial R, folio 244 recto of a Passional, from Weissenau, Germany, ca. 1170–1200. Bibliotheca Bodmeriana, Geneva.

BEFORE 1300
Contents

The Gods and Goddesses of Mount Olympus

The chief deities of the Greeks ruled the world from their home on Mount Olympus, Greece's highest peak. They figure prominently not only in Greek, Etruscan, and Roman art but also in art from the Renaissance to the present.

The 12 Olympian gods (and their Roman equivalents) were

- *Zeus* (*Jupiter*) King of the gods, Zeus ruled the sky and allotted the sea to his brother Poseidon and the Underworld to his other brother Hades. His weapon was the thunderbolt. Jupiter was also the chief god of the Romans.

- *Hera* (*Juno*) Wife and sister of Zeus, Hera was the goddess of marriage.

- *Poseidon* (*Neptune*) Poseidon was lord of the sea. He controlled waves, storms, and earthquakes with his three-pronged pitchfork (*trident*).

- *Hestia* (*Vesta*) Sister of Zeus, Poseidon, and Hera, Hestia was goddess of the hearth.

- *Demeter* (*Ceres*) Third sister of Zeus, Demeter was the goddess of grain and agriculture.

- *Ares* (*Mars*) God of war, Ares was the son of Zeus and Hera and the lover of Aphrodite, and the father of the twin founders of Rome, Romulus and Remus.

- *Athena* (*Minerva*) Goddess of wisdom and warfare, Athena was a virgin born from the head of Zeus.

- *Hephaistos* (*Vulcan*) God of fire and of metalworking, Hephaistos was the son of Zeus and Hera. Born lame and, uncharacteristically for a god, ugly, he married Aphrodite, who was unfaithful to him.

- *Apollo* (*Apollo*) God of light and music and son of Zeus, the young, beautiful Apollo was sometimes identified with the sun (*Helios/Sol*).

- *Artemis* (*Diana*) Sister of Apollo, Artemis was goddess of the hunt. She was occasionally equated with the moon (*Selene/Luna*).

- *Aphrodite* (*Venus*) Daughter of Zeus and a *nymph* (goddess of springs and woods), Aphrodite was the goddess of love and beauty.

- *Hermes* (*Mercury*) Son of Zeus and another nymph, Hermes was the fleet-footed messenger of the gods. He carried the *caduceus*, a magical herald's rod.

Other important Greek gods and goddesses were

- *Hades* (*Pluto*), lord of the Underworld and god of the dead. Although the brother of Zeus and Poseidon, Hades never resided on Mount Olympus.

- *Dionysos* (*Bacchus*), god of wine.

- *Eros* (*Amor* or *Cupid*), the winged child-god of love, son of Aphrodite and Ares.

- *Asklepios* (*Aesculapius*), god of healing. His serpent-entwined staff is the emblem of modern medicine.

Zeus, from Cape Artemision, ca. 460–450 BCE

Athena, by Phidias, ca. 438 BCE

Aphrodite, by Praxiteles, ca. 350–340 BCE

Hermes and infant Dionysos, by Praxiteles, ca. 340 BCE

The Life of Jesus in Art

Christians believe that Jesus of Nazareth is the son of God, the *Messiah* (Savior, Christ) of the Jews prophesied in the Old Testament. His life—his miraculous birth from the womb of a virgin mother, his preaching and miracle working, his execution by the Romans and subsequent ascent to Heaven—has been the subject of countless artworks from Roman times through the present day.

INCARNATION AND CHILDHOOD

The first "cycle" of the life of Jesus consists of the events of his conception (Incarnation), birth, infancy, and childhood.

▐ *Annunciation to Mary* The archangel Gabriel announces to the Virgin Mary that she will miraculously conceive and give birth to God's son Jesus.

▐ *Visitation* The pregnant Mary visits her cousin Elizabeth, who is pregnant with John the Baptist. Elizabeth is the first to recognize that Mary is bearing the Son of God.

▐ *Nativity*, *Annunciation to the Shepherds*, and *Adoration of the Shepherds* Jesus is born at night in Bethlehem and placed in a basket. Mary and her husband Joseph marvel at the newborn, while an angel announces the birth of the Savior to shepherds in the field, who rush to adore the child.

▐ *Adoration of the Magi* A bright star alerts three wise men (*magi*) in the East that the King of the Jews has been born. They travel 12 days to present precious gifts to the infant Jesus.

▐ *Presentation in the Temple* In accordance with Jewish tradition, Mary and Joseph bring their firstborn son to the temple in Jerusalem, where the aged Simeon recognizes Jesus as the prophesied Savior of humankind.

▐ *Massacre of the Innocents* and *Flight into Egypt* King Herod, fearful that a rival king has been born, orders the massacre of all infants, but the Holy Family escapes to Egypt.

▐ *Dispute in the Temple* Joseph and Mary travel to Jerusalem for the feast of Passover. Jesus, only a boy, debates the astonished Jewish scholars in the temple, foretelling his ministry.

PUBLIC MINISTRY

The public-ministry cycle comprises the teachings of Jesus and the miracles he performed.

▐ *Baptism* The beginning of Jesus' public ministry is marked by his baptism at age 30 by John the Baptist in the Jordan River. God's voice is heard proclaiming Jesus as his son.

▐ *Calling of Matthew* Jesus summons Matthew, a tax collector, to follow him, and Matthew becomes one of his 12 disciples, or *apostles* (from the Greek for "messenger").

▐ *Miracles* Jesus performs many miracles, revealing his divine nature. These include acts of healing and raising the dead, turning water into wine, walking on water and calming storms, and creating wondrous quantities of food.

▐ *Delivery of the Keys to Peter* Jesus chooses the fisherman Peter (whose name means "rock") as his successor. He declares that Peter is the rock on which his church will be built and symbolically delivers to Peter the keys to the kingdom of Heaven.

▐ *Transfiguration* Jesus scales a mountain and, in the presence of Peter and two other disciples, is transformed into radiant light. God announces from a cloud that Jesus is his son.

▐ *Cleansing of the Temple* Jesus returns to Jerusalem, where he finds money changers and merchants conducting business in the temple. He rebukes them and drives them out.

Annunciation and Visitation, Reims Cathedral, ca. 1230

Annunciation to the Shepherds, *Lectionary of Henry II*, 1002–1014

PASSION

The Passion (Latin *passio*, "suffering") cycle includes the events leading to Jesus' death, Resurrection, and ascent to Heaven.

▌ *Entry into Jerusalem* On the Sunday before his Crucifixion (Palm Sunday), Jesus rides into Jerusalem on a donkey.

▌ *Last Supper* In Jerusalem, Jesus celebrates Passover with his disciples. During this Last Supper, Jesus foretells his imminent betrayal, arrest, and death and invites the disciples to remember him when they eat bread (symbol of his body) and drink wine (his blood). This ritual became the celebration of *Mass* (*Eucharist*).

▌ *Agony in the Garden* Jesus goes to the Mount of Olives in the Garden of Gethsemane, where he struggles to overcome his human fear of death by praying for divine strength.

▌ *Betrayal* and *Arrest* The disciple Judas Iscariot betrays Jesus to the Jewish authorities for 30 pieces of silver. Judas identifies Jesus to the soldiers by kissing him, and Jesus is arrested.

▌ *Trials of Jesus* Jesus is brought before Caiaphas, the Jewish high priest, who interrogates Jesus about his claim to be the Messiah. Jesus is then brought before the Roman governor of Judaea, Pontius Pilate, on the charge of treason because he had proclaimed himself King of the Jews. Pilate asks the crowd to choose between freeing Jesus or Barabbas, a murderer. The people choose Barabbas, and the judge condemns Jesus to death.

▌ *Flagellation* The Roman soldiers who hold Jesus captive whip (flagellate) him and mock him by dressing him as King of the Jews and placing a crown of thorns on his head.

▌ *Carrying of the Cross, Raising of the Cross*, and *Crucifixion* The Romans force Jesus to carry the cross on which he will be crucified from Jerusalem to Mount Calvary. Soldiers erect the cross and nail Jesus' hands and feet to it. Jesus' mother, John the Evangelist, and Mary Magdalene mourn at the foot of the cross, while soldiers torment Jesus. One of them stabs Jesus in the side with a spear. After suffering great pain, Jesus dies on Good Friday.

▌ *Deposition, Lamentation*, and *Entombment* Two disciples, Joseph of Arimathea and Nicodemus, remove Jesus' body from the cross (Deposition) and take him to his tomb. Joseph, Nicodemus, the Virgin Mary, Saint John the Evangelist, and Mary Magdalene mourn over the dead Jesus (Lamentation). (When in art the isolated figure of the Virgin Mary cradles her dead son in her lap, it is called a *Pietà*—Italian for "pity.") Then his followers lower Jesus into a sarcophagus in the tomb (Entombment).

▌ *Descent into Limbo* During the three days he spends in the tomb, Jesus (after death, Christ) descends into Hell, or Limbo, and frees the souls of the righteous, including Adam, Eve, Moses, David, Solomon, and John the Baptist.

▌ *Resurrection* and *Three Marys at the Tomb* On the third day (Easter Sunday), Christ rises from the dead and leaves the tomb. The Virgin Mary, Mary Magdalene, and Mary, the mother of James, visit the tomb, find it empty, and learn from an angel that Christ has been resurrected.

▌ *Noli Me Tangere, Supper at Emmaus,* and *Doubting of Thomas* During the 40 days between Christ's Resurrection and his ascent to Heaven, he appears on several occasions to his followers. Christ warns Mary Magdalene, weeping at his tomb, with the words "Don't touch me" (*Noli me tangere* in Latin). At Emmaus he eats supper with two astonished disciples. Later, Thomas, who cannot believe that Christ has risen, touches the wound in his side inflicted at the Crucifixion.

▌ *Ascension* On the 40th day, on the Mount of Olives, with his mother and apostles as witnesses, Christ gloriously ascends to Heaven in a cloud.

Crucifixion, Church of the Dormition, Daphni, ca. 1090–1100

Ascension, *Rabbula Gospels*, 586

Greco-Roman Temple Design and the Classical Orders

The gable-roofed columnar stone temples of the Greeks and Romans have had more influence on the later history of architecture in the Western world than any other building type ever devised. Many of the elements of classical temple architecture are present in buildings from the Renaissance to the present day. The basic design principles of Greek and Roman temples and the most important components of the classical orders can be summarized as follows.

■ *Temple design* The core of a Greco-Roman temple was the *cella,* a room with no windows that usually housed the statue of the god or goddess to whom the shrine was dedicated. Generally, only the priests, priestesses, and chosen few would enter the cella. Worshipers gathered in front of the building, where sacrifices occurred at open-air altars. In most Greek temples, for example, the second temple erected in honor of Hera at Paestum, a *colonnade* was erected all around the cella to form a *peristyle.* In contrast, Roman temples, for example, the Temple of Portunus in Rome, usually have freestanding columns only in a porch at the front of the building. Sometimes, as in the Portunus temple, *engaged* (attached) half-columns adorn three sides of the cella to give the building the appearance of a *peripteral* temple. Architectural historians call this a *pseudoperipteral* design.

■ *Classical orders* The Greeks developed two basic architectural orders, or design systems: the *Doric* and the *Ionic.* The forms of the columns and *entablature* (superstructure) generally differentiate the orders. Classical columns have two or three parts, depending on the order: the shaft, which is usually marked with vertical channels (*flutes*); the *capital*; and, in the Ionic order, the *base.* The Doric capital consists of a round *echinus* beneath a square abacus block. Spiral *volutes* constitute the distinctive feature of the Ionic capital. Classical entablatures have three parts: the *architrave,* the *frieze,* and the triangular *pediment* of the gabled roof, framed by the *cornice.* In the Doric order, the frieze is subdivided into *triglyphs* and *metopes,* whereas in the Ionic, the frieze is left open.

The *Corinthian capital,* a later Greek invention very popular in Roman times, is more ornate than either the Doric or Ionic. It consists of a double row of acanthus leaves, from which tendrils and flowers emerge. Although this capital often is cited as the distinguishing element of the Corinthian order, in strict terms no Corinthian order exists. Architects simply substituted the new capital type for the volute capital in the Ionic order, as in the *tholos* (round temple) at Epidauros.

Sculpture played a major role on the exterior of classical temples, partly to embellish the deity's shrine and partly to tell something about the deity to those gathered outside. Sculptural ornament was concentrated on the upper part of the building, in the pediment and frieze.

Doric and Ionic orders

Greek Doric peripteral temple (Temple of Hera II, Paestum, Italy, ca. 460 BCE)

Roman Ionic pseudoperipteral temple
(Temple of Portunus, Rome, ca. 75 BCE)

Corinthian capital (Tholos, Epidauros, Greece, ca. 350 BCE)

Arches and Vaults

Although earlier architects used both arches and vaults, the Romans employed them more extensively and effectively than any other ancient civilization. The Roman forms became staples of architectural design from the Middle Ages until today.

▌ *Arch* The arch is one of several ways of spanning a passageway. The Romans preferred it to the *post-and-lintel* (column-and-architrave) system used in the Greek orders. Builders construct arches using wedge-shaped stone blocks called *voussoirs*. The central voussoir is the arch's *keystone*.

▌ *Barrel vault* Also called the *tunnel vault*, the barrel vault is an extension of a simple arch, creating a semicylindrical ceiling over parallel walls.

▌ *Groin vault* The groin vault, or *cross vault*, is formed by the intersection at right angles of two barrel vaults of equal size. When a series of groin vaults covers an interior hall, the open lateral arches of the vaults function as windows admitting light to the building.

▌ *Dome* The hemispherical dome may be described as a round arch rotated around the full circumference of a circle, usually resting on a cylindrical *drum*. The Romans normally constructed domes using *concrete*, a mix of lime mortar, volcanic sand, water, and small stones, instead of with large stone blocks. Concrete dries to form a solid mass of great strength, which allowed the Romans to puncture the apex of a concrete dome with an *oculus* (eye), so that much-needed light could reach the interior of the building.

Barrel vaults, as noted, resemble tunnels, and groin vaults are usually found in a series covering a similar *longitudinally* oriented interior space. Domes, in contrast, crown *centrally* planned buildings, so named because the structure's parts are of equal or almost equal dimensions around the center.

Arch

Barrel vault

Groin vault

Hemispherical dome with oculus

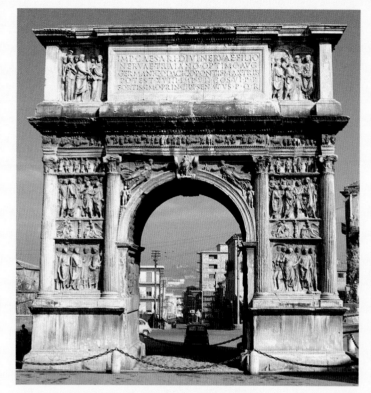

Roman arch (Arch of Trajan, Benevento, Italy, ca. 114–118)

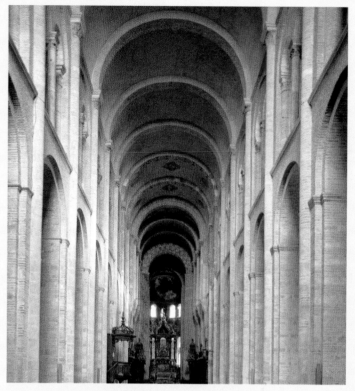

Medieval barrel-vaulted church
(Saint-Sernin, Toulouse, France, ca. 1070–1120)

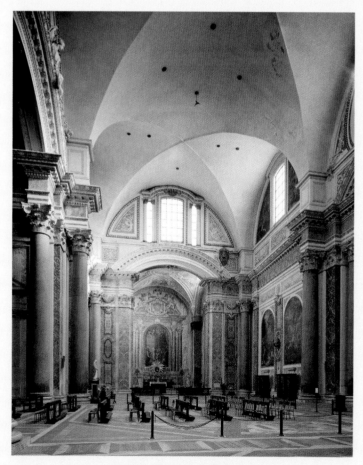

Roman hall with groin vaults
(Baths of Diocletian [Santa Maria degli Angeli],
Rome, Italy, ca. 298–306)

Roman dome with oculus (Pantheon, Rome, Italy, 118–125)

Medieval Church Design

Church design during the Middle Ages set the stage for ecclesiastical architecture from the Renaissance to the present. Both the longitudinal- and central-plan building types of antiquity had a long postclassical history.

▌ *Basilican churches* In Western Christendom, the typical medieval church had a *basilican* plan, which evolved from the Roman columnar hall, or basilica. The great European cathedrals of the Gothic age, which were the immediate predecessors of the churches of the Renaissance and Baroque eras, shared many elements with the earliest basilican churches constructed during the fourth century, including a wide central *nave* flanked by *aisles* and ending in an *apse*. Some basilican churches also have a *transept*, an area perpendicular to the nave. The nave and transept intersect at the *crossing*. Gothic

churches, however, have many additional features. The key components of Gothic design are labeled in the drawing of a typical French Gothic cathedral and the plan of Chartres Cathedral.

Gothic architects frequently extended the aisles around the apse to form an *ambulatory*, onto which opened *radiating chapels* housing sacred relics. Groin vaults formed the ceiling of the nave, aisles, ambulatory, and transept alike, replacing the timber roof of the typical Early Christian basilica. These vaults rested on *diagonal* and *transverse ribs* in the form of pointed arches. On the exterior, *flying buttresses* held the nave vaults in place. These masonry struts transferred the thrust of the nave vaults across the roofs of the aisles to tall piers frequently capped by pointed ornamental *pinnacles*. This structural system made it possible to open up the walls above the *nave arcade* with huge *stained-glass* windows in the nave *clerestory*.

Plan of Chartres Cathedral, Chartres, France, rebuilt after 1194

Left: Cutaway view of a typical French Gothic cathedral
(1) pinnacle, (2) flying buttress, (3) vaulting web,
(4) diagonal rib, (5) transverse rib, (6) springing,
(7) clerestory, (8) oculus, (9) lancet, (10) triforium,
(11) nave arcade, (12) compound pier with responds

Central-plan churches The domed central plan of classical antiquity dominated the architecture of the Byzantine Empire but with important modifications. Because the dome covered the crossing of a Byzantine church, architects had to find a way to erect domes on square bases instead of on the circular bases (cylindrical drums) of Roman buildings. The solution was *pendentive* construction in which the dome rests on what is in effect a second, larger dome. The top portion and four segments around the rim of the larger dome are omitted, creating four curved triangles, or pendentives. The pendentives join to form a ring and four arches whose planes bound a square. The first use of pendentives on a grand scale occurred in the sixth-century church of Hagia Sophia (Holy Wisdom) in Constantinople.

The interiors of Byzantine churches differed from those of basilican churches in the West not only in plan and the use of domes but also in the manner in which they were adorned. The original mosaic decoration of Hagia Sophia is lost, but at Saint Mark's in Venice, some 40,000 square feet of mosaics cover all the walls, arches, vaults, and domes.

Hagia Sophia, Constantinople (Istanbul), Turkey, 532–537

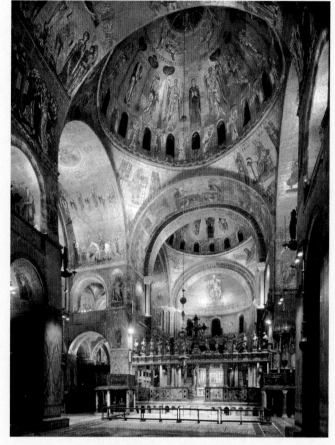

Saint Mark's, Venice, Italy, begun 1063

Pendentives

Dome on pendentives

1 ft.

I-1 CLYFFORD STILL, *1948-C, PH-15,* 1948. Oil on canvas, 6′ 8$\frac{7}{8}$″ × 5′ 10$\frac{3}{4}$″. Hirshhorn Museum and Sculpture Garden, Smithsonian Institution, Washington, D.C. (purchased with funds of Joseph H. Hirshhorn, 1992).

Clyfford Still painted this abstract composition without knowing who would purchase it or where it would be displayed, but throughout history most artists created works for specific patrons and settings.

INTRODUCTION: WHAT IS ART HISTORY?

Except when referring to the modern academic discipline, people do not often juxtapose the words "art" and "history." They tend to think of history as the record and interpretation of past human actions, particularly social and political actions. Most think of art, quite correctly, as part of the present—as something people can see and touch. Of course, people cannot see or touch history's vanished human events, but a visible, tangible artwork is a kind of persisting event. One or more artists made it at a certain time and in a specific place, even if no one today knows just who, when, where, or why. Although created in the past, an artwork continues to exist in the present, long surviving its times. The first painters and sculptors died 30,000 years ago, but their works remain, some of them exhibited in glass cases in museums built only a few years ago.

Modern museum visitors can admire these objects from the remote past—and countless others humankind has produced over the millennia—without any knowledge of the circumstances that led to the creation of those works. The beauty or sheer size of an object can impress people, the artist's virtuosity in the handling of ordinary or costly materials can dazzle them, or the subject depicted can move them. Viewers can react to what they see, interpret the work in the light of their own experience, and judge it a success or a failure. These are all valid responses to a work of art. But the enjoyment and appreciation of artworks in museum settings are relatively recent phenomena, as is the creation of artworks solely for museum-going audiences to view.

Today, it is common for artists to work in private studios and to create paintings, sculptures, and other objects commercial art galleries will offer for sale. This is what the American painter CLYFFORD STILL (1904–1980) did when he created large canvases of pure color (FIG. I-1) titled simply with the year of their creation. Usually, someone the artist has never met will purchase the artwork and display it in a setting the artist has never seen. This practice is not a new phenomenon in the history of art—an ancient potter decorating a vase for sale at a village market stall probably did not know who would buy the pot or where it would be housed—but it is not at all typical. In fact, it is exceptional. Throughout history, most artists created paintings, sculptures, and other objects for specific patrons and settings and to fulfill a specific purpose, even if today no one knows the original contexts of most of those works. Museum visitors can appreciate the visual and tactile qualities of these objects, but they cannot understand why they were made or why they appear as they do without knowing the circumstances of their creation. Art *appreciation* does not require knowledge of the historical context of an artwork (or a building). Art *history* does.

Thus, a central aim of art history is to determine the original context of artworks. Art historians seek to achieve a full understanding not only of why these "persisting events" of human history look the way they do but also of why the artistic events happened at all. What unique set of circumstances gave rise to the erection of a particular building or led an individual patron to commission a certain artist to fashion a singular artwork for a specific place? The study of history is therefore vital to art history. And art history is often very important to the study of history. Art objects and buildings are historical documents that can shed light on the peoples who made them and on the times of their creation in a way other historical documents cannot. Furthermore, artists and architects can affect history by reinforcing or challenging cultural values and practices through the objects they create and the structures they build. Thus, the history of art and architecture is inseparable from the study of history, although the two disciplines are not the same.

The following pages introduce some of the distinctive subjects art historians address and the kinds of questions they ask, and explain some of the basic terminology they use when answering these questions. Readers armed with this arsenal of questions and terms will be ready to explore the multifaceted world of art through the ages.

ART HISTORY IN THE 21ST CENTURY

Art historians study the visual and tangible objects humans make and the structures humans build. Scholars traditionally have classified such works as architecture, sculpture, the pictorial arts (painting, drawing, printmaking, and photography), and the craft arts, or arts of design. The craft arts comprise utilitarian objects, such as ceramics, metalwork, textiles, jewelry, and similar accessories of ordinary living. Artists of every age have blurred the boundaries among these categories, but this is especially true today, when multimedia works abound.

From the earliest Greco-Roman art critics on, scholars have studied objects that their makers consciously manufactured as "art" and to which the artists assigned formal titles. But today's art historians also study a vast number of objects that their creators and owners almost certainly did not consider to be "works of art." Few ancient Romans, for example, would have regarded a coin bearing their emperor's portrait as anything but money. Today, an art museum may exhibit that coin in a locked case in a climate-controlled room, and scholars may subject it to the same kind of art historical analysis as a portrait by an acclaimed Renaissance or modern sculptor or painter.

The range of objects art historians study is constantly expanding and now includes, for example, computer-generated images, whereas in the past almost anything produced using a machine would not have been regarded as art. Most people still consider the performing arts—music, drama, and dance—as outside art history's realm because these arts are fleeting, impermanent media. But recently even this distinction between "fine art" and "performance art" has become blurred. Art historians, however, generally ask the same kinds of questions about what they study, whether they employ a restrictive or expansive definition of art.

The Questions Art Historians Ask

HOW OLD IS IT? Before art historians can construct a history of art, they must be sure they know the date of each work they study. Thus, an indispensable subject of art historical inquiry is *chronology,*

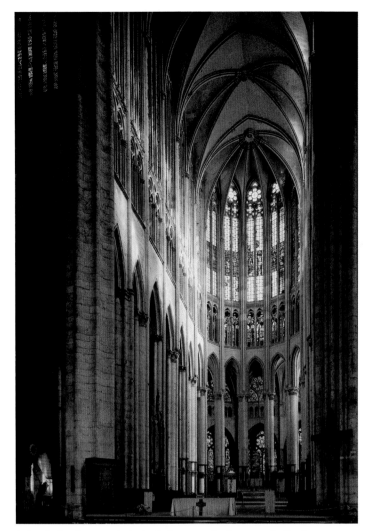

I-2 Choir of Beauvais Cathedral, Beauvais, France, rebuilt after 1284.

The style of an object or building often varies from region to region. This cathedral has towering stone vaults and large stained-glass windows typical of 13th-century French architecture.

the dating of art objects and buildings. If researchers cannot determine a monument's age, they cannot place the work in its historical context. Art historians have developed many ways to establish, or at least approximate, the date of an artwork.

Physical evidence often reliably indicates an object's age. The material used for a statue or painting—bronze, plastic, or oil-based pigment, to name only a few—may not have been invented before a certain time, indicating the earliest possible date someone could have fashioned the work. Or artists may have ceased using certain materials—such as specific kinds of inks and papers for drawings—at a known time, providing the latest possible dates for objects made of those materials. Sometimes the material (or the manufacturing technique) of an object or a building can establish a very precise date of production or construction. Studying tree rings, for instance, usually can help scholars determine within a narrow range the date of a wood statue or a timber roof beam.

Documentary evidence can help pinpoint the date of an object or building when a dated written document mentions the work. For example, official records may note when church officials commissioned a new altarpiece—and how much they paid to which artist.

Internal evidence can play a significant role in dating an artwork. A painter might have depicted an identifiable person or a kind of hairstyle, clothing, or furniture fashionable only at a certain

I-3 Interior of Santa Croce, Florence, Italy, begun 1294.

In contrast to Beauvais Cathedral (FIG. I-2), this contemporaneous Florentine church conforms to the quite different regional style of Italy. The building has a low timber roof and small windows.

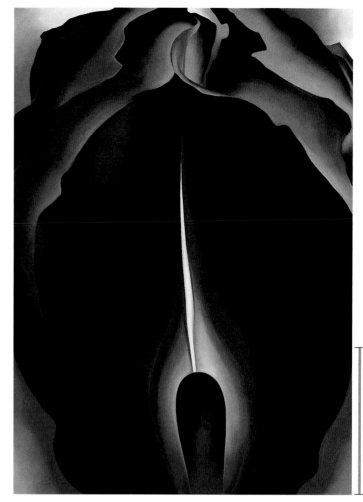

1 ft.

I-4 GEORGIA O'KEEFFE, *Jack-in-the-Pulpit No. 4*, 1930. Oil on canvas, 3′ 4″ × 2′ 6″. National Gallery of Art, Washington, D.C. (Alfred Stieglitz Collection, bequest of Georgia O'Keeffe).

O'Keeffe's paintings feature close-up views of petals and leaves in which the organic forms become powerful abstract compositions. This approach to painting typifies the artist's distinctive personal style.

time. If so, the art historian can assign a more accurate date to that painting.

Stylistic evidence is also very important. The analysis of *style*—an artist's distinctive manner of producing an object—is the art historian's special sphere. Unfortunately, because it is a subjective assessment, stylistic evidence is by far the most unreliable chronological criterion. Still, art historians find style a very useful tool for establishing chronology.

WHAT IS ITS STYLE? Defining artistic style is one of the key elements of art historical inquiry, although the analysis of artworks solely in terms of style no longer dominates the field as it once did. Art historians speak of several different kinds of artistic styles.

Period style refers to the characteristic artistic manner of a specific time, usually within a distinct culture, such as "Archaic Greek" or "Late Byzantine." But many periods do not manifest any stylistic unity at all. How would someone define the artistic style of the opening decade of the new millennium in North America? Far too many crosscurrents exist in contemporary art for anyone to describe a period style of the early 21st century—even in a single city such as New York.

Regional style is the term art historians use to describe variations in style tied to geography. Like an object's date, its *provenance,* or place of origin, can significantly determine its character. Very often two artworks from the same place made centuries apart are more similar than contemporaneous works from two different regions. To cite one example, usually only an expert can distinguish between an Egyptian statue carved in 2500 BCE and one made in 500 BCE. But no

one would mistake an Egyptian statue of 500 BCE for one of the same date made in Greece or Mexico.

Considerable variations in a given area's style are possible, however, even during a single historical period. In late medieval Europe, French architecture differed significantly from Italian architecture. The interiors of Beauvais Cathedral (FIG. I-2) and the Florentine church of Santa Croce (FIG. I-3) typify the architectural styles of France and Italy, respectively, at the end of the 13th century. The rebuilding of the east end of Beauvais Cathedral began in 1284. Construction commenced on Santa Croce only 10 years later. Both structures employ the *pointed arch* characteristic of this era, yet the two churches differ strikingly. The French church has towering stone ceilings and large expanses of colored windows, whereas the Italian building has a low timber roof and small, widely separated windows. Because the two contemporaneous churches served similar purposes, regional style mainly explains their differing appearance.

Personal style, the distinctive manner of individual artists or architects, often decisively explains stylistic discrepancies among monuments of the same time and place. In 1930 the American painter GEORGIA O'KEEFFE (1887–1986) produced a series of paintings of flowering plants. One of them was *Jack-in-the-Pulpit No. 4* (FIG. I-4), a sharply focused close-up view of petals and leaves. O'Keeffe captured the growing plant's slow, controlled motion while converting

1 ft.

I-5 BEN SHAHN, *The Passion of Sacco and Vanzetti*, 1931–1932. Tempera on canvas, 7′ $\frac{1}{2}$″ × 4′. Whitney Museum of American Art, New York (gift of Edith and Milton Lowenthal in memory of Juliana Force).

A contemporary of O'Keeffe's, Shahn developed a style of painting that differed markedly from hers. His paintings are often social commentaries on current events and incorporate readily identifiable people.

I-6 GISLEBERTUS, The weighing of souls, detail of Last Judgment (FIG. 12-12), west tympanum of Saint-Lazare, Autun, France, ca. 1120–1135.

In this high relief portraying the weighing of souls on Judgment Day, Gislebertus used disproportion and distortion to dehumanize the devilish figure yanking on the scales of justice.

the plant into a powerful abstract composition of lines, forms, and colors (see the discussion of art historical vocabulary in the next section). Only a year later, another American artist, BEN SHAHN (1898–1969), painted *The Passion of Sacco and Vanzetti* (FIG. I-5), a stinging commentary on social injustice inspired by the trial and execution of two Italian anarchists, Nicola Sacco and Bartolomeo Vanzetti. Many people believed Sacco and Vanzetti had been unjustly convicted of killing two men in a holdup in 1920. Shahn's painting compresses time in a symbolic representation of the trial and its aftermath. The two executed men lie in their coffins. Presiding over them are the three members of the commission (headed by a college president wearing academic cap and gown) that declared the original trial fair and cleared the way for the executions. Behind, on the wall of a stately government building, hangs the framed portrait of the judge who pronounced the

initial sentence. Personal style, not period or regional style, sets Shahn's canvas apart from O'Keeffe's. The contrast is extreme here because of the very different subjects the artists chose. But even when two artists depict the same subject, the results can vary widely. The *way* O'Keeffe painted flowers and the *way* Shahn painted faces are distinctive and unlike the styles of their contemporaries. (See the "Who Made It?" discussion on page xxix.)

The different kinds of artistic styles are not mutually exclusive. For example, an artist's personal style may change dramatically during a long career. Art historians then must distinguish among the different period styles of a particular artist, such as the "Blue Period" and the "Cubist Period" of the prolific 20th-century artist Pablo Picasso.

WHAT IS ITS SUBJECT? Another major concern of art historians is, of course, subject matter, encompassing the story, or narrative; the scene presented; the action's time and place; the persons involved; and the environment and its details. Some artworks, such as modern abstract paintings (FIG. I-1), have no subject, not even a setting. The "subject" is the artwork itself. But when artists represent people, places, or actions, viewers must identify these aspects to achieve complete understanding of the work. Art historians traditionally separate pictorial subjects into various categories, such as religious, historical, mythological, *genre* (daily life), portraiture, *landscape* (a depiction of a place), *still life* (an arrangement of inanimate objects), and their numerous subdivisions and combinations.

Iconography—literally, the "writing of images"—refers both to the content, or subject of an artwork, and to the study of content in art. By extension, it also includes the study of *symbols,* images that stand for other images or encapsulate ideas. In Christian art, two intersecting

I-7 The four evangelists, folio 14 verso of the *Aachen Gospels,* ca. 810. Ink and tempera on vellum, 1′ × 9½″. Cathedral Treasury, Aachen.

Artists depict figures with attributes in order to identify them for viewers. The authors of the four gospels have distinctive attributes—John an eagle, Luke an ox, Mark a lion, and Matthew a winged man.

I-8 ALBRECHT DÜRER, *The Four Horsemen of the Apocalypse,* ca. 1498. Woodcut, 1′ 3¼″ × 11″. Metropolitan Museum of Art, New York (gift of Junius S. Morgan, 1919).

Personifications are abstract ideas codified in human form. Here, Albrecht Dürer represented Death, Famine, War, and Pestilence as four men on charging horses, each carrying an identifying attribute.

lines of unequal length or a simple geometric cross can serve as an emblem of the religion as a whole, symbolizing the cross of Jesus Christ's crucifixion. A symbol also can be a familiar object the artist imbued with greater meaning. A balance or scale, for example, may symbolize justice or the weighing of souls on Judgment Day (FIG. I-6).

Artists may depict figures with unique *attributes* identifying them. In Christian art, for example, each of the authors of the New Testament Gospels, the four evangelists (FIG. I-7), has a distinctive attribute. People can recognize Saint John by the eagle associated with him, Luke by the ox, Mark by the lion, and Matthew by the winged man.

Throughout the history of art, artists have used *personifications*—abstract ideas codified in human form. Worldwide, people visualize Liberty as a robed woman with a torch because of the fame of the colossal statue set up in New York City's harbor in the 19th century. *The Four Horsemen of the Apocalypse* (FIG. I-8) is a terrifying late-15th-century depiction of the fateful day at the end of time when, according to the Bible's last book, Death, Famine, War, and Pestilence will annihilate the human race. The German artist ALBRECHT DÜRER (1471–1528) personified Death as an emaciated old man with a pitchfork. Dürer's Famine swings the scales that will weigh human souls (compare FIG. I-6), War wields a sword, and Pestilence draws a bow.

Even without considering style and without knowing a work's maker, informed viewers can determine much about the work's period and provenance by iconographical and subject analysis alone. In *The Passion of Sacco and Vanzetti* (FIG. I-5), for example, the two

coffins, the trio headed by an academic, and the robed judge in the background are all pictorial clues revealing the painting's subject. The work's date must be after the trial and execution, probably while the event was still newsworthy. And because the two men's deaths caused the greatest outrage in the United States, the painter–social critic was probably American.

WHO MADE IT? If Ben Shahn had not signed his painting of Sacco and Vanzetti, an art historian could still assign, or *attribute* (make an *attribution* of), the work to him based on knowledge of the artist's personal style. Although signing (and dating) works is quite common (but by no means universal) today, in the history of art countless works exist whose artists remain unknown. Because personal style can play a large role in determining the character of an artwork, art historians often try to attribute anonymous works to known artists. Sometimes they assemble a group of works all thought to be by the same person, even though none of the objects in the group is the known work of an artist with a recorded name. Art historians thus reconstruct the careers of artists such as "the Achilles Painter," the anonymous ancient Greek vase painter whose masterwork is a depiction of the hero Achilles. Scholars base their attributions on internal evidence, such as the distinctive way an artist draws or carves drapery folds, earlobes, or flowers. It requires a keen, highly trained eye and long experience to become a *connoisseur,* an expert in

I-9 Augustus wearing the corona civica, early first century CE. Marble, 1′ 5″ high. Glyptothek, Munich.

Patrons frequently dictate the form their portraits will take. The Roman emperor Augustus demanded that he always be portrayed as a young, godlike head of state even though he lived to age 76.

In the art of portraiture, to name only one category of painting and sculpture, the patron has often played a dominant role in deciding how the artist represented the subject, whether that person was the patron or another individual, such as a spouse, son, or mother. Many Egyptian pharaohs and some Roman emperors, for example, insisted that artists depict them with unlined faces and perfect youthful bodies no matter how old they were when portrayed. In these cases, the state employed the sculptors and painters, and the artists had no choice but to depict their patrons in the officially approved manner. This is why Augustus, who lived to age 76, looks so young in his portraits (FIG. I-9). Although Roman emperor for more than 40 years, Augustus demanded that artists always represent him as a young, godlike head of state.

All modes of artistic production reveal the impact of patronage. Learned monks provided the themes for the sculptural decoration of medieval church portals (FIG. I-6). Renaissance princes and popes dictated the subject, size, and materials of artworks destined for buildings constructed according to their specifications. An art historian could make a very long list of commissioned works, and it would indicate that throughout the history of art, patrons have had diverse tastes and needs and demanded different kinds of art. Whenever a patron contracts an artist or architect to paint, sculpt, or build in a prescribed manner, personal style often becomes a very minor factor in the ultimate appearance of the painting, statue, or building. In these cases, the identity of the patron reveals more to art historians than does the identity of the artist or school. The portrait of Augustus wearing a *corona civica*, or civic crown (FIG. I-9), was the work of a virtuoso sculptor, a master wielder of hammer and chisel. But scores of similar portraits of that emperor exist today. They differ in quality but not in kind from this one. The patron, not the artist, determined the character of these artworks. Augustus's public image never varied.

The Words Art Historians Use

Like all specialists, art historians have their own specialized vocabulary. That vocabulary consists of hundreds of words, but certain basic terms are indispensable for describing artworks and buildings of any time and place. They make up the essential vocabulary of *formal analysis*, the visual analysis of artistic form. Definitions of the most important of these art historical terms follow.

FORM AND COMPOSITION *Form* refers to an object's shape and structure, either in two dimensions (for example, a figure painted on a canvas) or in three dimensions (such as a statue carved from a marble block). Two forms may take the same shape but may differ in their color, texture, and other qualities. *Composition* refers to how an artist organizes (*composes*) forms in an artwork, either by placing shapes on a flat surface or by arranging forms in space.

MATERIAL AND TECHNIQUE To create art forms, artists shape materials (pigment, clay, marble, gold, and many more) with tools (pens, brushes, chisels, and so forth). Each of the materials and tools available has its own potentialities and limitations. Part of all artists' creative activity is to select the *medium* and instrument most suitable to the artists' purpose—or to develop new media and tools, such as bronze and concrete in antiquity and cameras and computers in modern times. The processes artists employ, such as applying paint to canvas with a brush, and the distinctive, personal ways they handle materials constitute their *technique*. Form, material, and technique interrelate and are central to analyzing any work of art.

LINE Among the most important elements defining an artwork's shape or form is *line*. A line can be understood as the path of a point moving in space, an invisible line of sight. More commonly, however, artists and architects make a line tangible by drawing (or chiseling) it

assigning artworks to "the hand" of one artist rather than another. Attribution is subjective, of course, and ever open to doubt. At present, for example, international debate rages over attributions to the famous 17th-century Dutch painter Rembrandt.

Sometimes a group of artists works in the same style at the same time and place. Art historians designate such a group as a *school*. "School" does not mean an educational institution. The term connotes only chronological, stylistic, and geographic similarity. Art historians speak, for example, of the Dutch school of the 17th century and, within it, of subschools such as those of the cities of Haarlem, Utrecht, and Leyden.

WHO PAID FOR IT? The interest many art historians show in attribution reflects their conviction that the identity of an artwork's maker is the major reason the object looks the way it does. For them, personal style is of paramount importance. But in many times and places, artists had little to say about what form their work would take. They toiled in obscurity, doing the bidding of their *patrons*, those who paid them to make individual works or employed them on a continuing basis. The role of patrons in dictating the content and shaping the form of artworks is also an important subject of art historical inquiry.

on a *plane,* a flat surface. A line may be very thin, wirelike, and delicate. It may be thick and heavy. Or it may alternate quickly from broad to narrow, the strokes jagged or the outline broken. When a continuous line defines an object's outer shape, art historians call it a *contour line.* All of these line qualities are present in Dürer's *Four Horsemen of the Apocalypse* (FIG. I-8). Contour lines define the basic shapes of clouds, human and animal limbs, and weapons. Within the forms, series of short broken lines create shadows and textures. An overall pattern of long parallel strokes suggests the dark sky on the frightening day when the world is about to end.

COLOR Light reveals all colors. Light in the world of the painter and other artists differs from natural light. Natural light, or sunlight, is whole or *additive light.* As the sum of all the wavelengths composing the visible *spectrum,* natural light may be disassembled or fragmented into the individual colors of the spectral band. The painter's light in art—the light reflected from pigments and objects—is *subtractive light.* Paint pigments produce their individual colors by reflecting a segment of the spectrum while absorbing all the rest. Green pigment, for example, subtracts or absorbs all the light in the spectrum except that seen as green.

Hue is the property that gives a color its name. Although the spectrum colors merge into each other, artists usually conceive of their hues as distinct from one another. Color has two basic variables—the apparent amount of light reflected and the apparent purity. A change in one must produce a change in the other. Some terms for these variables are *value,* or *tonality* (the degree of lightness or darkness), and *intensity,* or *saturation* (the purity of a color, or its brightness or dullness).

Artists call the three basic colors—red, yellow, and blue—the *primary colors.* The *secondary colors* result from mixing pairs of primaries: orange (red and yellow), purple (red and blue), and green (yellow and blue). *Complementary colors* represent the pairing of a primary color and the secondary color created from mixing the two other primary colors—red and green, yellow and purple, and blue and orange. They "complement," or complete, each other, one absorbing colors the other reflects.

Artists can manipulate the appearance of colors, however. One artist who made a systematic investigation of the formal aspects of art, especially color, was JOSEF ALBERS (1888–1976), a German-born artist who emigrated to the United States in 1933. In connection with his studies, Albers created the series *Homage to the Square*—hundreds of paintings, most of which are color variations on the same composition of concentric squares, as in the illustrated example (FIG. I-10). The series reflected Albers's belief that art originates in "the discrepancy between physical fact and psychic effect."[1] Because the composition in most of these paintings remains constant, the works succeed in revealing the relativity and instability of color perception. Albers varied the hue, saturation, and value of each square in the paintings in this series. As a result, the sizes of the squares from painting to painting appear to vary (although they remain the same), and the sensations emanating from the paintings range from clashing dissonance to delicate serenity. Albers explained his motivation for focusing on color juxtapositions:

> They [the colors] are juxtaposed for various and changing visual effects. . . . Such action, reaction, interaction . . . is sought in order to make obvious how colors influence and change each other; that the same color, for instance—with different grounds or neighbors—looks different. . . . Such color deceptions prove that we see colors almost never unrelated to each other.[2]

Albers's quotation is only one example of how artists' comments on their own works are often invaluable to art historians. In *Art through*

I-10 JOSEF ALBERS, *Homage to the Square: "Ascending,"* 1953. Oil on composition board, 3′ 7½″ × 3′ 7½″. Whitney Museum of American Art, New York.

Josef Albers painted hundreds of canvases with the same composition but employed variations in hue, saturation, and value in order to reveal the relativity and instability of color perception.

the Ages: The Western Perspective, artist commentaries appear frequently in boxed features called "Artists on Art."

TEXTURE The term *texture* refers to the quality of a surface, such as rough or shiny. Art historians distinguish between true texture, or the tactile quality of the surface, and represented texture, as when painters depict an object as having a certain texture even though the pigment is the true texture. Sometimes artists combine different materials of different textures on a single surface, juxtaposing paint with pieces of wood, newspaper, fabric, and so forth. Art historians refer to this mixed-media technique as *collage.* Texture is, of course, a key determinant of any sculpture's character. A viewer's first impulse is usually to handle a piece of sculpture—even though museum signs often warn "Do not touch!" Sculptors plan for this natural human response, using surfaces varying in texture from rugged coarseness to polished smoothness. Textures are often intrinsic to a material, influencing the type of stone, wood, plastic, clay, or metal sculptors select.

SPACE, MASS, AND VOLUME *Space* is the bounded or boundless "container" of objects. For art historians, space can be the literal three-dimensional space occupied by a statue or a vase or contained within a room or courtyard. Or space can be *illusionistic,* as when painters depict an image (or illusion) of the three-dimensional spatial world on a two-dimensional surface.

Mass and *volume* describe three-dimensional objects and space. In both architecture and sculpture, mass is the bulk, density, and weight of matter in space. Yet the mass need not be solid. It can be the exterior form of enclosed space. Mass can apply to a solid Egyptian pyramid or stone statue, to a church, synagogue, or mosque—architectural shells enclosing sometimes vast spaces—and to a hollow metal statue or baked clay pot. Volume is the space that mass organizes, divides, or encloses. It may be a building's interior spaces, the

I-11 CLAUDE LORRAIN, *Embarkation of the Queen of Sheba*, 1648. Oil on canvas, 4′ 10″ × 6′ 4″. National Gallery, London.

To create the illusion of a deep land-scape, Claude Lorrain employed perspective, reducing the size of and blurring the most distant forms. Also, all diagonal lines converge on a single point.

1 ft.

intervals between a structure's masses, or the amount of space occupied by three-dimensional objects such as sculpture, pottery, or furniture. Volume and mass describe both the exterior and interior forms of a work of art—the forms of the matter of which it is composed and the spaces immediately around the work and interacting with it.

PERSPECTIVE AND FORESHORTENING *Perspective* is one of the most important pictorial devices for organizing forms in space. Throughout history, artists have used various types of perspec-

tive to create an illusion of depth or space on a two-dimensional surface. The French painter CLAUDE LORRAIN (1600–1682) employed several perspectival devices in *Embarkation of the Queen of Sheba* (FIG. I-11), a painting of a biblical episode set in a 17th-century European harbor with a Roman ruin in the left foreground. For example, the figures and boats on the shoreline are much larger than those in the distance. Decreasing the size of an object makes it appear farther away. Also, the top and bottom of the port building at the painting's right side are not parallel horizontal lines, as they are

I-12 OGATA KORIN, *White and Red Plum Blossoms*, Edo period, ca. 1710–1716. Pair of twofold screens. Ink, color, and gold leaf on paper, each screen 5′ 1⅝″ × 5′ 7⅞″. MOA Art Museum, Shizuoka-ken.

Ogata Korin was more concerned with creating an interesting composition of shapes on a surface than with locating objects in space. Asian artists rarely employed Western perspective.

1 ft.

I-13 PETER PAUL RUBENS, *Lion Hunt,* 1617–1618. Oil on canvas, 8′ 2″ × 12′ 5″. Alte Pinakothek, Munich.

Foreshortening—the representation of a figure or object at an angle to the picture plane—is a common device in Western art for creating the illusion of depth. Foreshortening is a type of perspective.

in a real building. Instead, the lines converge beyond the structure, leading viewers' eyes toward the hazy, indistinct sun on the horizon. These perspectival devices—the reduction of figure size, the convergence of diagonal lines, and the blurring of distant forms—have been familiar features of Western art since the ancient Greeks. But it is important to note at the outset that all kinds of perspective are only pictorial conventions, even when one or more types of perspective may be so common in a given culture that people accept them as "natural" or as "true" means of representing the natural world.

In *White and Red Plum Blossoms* (FIG. I-12), a Japanese landscape painting on two folding screens, OGATA KORIN (1658–1716) used none of these Western perspective conventions. He showed the two plum trees as seen from a position on the ground, but viewers look down on the stream between them from above. Less concerned with locating the trees and stream in space than with composing shapes on a surface, the painter played the water's gently swelling curves against the jagged contours of the branches and trunks. Neither the French nor the Japanese painting can be said to project "correctly" what viewers "in fact" see. One painting is not a "better" picture of the world than the other. The European and Asian artists simply approached the problem of picture-making differently. Claude Lorrain's approach is, however, one of the most distinctive features of the Western tradition in art examined exclusively in this book.

Artists also represent single figures in space in varying ways. When the Flemish artist PETER PAUL RUBENS (1577–1640) painted *Lion Hunt* (FIG. I-13), he used *foreshortening* for all the hunters and animals—that is, he represented their bodies at angles to the picture plane. When in life one views a figure at an angle, the body appears to contract as it extends back in space. Foreshortening is a kind of perspective. It produces the illusion that one part of the body is farther away than another, even though all the forms are on the same surface. Especially noteworthy in *Lion Hunt* are the gray horse at the left, seen from behind with the bottom of its left rear hoof facing viewers and most of its head hidden by its rider's shield, and the fallen hunter at the painting's lower right corner, whose barely visible legs and feet recede into the distance.

The artist who carved the portrait of the ancient Egyptian official Hesire (FIG. I-14) did not employ foreshortening. That artist's purpose was to present the various human body parts as clearly as possible, without overlapping. The lower part of Hesire's body is in

I-14 Hesire, relief from his tomb at Saqqara, Egypt, Third Dynasty, ca. 2650 BCE. Wood, 3′ 9″ high. Egyptian Museum, Cairo.

Egyptian artists combined frontal and profile views to give a precise picture of the parts of the human body, as opposed to depicting how an individual body appears from a specific viewpoint.

I-15 King on horseback with attendants, from Benin, Nigeria, ca. 1550–1680. Bronze, 1′ 7½″ high. Metropolitan Museum of Art, New York (Michael C. Rockefeller Memorial Collection, gift of Nelson A. Rockefeller).

This African artist used hierarchy of scale to distinguish the relative rank of the figures, making the king the largest. The sculptor created the relief by casting (pouring bronze into a mold).

ures, constituent parts of buildings, and so forth. In ancient Greece, many sculptors devised canons of proportions so strict and all-encompassing that they calculated the size of every body part in advance, even the fingers and toes, according to mathematical ratios.

Proportional systems can differ sharply from period to period, culture to culture, and artist to artist. Part of the task art history students face is to perceive and adjust to these differences. In fact, many artists have used disproportion and distortion deliberately for expressive effect. In the medieval French depiction of the weighing of souls on Judgment Day (FIG. I-6), the devilish figure yanking down on the scale has distorted facial features and stretched, lined limbs with animal-like paws for feet. Disproportion and distortion make him appear "inhuman," precisely as the sculptor intended.

In other cases, artists have used disproportion to focus attention on one body part (often the head) or to single out a group member (usually the leader). These intentional "unnatural" discrepancies in proportion constitute what art historians call *hierarchy of scale,* the enlarging of elements considered the most important. On a bronze plaque from Benin, Nigeria (FIG. I-15), the sculptor enlarged all the heads for emphasis and also varied the size of each figure according to its social status. Central, largest, and therefore most important is the Benin king, mounted on horseback. The horse has been a symbol of power and wealth in many societies from prehistory to the present. That the Benin king is disproportionately larger than his horse, contrary to nature, further aggrandizes him. Two large attendants fan the king. Other figures of smaller size and status at the Benin court stand on the king's left and right and in the plaque's upper corners. One tiny figure next to the horse is almost hidden from view beneath the king's feet.

One problem that students of art history—and professional art historians too—confront when studying illustrations in art history books is that although the relative sizes of figures and objects in a painting or sculpture are easy to discern, it is impossible to determine the absolute size of the works reproduced because they all appear at approximately the same size on the page. Readers of *Art through the Ages* can learn the size of all artworks from the dimensions given in the captions and, more intuitively, from the scales that appear—for the first time in this 13th edition—at the lower left or right corner of the illustration.

profile to give the most complete view of the legs, with both the heels and toes of the foot visible. The frontal torso, however, allows viewers to see its full shape, including both shoulders, equal in size, as in nature. (Compare the shoulders of the hunter on the gray horse or those of the fallen hunter in *Lion Hunt*'s left foreground.) The result, an "unnatural" 90-degree twist at the waist, provides a precise picture of human body parts. Rubens and the Egyptian sculptor used very different means of depicting forms in space. Once again, neither is the "correct" manner, although foreshortening, like perspective, is one of the characteristic features of the Western artistic tradition.

PROPORTION AND SCALE *Proportion* concerns the relationships (in terms of size) of the parts of persons, buildings, or objects. People can judge "correct proportions" intuitively ("that statue's head seems the right size for the body"). Or proportion can be a mathematical relationship between the size of one part of an artwork or building and the other parts within the work. Proportion in art implies using a *module,* or basic unit of measure. When an artist or architect uses a formal system of proportions, all parts of a building, body, or other entity will be fractions or multiples of the module. A module might be a *column*'s diameter, the height of a human head, or any other component whose dimensions can be multiplied or divided to determine the size of the work's other parts.

In certain times and places, artists have formulated *canons,* or systems, of "correct" or "ideal" proportions for representing human fig-

CARVING AND CASTING Sculptural technique falls into two basic categories, *subtractive* and *additive. Carving* is a subtractive technique. The final form is a reduction of the original mass of a block of stone, a piece of wood, or another material. Wooden statues were once tree trunks, and stone statues began as blocks pried from mountains. An unfinished marble statue of a bound slave (FIG. I-16) by the Italian artist MICHELANGELO BUONARROTI (1475–1564) clearly reveals the original shape of the stone block. Michelangelo thought of sculpture as a process of "liberating" the statue within the block. All sculptors of stone or wood cut away (subtract) "excess material." When they finish, they "leave behind" the statue—in this example, a twisting nude male form whose head Michelangelo never freed from the stone block.

In additive sculpture, the artist builds up the forms, usually in clay around a framework, or *armature.* Or a sculptor may fashion a *mold,* a hollow form for shaping, or *casting,* a fluid substance such as bronze or plaster. The ancient Greek sculptor who made the bronze statue of a warrior found in the sea near Riace, Italy, cast the head (FIG. I-17), limbs, torso, hands, and feet in separate molds and then *welded* them together (joined them by heating). Finally, the artist added features, such as the pupils of the eyes (now missing), in other materials. The warrior's teeth are silver, and his lower lip is copper.

1 ft.

I-16 MICHELANGELO BUONARROTI, unfinished captive, 1527–1528. Marble, 8′ 7½″ high. Galleria dell'Accademia, Florence.

Carving a freestanding figure from stone or wood is a subtractive process. Michelangelo thought of sculpture as a process of "liberating" the statue within the block of marble.

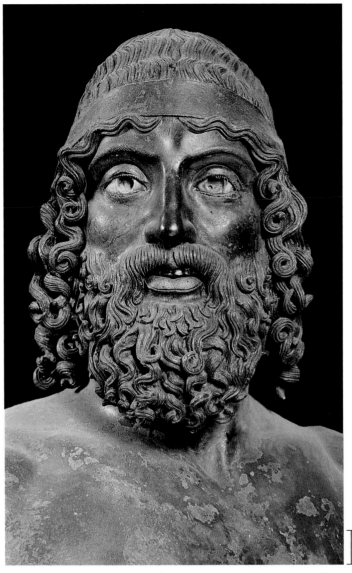

1 in.

I-17 Head of a warrior, detail of a statue (FIG. 5-35) from the sea off Riace, Italy, ca. 460–450 BCE. Bronze, full statue 6′ 6″ high. Museo Nazionale della Magna Grecia, Reggio Calabria.

The sculptor of this life-size statue of a bearded Greek warrior cast the head, limbs, torso, hands, and feet in separate molds, then welded the pieces together and added the eyes in a different material.

RELIEF SCULPTURE *Statues* that exist independent of any architectural frame or setting and that viewers can walk around are *freestanding* sculptures, or *sculptures in the round,* whether the artist produced the piece by carving (FIG. I-9) or casting (FIG. I-17). In *relief* sculpture, the subjects project from the background but remain part of it. In *high-relief* sculpture, the images project boldly. In the medieval weighing-of-souls scene (FIG. I-6), the relief is so high that not only do the forms cast shadows on the background, but some parts are even in the round, which explains why some pieces, for example the arms of the scale, broke off centuries ago. In *low relief,* or *basrelief,* such as the portrait of Hesire (FIG. I-14), the projection is slight. Relief sculpture, like sculpture in the round, can be produced either by carving or casting. The plaque from Benin (FIG. I-15) is an example of bronze casting in high relief.

ARCHITECTURAL DRAWINGS Buildings are groupings of enclosed spaces and enclosing masses. People experience architecture both visually and by moving through and around it, so they perceive architectural space and mass together. Architects can represent these spaces and masses graphically in several ways, including as plans, sections, elevations, and cutaway drawings.

A *plan,* essentially a map of a floor, shows the placement of a structure's masses and, therefore, the spaces they circumscribe and enclose. A *section,* like a vertical plan, depicts the placement of the masses as if someone cut through the building along a plane. Drawings showing a theoretical slice across a structure's width are *lateral sections.* Those cutting through a building's length are *longitudinal sections.* Illustrated here are the plan and lateral section of Beauvais Cathedral (FIG. I-18), which may be compared to the photograph of the church's *choir* (FIG. I-2). The plan shows not only the choir's shape and the location of the *piers* dividing the *aisles* and supporting the *vaults* above but also the pattern of the crisscrossing vault *ribs.* The lateral section shows both the interior of the choir with its vaults and tall *stained-glass* windows as well as the roof structure and the form of the exterior *flying buttresses* that hold the vaults in place.

I-18 Plan (*left*) and lateral section (*right*) of Beauvais Cathedral, Beauvais, France, rebuilt after 1284.

Architectural drawings are indispensable aids for the analysis of buildings. Plans are maps of floors, recording the structure's masses. Sections are vertical "slices," across either a building's width or length.

Other types of architectural drawings appear throughout this book. An *elevation* drawing is a head-on view of an external or internal wall. A *cutaway* combines in a single drawing an exterior view with an interior view of part of a building.

This overview of the art historian's vocabulary is not exhaustive, nor have artists used only painting, drawing, sculpture, and architecture as media over the millennia. Ceramics, jewelry, textiles, photography, and computer art are just some of the numerous other arts. All of them involve highly specialized techniques described in distinct vocabularies. As in this introductory chapter, new terms are in *italics* where they first appear. The comprehensive Glossary at the end of the book contains definitions of all italicized terms.

Art History and Other Disciplines

By its very nature, the work of art historians intersects with that of others in many fields of knowledge, not only in the humanities but also in the social and natural sciences. To do their job well today, art historians regularly must go beyond the boundaries of what the public and even professional art historians of previous generations traditionally considered the specialized discipline of art history. In short, art historical research in the 21st century is typically interdisciplinary in nature. To cite one example, in an effort to unlock the secrets of a particular statue, an art historian might conduct archival research hoping to uncover new documents shedding light on who paid for the work and why, who made it and when, where it originally stood, how its contemporaries viewed it, and a host of other questions. Realizing, however, that the authors of the written documents often were not objective recorders of fact but rather observers with their own biases and agendas, the art historian may also use methodologies developed in

such fields as literary criticism, philosophy, sociology, and gender studies to weigh the evidence the documents provide.

At other times, rather than attempt to master many disciplines at once, art historians band together with other specialists in multidisciplinary inquiries. Art historians might call in chemists to date an artwork based on the composition of the materials used or might ask geologists to determine which quarry furnished the stone for a particular statue. X-ray technicians might be enlisted in an attempt to establish whether a painting is a forgery. Of course, art historians often reciprocate by contributing their expertise to the solution of problems in other disciplines. A historian, for example, might ask an art historian to determine—based on style, material, iconography, and other criteria—if any of the portraits of a certain king date to after his death. That would help establish the ruler's continuing prestige during the reigns of his successors. (Some portraits of Augustus, FIG. I-9, the founder of the Roman Empire, postdate his death by decades, even centuries.)

DIFFERENT WAYS OF SEEING

The history of art can be a history of artists and their works, of styles and stylistic change, of materials and techniques, of images and themes and their meanings, and of contexts and cultures and patrons. The best art historians analyze artworks from many viewpoints. But no art historian (or scholar in any other field), no matter how broad-minded in approach and no matter how experienced, can be truly objective. Like artists, art historians are members of a society, participants in its culture. How can scholars (and museum visitors and travelers to foreign locales) comprehend cultures unlike their own? They can try to reconstruct the original cultural contexts of artworks, but they are limited by their distance from the thought

1 in.

I-19 *Left:* John Henry Sylvester, *Portrait of Te Pehi Kupe* (detail), 1826. Watercolor, $8\frac{1}{4}'' \times 6\frac{1}{4}''$. National Library of Australia, Canberra (Rex Nan Kivell Collection). *Right:* Te Pehi Kupe, *Self-Portrait*, 1826. From Leo Frobenius, *The Childhood of Man* (New York: J. B. Lippincott, 1909).

These strikingly different portraits of the same Maori chief reveal how differently Western and non-Western artists "see" a subject. Understanding the cultural context of artworks is vital to art history.

patterns of the cultures they study and by the obstructions to understanding—the assumptions, presuppositions, and prejudices peculiar to their own culture—their own thought patterns raise. Art historians may reconstruct a distorted picture of the past because of culture-bound blindness.

A single instance underscores how differently people of diverse cultures view the world and how various ways of seeing can cause sharp differences in how artists depict the world. Illustrated here are two contemporaneous portraits of a 19th-century Maori chieftain (FIG. I-19)—one by an Englishman, John Sylvester (active early 19th century), and the other by the New Zealand chieftain himself, Te Pehi Kupe (d. 1829). Both reproduce the chieftain's facial tattooing. The European artist (FIG. I-19, *left*) included the head and shoulders and underplayed the tattooing. The tattoo pattern is one aspect of the likeness among many, no more or less important than the chieftain's European attire. Sylvester also recorded his subject's momentary glance toward the right and the play of light on his hair, fleeting aspects that have nothing to do with the figure's identity.

In contrast, Te Pehi Kupe's self-portrait (FIG. I-19, *right*)—made during a trip to Liverpool, England, to obtain European arms to take back to New Zealand—is not a picture of a man situated in space and bathed in light. Rather, it is the chieftain's statement of the supreme importance of the tattoo design that symbolizes his rank among his people. Remarkably, Te Pehi Kupe created the tattoo patterns from memory, without the aid of a mirror. The splendidly composed insignia, presented as a flat design separated from the body and even from the head, is Te Pehi Kupe's image of himself. Only by understanding the cultural context of each portrait can viewers hope to understand why the English representation differs so strikingly from the Maori representation.

As noted at the outset, the study of the context of artworks and buildings is one of the central concerns of art historians. Western art differs in many fundamental ways from other artistic traditions, but even within the Western world, each culture and each period is distinctive. Paintings, sculptures, buildings—indeed, all art forms—changed dramatically with each change of culture, locale, and date. *Art through the Ages: The Western Perspective* seeks to present a history of art and architecture that will help readers understand not only the subjects, styles, and techniques of paintings, sculptures, buildings, and other art forms created in the Western world across 30 millennia but also their cultural and historical contexts. That story now begins.

14-1 Gɪᴏᴛᴛᴏ ᴅɪ Bᴏɴᴅᴏɴᴇ, Arena Chapel (Cappella Scrovegni; interior looking west), Padua, Italy, 1305–1306.

Giotto, widely regarded as the first Renaissance painter, was a pioneer in pursuing a naturalistic approach to representation based on observation. The frescoes in the Arena Chapel show his art at its finest.

14

ITALY, 1200 TO 1400

When the Italian humanists of the 16th century condemned the art of the late Middle Ages in northern Europe as "*Gothic*" (see Chapter 13), they did so by comparing it with the contemporary art of Italy, which was a conscious revival of *classical** art. Italian artists and scholars regarded medieval artworks as distortions of the noble art of the Greeks and Romans. But interest in the art of classical antiquity was not entirely absent during the medieval period, even in France, the center of the Gothic style. For example, on the west front of Reims Cathedral, the statues of Christian *saints* and angels (FIG. 13-24) reveal the unmistakable influence of Roman art on French sculptors. However, the classical revival that took root in Italy during the 13th and 14th centuries (MAP 14-1) was much more pervasive and long-lasting.

THE 13TH CENTURY

Italian admiration for classical art surfaced early on at the court of Frederick II, king of Sicily (r. 1197–1250) and Holy Roman Emperor (r. 1220–1250). Frederick's nostalgia for the past grandeur of Rome fostered a revival of Roman sculpture in Sicily and southern Italy not unlike the neoclassical *renovatio* (renewal) that Charlemagne encouraged in Germany four centuries earlier (see Chapter 11).

Sculpture

NICOLA PISANO The sculptor Nicola d'Apulia (Nicholas of Apulia), better known as NICOLA PISANO (active ca. 1258–1278) after his adopted city (see "Italian Artists' Names," page 376), received his early training in southern Italy under Frederick's rule. In 1250, Nicola traveled northward and eventually settled in Pisa. Then at the height of its political and economic power, Pisa was a magnet for artists seeking lucrative commissions. Nicola specialized in carving marble reliefs and ornamentation for large *pulpits* (raised platforms from which priests lead church services), completing the first (FIG. 14-2) in 1260 for Pisa's baptistery (FIG. 12-25, *left*). Some elements of the pulpit's design carried on medieval traditions (for example, the *trefoil arches* and the lions supporting some of the *columns*), but Nicola also incorporated

---

* In *Art through the Ages* the adjective "Classical," with uppercase *C*, refers specifically to the Classical period of ancient Greece, 480–323 BCE. Lowercase "classical" refers to Greco-Roman antiquity in general, that is, the period treated in Chapters 5, 6, and 7.

Italian Artists' Names

In contemporary societies, people have become accustomed to a standardized method of identifying individuals, in part because of the proliferation of official documents such as driver's licenses, passports, and student identification cards. Given names are coupled with family names, although the order of the two (or more) names varies from country to country. This kind of regularity in names was not, however, the norm in premodern Italy. Many individuals were known by their place of birth or adopted hometown. Nicola Pisano was known as "Nicholas the Pisan," Giulio Romano was "Julius the Roman," and Domenico Veneziano was "the Venetian." Leonardo da Vinci ("Leonard from Vinci") hailed from the small town of Vinci.

Art historians therefore refer to these artists by their given name, not the name of their town: "Leonardo," not "da Vinci."

Nicknames were also common. Giorgione was "Big George." People usually referred to Tommaso di Cristoforo Fini as Masolino ("Little Thomas") to distinguish him from his more famous pupil Masaccio ("Brutish Thomas"). Guido di Pietro was called Fra Angelico (the Angelic Friar). Cenni di Pepo is remembered as Cimabue ("bull's head"). Names were also impermanent and could be changed at will. This flexibility has resulted in significant challenges for historians, who often must deal with archival documents and records that refer to the same artist by different names.

classical elements. The large, bushy *capitals* are a Gothic variation of the highly ornate *Corinthian capital.* The arches are round, as in Roman architecture, rather than pointed (*ogival*) as in Gothic buildings. And each of the large rectangular relief panels resembles the sculptured front of a Roman *sarcophagus,* or coffin (for example, FIG. 7-70).

The densely packed large-scale figures of the individual panels also seem to derive from the compositions found on Roman sarcophagi. One of these panels (FIG. 14-3) depicts scenes from the Infancy cycle of Christ (see "The Life of Jesus in Art," Chapter 8,

pages 216–217, or in the "Before 1300" section), including the *Annunciation* (*top left*), the *Nativity* (*center* and *lower half*), and the *Adoration of the Shepherds* (*top right*). Mary appears twice, and her size varies. The focus of the composition is the reclining Virgin of the *Nativity,* whose posture and drapery are reminiscent of those of the lid figures on Etruscan (FIGS. 6-5 and 6-15) and Roman (FIG. 7-61) sarcophagi. The face types, beards, and coiffures as well as the bulk and weight of Nicola's figures also reveal the influence of classical relief sculpture. Scholars have even been able to pinpoint the models of some of the pulpit figures on Roman sarcophagi in Pisa.

MAP 14-1 Italy around 1400.

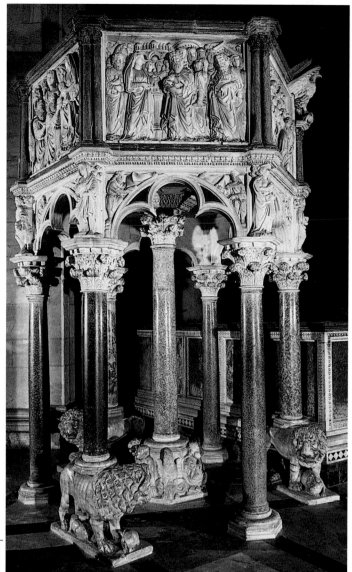

Nicola Pisano's baptistery pulpit at Pisa retains many medieval design elements, for example, the trefoil arches and the lions supporting columns, but the panels draw on ancient Roman sarcophagus reliefs.

GIOVANNI PISANO Nicola Pisano's son, Giovanni Pisano (ca. 1250–1320), likewise became a sought-after sculptor of church pulpits. Giovanni's pulpit in Sant'Andrea at Pistoia also has a panel (FIG. **14-4**) featuring the Nativity and related scenes. The son's version of the subject is in striking contrast to his father's thick carving and placid, almost stolid, presentation of the religious narrative. Giovanni arranged the figures loosely and dynamically. They twist and bend in excited animation, and the spaces that open deeply between them suggest their motion. In the *Annunciation* episode (*top left*), the Virgin shrinks from the angel's sudden appearance in a posture of alarm touched with humility. The same spasm of apprehension contracts her supple body as she reclines in the *Nativity* scene (*center*). The drama's principals share in a peculiar nervous agitation, as if they all suddenly are moved by spiritual passion. Only the shepherds and the sheep (*right*) do not yet experience the miraculous event. The swiftly turning, sinuous draperies, the slender figures they enfold, and the general emotionalism of the scene are features not found in Nicola Pisano's interpretation. The father worked in the classical tradition, the son in a style derived from French Gothic. Both styles were important ingredients in the formation of the distinctive and original art of 14th-century Italy.

Painting and Architecture

A third contributing component of 14th-century Italian art was the Byzantine tradition (see Chapter 9). Throughout the Middle Ages, the Byzantine style dominated Italian painting, but its influence was especially strong after the fall of Constantinople in 1204, which precipitated a migration of Byzantine artists to Italy.

14-3 Nicola Pisano, *Annunciation, Nativity, and Adoration of the Shepherds,* relief panel on the baptistery pulpit, Pisa, Italy, 1259–1260. Marble, 2′ 10″ × 3′ 9″.

Classical sculpture inspired the face types, beards, coiffures, and draperies, as well as the bulk and weight of Nicola's figures. The Madonna of the *Nativity* resembles lid figures on Roman sarcophagi.

14-4 Giovanni Pisano, *Annunciation, Nativity, and Adoration of the Shepherds,* relief panel on the pulpit of Sant'Andrea, Pistoia, Italy, 1297–1301. Marble, 2′ 10″ × 3′ 4″.

The French Gothic style had a greater influence on Giovanni Pisano, Nicola's son. Giovanni arranged his figures loosely and dynamically. They display a nervous agitation, as if moved by spiritual passion.

14-5 BONAVENTURA BERLINGHIERI, panel from the *Saint Francis Altarpiece,* San Francesco, Pescia, Italy, 1235. Tempera on wood, 5′ × 3′ × 6′.

Berlinghieri was one of the leading painters working in the Italo-Byzantine style, or *maniera greca.* The frontal pose of Saint Francis and the use of gold leaf reveal the painter's Byzantine sources.

BONAVENTURA BERLINGHIERI

One of the leading painters working in the Italo-Byzantine style, or *maniera greca* (Greek style), was BONAVENTURA BERLINGHIERI (active ca. 1235–1244) of Lucca. He created the *Saint Francis Altarpiece* (FIG. 14-5) for the church of San Francesco (Saint Francis) in Pescia in 1235. Painted in *tempera* on wood panel (see "Tempera and Oil Painting," Chapter 15, page 401), the *altarpiece* honors Saint Francis of Assisi (ca. 1181–1226). Francis wears the coarse clerical robe, tied at the waist with a rope, which became the costume of Franciscan monks. The saint displays the *stigmata*—marks resembling Christ's wounds—that appeared on his hands and feet. Flanking Francis are two angels, whose frontal poses, prominent halos, and lack of modeling reveal the Byzantine roots of Berlinghieri's style. So too does his use of *gold leaf* (gold beaten into tissue-paper-thin sheets, then applied to surfaces), which emphasizes the image's flatness and spiritual nature. The narrative scenes that run along the sides of the panel provide an active contrast to the stiff formality of the large central image of Francis. At the upper left, taking pride of place at the saint's right, Francis miraculously acquires the stigmata. Directly below, the saint preaches to the birds. These and the scenes depicting Francis's miracle cures strongly suggest that Berlinghieri's source was one or more Byzantine *illuminated manuscripts* (compare FIG. 9-17) having biblical narrative scenes.

Berlinghieri's *Saint Francis Altarpiece* also highlights the increasingly prominent role of religious orders in late medieval Italy (see "The Great Schism, Mendicant Orders, and Confraternities," page 379). Saint Francis's Franciscan order worked diligently to impress on the public the saint's valuable example and to demonstrate its monks' commitment to teaching and to alleviating suffering. Berlinghieri's Pescia altarpiece, painted nine years after Francis's death, is the earliest known signed and dated representation of the saint. Appropriately, the panel focuses on the aspects of the saint's life that the Franciscans wanted to promote, thereby making visible (and thus more credible) the legendary life of this holy man. Saint Francis believed he could get closer to God by rejecting worldly goods, and to achieve this he stripped himself bare in a public square and committed himself to a strict life of fasting, prayer, and meditation. The appearance of stigmata on his hands and feet (clearly visible in the saint's frontal image, which resembles an *icon*) was perceived as God's blessing and led some followers to see Francis as a second Christ. Fittingly, four of the six narrative scenes on the altarpiece depict miraculous healings, connecting him more emphatically to Christ.

SANTA MARIA NOVELLA The increased importance of the mendicant orders during the 13th century led to the construction of large churches in Florence by the Franciscans (Santa Croce; FIG. I-3) and the Dominicans. The Florentine government and contributions from private citizens subsidized the commissioning of the Dominicans' Santa Maria Novella (FIG. 14-6) around 1246. The large congregations these orders attracted necessitated the expansive scale of this church. Small *oculi* (round windows) and marble striping along

The Great Schism, Mendicant Orders, and Confraternities

In 1305 the College of Cardinals (the collective body of all cardinals) elected a French pope, Clement V, who settled in Avignon. Subsequent French popes remained in Avignon, despite their announced intentions to return to Rome. Understandably, this did not please the Italians, who saw Rome as the rightful capital of the universal church. The conflict between the French and Italians resulted in the election in 1378 of two popes— Clement VII, who resided in Avignon (and who does not appear in the Catholic Church's official list of popes), and Urban VI (r. 1378–1389), who remained in Rome. Thus began what became known as the Great Schism. After 40 years, the Holy Roman Emperor Sigismund (r. 1410–1437) convened a council that managed to resolve this crisis by electing a new Roman pope, Martin V (r. 1417–1431), who was acceptable to all.

The pope's absence from Italy during much of the 14th century (the Avignon papacy) contributed to an increase in prominence of *monastic orders*. The Augustinians, Carmelites, and Servites became very active, ensuring a constant religious presence in the daily life of Italians, but the largest and most influential monastic orders were the *mendicants* (begging friars)—the Franciscans, founded by Francis of Assisi (FIG. **14-5**), and the Dominicans, founded by the Spaniard Dominic de Guzman (ca. 1170–1221). These mendicants renounced all worldly goods and committed themselves to spreading God's word, performing good deeds, and ministering to the sick and dying. The Dominicans, in particular, contributed significantly to establishing urban educational institutions. The Franciscans and Dominicans became very popular among Italian citizens because of their devotion to their faith and the more personal relationship with God they encouraged. Although both mendicant orders were working for the same purpose—the glory of God—a degree of rivalry nevertheless existed between the two. They established their churches on opposite sides of Florence—Santa Croce (FIG. I-3), the Franciscan church, on the eastern side, and the Dominicans' Santa Maria Novella (FIG. **14-6**) on the western (MAP **16-1**).

Confraternities, organizations consisting of laypersons who dedicated themselves to strict religious observance, also grew in popularity during the 14th and 15th centuries. The mission of confraternities included tending the sick, burying the dead, singing hymns, and per-

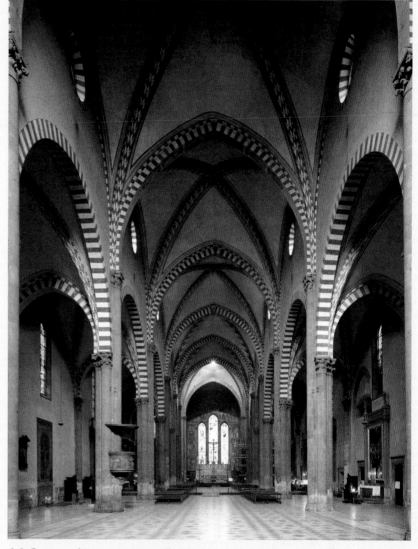

14-6 Nave of Santa Maria Novella, Florence, Italy, ca. 1246–1470.

The basilicas of Santa Maria Novella and Santa Croce (FIG. I-3) testify to the growing influence of the Dominican and Franciscan mendicant orders, respectively, in 13th-century Florence.

forming other good works. The confraternities as well as the mendicant orders continued to play an important role in Italian religious life through the 16th century. Further, the numerous artworks and monastic churches they commissioned ensured their enduring legacy.

the ogival arches punctuate the *nave,* or central *aisle.* (For the nomenclature of *basilican* church architecture, see FIG. **8-9** or in the "Before 1300" section.) Originally, a screen (*tramezzo*) placed across the nave separated the friars from the lay audience. The priests performed the *Mass* at separate altars on each side of the screen. Church officials removed this screen in the mid-16th century to encourage greater lay participation in the Mass.

CIMABUE One of the first artists to begin to break away from the Italo-Byzantine style that dominated 13th-century Italian painting was Cenni di Pepo, better known as CIMABUE (ca. 1240–1302). Although his works reveal the unmistakable influence of Gothic sculpture, Cimabue challenged some of the conventions that dominated late medieval art in pursuit of a new *naturalism*, the close observation of the natural world that was at the core of the classical

THE 14TH CENTURY

In the 14th century, Italy consisted of numerous independent *city-states,* each corresponding to a geographic region centered on a major city (MAP **14-1**). Most of the city-states, such as Venice, Florence, Lucca, and Siena, were republics. These republics were constitutional oligarchies—governed by executive bodies, advisory councils, and special commissions. Other powerful 14th-century states included the Papal States, the Kingdom of Naples, and the Duchies of Milan, Modena, Ferrara, and Savoy. As their names indicate, these states were politically distinct from the republics, but all the states shared in the prosperity of the period. The sources of wealth varied from state to state. Italy's port cities expanded maritime trade, whereas the economies of other cities depended on banking or the manufacture of arms or textiles.

The eruption of the Black Death (bubonic plague) in the late 1340s threatened this prosperity, however. Originating in China, the Black Death swept across the entire European continent. The most devastating natural disaster in European history, the plague killed between 25 and 50 percent of Europe's population in about five years. Italy was particularly hard hit. In large cities, where people lived in relatively close proximity, the death tolls climbed as high as 50 or 60 percent of the population. The Black Death had a significant effect on art. It stimulated religious bequests and encouraged the commissioning of devotional images. The focus on sickness and death also led to a burgeoning in hospital construction.

Another significant development in 14th-century Italy was the blossoming of a vernacular (commonly spoken) literature, which dramatically affected Italy's intellectual and cultural life. Latin remained the official language of church liturgy and state documents. However, the creation of an Italian vernacular literature (based on the Tuscan dialect common in Florence) expanded the audience for philosophical and intellectual concepts because of its greater accessibility. Dante Alighieri (1265–1321; author of *The Divine Comedy*), poet and scholar Francesco Petrarch (1304–1374), and Giovanni Boccaccio (1313–1375; author of *Decameron*) were among those most responsible for establishing this vernacular literature.

RENAISSANCE HUMANISM The development of a vernacular literature was one important sign that the essentially religious view of the world that dominated medieval Europe was about to change dramatically in what historians call the *Renaissance.* Although religion continued to occupy a primary position in the lives of Europeans, a growing concern with the natural world, the individual, and humanity's worldly existence characterized the Renaissance period—the 14th through the 16th centuries. The word *renaissance* in French and English (*rinascità* in Italian) refers to a "rebirth" of art and culture. A revived interest in classical cultures—indeed, the veneration of classical antiquity as a model—was central to this rebirth. The notion that the Renaissance represented the restoration of the glorious past of Greece and Rome gave rise to the concept of the "Middle Ages" as the era spanning the time between antiquity and the Renaissance. The transition from the medieval to the Renaissance, though dramatic, did not come about abruptly, however. In fact, much that is medieval persisted in the Renaissance and in later periods.

Fundamental to the development of the Italian Renaissance was *humanism,* a concept that emerged during the 14th century and became a central component of Italian art and culture in the 15th and 16th centuries. Humanism was more a code of civil conduct, a theory of education, and a scholarly discipline than a philosophical system. As their name suggests, Italian humanists were concerned chiefly with human values and interests as distinct from—but not opposed to—religion's otherworldly values. Humanists pointed to

14-7 CIMABUE, *Madonna Enthroned with Angels and Prophets,* from Santa Trinità, Florence, Italy, ca. 1280–1290. Tempera and gold leaf on wood, 12′ 7″ × 7′ 4″. Galleria degli Uffizi, Florence.

Cimabue was one of the first artists to break away from the Italo-Byzantine style. Although he relied on Byzantine models, Cimabue depicted the Madonna's massive throne as receding into space.

1 ft.

tradition. Cimabue's *Madonna Enthroned with Angels and Prophets* (FIG. **14-7**), created for the church of Santa Trinità (Holy Trinity) in Florence, nonetheless reveals the painter's reliance on Byzantine models for the composition as well as the gold background (compare FIG. 9-18). Cimabue used the gold embellishments common to Byzantine art for the folds of the Madonna's robe, but they are no longer merely decorative patterns. Here they enhance the three-dimensionality of the drapery. Cimabue also constructed a deeper space for the Madonna and the surrounding figures to inhabit than is common in Byzantine art. The Virgin's throne, for example, is a massive structure that Cimabue convincingly depicted as receding into space. The overlapping bodies of the angels on each side of the throne and the half-length prophets who look outward or upward from beneath it reinforce the sense of depth.

14-8 GIOTTO DI BONDONE, *Madonna Enthroned,* from the Church of Ognissanti, Florence, Italy, ca. 1310. Tempera and gold leaf on wood, 10′ 8″ × 6′ 8″. Galleria degli Uffizi, Florence.

Giotto displaced the Byzantine style in Italian painting and revived the naturalism of classical art. His figures have substance, dimensionality, and bulk and give the illusion that they could throw shadows.

classical cultures as particularly praiseworthy. This enthusiasm for antiquity, represented by the elegant Latin of Cicero (106–43 BCE) and the Augustan age, involved study of Latin literature and a conscious emulation of what proponents thought were the Roman civic virtues. These included self-sacrificing service to the state, participation in government, defense of state institutions (especially the administration of justice), and stoic indifference to personal misfortune in the performance of duty. With the help of a new interest in and knowledge of Greek, the humanists of the late 14th and 15th centuries recovered a large part of the Greek as well as the Roman literature and philosophy that had been lost, left unnoticed, or cast aside in the Middle Ages. Indeed, classical cultures provided humanists with a model for living in this world, a model primarily of human focus that derived not from an authoritative and traditional religious dogma but from reason.

Ideally, humanists sought no material reward for services rendered. The sole reward for heroes of civic virtue was fame, just as the reward for leaders of the holy life was sainthood. For the educated, the lives of heroes and heroines of the past became as edifying as the

lives of the saints. Petrarch wrote a book on illustrious men, and his colleague Boccaccio complemented it with biographies of famous women—from Eve to his contemporary, Joanna, queen of Naples. Both Petrarch and Boccaccio were famous in their own day as poets, scholars, and men of letters—their achievements equivalent in honor to those of the heroes of civic virtue. In 1341 in Rome, Petrarch received the laurel wreath crown, the ancient symbol of victory and merit. The humanist cult of fame emphasized the importance of creative individuals and their role in contributing to the renown of the city-state and of all Italy.

Giotto

GIOTTO DI BONDONE (ca. 1266–1337) of Florence made a much more radical break with the past than did Cimabue. Art historians from Giorgio Vasari[†] to the present day have regarded Giotto as the first Renaissance painter, a pioneer in pursuing a naturalistic approach to representation based on observation. Scholars still debate the sources of Giotto's style, however. One formative influence must have been the work of the man Vasari said was his teacher, Cimabue, although Vasari lauded Giotto as having eclipsed Cimabue by abandoning the "crude *maniera greca.*" Some late-13th-century *murals* in Rome with fully modeled figures of saints may also have influenced the young Giotto. French Gothic sculpture (which Giotto may have seen, but certainly familiar to him from the work of Giovanni Pisano, who had spent time in Paris) and ancient Roman art must also have contributed to Giotto's artistic education. Yet no mere synthesis of these varied influences could have produced the significant shift in artistic approach that has led some scholars to describe Giotto as the father of Western pictorial art. Renowned in his own day, he established a reputation that has never faltered. Regardless of the other influences on his artistic style, his true teacher was nature—the world of visible things.

Giotto's revolution in painting did not consist only of displacing the Byzantine style, establishing painting as a major art form for the next seven centuries, and restoring the naturalistic approach the ancients developed and medieval artists largely abandoned. He also inaugurated a method of pictorial expression based on observation and initiated an age that might be called "early scientific." By stressing the preeminence of sight for gaining knowledge of the world, Giotto and his successors contributed to the foundation of empirical science. They recognized that the visual world must be observed before it can be analyzed and understood. Praised in his own and later times for his fidelity to nature, Giotto was more than a mere imitator of it. He revealed nature while observing it and divining its visible order. In fact, he showed his generation a new way of seeing. With Giotto, Western artists turned resolutely toward the visible world as their source of knowledge of nature.

MADONNA ENTHRONED On nearly the same great scale as Cimabue's enthroned Madonna (FIG. **14-7**) is Giotto's panel (FIG. **14-8**) depicting the same subject, painted for the high altar of the Ognissanti (All Saints) church in Florence. Although still seen against the traditional gold background, Giotto's Madonna rests within her Gothic throne with the unshakable stability of an ancient

[†]Giorgio Vasari (1511–1574) established himself as both a painter and architect during the 16th century. However, people today usually associate him with his landmark book *Lives of the Most Eminent Painters, Sculptors, and Architects,* first published in 1550. Scholars long have considered this book a major source of information about Italian art and artists, although many of the details have proven inaccurate. Regardless, Vasari's *Lives* remains a tour de force—an ambitious, comprehensive book dedicated to recording the biographies of artists.

Fresco Painting

Fresco painting has a long history, particularly in the Mediterranean region, where the Minoans (FIGS. 4-7 to 4-9) used it as early as 1650 BCE. *Fresco* (Italian for "fresh") is a mural-painting technique that involves applying permanent limeproof pigments, diluted in water, on freshly laid lime plaster. Because the surface of the wall absorbs the pigments as the plaster dries, fresco is one of the most permanent painting techniques. The stable condition of frescoes such as those in the Arena Chapel (FIGS. 14-1 and 14-9) and in the Sistine Chapel (FIGS. 17-1, 17-18, and 17-19), now hundreds of years old, attest to the longevity of this painting method. The colors have remained vivid (although dirt and soot have necessitated cleaning) because of the chemically inert pigments the artists used. In addition to this *buon fresco* ("true" fresco) technique, artists used *fresco secco* (dry fresco). Fresco secco involves painting on dried lime plaster. Although the finished product visually approximates buon fresco, the plaster wall does not absorb the pigments, which simply adhere to the surface. Thus fresco secco does not have buon fresco's longevity.

The buon fresco process is time-consuming and demanding and requires several layers of plaster. Although buon fresco methods vary, generally the artist prepares the wall with a rough layer of lime plaster called the *arriccio* (brown coat). The artist then transfers the composition to the wall, usually by drawing directly on the arriccio with a burnt-orange pigment called *sinopia* (most popular during the 14th century) or by transferring a *cartoon* (a full-sized preparatory drawing). Cartoons increased in usage in the 15th and 16th centuries, largely replacing sinopia underdrawings. Finally, the painter lays the *intonaco* (painting coat) smoothly over the drawing in sections (called *giornate*, Italian for "days") only as large as the artist expects to complete in that session. The buon fresco painter must apply the colors fairly quickly, because once the plaster is dry, it will no longer absorb the pigment. Any

14-9 GIOTTO DI BONDONE, *Lamentation*, Arena Chapel (Cappella Scrovegni), Padua, Italy, ca. 1305. Fresco, 6' 6¾" × 6' ¾".

In this fresco painted in several sections, Giotto used the diagonal slope of the rocky landscape to direct the viewer's attention toward the head of the sculpturesque figure of the dead Christ.

areas of the intonaco that remain unpainted after a session must be cut away so that fresh plaster can be applied for the next giornata.

In areas of high humidity, such as Venice, fresco was less appropriate because moisture is an obstacle to the drying process. Over the centuries, fresco became less popular, although it did experience a revival in the 1930s with the Mexican muralists (FIGS. 24-67 and 24-68).

marble goddess. Giotto replaced Cimabue's slender Virgin, fragile beneath the thin ripplings of her drapery, with a weighty, queenly mother. In Giotto's painting, the Madonna's body is not lost. It is asserted. Giotto even shows Mary's breasts pressing through the thin fabric of her white undergarment. Gold highlights have disappeared from her heavy robe. Giotto aimed, before all else, to construct a figure that has substance, dimensionality, and bulk—qualities suppressed in favor of a spiritual immateriality in Byzantine and Italo-Byzantine art. Works painted in the new style portray sculpturesque figures—projecting into the light and giving the illusion that they could throw shadows. Giotto's *Madonna Enthroned* marks the end of medieval painting in Italy and the beginning of a new naturalistic approach to art.

ARENA CHAPEL, PADUA To project onto a flat surface the illusion of solid bodies moving through space presents a double challenge. Constructing the illusion of a body also requires constructing the illusion of a space sufficiently ample to contain that body. In his *fresco* cycles (see "Fresco Painting," above), Giotto constantly strove to reconcile these two aspects of illusionistic painting. His murals in the Arena Chapel (Cappella Scrovegni; FIG. 14-1) at Padua show his art at its finest. Enrico Scrovegni, a wealthy Paduan banker, built the chapel on a site adjacent to his now-razed palace. Consecrated in 1305, the Arena Chapel takes its name from an ancient Roman amphitheater nearby. Scrovegni erected the chapel, which he intended for his family's private use, in part to expiate the bankers' sin of usury. Some scholars have suggested that Giotto himself may have been the chapel's architect because its design is so perfectly suited to its interior decoration.

The rectangular *barrel-vaulted* hall has six narrow windows only in its south wall (FIG. 14-1, *left*), which left the entire north wall an unbroken and well-illuminated surface for painting. The building seems to have been designed to provide Giotto with as much flat surface as possible for presenting one of the most impressive and complete Christian pictorial cycles ever rendered. In 38 framed pictures, arranged on three levels, the artist related the most poignant incidents from the lives of the Virgin and her parents, Joachim and Anna (top level), the life and mission of Christ (middle level), and his Passion, Crucifixion, and Resurrection (bottom level). These three pictorial levels rest on a coloristically neutral base. Imitation marble veneer—reminiscent of ancient Roman decoration (FIG. 7-51), which Giotto may have seen—alternates with the Virtues and Vices painted in *grisaille* (monochrome grays, often used for modeling in paintings) to resemble sculpture. The climactic event of the cycle of human salvation, the Last Judgment, covers most of the west wall above the chapel's entrance (FIG. 14-1).

The hall's vaulted ceiling is blue, an azure sky dotted with golden stars symbolic of Heaven. Medallions bearing images of Christ, Mary, and various prophets also appear on the vault. Giotto painted the same blue in the backgrounds of the narrative panels on the walls below. The color thereby functions as a unifying agent for the entire decorative scheme and renders the scenes more realistic.

Decorative borders frame the individual panels. They offer a striking contrast to the sparse simplicity of the images they surround. Subtly scaled to the chapel's space (only about half life-size), Giotto's stately and slow-moving actors present their dramas convincingly and with great restraint. *Lamentation* (FIG. 14-9) reveals the essentials of his style. In the presence of boldly *foreshortened* angels, seen head-on with their bodies receding into the background and darting about in hysterical grief, a congregation mourns over the dead body of the Savior just before its entombment. Mary cradles her son's body, while Mary Magdalene looks solemnly at the wounds in Christ's feet and Saint John the Evangelist throws his arms back dramatically. Giotto arranged a shallow stage for the figures, bounded by a thick diagonal rock incline that defines a horizontal ledge in the foreground. Though narrow, the ledge provides firm visual support for the figures, and the steep slope indicates the picture's dramatic focal point at the lower left. The rocky setting, which recalls that of a 12th-century Byzantine mural (FIG. 9-27), also links this scene with the adjoining one. Giotto connected the framed scenes throughout the fresco cycle with such formal elements. The figures are sculpturesque, simple, and weighty, but this mass did not preclude motion and emotion. Postures and gestures that might have been only rhetorical and mechanical convey, in *Lamentation,* a broad spectrum of grief. They range from Mary's almost fierce despair to the passionate outbursts of Mary Magdalene and John to the philosophical resignation of the two disciples at the right and the mute sorrow of the two hooded mourners in the foreground. Giotto constructed a kind of stage that served as a model for artists who depicted human dramas in many subsequent paintings. His style broke sharply from the isolated episodes and figures seen in art until the late 13th century. In *Lamentation,* a single event provokes an intense response. Painters before Giotto rarely attempted, let alone achieved, this combination of compositional complexity and emotional resonance.

The formal design of the *Lamentation* fresco—the way the figures are grouped within the constructed space—is worth close study. Each group has its own definition, and each contributes to the rhythmic order of the composition. The strong diagonal of the rocky ledge, with its single dead tree (the tree of knowledge of good and evil, which withered at the fall of Adam), concentrates the viewer's attention on the group around the head of Christ, whose positioning is dynamically off center. The massive bulk of the seated mourner in the painting's left corner arrests and contains all movement beyond this group. The seated mourner to the right establishes a relation with the center figures, who, by gazes and gestures, draw the viewer's attention back to Christ's head. Figures seen from the back, which are frequent in Giotto's compositions, represent an innovation in the development away from the formal Italo-Byzantine style. These figures emphasize the foreground, aiding the visual placement of the intermediate figures farther back in space. This device, the very contradiction of the old frontality, in effect puts viewers behind the "observer figures," who, facing the action as spectators, reinforce the sense of stagecraft as a model for painting.

Giotto's new devices for depicting spatial depth and body mass could not, of course, have been possible without his management of light and shade. He shaded his figures to indicate both the direction of the light that illuminates them and the shadows (the diminished light), giving the figures volume. In *Lamentation,* light falls upon the upper surfaces of the figures (especially the two central bending figures) and passes down to dark in their draperies, separating the volumes one from the other and pushing one to the fore, the other to the rear. The graded continuum of light and shade, directed by an even, neutral light from a single steady source—not shown in the picture—was the first step toward the development of *chiaroscuro* (the use of contrasts of dark and light to produce modeling) in later Renaissance painting.

The stagelike settings made possible by Giotto's innovations in *perspective* (the depiction of three-dimensional objects in space on a two-dimensional surface) and lighting suited perfectly the dramatic narrative the Franciscans emphasized then as a principal method for educating the faithful in their religion. In the age of humanism, the old stylized presentations of the holy mysteries had evolved into what were called *mystery plays.* The drama of the Mass was extended into one- and two-act tableaus and scenes and then into simple narratives offered at church portals and in city squares. (Eventually, confraternities also presented more elaborate religious dramas called *sacre rappresentazioni*—holy representations.) The great increase in popular sermons addressed to huge city audiences prompted a public taste for narrative, recited as dramatically as possible. The arts of illusionistic painting, of drama, and of sermon rhetoric with all their theatrical flourishes developed simultaneously and were mutually influential. Giotto's art masterfully synthesized dramatic narrative, holy lesson, and truth to human experience in a visual idiom of his own invention, accessible to all. Not surprisingly, Giotto's frescoes served as textbooks for generations of Renaissance painters.

Siena

Among 14th-century Italian city-states, the Republics of Siena and Florence were the most powerful. Both Siena and Florence (the major cities of these two republics) were urban centers of bankers and merchants with widespread international contacts and large sums available for the commissioning of artworks (see "Artists' Guilds, Commissions, and Contracts," page 384).

DUCCIO The works of DUCCIO DI BUONINSEGNA (active ca. 1278–1318) represent Sienese art in its supreme achievement. His most famous painting, the immense altarpiece called the *Maestà*

Artists' Guilds, Commissions, and Contracts

The structured organization of economic activity during the 14th century, when Italy had established a thriving international trade and held a commanding position in the Mediterranean world, extended to many trades and professions. *Guilds* (associations of master craftspeople, apprentices, and tradespeople), which had emerged during the 12th century, became prominent. These associations not only protected members' common economic interests against external pressures, such as taxation, but also provided them with the means to regulate their internal operations (for example, work quality and membership training).

Because of today's international open art market, the notion of an "artists' union" may seem strange. The general public tends to see art as the creative expression of an individual artist. However, artists did not always enjoy this degree of freedom. Historically, artists rarely undertook major artworks without a patron's concrete commission. The patron could be a civic group, religious entity, private individual, or even the artists' guild itself. Guilds, although primarily economic commercial organizations, contributed to their city's religious and artistic life by subsidizing the building and decoration of numerous churches and hospitals. For example, the Arte della Lana (wool manufacturers' guild) oversaw the start of Florence Cathedral (FIGS. 14-18 and 14-19) in 1296, and the Arte di Calimala (wool merchants' guild) supervised the completion of its dome.

Monastic orders, confraternities, and the popes were also major art patrons. In addition, wealthy families and individuals commissioned artworks for a variety of reasons. Besides the aesthetic pleasure these patrons derived from art, the images often served as testaments to the patron's wealth, status, power, and knowledge. Because artworks during this period were the product of what was, in effect, a service contract, a patron's needs or wishes played a crucial role in the final form of any painting, sculpture, or building. Some contracts between patrons and artists are preserved in European municipal and church archives. The patrons normally asked artists to submit drawings or models for approval, and they expected the artists they hired to adhere to the approved designs fairly closely. These contracts usually stipulated certain conditions, such as the insistence on the artist's own hand in the production of the work, the quality of pigment and amount of gold or other precious items to be used, completion date, payment terms, and penalties for failure to meet the contract's terms.

A few extant 13th- and 14th-century painting contracts are especially illuminating. Although they may specify the subject to be represented, the focus of these binding legal documents is always the financial aspects of the commission and the responsibilities of the painter to the patron (and vice versa). In a contract dated November 1, 1301, between Cimabue and another artist and the Hospital of Santa Chiara in Pisa, the artists agree to supply an altarpiece

> with colonnettes, tabernacles, and predella, painted with histories of the divine majesty of the Blessed Virgin Mary, of the apostles, of the angels, and with other figures and pictures, as shall be seen fit and shall please the said master of or other legitimate persons for the hospital.*

Other contract terms specify the size of the panel and require that gold and silver gilding be used for parts of the altarpiece.

The contract for the construction of an altarpiece was usually a separate document, for that required the services of a master carpenter. For example, Duccio's April 15, 1285, contract with the rectors of the Confraternity of the Laudesi, the lay group associated with the Dominican church of Santa Maria Novella (FIG. 14-6) in Florence, specifies only that he is to provide the painting, not its frame—and it imposes conditions that he must meet if he is to be paid.

> [The rectors] promise . . . to pay the same Duccio . . . as the payment and price of the painting of the said panel that is to be painted and done by him in the way described below . . . 150 lire of the small florins. . . . [Duccio, in turn, promises] to paint and embellish the panel with the image of the blessed Virgin Mary and of her omnipotent Son and other figures, according to the wishes and pleasure of the lessors, and to gild [the panel] and do everything that will enhance the beauty of the panel, his being all the expenses and the costs. . . . If the said panel is not beautifully painted and it is not embellished according to the wishes and desires of the same lessors, they are in no way bound to pay him the price or any part of it.†

Sometimes patrons furnished the materials and paid artists by the day instead of a fixed amount. That was the arrangement Duccio made on October 9, 1308, when he agreed to paint the *Maestà* (FIG. 14-10) for the high altar of Siena Cathedral.

> Duccio has promised to paint and make the said panel as well as he can and knows how, and he further agreed not to accept or receive any other work until the said panel is done and completed. . . . [The church officials promise] to pay the said Duccio sixteen solidi of the Sienese denari as his salary for the said work and labor for each day that the said Duccio works with his own hands on the said panel . . . [and] to provide and give everything that will be necessary for working on the said panel so that the said Duccio need contribute nothing to the work save his person and his effort.‡

In all cases, the artists worked for their patrons and could count on being compensated for their talents and efforts only if the work they delivered met the standards of those who ordered it.

---

* Translated by John White, *Duccio: Tuscan Art and the Medieval Workshop* (London: Thames & Hudson, 1979), 34.
† Translated by James H. Stubblebine, *Duccio di Buoninsegna and His School* (Princeton, N.J.: Princeton University Press, 1979), 1: 192.
‡ Stubblebine, *Duccio*, 1: 201.

14-10 DUCCIO DI BUONINSEGNA, *Virgin and Child Enthroned with Saints,* principal panel of the *Maestà* altarpiece, from Siena Cathedral, Siena, Italy, 1308–1311. Tempera and gold leaf on wood, 7′ × 13′ (center panel). Museo dell'Opera del Duomo, Siena.

Duccio derived the formality and symmetry of his composition from Byzantine tradition, but relaxed the rigidity and frontality of the figures, softened the drapery, and individualized the faces.

(*Virgin Enthroned in Majesty;* FIG. **14-10**), replaced a much smaller painting of the Virgin Mary on the high altar of Siena Cathedral. The Sienese believed the Virgin had brought them their victory over the Florentines at the battle of Monteperti in 1260, and she was the focus of the religious life of the republic. Duccio and his assistants began work on the prestigious commission in 1308 and completed the *Maestà* in 1311. As originally executed, it consisted of a seven-foot-high central panel (FIG. **14-10**), surmounted by seven *pinnacles* above, and a *predella,* or raised shelf, of panels at the base, altogether some 13 feet high. Painted in tempera front and back, the work unfortunately is no longer viewable in its entirety because of its dismantling in subsequent centuries. Many of Duccio's panels are now scattered as single masterpieces among the world's museums.

The main panel of the front side represents the Virgin enthroned as Queen of Heaven amid choruses of angels and saints. Duccio derived the composition's formality and symmetry, along with the figures and facial types of the principal angels and saints, from Byzantine tradition. But the artist relaxed the strict frontality and rigidity of the figures. They turn to each other in quiet conversation. Further, Duccio individualized the faces of the four saints kneeling in the foreground, who perform their ceremonial gestures without stiffness. Similarly, he softened the usual Byzantine hard body outlines and drapery patterning. The drapery, particularly that of the female saints at both ends of the panel, falls and curves loosely. This is a feature familiar in northern Gothic works (FIG. **13-37**) and is a mark of the artistic dialogue between Italy and the north in the 14th century.

Despite these changes that reveal Duccio's interest in the new naturalism, he respected the age-old requirement that as an altarpiece, the *Maestà* would be the focus of worship in Siena's largest

and most important church, its *cathedral,* the seat of the bishop of Siena. As such, Duccio knew the *Maestà* should be an object holy in itself—a work of splendor to the eyes, precious in its message and its materials. Duccio thus recognized that he could not be too radical—that the function of this work naturally limited experimentation with depicting narrative action and producing illusionistic effects (such as Giotto's) by modeling forms and adjusting their placement in pictorial space.

Instead, the Queen of Heaven panel is a miracle of color composition and *texture* manipulation, unfortunately not apparent in a photograph. Close inspection of the original reveals what the Sienese artist learned from other sources. In the 13th and 14th centuries, Italy was the distribution center for the great silk trade from China and the Middle East. After processing the silk in city-states such as Lucca and Florence, the Italians exported the precious fabric throughout Europe to satisfy an immense market for sumptuous dress. (Dante, Petrarch, and many of the humanists decried the appetite for luxury in costume, which to them represented a decline in civic and moral virtue.) People throughout Europe (Duccio and other artists among them) prized fabrics from China, Persia, Byzantium, and the Islamic realms. In the *Maestà* panel, Duccio created the glistening and shimmering effects of textiles, adapting the motifs and design patterns of exotic materials. Complementing the luxurious fabrics and the (lost) gilded wood frame are the gold haloes of the holy figures, which feature tooled decorative designs in gold leaf (*punchwork*). But Duccio, like Giotto (FIG. **14-8**), eliminated almost all the gold patterning of the figures' garments in favor of creating three-dimensional volume. Traces remain only in the Virgin's red dress.

The 14th Century   **385**

14-11 Duccio di Buoninsegna, *Betrayal of Jesus*, detail from the back of the *Maestà* altarpiece, from Siena Cathedral, Siena, Italy, 1309–1311. Tempera and gold leaf on wood, detail 1′ 10½″ × 3′ 4″. Museo dell'Opera del Duomo, Siena.

On the back of the *Maestà*, Duccio painted a religious drama in which the actors display a variety of individual emotions. Duccio here took a decisive step toward the humanization of religious subject matter.

1 in.

On the front panel of the *Maestà*, Duccio showed himself as the great master of the formal altarpiece. However, he allowed himself greater latitude for experimentation in the small accompanying panels, front and back. (Both sides of the altarpiece were always on view because the high altar stood at the very center of the sanctuary.) These images reveal Duccio's powers as a narrative painter. In the numerous panels on the back, he illustrated the later life of Christ—his ministry (on the *predella*), his Passion (on the main panel), and his Resurrection and appearances to the disciples (on the pinnacles). On one of the small panels, *Betrayal of Jesus* (FIG. **14-11**), the artist represented several episodes of the event—the betrayal of Jesus by Judas's false kiss, the disciples fleeing in terror, and Peter cutting off the ear of the high priest's servant. Although the background, with its golden sky and rock formations, remains traditional, the style of the figures before it has changed quite radically. The bodies are not the flat frontal shapes of Italo-Byzantine art. Duccio imbued them with mass, modeled them with a range from light to dark, and arranged their draperies around them convincingly. Even more novel and striking is the way the figures seem to react to the central event. Through posture, gesture, and even facial expression, they display a variety of emotions. Duccio carefully differentiated among the anger of Peter, the malice of Judas (echoed in the faces of the throng about Jesus), and the apprehension and timidity of the fleeing disciples. These figures are actors in a religious drama that the artist interpreted in terms of thoroughly human actions and reactions. In this and similar narrative panels, Duccio took a decisive step toward the humanization of religious subject matter.

ORVIETO CATHEDRAL While Duccio was working on the *Maestà* for Siena Cathedral, a Sienese architect, Lorenzo Maitani, was called to Orvieto to design that city's cathedral (FIG. **14-12**). The Orvieto *facade* imitates some elements of the French Gothic

architectural vocabulary (see Chapter 13), especially the pointed gables over the three doorways, the *rose window* and statues in niches in the upper zone, and the four large *pinnacles* that divide the facade into three bays. The outer pinnacles serve as miniature substitutes for the large northern European west-front towers. Maitani's facade, however, is merely a Gothic overlay masking a marble-revetted basil-

14-12 Lorenzo Maitani, west facade of Orvieto Cathedral, Orvieto, Italy, begun 1310.

The pointed gables over the doorways, the rose window, and the large pinnacles derive from French architecture, but the facade of Orvieto Cathedral is merely a Gothic overlay masking a timber-roofed basilica.

14-13 SIMONE MARTINI and LIPPO MEMMI(?), *Annunciation* altarpiece, from Siena Cathedral, Siena, Italy, 1333 (frame reconstructed in the 19th century). Tempera and gold leaf on wood, center panel 10′ 1″ × 8′ 8¾″. Galleria degli Uffizi, Florence.

A pupil of Duccio, Martini was instrumental in the creation of the International Style. Its hallmarks are elegant shapes, radiant color, flowing line, and weightless figures in golden, spaceless settings.

1 ft.

ican structure in the Tuscan Romanesque tradition, as the three-quarter view of the cathedral in FIG. 14-12 reveals. Few Italian architects fully accepted the northern Gothic style. Some architectural historians even have questioned whether it is proper to speak of late medieval Italian buildings as Gothic structures. The Orvieto facade resembles a great altar screen, its single plane covered with carefully placed carved and painted ornament. In principle, Orvieto belongs with Pisa Cathedral (FIG. 12-25) and other Italian buildings rather than with the French cathedrals at Amiens (FIG. 13-21) and Reims (FIG. 13-23). Inside, Orvieto Cathedral has a timber-roofed nave with a two-story elevation (columnar *arcade* and *clerestory*) in the Early Christian manner. Both the *chancel arch* framing the semicircular *apse* and the nave arcade's arches are round as opposed to pointed.

SIMONE MARTINI Duccio's successors in the Sienese school also produced innovative works. SIMONE MARTINI (ca. 1285–1344) was a pupil of Duccio and may have assisted him in painting the *Maestà*. Martini was a close friend of Petrarch, and the poet praised him highly for his portrait of "Laura" (the woman to whom Petrarch dedicated his sonnets). Martini worked for the French kings in Naples and Sicily and, in his last years, produced paintings for the papal court at Avignon, where he came in contact with Northern European painters. By adapting the insubstantial but luxuriant patterns of the French Gothic manner to Sienese art and, in turn, by acquainting painters north of the Alps with the Sienese style, Martini was instrumental in creating the so-called *International Style*. This new style swept Europe during the late 14th and early 15th centuries because it appealed to the aristocratic taste for brilliant colors, lavish costumes, intricate ornamentation, and themes involving splendid processions.

Martini's *Annunciation* altarpiece (FIG. 14-13) features elegant shapes and radiant color, fluttering line, and weightless figures in a spaceless setting—all hallmarks of the artist's style. The complex etiquette of the European chivalric courts probably dictated the presentation. The angel Gabriel has just alighted, the breeze of his passage lifting his mantle, his iridescent wings still beating. The gold of his sumptuous gown is representative of the celestial realm from which he has descended to deliver his message. The Virgin, putting down her book of devotions, shrinks demurely from Gabriel's reverent genuflection, an appropriate gesture in the presence of royalty. She draws about her the deep blue, golden-hemmed mantle, the heraldic colors she wears as Queen of Heaven. Between the two figures is a vase of white lilies, symbolic of the Virgin's purity. Despite the Virgin's modesty and diffidence and the tremendous import of the angel's message, the scene subordinates drama to court ritual, and structural experimentation to surface splendor. The intricate *tracery* of the richly tooled (reconstructed) French Gothic–inspired frame and the elaborate punchwork halos, now a characteristic feature of Sienese panel painting, enhance the tactile magnificence of the *Annunciation.*

Simone Martini and his student and assistant, LIPPO MEMMI (active ca. 1317–1350), signed the altarpiece and dated it (1333). The latter's contribution to the *Annunciation* is still a matter of debate, but art historians now generally agree he painted the two lateral saints. These figures, which are reminiscent of the jamb statues of Gothic church portals, have greater solidity and lack the linear elegance of Martini's central pair. Given the nature of medieval and Renaissance workshop practices, it is often next to impossible to distinguish the master's hand from that of an assistant, especially if the master corrected or redid part of the latter's work (see "Artistic Training in Renaissance Italy," page 388).

Artistic Training in Renaissance Italy

In 14th- through 16th-century Italy, training to become a professional artist (earning membership in the appropriate guild) was a laborious and lengthy process. Because Italians perceived art as a trade, they expected artists to be trained as they would be in any other profession. Accordingly, aspiring artists started their training at an early age, anywhere from 7 to 15 years old. Their fathers would negotiate arrangements with specific master artists whereby each youth lived with a master for a specified number of years, usually five or six. During that time, they served as apprentices to the masters in the workshop, learning the trade. (This living arrangement served as a major obstacle for aspiring female artists, as it was considered inappropriate for young girls to live in a master's household.)

The skills apprentices learned varied with the type of studio they joined. Those apprenticed to painters learned to grind pigments, draw, prepare wood panels for painting, gild, and lay plaster for fresco. Sculptors in training learned to manipulate different materials (for example, wood, stone, *terracotta* [baked clay], wax, bronze, or stucco), although many sculpture workshops specialized in only one or two of these materials. For stone carving, apprentices learned their craft by blocking out the master's designs for statues.

The guilds supervised this rigorous training. They wanted not only to ensure their professional reputations by admitting only the most talented members but also to control the number of artists (to limit undue competition). Toward this end they frequently tried to regulate the number of apprentices working under a single master. Surely, the quality of the apprentices a master trained reflected the master's competence. When encouraging a prospective apprentice to join his studio, the Paduan painter Francesco Squarcione (1397–1468) boasted he could teach "the true art of perspective and everything necessary to the art of painting. . . . I made a man of Andrea Mantegna [see Chapter 16] who stayed with me and I will also do the same to you."*

As their skills developed, apprentices took on increasingly difficult tasks. After completing their apprenticeships, artists entered the appropriate guilds. For example, painters, who ground pigments, joined the guild of apothecaries; sculptors were members of the guild of stoneworkers; and goldsmiths entered the silk guild, because gold often was stretched into threads wound around silk for weaving. Such memberships served as certification of the artists' competence. Once "certified," artists often affiliated themselves with established workshops, as assistants to master artists. This was largely for practical reasons. New artists could not expect to receive many commissions, and the cost of establishing their own workshops was high. In any case, this arrangement was not permanent, and workshops were not necessarily static enterprises. Although well-established and respected studios existed, workshops could be organized around individual masters (with no set studio locations) or organized for a specific project, especially an extensive decoration program.

Generally, assistants were responsible for gilding frames and backgrounds, completing decorative work, and, occasionally, rendering architectural settings. Artists regarded figures, especially those central to the represented subject, as the most important and difficult parts of a painting, and the master therefore reserved these for himself. Sometimes assistants painted secondary or marginal figures, but only under the master's close supervision.

Eventually, of course, artists hoped to attract patrons and establish themselves as masters. Artists, who were largely anonymous during the medieval period, began to enjoy greater emancipation during the 15th and 16th centuries, when they rose in rank from artisan to artist-scientist. The value of their individual skills—and their reputations—became increasingly important to their patrons and clients.

* Quoted in Giuseppe Fiocco, *Mantegna: La cappella Ovetari nella chiesa degli Eremitani* (Milan: A. Pizzi, 1974), 7.

PIETRO LORENZETTI One of Duccio's students, PIETRO LORENZETTI (active 1320–1348), contributed significantly to the general experiments in pictorial realism that characterized the 14th century. Going well beyond his master, Lorenzetti achieved a remarkable degree of spatial illusionism in his large *triptych* (three-part panel painting) *Birth of the Virgin* (FIG. **14-14**), created for the altar of Saint Savinus in Siena Cathedral. Lorenzetti painted the wooden architectural members that divide the panel as though they extend back into the painted space. Viewers seem to look through the wooden frame (apparently added later) into a boxlike stage, where the event takes place. That one of the vertical members cuts across one of the figures, blocking part of it from view, strengthens the illusion. In subsequent centuries, artists exploited this use of architectural elements to enhance the pictorial illusion that the painted figures are acting out a drama just a few feet away. This kind of pictorial illusionism characterized ancient Roman mural painting (FIGS. 7-18 and 7-19, *right*), but had not been practiced in Italy for a thousand years.

Lorenzetti's setting for his holy subject also represented a marked step in the advance of worldly realism. Saint Anne—who, like Nicola Pisano's Virgin of the *Nativity* (FIG. 14-3), resembles a reclining figure on the lid of a Roman sarcophagus (FIG. 7-61)—props herself up

wearily as the midwives wash the child and the women bring gifts. She is the center of an episode that occurs in an upper-class Italian house of the period. A number of carefully observed domestic details and the scene at the left, where Joachim eagerly awaits the news of the delivery, place the event in an actual household, as if viewers had moved the panels of the walls back and peered inside. Lorenzetti joined structural innovation in illusionistic space with the new curiosity that led to careful inspection and recording of what lay directly before the artist's eye in the everyday world.

PALAZZO PUBBLICO Not all Sienese painting of the early 14th century was religious in character. One of the most important fresco cycles of the period (discussed next) was a civic commission for Siena's Palazzo Pubblico ("public palace" or city hall). Siena was a proud commercial and political rival of Florence. As the secular center of the community, the civic meeting hall in the main square (the Campo, or Field; FIG. **14-15**) was almost as great an object of civic pride as the city's cathedral. The Palazzo Pubblico has a slightly concave facade (to conform to the irregular shape of the Campo) and a gigantic tower visible from miles around. The imposing building and tower must have earned the admiration of Siena's citizens as well as of

14-14 Pietro Lorenzetti, *Birth of the Virgin*, from the altar of Saint Savinus, Siena Cathedral, Siena, Italy, 1342. Tempera on wood, 6′ 1″ × 5′ 11″. Museo dell'Opera del Duomo, Siena.

In this triptych, Pietro Lorenzetti revived the pictorial illusionism of ancient Roman murals and painted the architectural members that divide the panel as though they extend back into the painted space.

1 ft.

14-15 Aerial view of the Campo with the Palazzo Pubblico, Siena, Italy, 1288–1309.

Siena's Palazzo Pubblico has a slightly concave facade and a gigantic tower visible from miles around. The tower served both as a defensive lookout over the countryside and a symbol of the city-state's power.

visitors to the city, inspiring in them respect for the republic's power and success. The tower served as lookout over the city and the countryside around it and as a bell tower (*campanile*) for ringing signals of all sorts to the populace. Siena, like other Italian city-states, had to defend itself against neighboring cities and often against kings and emperors. In addition, it had to be secure against the internal upheavals

common in the history of the Italian city-republics. Class struggle, feuds between rich and powerful families, and even uprisings of the whole populace against the city governors were constant threats. The heavy walls and *battlements* (fortified *parapets*) of the Italian town hall eloquently express how frequently the city governors needed to defend themselves against their own citizens. The Sienese tower, out

14-16 AMBROGIO LORENZETTI, *Peaceful City,* detail from *Effects of Good Government in the City and in the Country,* Sala della Pace, Palazzo Pubblico, Siena, Italy, 1338–1339. Fresco.

In the Hall of Peace of Siena's city hall, Ambrogio Lorenzetti painted an illusionistic panorama of the bustling city. The fresco served as an allegory of good government in the Sienese republic.

of reach of most missiles, includes *machicolated galleries* (galleries with holes in their floors to allow the dumping of stones or hot liquids on enemies below) built out on *corbels* (projecting supporting architectural members) for defense of the tower's base.

AMBROGIO LORENZETTI The painter entrusted with the vast fresco program in Siena's Palazzo Pubblico was Pietro Lorenzetti's brother, AMBROGIO LORENZETTI (active 1319–1348), who both elabo-

rated Pietro's advances in illusionistic representation in spectacular fashion and gave visual form to Sienese civic concerns. Ambrogio produced three frescoes for the walls of the Sala della Pace (Hall of Peace) in the Palazzo Pubblico: *Allegory of Good Government, Bad Government and the Effects of Bad Government in the City,* and *Effects of Good Government in the City and in the Country.* The turbulent politics of the Italian cities—the violent party struggles, the overthrow and reinstatement of governments—certainly would have called for solemn

14-17 AMBROGIO LORENZETTI, *Peaceful Country,* detail from *Effects of Good Government in the City and in the Country,* Sala della Pace, Palazzo Pubblico, Siena, Italy, 1338–1339. Fresco.

This sweeping view of the Sienese countryside is one of the first appearances of landscape in Western art since antiquity. An allegorical figure of winged Security promises safety to all who live under the rule of law.

reminders of fair and just administration. And the city hall was just the place for paintings such as Ambrogio Lorenzetti's. Indeed, the leaders of the Sienese government who commissioned this fresco series had undertaken the "ordering and reformation of the whole city and countryside of Siena."

In *Effects of Good Government in the City and in the Country*, the artist depicted the urban and rural effects of good government. *Peaceful City* (FIG. **14-16**) is a panoramic view of Siena, with its clustering palaces, markets, towers, churches, streets, and walls, reminiscent of the townscapes of ancient Roman murals (FIG. **7-19**, *left*). The city's traffic moves peacefully, guild members ply their trades and crafts, and several radiant maidens, hand in hand, perform a graceful circling dance. Dancers were regular features of festive springtime rituals. Here, their presence also serves as a metaphor for a peaceful commonwealth. The artist fondly observed the life of his city, and its architecture gave him an opportunity to apply Sienese artists' rapidly growing knowledge of perspective.

As an entourage passes through the city gate to the countryside beyond its walls, Ambrogio Lorenzetti's *Peaceful Country* (FIG. **14-17**) presents a bird's-eye view of the undulating Tuscan countryside—its villas, castles, plowed farmlands, and peasants going about their seasonal occupations. An allegorical figure of Security hovers above the landscape, unfurling a scroll that promises safety to all who live under the rule of law. In this sweeping view of an actual countryside, *Peaceful Country* represents one of the first appearances of *landscape* in Western art since antiquity (FIG. **7-20**). Whereas earlier depictions were fairly generic, Lorenzetti particularized the landscape—as well as the city view—by careful observation and endowed the painting with the character of a specific place and environment.

The Black Death may have ended the careers of both Lorenzettis. They disappear from historical records in 1348, the year that brought so much horror to defenseless Europe.

Florence

Like Siena, the Republic of Florence was a dominant city-state during the 14th century. The historian Giovanni Villani (ca. 1270–1348), for example, described Florence as "the daughter and the creature of Rome," suggesting a preeminence inherited from the Roman Empire. Florentines were fiercely proud of what they perceived as their economic and cultural superiority. Florence controlled the textile industry in Italy, and the republic's gold *florin* was the standard coin of exchange everywhere in Europe.

FLORENCE CATHEDRAL Florentines translated their pride in their predominance into landmark buildings, such as Florence Cathedral (FIG. **14-18**), recognized as the center for the most important religious observances in the city. ARNOLFO DI CAMBIO (ca. 1245–1302) began work on the cathedral in 1296. Intended as the "most beautiful and honorable church in Tuscany," this structure reveals the competitiveness Florentines felt with cities such as Siena and Pisa. Cathedral authorities planned for the church to hold the city's entire population, and although it holds only about 30,000 (Florence's population at the time was slightly less than 100,000), it seemed so large that even the noted architect Leon Battista Alberti (see Chapter 16) commented that it seemed to cover "all of Tuscany with its shade." The builders ornamented the church's surfaces, in the old Tuscan fashion, with marble-encrusted geometric designs, matching the cathedral's *revetment* (decorative wall paneling) to that

14-18 ARNOLFO DI CAMBIO and others, Florence Cathedral (aerial view looking northeast), Florence, Italy, begun 1296.

This basilican church with its marble-encrusted walls carries on the Tuscan Romanesque architectural tradition, linking Florence Cathedral more closely to Early Christian Italy than to contemporaneous France.

14-19 ARNOLFO DI CAMBIO and others, interior of Florence Cathedral (looking east), Florence, Italy, begun 1296.

Designed to hold 30,000 worshipers, Florence Cathedral has fewer but wider and deeper nave and aisle bays than do northern Gothic cathedrals. The result is an interior of unmatched spaciousness.

of the neighboring 11th-century Romanesque baptistery of San Giovanni (FIGS. 12-26 and 14-18, *bottom left*).

The vast gulf that separates Florence Cathedral from its northern European counterparts becomes evident in a comparison between the Italian church and a full-blown German representative of the High Gothic style, such as Cologne Cathedral (FIG. 13-45). Cologne Cathedral's emphatic stress on the vertical produces an awe-inspiring upward rush of almost unmatched vigor and intensity. The building has the character of an organic growth shooting heavenward, its toothed upper portions engaging the sky. The pierced, translucent stone tracery of the spires merges with the atmosphere. Florence Cathedral, in contrast, clings to the ground and has no aspirations toward flight. All emphasis is on the horizontal elements of the design, and the building rests firmly and massively earthbound. The clearly defined simple geometric volumes of the cathedral show no tendency to merge either into each other or into the sky.

Giotto di Bondone designed the cathedral's campanile in 1334. In keeping with Italian tradition (FIGS. 12-20 and 12-25), it stands apart from the church. In fact, it is essentially self-sufficient and could stand anywhere else in Florence without looking out of place. The same hardly can be said of the Cologne towers. They are essential elements of the building behind them, and it would be unthinkable to detach one of them and place it elsewhere. No individual element in the Cologne grouping seems capable of an independent existence. One form merges into the next in a series of rising movements that pull the

eye ever-upward and never permit it to rest until it reaches the sky. The Italian tower is entirely different. Neatly subdivided into cubic sections, Giotto's tower is the sum of its component parts. Not only could this tower be removed from the building without adverse effects, but also each of the parts—cleanly separated from each other by continuous moldings—seems capable of existing independently as an object of considerable aesthetic appeal. This compartmentalization is reminiscent of the Romanesque style, but it also forecasts the ideals of Renaissance architecture. Artists hoped to express structure in the clear, logical relationships of the component parts and to produce self-sufficient works that could exist in complete independence. Compared with Cologne's towers, Giotto's campanile has a cool and rational quality that appeals more to the intellect than to the emotions.

In Florence Cathedral's plan, the nave (FIG. 14-19) appears to have been added to the *crossing* complex almost as an afterthought. In fact, the nave was the first section to be built, mostly according to Arnolfo di Cambio's original plans (except for the vaulting). Midway through the 14th century, the Florentines redesigned the crossing to increase the cathedral's interior space. In its present form, the area beneath the *dome* is the design's focal point, and the nave leads to it. To visitors from north of the Alps, the nave may have seemed as strange as the plan. Neither has a northern European counterpart. The Florence nave *bays* are twice as deep as those of Amiens (FIG. 13-19), and the wide arcades permit the shallow aisles to become part of the central nave. The result is an interior of unmatched spaciousness. The accent here, as it is on the exterior, is on the horizontal elements. The substantial capitals of the *piers* prevent them from soaring into the vaults and emphasize their function as supports.

The facade of Florence Cathedral was not completed until the 19th century and then in a form much altered from its original design. In fact, until the 17th century, Italian builders exhibited little concern for the facades of their churches, and dozens remain unfinished to this day. One reason for this may be that Italian architects did not conceive the facades as integral parts of the structures but, as in the case of Orvieto Cathedral (FIG. 14-12), as screens that could be added to the church exterior at any time.

Pisa, Venice, and Milan

Italy's port cities—Genoa, Pisa, and Venice—controlled the ever busier and more extended avenues of maritime commerce that connected the West with the lands of Islam, with Byzantium and Russia, and overland with China. As a port city, Pisa established itself as a major shipping power and thus as a dominant Italian city-state. Yet Pisa was not immune from the disruption that the Black Death wreaked across all of Italy and Europe in the late 1340s. Concern with death was a significant theme in art even before the onset of the plague and became more prominent in the years after midcentury.

CAMPOSANTO, PISA *Triumph of Death* (FIG. 14-20) is a tour de force of death imagery. The creator of this large-scale (over 18 × 49 feet) fresco remains disputed. Some attribute the work to FRANCESCO TRAINI (active ca. 1321–1363), while others argue for BUONAMICO BUFFALMACCO (active 1320–1336). Painted on the wall of the Camposanto (Holy Field), the enclosed burial ground adjacent to Pisa's cathedral (FIG. 12-25), the fresco captures the horrors of death and forces viewers to confront their mortality. In the left foreground (FIG. 14-20, *left*), young aristocrats, mounted in a stylish cavalcade, encounter three coffin-encased corpses in differing stages of decomposition. As the horror of the confrontation with death strikes them, the ladies turn away with delicate disgust, while a gentleman holds his nose (the animals, horses and dogs, sniff excitedly). At the far left, the hermit Saint Macarius unrolls a scroll bearing an inscription commenting on

14-20 FRANCESCO TRAINI or BUONAMICO BUFFALMACCO, two details of *Triumph of Death*, 1330s. Full fresco, 18′ 6″ × 49′ 2″. Camposanto, Pisa.

Befitting its location on a wall in Pisa's Camposanto, the enclosed burial ground adjacent to the city's cathedral, this fresco captures the horrors of death and forces viewers to confront their mortality.

the folly of pleasure and the inevitability of death. On the far right (FIG. 14-20, *right*), ladies and gentlemen ignore dreadful realities, occupying themselves in an orange grove with music and amusements while all around them angels and demons struggle for the souls of the corpses heaped in the foreground.

In addition to these direct and straightforward scenes, the mural contains details that convey more subtle messages. For example, the painter depicted those who appear unprepared for death—and thus unlikely to achieve salvation—as wealthy and reveling in luxury. Given that the Dominicans—an order committed to a life of poverty—participated in the design for this fresco program, the imagery surely was a warning against greed and lust. Although *Triumph of Death* is a compilation of disparate scenes, the artist rendered each scene with natural-

ism and emotive power. It is an irony of history that as Western humanity drew both itself and the world into ever sharper visual focus, it perceived ever more clearly that corporeal things were perishable.

DOGE'S PALACE, VENICE One of the wealthiest cities of late medieval Italy—and of Europe—was Venice, renowned for its streets of water. Situated on a lagoon on the northeastern coast of Italy, Venice was secure from land attack and could rely on a powerful navy for protection against invasion from the sea. Internally, Venice was a tight corporation of ruling families who, for centuries, provided stable rule and fostered economic growth. The Venetian republic's seat of government was the Doge's (Duke's) Palace (FIG. 14-21). Begun around 1340–1345 and significantly remodeled

14-21 Doge's Palace, Venice, Italy, begun ca. 1340–1345; expanded and remodeled, 1424–1438.

The delicate patterning in cream- and rose-colored marbles, the pointed and ogee arches, and the quatrefoil medallions of the Doge's Palace constitute a distinctive Venetian variation of northern Gothic architecture.

14-22 Milan Cathedral, Milan, Italy, begun 1386.

Milan Cathedral's elaborate facade is a confused mixture of Late Gothic pinnacles and tracery and Renaissance pediment-capped rectilinear portals. It marks the waning of the Gothic style.

after 1424, it was the most ornate public building in medieval Italy. In a stately march, the first level's short and heavy columns support rather severe pointed arches that look strong enough to carry the weight of the upper structure. Their rhythm doubles in the upper arcades, where slimmer columns carry *ogee arches* (made up of double-curving lines), which terminate in flamelike tips between medallions pierced with *quatrefoils* (cloverleaf-shaped). Each story is taller than the one beneath it, the topmost as high as the two lower arcades combined. Yet the building does not look top-heavy. This is due in part to the complete absence of articulation in the top story and in part to the walls' delicate patterning, in cream- and rose-colored marbles, which makes them appear paper-thin. The Doge's Palace represents a delightful and charming variant of Late Gothic architecture. Colorful, decorative, light and airy in appearance, the Venetian Gothic is ideally suited to Venice, which floats between water and air.

MILAN CATHEDRAL Since Romanesque times, northern European influences had been felt more strongly in Lombardy than in the rest of Italy. When Milan's citizens decided to build their own cathedral (FIG. **14-22**) in 1386, they invited experts from France, Germany, and England, as well as from Italy. These masters argued among themselves and with the city council, and no single architect ever played a dominant role. The result of this attempt at "architecture by committee" was, not surprisingly, a compromise. The building's proportions, particularly the nave's, became Italian (that is, wide in relation to height), and the surface decorations and details remained Gothic. Clearly derived from France are the cathedral's multitude of pinnacles and the elaborate tracery on the facade, flank, and *transept*. But long before the completion of the building, the new classical style of the Italian Renaissance had been well launched (see Chapter 16), and the Gothic design had become outdated. Thus, Milan Cathedral's elaborate facade represents a confused mixture of Late Gothic and Renaissance elements. With its pediment-capped rectilinear portals amid Gothic pinnacles, the cathedral stands as a symbol of the waning of the Gothic style and the advent of the Renaissance.

ITALY, 1200 TO 1400

THE 13TH CENTURY

▌ Diversity of style characterizes the art of 13th-century Italy, with some artists working in the newly revived classical tradition, some in the mode of Gothic France, and others in the *maniera greca,* or Italo-Byzantine style.

▌ Trained in southern Italy in the court style of Frederick II (r. 1197–1250), Nicola Pisano was a master sculptor who settled in Pisa and carved pulpits incorporating marble panels that, both stylistically and in individual motifs, depend on ancient Roman sarcophagi.

▌ Nicola's son, Giovanni Pisano, also was a sculptor of church pulpits, but his work more closely reflects the Gothic sculpture of France.

▌ The leading painters working in the Italo-Byzantine style were Bonaventura Berlinghieri and Cimabue. Both artists drew inspiration from Byzantine icons and illuminated manuscripts. Berlinghieri's *Saint Francis Altarpiece* is the earliest dated portrayal of Saint Francis of Assisi, who died in 1226.

Nicola Pisano, Pisa baptistery pulpit, 1259–1260

Berlinghieri, *Saint Francis Altarpiece,* 1235

THE 14TH CENTURY

▌ During the 14th century, Italy suffered the most devastating natural disaster in European history— the Black Death that swept through Europe—but it was also the time when Renaissance humanism took root. Although religion continued to occupy a primary position in Italian life, scholars and artists became much more concerned with the natural world.

▌ Giotto di Bondone of Florence, widely regarded as the first Renaissance painter, was a pioneer in pursuing a naturalistic approach to representation based on observation, which was at the core of the classical tradition in art. The Renaissance marked the rebirth of classical values in art and society.

▌ The greatest master of the Sienese school of painting was Duccio di Buoninsegna, whose *Maestà* still incorporates many elements of the *maniera greca.* He relaxed the frontality and rigidity of his figures, however, and in narrative scenes took a decisive step toward humanizing religious subject matter by depicting actors displaying individual emotions.

▌ Secular themes also came to the fore in 14th-century Italy, most notably in Ambrogio Lorenzetti's frescoes for Siena's Palazzo Pubblico. His depictions of the city and its surrounding countryside are among the first landscapes in Western art since antiquity.

▌ The 14th-century architecture of Italy underscores the regional character of late medieval art. Some architectural historians even have questioned whether it is proper to speak of Italian buildings of this period as Gothic structures. Orvieto Cathedral's facade, for example, imitates some elements of the French Gothic vocabulary, but it is merely an overlay masking a traditional timber-roofed structure with round arches in the nave arcade.

Giotto, Arena Chapel, Padua, ca. 1305

Duccio, *Maestà,* Siena Cathedral, 1308–1311

Orvieto Cathedral, begun 1310

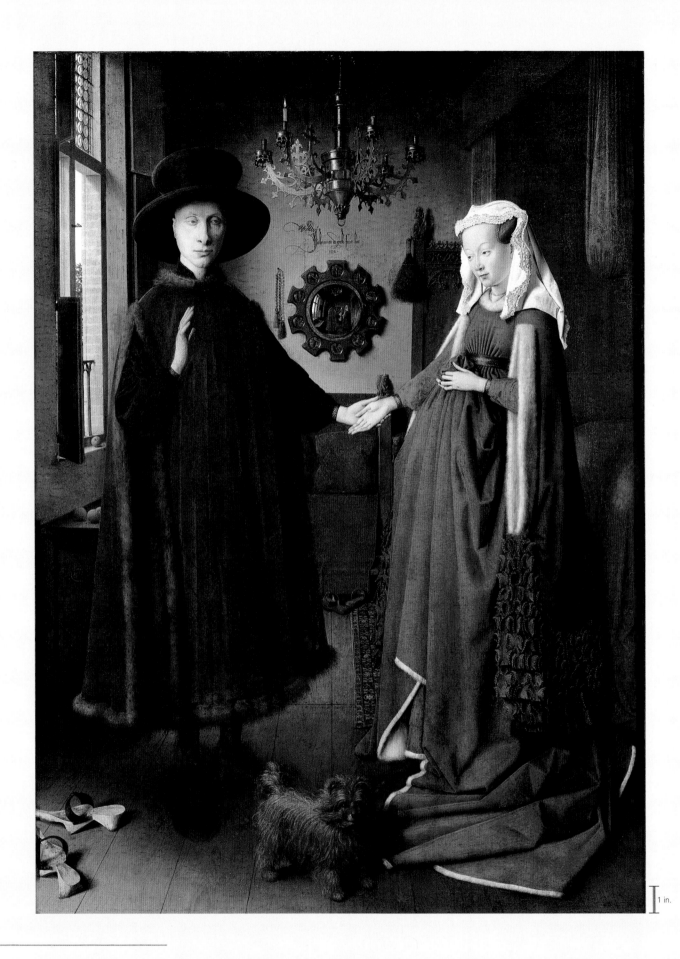

15-1 Jan van Eyck, *Giovanni Arnolfini and His Bride,* 1434. Oil on wood, 2′ 9″ × 1′ 10½″. National Gallery, London.

Van Eyck played a major role in popularizing oil painting and in establishing portraiture as an important art form. In this portrait of an Italian financier and his wife, he also portrayed himself in the mirror.

15

NORTHERN EUROPE, 1400 TO 1500

As the 15th century opened, two competing popes still resided in Rome and Avignon during the Great Schism (1378–1417), and France and England still fought each other in the Hundred Years' War (1337–1453). Social turmoil accompanied dying *feudalism* as the widespread European movement toward centralized royal governments, begun in the 12th century, continued apace. But out of conflict and turmoil also emerged a new economic system—the early stage of European capitalism. In response to the financial requirements of trade, new credit and exchange systems created an economic network of enterprising European cities. Trade in money accompanied trade in commodities, and the former financed industry. Both were in the hands of international trading companies such as those of Jacques Coeur in Bourges (see Chapter 13) and the Medici in Florence (see Chapter 16). In 1460 the Flemish established the first international commercial stock exchange in Antwerp. In fact, the French word for stock market (*bourse*) comes from the name of the van der Beurse family of Bruges, the wealthiest city in 15th-century Flanders—a region corresponding to what is today Belgium, the Netherlands, Luxembourg, and part of northern France (MAP **15-1**).

Art also thrived in Northern Europe during this time under royal, ducal, church, and private patronage. Two developments in particular were of special significance: the adoption of oil-based pigment as the leading medium for painting and the blossoming of printmaking as a major art form, which followed the invention of movable type. These new media had a dramatic impact on artistic production worldwide.

BURGUNDY AND FLANDERS

In the 15th century, Flanders was not an independent state but a region under the control of the duke of Burgundy, the ruler of the fertile east-central region of France still famous for its wines. Duke Philip the Bold (r. 1363–1404) was one of four sons of King John II (r. 1350–1364) of France. In 1369, Philip married Margaret of Mâle, the daughter of the count of Flanders, and acquired territory in the Netherlands. Thereafter, the major source of Burgundian wealth was Bruges, the city that made Burgundy a dangerous rival of France, which then, as in the Gothic age, was a smaller kingdom geographically than the modern nation-state. Bruges initially derived its wealth from the wool trade and soon expanded into banking, becoming the financial clearinghouse for all of Northern Europe. Indeed, Bruges so dominated Flanders that the duke of Burgundy eventually chose to make the city his capital and moved his court there from Dijon in the early 15th century.

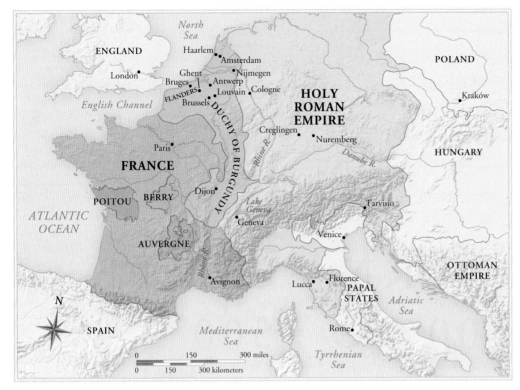

MAP 15-1 France, the duchy of Burgundy, and the Holy Roman Empire in 1477.

spouted water, because the Carthusian commitment to silence and prayer would have precluded anything that produced sound. Although the sculptor died before completing the entire fountain, he did finish *Well of Moses* (FIG. 15-2). Moses and five other prophets (David, Daniel, Isaiah, Jeremiah, and Zachariah) surround a base that once supported a 25-foot-tall group of Christ on the Cross, the Virgin Mary, John the Evangelist, and Mary Magdalene. The *Well of Moses* is a modern name. The Carthusians called it a *fons vitae*, a fountain of everlasting life. The blood of the crucified Christ symbolically flowed down over the grieving angels and Old Testament prophets, spilling into the well below, washing over Christ's prophetic predecessors and redeeming anyone who would drink water from the well. The inspiration for the well may have come in part from contemporaneous *mystery plays* in which actors portraying prophets frequently delivered commentaries on events in Christ's life.

Although the six figures recall the jamb statues (FIGS. 13-17 and 13-24) of Gothic portals, they are much more realistically rendered, and the prophets have almost portraitlike features and distinct individual personalities and costumes. David is an elegantly garbed Gothic king, Moses an elderly horned prophet (compare FIG. 12-36) with a waist-length beard. Sluter's intense observation of natural appearance provided him with the information necessary to sculpt the figures in minute detail. Heavy draperies with voluminous folds swathe the life-size figures. The artist succeeded in making their difficult, complex surfaces seem remarkably naturalistic. He enhanced this effect by skillfully differentiating textures, from coarse drapery to smooth flesh and silky hair. Originally, paint, much of which has flaked off, further augmented the naturalism of the figures. (The painter was Jean Malouel [ca. 1365–1415], another Netherlandish master.) This fascination with the specific and tangible in the visible world became one of the chief characteristics of 15th-century Flemish art.

MELCHIOR BROEDERLAM Philip the Bold also commissioned a major altarpiece for the main altar in the chapel of the Chartreuse. A collaborative project between two Flemish artists, this altarpiece consisted of a large sculptured shrine by Jacques de Baerze (active ca. 1384–1399) and a pair of exterior panels painted by MELCHIOR BROEDERLAM (active ca. 1387–1409).

Altarpieces were a major art form north of the Alps in the late 14th and 15th centuries. From their position behind the altar, they served as backdrops for the Mass. The Mass represents a ritual celebration of the Holy *Eucharist*. At the Last Supper, Christ commanded that his act of giving to his apostles his body to eat and his blood to drink be repeated in memory of him. This act serves as the nucleus of the Mass. The ritual of the Mass involves prayer, contemplation of the Word of God, and the reenactment of the Eucharistic sacrament. Because the Mass involves not only a memorial rite but complex Christian doctrinal tenets as well, art has traditionally played an important role in giving visual form to these often intricate theological concepts for the Christian faithful. Like sculpted

Due to the expanded territory and the prosperity of the duchy of Burgundy, Philip the Bold and his successors were probably the most powerful rulers in Northern Europe during the first three-quarters of the 15th century. Although members of the French royal family, they usually supported England (on which they relied for the raw materials used in their wool industry) during the Hundred Years' War and, at times, controlled much of northern France, including Paris, the seat of the French monarchy. At the height of Burgundian power, the reigning duke's lands stretched from the Rhône River to the North Sea.

Chartreuse de Champmol

The dukes of Burgundy were major patrons of the arts and understood how art could support their dynastic and political goals as well as adorn their castles and town houses. Philip the Bold's grandest artistic enterprise was the building of the Chartreuse de Champmol, near Dijon. A *chartreuse* ("charter house" in English) is a Carthusian *monastery*. The Carthusian order, founded by Saint Bruno in the late 11th century at Chartreuse, near Grenoble in southeastern France, consisted of monks who devoted their lives to solitary living and prayer. Unlike monastic orders that earned income from farming and other work, the Carthusians generated no revenues. Philip's generous endowment at Champmol was therefore the sole funding for an ambitious artistic program. Inspired by Saint-Denis, the royal abbey of France and burial site of the French kings (see Chapter 13), Philip intended the Dijon chartreuse to become a ducal *mausoleum* and serve both as a means of securing salvation in perpetuity for the Burgundian dukes (the monks prayed continuously for the souls of the ducal family) and as a dynastic symbol of Burgundian power.

CLAUS SLUTER In 1389, Philip the Bold placed the Haarlem (Netherlands) sculptor CLAUS SLUTER (active ca. 1380–1406) in charge of the sculptural program for the Chartreuse de Champmol. For the cloister of the Carthusian monastery, Sluter designed a large sculptural fountain located in a well. The well served as a water source for the monastery. It seems improbable, however, that the fountain actually

The *Well of Moses*, a symbolic fountain of life made for the duke of Burgundy, originally supported a Crucifixion group. Sluter's figures recall the jamb statues of French Gothic portals but are far more realistic.

1 ft.

medieval church portals, these altarpieces had a didactic role, especially for the illiterate. They also reinforced Church doctrines for viewers and stimulated devotion.

Given their function as backdrops to the Mass, it is not surprising that many altarpieces depict scenes directly related to Christ's sacrifice. The Champmol altarpiece, or *retable*, for example, features sculpted Passion scenes on the interior. These public altarpieces most often took the form of *polyptychs* (hinged multipaneled paintings) or carved relief panels. The hinges allowed the clergy to close the polyptych's side wings over the central panel(s). Artists decorated both the exterior and interior of the altarpieces. This multi-image format provided artists the opportunity to construct narratives through a sequence of images, somewhat as in manuscript illustration. Although scholars do not have concrete information about when the clergy opened and closed these altarpieces, evidence suggests they remained closed on regular days and were opened on Sundays and feast days. This schedule would have allowed viewers to see both the interior and exterior—diverse imagery at various times according to the liturgical calendar. Over time, however, differing Protestant conceptions of the Eucharist (see Chapter 18) ultimately led to a decline of the altarpiece as a dominant art form in Northern Europe.

The painted wings of the *Retable de Champmol* (FIG. 15-3) depict the *Annunciation* and *Visitation* on the left panel and the

1 ft.

15-3 Melchior Broederlam, *Retable de Champmol*, from the chapel of the Chartreuse de Champmol, Dijon, France, installed 1399. Oil on wood, each wing 5′ 5¾″ × 4′ 1¼″. Musée des Beaux-Arts, Dijon.

This early example of oil painting reveals an attempt to represent the three-dimensional world on a two-dimensional surface, but the gold background and flat halos recall medieval pictorial conventions.

Presentation in the Temple and *Flight into Egypt* on the right panel (see "The Life of Jesus in Art," Chapter 8, pages 216–217, or in the "Before 1300" section). Broederlam's painted images on the altarpiece's exterior deal with Christ's birth and infancy and set the stage for de Baerze's interior sculpted Passion scenes (not illustrated). The exterior panels are an unusual amalgam of different styles, locales, and religious symbolism. The two paintings include both landscape and interior scenes. The style of the buildings Broederlam depicted varies from Romanesque to Gothic (see Chapters 12 and 13). Scholars have suggested that the juxtaposition of different architectural styles in the left panel is symbolic. The *rotunda* (round building, usually with a dome) refers to the Old Testament, whereas the Gothic porch relates to the New Testament. In the right panel, a statue of a pagan god falls from the top of a column as the Holy Family approaches. These and other details symbolically announce the coming of the new order under Christ. Stylistically, Broederlam's representation of parts of the landscape and architecture reveals an attempt to render the three-dimensional world on a two-dimensional surface. Yet the gold background and the flat halos of the figures, regardless of the positions of their heads, recall medieval pictorial conventions. Despite this interplay of various styles and diverse imagery, the altarpiece was a precursor of many of the artistic developments (such as the illusionistic depiction of three-dimensional objects and the representation of landscape) that preoccupied European artists throughout the 15th century.

Robert Campin, Jan van Eyck, and Rogier van der Weyden

Melchior Broederlam's Champmol retable also foreshadowed another significant development in 15th-century art—the widespread adoption of *oil paints*. Oil paints facilitated the exactitude in rendering details so characteristic of Northern European painting. Although the Italian biographer Giorgio Vasari and other 16th-century commentators credited Jan van Eyck with the invention of oil painting, recent evidence has revealed that oil paints had been known for some time, well before Melchior Broederlam used oils in his work for Philip the Bold. Flemish painters built up their pictures by superimposing translucent paint layers on a layer of underpainting, which in turn had been built up from a carefully planned drawing made on a panel prepared with a white ground. With the oil medium, artists created richer colors than previously had been possible, giving their paintings an intense tonality, the illusion of glowing light, and enamel-like surfaces. These traits differed significantly from the high-keyed color, sharp light, and rather *matte* (dull) surface of *tempera* (see "Tempera and Oil Painting," page 401). The brilliant and versatile oil medium suited perfectly the formal intentions of the generation of Flemish painters after Broederlam, including Robert Campin, Jan van Eyck, and Rogier van der Weyden, who aimed for sharply focused clarity of detail in their representation of thousands of objects ranging in scale from large to almost invisible.

ROBERT CAMPIN One of the earliest masters of oil painting was the artist known as the "Master of Flémalle," who scholars generally agree was ROBERT CAMPIN (ca. 1378–1444), the leading painter of the city of Tournai. His most famous work is the *Mérode Altarpiece* (FIG. **15-4**). Similar in format to, but much smaller than, the Champmol retable, the *Mérode Altarpiece* was a private commission for household prayer. It was not unusual in that respect. Based on an accounting of extant Flemish religious paintings, lay patrons outnumbered clerical patrons by a ratio of two to one. At the time, various reform movements advocated personal devotion, and in the

years leading up to the Protestant Reformation in the early 16th century, private devotional exercises and prayer grew in popularity. One of the more prominent features of these images commissioned for private use is the integration of religious and secular concerns. For example, artists often presented biblical scenes as taking place in a Flemish house. Although this might seem inappropriate or even sacrilegious today, religion was such an integral part of Flemish life that separating the sacred from the secular became virtually impossible. Moreover, the presentation in religious art of familiar settings and objects no doubt strengthened the direct bond the patron or viewer felt with biblical figures.

The popular *Annunciation* theme, as prophesied in Isaiah 7:14, occupies the Mérode triptych's central panel. The archangel Gabriel approaches Mary, who sits reading. The artist depicted a well-kept middle-class Flemish home as the site of the event. The carefully rendered architectural scene in the background of the right wing confirms this identification of the locale. The depicted accessories, furniture, and utensils contribute to the identification of the setting as Flemish. However, the objects represented are not merely decorative. They also function as religious symbols. The book, extinguished candle, and lilies on the table, the copper basin in the corner niche, the towels, fire screen, and bench all symbolize, in different ways, the Virgin's purity and her divine mission. In the right panel, Joseph has made a mousetrap, symbolic of the theological tradition that Christ is bait set in the trap of the world to catch the Devil. Campin completely inventoried a carpenter's shop. The ax, saw, and rod in the foreground not only are tools of the carpenter's trade but also are mentioned in Isaiah 10:15.

In the left panel, the closed garden is symbolic of Mary's purity, and the flowers depicted all relate to Mary's virtues, especially humility. The altarpiece's donor, Peter Inghelbrecht, a wealthy merchant, and his wife kneel in the garden and witness the momentous event through an open door. *Donor portraits*—portraits of the individual(s) who commissioned (or "donated") the work—became very popular in the 15th century. In this instance, in addition to asking to be represented in their altarpiece, the Inghelbrechts probably specified the subject. Inghelbrecht means "angel bringer," a reference to the *Annunciation* theme of the central panel. The wife's name, Scrynmakers, means "cabinet- or shrine-makers," referring to the workshop scene in the right panel.

JAN VAN EYCK The first Netherlandish painter to achieve international fame was JAN VAN EYCK (ca. 1390–1441), who in 1425 became the court painter of Philip the Good, duke of Burgundy (r. 1419–1467). The artist moved his studio to Bruges, where the duke maintained his official residence, in 1432, the year he completed the *Ghent Altarpiece* (FIGS. **15-5** and **15-6**). This retable is one of the largest (nearly 12 feet tall) of the 15th century. Jodocus Vyd, diplomat-retainer of Philip the Good, and his wife Isabel Borluut commissioned this polyptych as the centerpiece of the chapel Vyd built in the church originally dedicated to Saint John the Baptist (since 1540 Saint Bavo Cathedral). Vyd's largesse and the political and social connections that the *Ghent Altarpiece* revealed to its audience contributed to Vyd's appointment as burgomeister (chief magistrate) of Ghent shortly after the unveiling of the work. Two of the exterior panels (FIG. **15-5**) depict the donors. The husband and wife, painted in illusionistically rendered niches, kneel with their hands clasped in prayer. They gaze piously at illusionistic stone sculptures of Ghent's patron saints, Saint John the Baptist and Saint John the Evangelist (who was probably also Vyd's patron saint). An *Annunciation* scene appears on the upper register, with a careful representation of a Flemish town outside the painted window of the center

Tempera and Oil Painting

The generic words "paint" and "pigment" encompass a wide range of substances artists have used over the years. Fresco aside (see "Fresco Painting," Chapter 14, page 382), during the 14th century, egg *tempera* was the material of choice for most painters, both in Italy and Northern Europe.

Tempera consists of egg combined with a wet paste of ground pigment. In his influential guidebook *Il libro dell'arte* (*The Artist's Handbook,* 1437), Cennino Cennini mentioned that artists mixed only the egg yolk with the ground pigment, but analyses of paintings from this period have revealed that some artists used the whole egg. Images painted with tempera have a velvety sheen. Artists usually applied tempera to the painting surface with a light touch because thick application of the pigment mixture results in premature cracking and flaking.

Scholars have discovered that artists used oil paints as far back as the 8th century, but not until the early 15th century did oil painting become widespread. Flemish artists such as Melchior Broederlam (FIG. 15-3) were among the first to employ oils extensively (often mixing them with tempera), and Italian painters quickly followed suit. The discovery of better drying components in the early 15th century enhanced the setting capabilities of oils. Rather than apply these oils in the light, flecked brushstrokes that tempera encouraged, artists laid the oils down in transparent layers, or *glazes,* over opaque or semiopaque underlayers. In this manner, painters could build up deep tones through repeated glazing. Unlike tempera, whose surface dries quickly due to water evaporation, oils dry more uniformly and slowly, providing the artist time to rework areas. This flexibility must have been particularly appealing to artists who worked very deliberately, such as Robert Campin (FIG. 15-4), Jan van Eyck (FIGS. 15-1, 15-5 to 15-7), and other Flemish masters discussed in this chapter and the Italian Leonardo da Vinci (see Chapter 17). Leonardo also preferred oil paint because its gradual drying process and consistency permitted him to blend the pigments, thereby creating the impressive *sfumato* (smoky effect) that contributed to his fame.

Both tempera and oils can be applied to various surfaces. Through the early 16th century, wooden panels served as the foundation for most paintings. Italians painted on poplar. Northern European artists used oak, lime, beech, chestnut, cherry, pine, and silver fir. Availability of these timbers determined the choice of wood. Linen canvas became increasingly popular in the late 16th century. Although evidence suggests that artists did not intend permanency for their early images on canvas, the material proved particularly useful in areas such as Venice where high humidity warped wood panels and made fresco unfeasible. Further, until artists began to use wooden bars to stretch the canvas to form a taut surface, canvas paintings were more portable than wood panels.

1 ft.

15-4 ROBERT CAMPIN (MASTER OF FLÉMALLE), *Mérode Altarpiece* (open), ca. 1425–1428. Oil on wood, center panel 2′ 1⅜″ × 2′ ⅞″, each wing 2′ 1⅜″ × 10⅞″. Metropolitan Museum of Art, New York (The Cloisters Collection, 1956).

Campin set the *Annunciation* in a Flemish merchant's home in which the everyday objects represented have symbolic significance. Oil paints permitted Campin to depict all the details with loving fidelity.

panel. In the uppermost arched panels, van Eyck depicted images of the Old Testament prophets Zachariah and Micah, along with *sibyls,* Greco-Roman mythological prophetesses whose writings the Christian Church interpreted as prophecies of Christ.

When opened (FIG. 15-6), the altarpiece reveals a sumptuous, superbly colored painting of humanity's redemption through Christ. In the upper register, God the Father—wearing the pope's triple tiara, with a worldly crown at his feet, and resplendent in a deep-scarlet mantle—presides in majesty. To God's right is the Virgin, represented, as in the Gothic age, as the Queen of Heaven, with a crown of 12 stars upon her head. Saint John the Baptist sits to God's left. To either side is a choir of angels, with an angel playing an organ on the right. Adam and Eve appear in the far panels. The inscriptions in the arches above Mary and Saint John extol the Virgin's virtue and purity and Saint John's greatness as the forerunner of Christ. The inscription above the Lord's head translates as "This is God, all-powerful in his divine majesty; of all the best, by the gentleness of his goodness; the most liberal giver, because of his infinite generosity." The step behind the crown at the Lord's feet bears the inscription "On his head, life without death. On his brow, youth without age. On his right, joy without sadness. On his left, security without fear." The entire altarpiece amplifies the central theme of salvation. Even though humans, symbolized by Adam and Eve, are sinful, they will be saved because God, in his infinite love, will sacrifice his own son for this purpose.

The panels of the lower register extend the symbolism of the upper. In the central panel, the community of saints comes from the four corners of the earth through an opulent, flower-spangled landscape. They proceed toward the altar of the Lamb and the octagonal fountain of life (compare FIG. 15-2). The Revelation passage recounting the Adoration of the Lamb is the main reading on All Saints' Day (November 1). The Lamb symbolizes the sacrificed Son of God, whose heart bleeds into a chalice, while into the fountain spills the "pure river of water of life, clear as crystal, proceeding out of the throne of God and of the Lamb" (Rev. 22:1). On the right, the 12 apostles and a group of martyrs in red robes advance. On the left appear prophets. In the right background come the virgin martyrs, and in the left background the holy confessors approach. On the lower wings, hermits, pilgrims, knights, and judges approach from left and right. They symbolize the four cardinal virtues: Temperance, Prudence, Fortitude, and Justice, respectively. The altarpiece celebrates the whole Christian cycle from the Fall to the Redemption, presenting the Church triumphant in heavenly Jerusalem.

Van Eyck used oil paints to render the entire altarpiece in a shimmering splendor of color that defies reproduction. No small detail escaped the painter. With pristine specificity, he revealed the beauty of the most insignificant object as if it were a work of piety as much as a work of art. He captured the soft texture of hair, the glitter of gold in the heavy brocades, the luster of pearls, and the flashing of gems, all with loving fidelity to appearance. This kind of meticulous attention to recording the exact surface appearance of humans, animals, objects, and landscapes, already evident in the *Mérode Altarpiece* (FIG. 15-4), became the hallmark of Flemish panel painting in the 15th century.

GIOVANNI ARNOLFINI Emerging capitalism led to an urban prosperity that fueled the growing bourgeois market for art objects, particularly in Bruges, Antwerp, and, later, Amsterdam. This prosperity contributed to a growing interest in secular art in addition to

15-5 JAN VAN EYCK, *Ghent Altarpiece* (closed), Saint Bavo Cathedral, Ghent, Belgium, completed 1432. Oil on wood, 11′ 5″ × 7′ 6″.

Monumental painted altarpieces were popular in 15th-century Flemish churches. Artists decorated both the interiors and exteriors of these hinged polyptychs, which often, as here, included donor portraits.

religious artworks. Both the *Mérode Altarpiece* and the *Ghent Altarpiece* include painted portraits of their donors. These paintings marked a significant revival of portraiture, a genre that had languished since antiquity.

A purely secular portrait, but one with religious overtones, is Jan van Eyck's oil painting *Giovanni Arnolfini and His Bride* (FIG. 15-1). Van Eyck depicted the Lucca financier (who had established himself in Bruges as an agent of the Medici family) and his betrothed in a Flemish bedchamber that is simultaneously mundane and charged with the spiritual. As in the *Mérode Altarpiece,* almost every object portrayed conveys the sanctity of the event, specifically, the holiness of matrimony. Arnolfini and his bride, Giovanna Cenami, hand in hand, take the marriage vows. The cast-aside clogs indicate that this event is taking place on holy ground. The little dog symbolizes fidelity (the common canine name Fido originated from the Latin *fido,* "to trust"). Behind the pair, the curtains of the marriage bed have been opened. The bedpost's *finial* (crowning ornament) is a tiny statue of Saint Margaret, patron saint of childbirth. (Giovanna is not yet pregnant, although the fashionable costume she wears makes her appear so.) From the finial hangs a whisk broom, symbolic of domestic care. The oranges on the chest below the window may refer to fertility. The single

15-6 Jan van Eyck, *Ghent Altarpiece* (open), Saint Bavo Cathedral, Ghent, Belgium, completed 1432. Oil on wood, 11′ 5″ × 15′ 1″.

In this sumptuous painting of salvation from the Original Sin of Adam and Eve, God the Father presides in majesty. Van Eyck rendered every figure, garment, and object with loving fidelity to appearance.

candle burning in the left rear holder of the ornate chandelier and the mirror, in which the viewer sees the entire room reflected, symbolize the all-seeing eye of God. The small medallions set into the mirror frame show tiny scenes from the Passion of Christ and represent God's promise of salvation for the figures reflected on the mirror's convex surface. Flemish viewers would have been familiar with many of the objects included in the painting because of traditional Flemish customs. Husbands traditionally presented brides with clogs, and the solitary lit candle in the chandelier was part of Flemish marriage practices. Van Eyck's placement of the two figures suggests conventional gender roles—the woman stands near the bed and well into the room, whereas the man stands near the open window, symbolic of the outside world.

Van Eyck enhanced the documentary nature of this scene by exquisitely painting each object. He carefully distinguished textures and depicted the light from the window on the left reflecting off various surfaces. He augmented the scene's credibility by including the convex mirror (complete with its spatial distortion, brilliantly recorded), because viewers can see not only the principals, Arnolfini and his wife, but also two persons who look into the room through the door. (Arnolfini's raised right hand may be a gesture of greeting to the two men.) One of these must be the artist himself, as the florid inscription above the mirror, "Johannes de Eyck fuit hic" (Jan van Eyck was here),

announces he was present. The picture's purpose, then, seems to have been to record and sanctify this marriage. However, some scholars have taken issue with this traditional reading of the painting, suggesting instead that Arnolfini is conferring legal privileges on his wife to conduct business in his absence. In either case, the artist functions as a witness. The self-portrait of van Eyck in the mirror also underscores the painter's self-consciousness as a professional artist whose role deserves to be recorded and remembered. (Compare the 12th-century monk Eadwine's self-portrait as "prince of scribes" [FIG. 12-37], a very early instance of an artist engaging in "self-promotion.")

MAN IN A RED TURBAN In 15th-century Flanders, artists also painted secular portraits without the layer of religious interpretation present in the Arnolfini double portrait. These private commissions began to multiply as both artists and patrons became interested in the reality (both physical and psychological) that portraits could reveal. For various reasons, great patrons embraced the opportunity to have their likenesses painted. They wanted to memorialize themselves in their dynastic lines and to establish their identities, ranks, and stations with images far more concrete than heraldic coats of arms. Portraits also served to represent state officials at events they could not attend. Sometimes, royalty, nobility, and the very rich would send artists to

Framed Paintings

Until recent decades, when painters began to be content with simply affixing canvas to wooden *stretcher bars* to provide a taut painting surface devoid of any ornamentation, artists considered the frame an integral part of the painting. Frames served a number of functions, some visual, others conceptual. For paintings such as large-scale altarpieces that were part of a larger environment, frames often served to integrate the painting with its surroundings. Frames could also be used to reinforce the illusionistic nature of the painted image. For example, the Italian painter Giovanni Bellini duplicated the carved pilasters of the architectural frame in his *San Zaccaria Altarpiece* (FIG. **17-33**) in the painting itself, thereby enhancing the illusion of space and giving the painted figures an enhanced physical presence. In Jan van Eyck's *Ghent Altarpiece*, the frame seems to cast shadows on the floor between the angel and Mary in the *Annunciation* scene (FIG. **15-5**, *top*.) More commonly, artists used frames specifically to distance the viewer from the (often otherworldly) scene by calling attention to the separation of the image from the viewer's space.

Most 15th- and 16th-century paintings included elaborate frames that the artists themselves helped design and construct. Frequently, the artists painted or gilded the frames, adding to the expense. Surviving contracts reveal that the frame accounted for as much as half the cost of an altarpiece. For small works, artists sometimes affixed the frames to the panels before painting, creating an insistent visual presence as they worked. Occasionally, a single piece of wood served as both panel and frame, and the artist carved the painting surface from the wood, leaving the edges as a frame. Larger images with elaborate frames, such as altarpieces, required the services of a woodcarver or stonemason. The painter worked closely with the individual constructing the frame to ensure its appropriateness for the image(s) produced.

Unfortunately, over time, many frames have been removed from their paintings. For instance, in 1566 church officials dismantled the *Ghent Altarpiece* and detached its elaborately carved frame in order to protect the sacred work from Protestant *iconoclasts* (see "Protes-

15-7 JAN VAN EYCK, *Man in a Red Turban*, 1433. Oil on wood, $1' 1\frac{1}{8}'' \times 10\frac{1}{4}''$. National Gallery, London.

Man in a Red Turban seems to be the first Western painted portrait in a thousand years in which the sitter looks directly at the viewer. The inscribed frame suggests it is a self-portrait of Jan van Eyck.

1 in.

tantism and Iconoclasm," Chapter 18, page 510). As ill luck would have it, when the panels were reinstalled in 1587, no one could find the frame. Sadly, the absence of many of the original frames of old paintings deprives viewers today of the complete artistic vision of the artists. Conversely, when the original frames exist, they sometimes provide essential information, such as the subject, name of the painter, and date. For example, the inscriptions on the frame of Jan van Eyck's *Man in a Red Turban* (FIG. **15-7**) state that he painted it on October 21, 1433, and the inclusion of "As I can" and the omission of the sitter's name suggest that the painting is a self-portrait.

paint the likeness of a prospective bride or groom. When young King Charles VI (r. 1380–1422) of France sought a bride, a painter journeyed to three different royal courts to make portraits of the candidates for the king to use in making his choice.

In *Man in a Red Turban* (FIG. **15-7**), the man van Eyck portrayed looks directly at the viewer. This seems to be the first Western painted portrait in a thousand years where the sitter does so. The level, composed gaze, directed from a true three-quarter head pose, must have impressed observers deeply. The painter created the illusion that from whatever angle a viewer observes the face, the eyes return that gaze. Van Eyck, with his considerable observational skill and controlled painting style, injected a heightened sense of speci-

ficity into this portrait by including beard stubble, veins in the bloodshot left eye, and weathered and aged skin. Although a definitive identification of the sitter has yet to be made, most scholars consider *Man in a Red Turban* to be a self-portrait, which van Eyck painted by looking at his image in a mirror (as he depicted himself in the mirror in the Arnolfinis' bedroom). The inscriptions on the frame (see "Framed Paintings," above) reinforce this identification. Across the top, van Eyck wrote "As I can" in Flemish using Greek letters, and across the bottom in Latin appears the statement "Jan van Eyck made me" and the date. The use of both Greek and Latin suggests the artist's view of himself as a successor to the fabled painters of antiquity.

15-8 ROGIER VAN DER WEYDEN, *Deposition,* center panel of a triptych from Notre-Dame hors-les-murs, Louvain, Belgium, ca. 1435. Oil on wood, 7′ 2⅝″ × 8′ 7⅛″. Museo del Prado, Madrid.

Deposition resembles a relief carving in which the biblical figures act out a drama of passionate sorrow as if on a shallow theatrical stage. The emotional impact of the painting is unforgettable.

ROGIER VAN DER WEYDEN When Jan van Eyck received the commission for the *Ghent Altarpiece,* ROGIER VAN DER WEYDEN (ca. 1400–1464) was an assistant in the workshop of Robert Campin, but the younger painter's fame eventually rivaled van Eyck's. Rogier soon became renowned for his dynamic compositions stressing human action and drama. He concentrated on Christian themes such as the Crucifixion and the *Pietà* (the Virgin Mary cradling the dead body of her son), moving observers emotionally by relating the sufferings of Christ.

An early masterwork is his 1435 *Deposition* (FIG. **15-8**), the center panel of a triptych the Archers Guild of Louvain commissioned for the church of Notre-Dame hors-les-murs (Notre-Dame "outside the [town] walls") in Louvain. Rogier acknowledged the patrons of this large painting by incorporating the crossbow (the guild's symbol) into the decorative tracery in the corners. Instead of creating a deep landscape setting, as van Eyck might have, Rogier compressed the figures and action onto a shallow stage, imitating the large sculptured shrines so popular in the 15th century, especially in

the Holy Roman Empire (FIGS. **15-18** and **15-19**). The device admirably served his purpose of expressing maximum action within a limited space. The painting, with the artist's crisp drawing and precise modeling of forms, resembles a stratified relief carving. A series of lateral undulating movements gives the group a compositional unity, a formal cohesion the artist strengthened by depicting the desolating anguish that many of the figures share. The similar poses of Christ and the Virgin Mary further unify the composition.

Few painters have equaled Rogier van der Weyden in the rendering of passionate sorrow as it vibrates through a figure or distorts a tearstained face. His depiction of the agony of loss is among the most authentic in religious art. The emotional impact on the viewer is immediate and unforgettable. It was probably Rogier van der Weyden that Michelangelo had in mind when, according to the Portuguese painter Francisco de Hollanda (1517–1584), the Italian master observed that "Flemish painting [will] please the devout better than any painting of Italy, which will never cause him to shed a tear, whereas that of Flanders will cause him to shed many."[1]

The Artist's Profession in Flanders

As in Italy (see "Artistic Training," Chapter 14, page 388), guilds controlled the Flemish artist's profession. To pursue a craft, individuals had to belong to the guild controlling that craft. Painters, for example, sought admission to the Guild of Saint Luke, the patron saint of painters (FIG. 15-9), as well as saddlers, glassworkers, and mirror-workers. The path to eventual membership in the guild began, for men, at an early age, when the father apprenticed his son in boyhood to a master, with whom the young aspiring painter lived. The master taught the fundamentals of his craft—how to make implements, prepare panels with *gesso* (plaster mixed with a binding material), and mix colors, oils, and varnishes. Once the youth mastered these procedures and learned to work in the master's traditional manner, he usually spent several years working as a journeyman in various cities, observing and absorbing ideas from other masters. He then was eligible to become a master and to apply for admission to the guild. Through the guild, he obtained commissions. The guild inspected his paintings to ensure that he used quality materials and to evaluate workmanship. It also secured him adequate payment for his labor. As a result of this quality control, Flemish artists soon gained a favorable reputation for their solid artisanship.

Women clearly had many fewer opportunities than men to train as artists, in large part because of social and moral constraints that would have forbidden women's apprenticeship in the homes of male masters. Moreover, from the 16th century, when academic training courses supplemented and then replaced guild training, until the 20th century, women would not as a rule expect or be permitted instruction in figure painting, insofar as it involved dissection of cadavers and study of the nude male model. Flemish women interested in pursuing art as a career, for example, Caterina van Hemessen (FIG. 18-17), most often received tutoring from fathers and husbands who were professionals and whom the women assisted in all the technical procedures of the craft. Despite these obstacles, membership records of the art guilds of cities such as Bruges reveal that a substantial number of

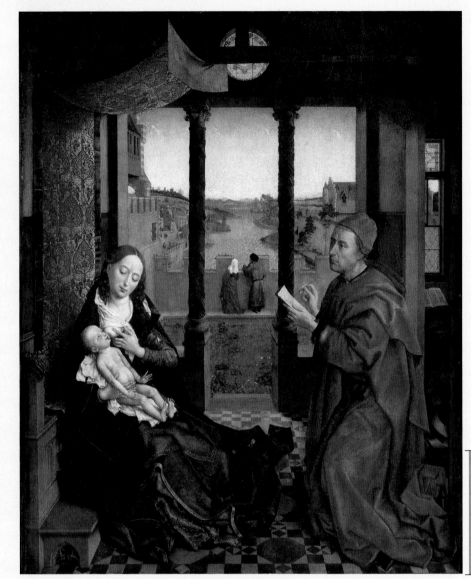

15-9 ROGIER VAN DER WEYDEN, *Saint Luke Drawing the Virgin,* ca. 1435–1440. Oil and tempera on wood, 4′ 6⅛″ × 3′ 7⅝″. Museum of Fine Arts, Boston. (Gift of Mr. and Mrs. Henry Lee Higginson)

Probably commissioned by the painters guild in Brussels, this panel honors the first Christian artist and the profession of painting. Saint Luke may be a self-portrait of Rogier van der Weyden.

Flemish women in the 15th century were able to establish themselves as artists. That they succeeded in negotiating the difficult path to acceptance as professionals is a testament to both their tenacity and their artistic skill.

SAINT LUKE Slightly later in date is Rogier's *Saint Luke Drawing the Virgin* (FIG. 15-9), probably painted for the Guild of Saint Luke, the artists guild in Brussels. The panel depicts the patron saint of painters drawing the Virgin Mary using a *silverpoint* (a sharp *stylus* that creates a fine line). The theme paid tribute to the profession of painting in Flanders (see "The Artist's Profession in Flanders," above) by drawing attention to the venerable history of the painter's craft. Many scholars believe that Rogier's *Saint Luke* is a self-portrait, iden-tifying the Flemish painter with the first Christian artist and under-scoring the holy nature of painting. Here, Rogier shares with Jan van Eyck the aim of recording every detail of the scene with loving fidelity to optical appearance, from the rich fabrics to the floor pattern to the landscape seen through the window. And, like Campin and van Eyck, Rogier imbued much of the representation with symbolic significance. At the right, the ox identifies the figure recording the Virgin's features as Saint Luke (see "The Four Evangelists," Chapter 11,

1 in.

15-10 ROGIER VAN DER WEYDEN, *Portrait of a Lady*, ca. 1460. Oil on panel, 1′ 1$\frac{3}{8}$″ × 10$\frac{1}{16}$″. National Gallery, Washington, D.C. (Andrew W. Mellon Collection).

Rogier van der Weyden won renown for his penetrating portrayals of character. The lowered eyes, tightly locked thin fingers, and fragile physique convey this unnamed lady's reserved demeanor.

page 290). The carved armrest of the Virgin's bench depicts Adam, Eve, and the serpent, reminding the viewer that Mary is the new Eve and Christ the new Adam who will redeem humanity from the Original Sin.

PORTRAIT OF A LADY Rogier, like van Eyck, also painted private portraits. The identity of the young woman he portrayed in FIG. **15-10** is unknown. Her dress and bearing imply noble rank. The portrait also reveals the lady's individual character. Her lowered eyes, tightly locked thin fingers, and fragile physique bespeak a reserved and pious demeanor. This style contrasted with the formal Italian approach (FIG. **16-25**), derived from the profiles common to coins and medallions, which was sterner and conveyed little of the sitter's personality. Rogier was perhaps chief among the Flemish in his penetrating readings of his subjects. As a great pictorial composer, he made beautiful use here of flat, sharply pointed angular shapes that so powerfully suggest this subject's composure. In this portrait, unlike in his *Saint Luke*, the artist placed little emphasis on minute description of surface detail. Instead, he defined large, simple planes and volumes and focused on capturing the woman's dignity and elegance.

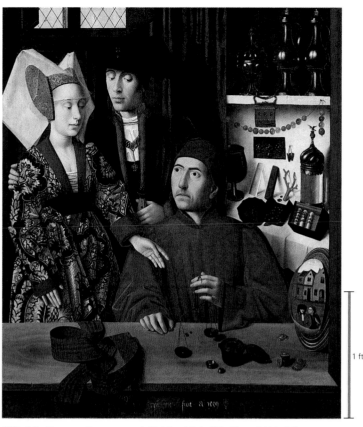

1 ft.

15-11 PETRUS CHRISTUS, *A Goldsmith in His Shop*, 1449. Oil on wood, 3′ 3″ × 2′ 10″. Metropolitan Museum of Art, New York (Robert Lehman Collection, 1975).

Once thought to depict Eligius, the patron saint of goldsmiths, Christus's painting, made for the Bruges goldsmiths' guild chapel, is more likely a generic scene of a couple shopping for a wedding ring.

Later Flemish Panel Painters

Robert Campin, Jan van Eyck, and Rogier van der Weyden were the leading figures of the first generation of "Northern Renaissance" painters. (Art historians usually transfer to Northern Europe, with less validity than in its original usage, the term "Renaissance," coined to describe the conscious revival of classical art in Italy.) The second generation of Flemish masters, active during the latter half of the 15th century, shared many of the concerns of their illustrious predecessors, especially the use of oil paints to create naturalistic representations, often, although not always, of traditional Christian subjects for installation in churches.

PETRUS CHRISTUS One work of uncertain Christian content is *A Goldsmith in His Shop* (FIG. **15-11**) by PETRUS CHRISTUS (ca. 1410–1472), who settled in Bruges in 1444. According to the traditional interpretation, *A Goldsmith in His Shop* portrays Saint Eligius (who was initially a master goldsmith before committing his life to God) sitting in his stall, showing an elegantly attired couple a selection of rings. The bride's betrothal girdle lies on the table as a symbol of chastity, and the woman reaches for the ring the goldsmith weighs. The artist's inclusion of a crystal container for Eucharistic wafers (on the lower shelf to the right of Saint Eligius) and the scales (a reference to the Last Judgment) supports a religious interpretation of this painting and continues the Flemish habit of imbuing everyday objects with symbolic significance. A halo once circled the goldsmith's head, seemingly confirming the religious nature of this scene, but when scientific analysis revealed that the halo was a later addition by an artist other than Christus, restorers removed it.

1 ft.

15-12 DIRK BOUTS, *Last Supper,* center panel of the *Altarpiece of the Holy Sacrament,* Saint Peter's, Louvain, Belgium, 1464–1468. Oil on wood, 6′ × 5′.

One of the earliest Northern European paintings to employ single-vanishing-point perspective, this *Last Supper* includes four servants in Flemish attire, probably portraits of the altarpiece's patrons.

DIRK BOUTS A different means of suggesting spatial recession is evident in *Last Supper* (FIG. 15-12) by DIRK BOUTS (ca. 1415–1475), who became the official painter of Louvain in 1468. The painting is the central panel of *Altarpiece of the Holy Sacrament,* which the Louvain Confraternity of the Holy Sacrament commissioned in 1464. It is one of the earliest Northern European paintings to demonstrate the use of a single *vanishing point* (see "Renaissance Perspectival Systems," Chapter 16, page 425) for creating *perspective.* All of the central room's *orthogonals* (converging diagonal lines imagined to be behind and perpendicular to the picture plane) lead to a single vanishing point in the center of the mantelpiece above Christ's head. However, the small side room has its own vanishing point, and neither it nor the vanishing point of the main room falls on the horizon of the landscape seen through the windows, as in Italian Renaissance paintings.

In *Last Supper,* Bouts did not focus on the biblical narrative itself but instead presented Christ in the role of a priest performing a ritual from the liturgy of the Christian Church—the consecration of the Eucharistic wafer. This contrasts strongly with other Last Supper depictions, which often focused on Judas's betrayal or on Christ's comforting of John. Bouts also added to the complexity of this image by including four servants (two in the pass-through window and two standing), all dressed in Flemish attire. These servants are most likely portraits of the confraternity's members responsible for commissioning the altarpiece, continuing the Flemish tradition of inserting into biblical representations portraits of the painting's patrons, first noted in the *Mérode Altarpiece* (FIG. 15-4).

HUGO VAN DER GOES By the mid-15th century, Flemish art had achieved renown throughout Europe. The *Portinari Altarpiece* (FIG. 15-13), for example, is a large-scale Flemish work in a family chapel in Florence, Italy. The artist who received the commission was HUGO VAN DER GOES (ca. 1440–1482), the dean of the painters guild of Ghent from 1468 to 1475. Hugo painted the triptych for Tommaso Portinari, an Italian shipowner and agent for the powerful Medici family of Florence. Portinari appears on the wings of the altarpiece with his family and their patron saints. The central panel depicts the *Adoration of the Shepherds.* On this large surface, Hugo displayed a scene of solemn grandeur, muting the high drama of the joyous occasion. The Virgin, Joseph, and the angels seem to brood on the suffering to come rather than to meditate on the Nativity miracle. Mary kneels, somber and monumental, on a tilted ground that has the expressive function of centering the main actors. The composition may also reflect the tilted stage floors of contemporary mystery plays. From the right rear enter three shepherds, represented with powerful realism in attitudes of wonder, piety, and gaping curiosity. Their lined faces, work-worn hands, and uncouth dress and manner seem immediately familiar.

The symbolic architecture and a continuous wintry northern landscape unify the three panels. Symbols surface throughout the altarpiece. Iris and columbine flowers symbolize the Sorrows of the Virgin. The 15 angels represent the Fifteen Joys of Mary. A sheaf of wheat stands for Bethlehem (the "house of bread" in Hebrew), a reference to the Eucharist. The harp of David, emblazoned over the building's portal in the middle distance (just to the right of the Virgin's head), signifies the ancestry of Christ. To stress the meaning and significance of the depicted event, Hugo revived medieval pictorial devices. Small scenes shown in the background of the altarpiece represent (from left to right) the flight into Egypt, the annunciation to the shepherds, and the arrival of the magi. Hugo's variation in the scale of his figures to differentiate them by their importance to the central event also reflects older traditions. Still, he put a vigorous, penetrating realism to work in a new direction, characterizing human beings according to their social level while showing their common humanity.

More recent scholarship has argued that this painting, although not devoid of religious content, should be seen in the context of the tradition of vocational paintings produced for installation in guild chapels. Although the couple's presence suggests a marriage portrait, most scholars now believe that the goldsmiths' guild in Bruges commissioned this painting. Saint Eligius was the patron saint of gold- and silversmiths, blacksmiths, and metalworkers, all of whom shared a chapel in a building adjacent to their meetinghouse. The reconsecration of this chapel took place in 1449, the same date as this painting. Therefore, it seems probable that Christus painted *A Goldsmith in His Shop,* which depicts an economic transaction and focuses on the goldsmith's profession, specifically for the guild chapel.

Christus went to great lengths to produce a historically credible image. For example, the variety of objects depicted in the painting serves as advertisement for the goldsmiths guild. Included are the profession's raw materials—precious stones, beads, crystal, coral, and seed pearls—scattered among finished products—rings, buckles, and brooches. The pewter vessels on the upper shelves are donation pitchers, which town leaders gave to distinguished guests. All these meticulously painted objects attest to the centrality and importance of the goldsmiths to both the secular and sacred communities as well as enhance the naturalism of the painting. The convex mirror in the foreground showing another couple and a street with houses serves to extend the painting's space into the viewer's space, further creating the illusion of reality.

15-13 Hugo van der Goes, *Portinari Altarpiece* (open), from Sant'Egidio, Florence, Italy, ca. 1476. Tempera and oil on wood, center panel 8′ 3½″ × 10′, each wing 8′ 3½″ × 4′ 7½″. Galleria degli Uffizi, Florence.

This altarpiece is a rare instance of the awarding of a major commission in Florence to a Flemish painter. The Italians admired the incredibly realistic details and Hugo's brilliant portrayal of human character.

After Portinari placed his altarpiece in the family chapel in the Florentine church of Sant'Egidio, it created a considerable stir among Italian artists. Although the painting as a whole may have seemed unstructured to them, Hugo's masterful technique and what the Florentines regarded as extraordinary realism in representing drapery, flowers, animals, and, above all, human character and emotion made a deep impression on them. At least one Florentine artist, Domenico Ghirlandaio (see Chapter 16), paid tribute to the Northern European master by using Hugo's most striking motif, the adoring shepherds, in one of his own Nativity paintings.

HANS MEMLING A contemporary of Hugo van der Goes was Hans Memling (ca. 1430–1494), who became a citizen of Bruges in 1465 and received numerous commissions from the city's wealthy merchants, Flemish and foreign alike. Memling specialized in portraits and images of the Madonna. The many that survive depict young, slight, pretty princesses, each holding a doll-like infant Christ. The center panel of the *Saint John Altarpiece* depicts the *Virgin with Saints and Angels* (FIG. 15-14). The patrons of this altarpiece—two brothers and two sisters of the order of the Hospital of Saint John in Bruges—appear on the exterior side panels (not illustrated). In the central panel, two

15-14 Hans Memling, *Virgin with Saints and Angels,* center panel of the *Saint John Altarpiece,* Hospitaal Sint Jan, Bruges, Belgium, 1479. Oil on wood, 5′ 7¾″ × 5′ 7¾″ (center panel), 5′ 7¾″ × 2′ 7⅛″ (each wing).

Memling specialized in images of the Madonna. His *Saint John Altarpiece* exudes an opulence that results from the sparkling and luminous colors and the realistic depiction of rich tapestries and brocades.

angels, one playing a musical instrument and the other holding a book, flank the Virgin. To the sides of Mary's throne stand Saint John the Baptist on the left and Saint John the Evangelist on the right, and seated in the foreground are Saints Catherine and Barbara. This gathering celebrates the *mystic marriage* of Saint Catherine of Alexandria, one of many virgin saints who were believed to have entered into a special spiritual marriage with Christ. As one of the most revered virgins of Christ, Saint Catherine provided a model of devotion especially resonant with women viewers (particularly nuns). The altarpiece exudes an opulence that results from the rich colors, carefully depicted tapestries and brocades, and the serenity of the figures. The composition is balanced and serene, the color sparkling and luminous, and the execution of the highest technical quality—all characteristics of 15th-century Flemish painting in general.

FRANCE

In contrast to the prosperity and peace Flanders enjoyed during the 15th century, in France the Hundred Years' War crippled economic enterprise and brought political instability. The anarchy of war and the weakness of the kings gave rise to a group of duchies, each with significant power. The strongest and wealthiest of these was the duchy of Burgundy, which controlled Flanders and where artists prospered. But the dukes of Berry, Bourbon, and Nemours, as well as members of the French royal court, were also major art patrons.

Manuscript Painting

During the 15th century, French artists built on the achievements of Gothic painters (see Chapter 13) and produced exquisitely refined *illuminated manuscripts*. Among the most significant developments in French manuscript painting was a new conception and presentation of space. Paintings in manuscripts took on more pronounced characteristics as illusionistic scenes. Increased contact with Italy, where Renaissance artists had revived the pictorial principles of classical antiquity, may have influenced French painters' interest in illusionism.

LIMBOURG BROTHERS Among the early-15th-century artists who furthered the maturation of manuscript painting were the three LIMBOURG BROTHERS—POL, HERMAN, and JEAN—from Nijmegen in the Netherlands. They were nephews of Jean Malouel, the court artist of Philip the Bold. Following in the footsteps of earlier illustrators such as Jean Pucelle (FIG. 13-36), the Limbourg brothers expanded the illusionistic capabilities of illumination. Trained in the Netherlands, the brothers moved to Paris no later than 1402, and between 1405 and their death in 1416, probably from the plague, they worked in Paris and Bourges for Jean, duke of Berry (r. 1360–1416)

15-15 LIMBOURG BROTHERS (POL, JEAN, HERMAN), *January,* from *Les Très Riches Heures du Duc de Berry,* 1413–1416. Ink on vellum, $8\frac{7}{8}'' \times 5\frac{3}{8}''$. Musée Condé, Chantilly.

The sumptuous pictures in *Les Très Riches Heures* depict characteristic activities of each month and give unusual prominence to genre subjects, reflecting the increasing integration of religious and secular art.

and brother of King Charles V (r. 1364–1380) of France and of Philip the Bold of Burgundy. The duke ruled the western French regions of Berry, Poitou, and Auvergne. He was an avid art patron and focused much of his collecting energy on manuscripts, jewels, and rare artifacts. An inventory of the duke's libraries revealed that he owned more than 300 manuscripts, including Pucelle's *Belleville Breviary* (FIG. 13-36) and the *Hours of Jeanne d'Évreux.* For Jean, the Limbourg brothers produced a gorgeously illustrated Book of Hours, *Les Très Riches Heures du Duc de Berry (The Very Sumptuous* days usually preceded the Office of the Blessed Virgin. Penitential Psalms, devotional prayers, litanies to the saints, and other prayers, including those of the dead and of the Holy Cross, followed the centerpiece. Such books became favorite possessions of the Northern European aristocracy during the 14th and 15th centuries. They eventually became available to affluent burghers and contributed to the decentralization of religious practice that was one factor in the Protestant Reformation in the early 16th century (see Chapter 18).

The calendar pictures of *Les Très Riches Heures* are perhaps the most famous in the history of manuscript illumination. They represent the 12 months in terms of the associated seasonal tasks, alternating scenes of nobility and peasantry. Above each picture is a *lunette* (semicircular frame) in which the Limbourgs depicted the chariot of the sun as it makes its yearly cycle through the 12 months and zodiac signs. Beyond its function as a religious book, *Les Très Riches Heures* also visually captures the power of the duke and his relationship to the peasants. The colorful calendar picture for January (FIG. **15-15**) depicts a New Year's reception at court. The duke appears as magnanimous host, his head circled by the fire screen, almost halolike, behind him. His chamberlain stands next to him, urging the guests forward with the words "aproche, aproche." The lavish spread of food on the table and the large tapestry on the back wall augment the richness and extravagance of the setting and the occasion.

In contrast, the illustration for October (FIG. **15-16**) focuses on the peasantry. Here, the Limbourg brothers depicted a sower, a harrower on horseback, and washerwomen, along with city dwellers, who promenade in front of the Louvre (the French king's residence at the time, now one of the world's great art museums). The peasants do not appear particularly disgruntled as they go about their tasks. Surely, this imagery flattered the duke's sense of himself as a compassionate master. The growing artistic interest in naturalism is evident here in the careful way the brothers recorded the architectural details of the Louvre and in their convincing depiction of the shadows of the people and objects (such as the archer scarecrow and the horse) in the scene.

As a whole, *Les Très Riches Heures* reinforced the image of the duke of Berry as a devout man, cultured bibliophile, sophisticated art patron, and powerful and magnanimous leader. Further, the expanded range of subject matter, especially the prominence of *genre* subjects in a religious book, reflected the increasing integration of religious and secular concerns in both art and life at the time. Although all three Limbourg brothers worked on *Les Très Riches Heures*, art historians have never been able to ascertain definitively which brother painted which images. Given the common practice of collaboration on artistic projects at this time, this determination of specific authorship is not very important. The Limbourg brothers died before completing this Book of Hours, and another court illustrator finished the manuscript about 70 years later.

1 in.

15-16 LIMBOURG BROTHERS (POL, JEAN, HERMAN), *October,* from *Les Très Riches Heures du Duc de Berry,* 1413–1416. Ink on vellum, $8\frac{7}{8}'' \times 5\frac{3}{8}''$. Musée Condé, Chantilly.

The Limbourg brothers expanded the illusionistic capabilities of manuscript painting with their care in rendering architectural detail and convincing depiction of shadows cast by people and objects.

Hours of the Duke of Berry). A *Book of Hours,* like a *breviary,* was a book used for reciting prayers (see "Medieval Books," Chapter 11, page 289). As prayer books, they replaced the traditional *psalters* (book of Psalms), which were the only liturgical books in private hands until the mid-13th century. The centerpiece of a Book of Hours was the "Office [prayer] of the Blessed Virgin," which contained liturgical passages to be read privately at set times during the day, from *matins* (dawn prayers) to *compline* (the last of the prayers recited daily). An illustrated calendar listing local religious feast

1 ft.

15-17 JEAN FOUQUET, *Melun Diptych. Étienne Chevalier and Saint Stephen* (left wing), ca. 1450. Oil on wood, 3′ $\frac{1}{2}$″ × 2′ 9$\frac{1}{2}$″. Gemäldegalerie, Staatliche Museen, Berlin. *Virgin and Child* (right wing), ca. 1451. Oil on wood, 3′ 1$\frac{1}{4}$″ × 2′ 9$\frac{1}{2}$″. Koninklijk Museum voor Schone Kunsten, Antwerp.

Fouquet's meticulous representation of a pious kneeling donor with a standing patron saint recalls Flemish painting, as do the three-quarter stances and the sharp focus of the portraits.

Panel Painting

Images for private devotional use were popular in France, as in Flanders, and the preferred medium was oil paint on wooden panels.

JEAN FOUQUET Among the French artists whose paintings were in demand was JEAN FOUQUET (ca. 1420–1481), who worked for King Charles VII (r. 1422–1461, the patron and client of Jacques Coeur; FIG. 18-30) and for the duke of Nemours. Fouquet painted a *diptych* (two-paneled painting; FIG. 15-17) for Étienne Chevalier, who, despite his lowly origins, became Charles VII's treasurer in 1452. In the left panel, Chevalier appears with his patron saint, Saint Stephen (Étienne in French). Appropriately, Fouquet's donor portrait of Chevalier depicts his prominent patron as devout—kneeling, with hands clasped in prayer. The representation of the pious donor with his standing saint recalls Flemish art, as do the three-quarter stances and the sharp, clear focus of the portraits. The artist depicted Saint Stephen holding the stone of his martyrdom (death by stoning) atop a volume of the Scriptures, thereby ensuring that viewers properly identify the saint. Fouquet rendered the entire image in meticulous detail and included a highly ornamented architectural setting.

In its original diptych form (the two panels are now in different museums), the viewer would follow the gaze of Chevalier and Saint Stephen over to the right panel, which depicts the Virgin Mary and Christ Child. The juxtaposition of these two images allowed the patron to bear witness to the sacred. The integration of sacred and secular (especially the political or personal) prevalent in other Northern European artworks also emerges here, complicating the reading of this diptych. Agnès Sorel, the mistress of King Charles VII, was Fouquet's model for the Virgin Mary. Sorel was a pious individual,

and according to an inscription, Chevalier commissioned this painting to fulfill a vow he made after Sorel's death in 1450. Thus, in addition to the religious interpretation of this diptych, there is surely a personal narrative here as well.

HOLY ROMAN EMPIRE

Because the Holy Roman Empire (whose core was Germany) did not participate in the long, drawn-out saga of the Hundred Years' War, its economy remained stable and prosperous. Without a dominant court culture to commission artworks, wealthy merchants and clergy became the primary German patrons during the 15th century.

Sculpture

The art of the early "Northern Renaissance" in the Holy Roman Empire displays a pronounced stylistic diversity. Although some artists followed developments in Flemish painting, the works of artists who specialized in carving large wooden retables reveal most forcefully the power of the lingering Late Gothic style.

VEIT STOSS The sculptor VEIT STOSS (1447–1533) trained in the Upper Rhine region but settled in Kraków (in present-day Poland) in 1477. In that year, he began work on a great altarpiece (FIG. 15-18) for the church of Saint Mary in Kraków. In the central boxlike shrine, huge carved and painted figures, some nine feet high, represent *Death and Assumption of the Virgin*. On the wings, Stoss portrayed scenes from the lives of Christ and Mary. The altar expresses the intense piety of Gothic culture in its late phase, when artists used every figural and ornamental design resource from the vocabulary of Gothic art to heighten the emotion and to glorify the

15-18 Veit Stoss, *Death and Assumption of the Virgin* (wings open), altar of the Virgin Mary, church of Saint Mary, Kraków, Poland, 1477–1489. Painted and gilded wood, central panel 23′ 9″ high.

In this huge sculptured and painted altarpiece, Veit Stoss used every figural and ornamental element from the vocabulary of Gothic art to heighten the emotion and to glorify the sacred event.

sacred event. In the Kraków altarpiece, the disciples of Christ congregate around the Virgin, who sinks down in death. One of them supports her, while another, just above her, wrings his hands in grief. Stoss posed others in attitudes of woe and psychic shock, striving for realism in every minute detail. Moreover, he engulfed the figures in restless, twisting, and curving swaths of drapery whose broken and writhing lines unite the whole tableau in a vision of agitated emotion. The artist's massing of sharp, broken, and pierced forms that dart flamelike through the composition—at once unifying and animating it—recalls the design principles of Late Gothic architecture (FIG. 13-27). Indeed, in the Kraków altarpiece, Stoss merged sculpture and architecture, enhancing their union with paint and gilding.

TILMAN RIEMENSCHNEIDER The Virgin's Assumption also appears in the center panel (FIG. 15-19) of the *Creglingen Altarpiece*, created by TILMAN RIEMENSCHNEIDER (ca. 1460–1531) of Würzburg for a parish church in Creglingen, Germany. He also incorporated intricate Gothic forms, especially in the altarpiece's elaborate canopy, but unlike Stoss, he did not paint the figures or the background. By employing an endless and restless line that runs through the garments of the figures, Riemenschneider succeeded in setting the whole design into fluid motion, and no individual element functions without the rest. The draperies float and flow around bodies lost within them, serving not as descriptions but as design elements that tie the figures to one another and to the framework. A look of psychic strain, a facial expression common in Riemenschneider's work, heightens the spirituality of the figures, immaterial and weightless as they appear.

15-19 TILMAN RIEMENSCHNEIDER, *The Assumption of the Virgin*, center panel of the *Creglingen Altarpiece*, Herrgottskirche, Creglingen, Germany, ca. 1495–1499. Lindenwood, 6′ 1″ wide.

Tilman Riemenschneider specialized in carving large wooden retables. His works feature intricate Gothic tracery and religious figures whose bodies are almost lost within their swirling garments.

15-20 Konrad Witz, *Miraculous Draught of Fish,* from the *Altarpiece of Saint Peter,* from the Chapel of Notre-Dame des Maccabées, Cathedral of Saint Peter, Geneva, Switzerland, 1444. Oil on wood, 4′ 3″ × 5′ 1″. Musée d'Art et d'Histoire, Geneva.

Konrad Witz set this Gospel episode on Lake Geneva. The painting is one of the first 15th-century works depicting a specific landscape and is noteworthy for the painter's skill in rendering water effects.

1 ft.

Panel Painting

As in Flanders, large-scale altarpieces featuring naturalistically painted biblical themes were familiar sights in the Holy Roman Empire.

KONRAD WITZ Among the most notable 15th-century German altarpieces is the *Altarpiece of Saint Peter,* painted in 1444 for the chapel of Notre-Dame des Maccabées in the Cathedral of Saint Peter in Geneva, Switzerland. Konrad Witz (ca. 1400–1446), whose studio was in Basel, painted one exterior wing of this triptych with a representation of the *Miraculous Draught of Fish* (FIG. **15-20**). The other exterior wing (not illustrated) depicts the release of Saint Peter from prison. The central panel is lost. On the interior wings, Witz painted scenes of the adoration of the magi and of Saint Peter's presentation of the donor (Bishop François de Mies) to the Virgin and Child. *Miraculous Draught of Fish* shows Peter, the first pope, unsuccessfully trying to emulate Christ walking on water. Some scholars think the detail is a subtle commentary on the limited power of the pope in Rome on the part of the Swiss cardinal who commissioned the work. The painting is particularly significant because of the landscape's prominence. Witz showed precocious skill in the study of water effects—the sky glaze on the slowly moving lake surface, the mirrored reflections of the figures in the boat, and the transparency of the shallow water in the foreground. He observed and depicted the landscape so carefully that art historians have determined the exact location shown. Witz presented a view of the shores of Lake Geneva, with the town of Geneva on the right and Le Môle Mountain in the distance behind Christ's head. This painting is one of the first 15th-century works depicting a specific site.

Graphic Arts

A new age blossomed in the 15th century with a sudden technological advance that had widespread effects—the invention by Johannes Gutenberg (ca. 1400–1468) of movable type around 1450 and the development of the printing press. Printing had been known in China centuries before but had never fostered, as it did in 15th-century Europe, a revolution in written communication and in the generation and management of information. Printing provided new and challenging media for artists, and the earliest form was the *woodcut* (see "Woodcuts, Engravings, and Etchings," page 415). Using a gouging instrument, artists remove sections of wood blocks, sawing along the grain. They ink the ridges that carry the designs, and the hollows remain dry of ink and do not print. Artists produced woodcuts well before the development of movable-type printing. But when a rise in literacy and the improved economy necessitated production of illustrated books on a grand scale, artists met the challenge of bringing the woodcut picture onto the same page as the letterpress.

MICHEL WOLGEMUT The so-called *Nuremberg Chronicle,* a history of the world produced in Nuremberg by Anton Koberger (ca. 1445–1513) with more than 650 illustrations by the workshop of Michel Wolgemut (1434–1519), documents this achievement. The hand-colored page illustrated here (FIG. **15-21**) represents Tarvisium (modern Tarvisio), a town in the extreme northeast of Italy, as it was in the "fourth age of the world" according to the Latin inscription at the top. The blunt, simple lines of the woodcut technique give a detailed perspective of Tarvisium, its harbor and shipping, its walls and towers, its churches and municipal buildings, and the baronial

Woodcuts, Engravings, and Etchings

With the invention of movable type in the 15th century and the new widespread availability of paper from commercial mills, the art of printmaking developed rapidly in Europe. A *print* is an artwork on paper, usually produced in multiple impressions. The set of prints an artist creates from a single print surface is called an *edition*. (The same term is used to describe a single printed version of a book. This is the 13th edition of *Art through the Ages*.) As with books manufactured on a press, the printmaking process involves the transfer of ink from a printing surface to paper. This can be accomplished in several ways. During the 15th and 16th centuries, artists most commonly used the *relief* and *intaglio* methods of printmaking.

Artists produce relief prints, the oldest and simplest of the printing methods, by carving into a surface, usually wood. Relief printing requires artists to conceptualize their images negatively—that is, they remove the surface areas around the images. Thus, when the printmaker inks the surface, the carved-out areas remain clean, and a positive image results when the artist presses the printing block against paper. Because artists produce *woodcuts* through a subtractive process (removing parts of the material), it is difficult to create very thin, fluid, and closely spaced lines. As a result, woodcut prints (for example, FIG. 15-21) tend to exhibit stark contrasts and sharp edges.

In contrast to the production of relief prints, the intaglio method involves a positive process. The artist *incises* (cuts) an image on a metal plate, often copper. The image can be created on the plate manually (*engraving* or *drypoint*; for example, FIG. 15-22) using a tool (a *burin* or *stylus*) or chemically (*etching*; for example, FIG. 20-16). In the latter process, an acid bath eats into the exposed parts of the plate where the artist has drawn through an acid-resistant coating. When the artist inks the surface of the intaglio plate and wipes it clean, the ink is forced into the incisions. Then the artist runs the plate and paper through a roller press, and the paper absorbs the remaining ink, creating the print. Because the artist "draws" the image onto the plate, intaglio prints differ in character from relief prints. Engravings, drypoints, and etchings generally present a wider variety of linear effects. They also often reveal to a greater extent evidence of the artist's touch, the result of the hand's changing pressure and shifting directions.

The paper and inks artists use also affect the finished look of the printed image. During the 15th and 16th centuries, European printmakers used papers produced from cotton and linen rags that papermakers mashed with water into a pulp. The papermakers then applied a thin layer of this pulp to a wire screen and allowed it to dry to create the paper. As contact with Asia increased, printmakers made greater use of what was called Japan paper (of mulberry fibers) and China paper. Artists, then as now, could select from a wide variety of inks. The type and proportion of the ink ingredients affect the consistency, color, and oiliness of inks, which various papers absorb differently. Paper is lightweight, and the portability of prints has appealed to artists over the years. The opportunity to produce multiple impressions from the same print surface also made printmaking attractive to 15th- and 16th-century artists. In addition, prints can be sold at cheaper prices than paintings or sculptures. Consequently, prints can reach a much wider audience than one-of-a-kind artworks can. The number and quality of existing 15th- and 16th-century European prints attest to the importance of the new print medium.

1 in.

15-21 MICHEL WOLGEMUT and shop, *Tarvisium*, page from the *Nuremberg Chronicle*, 1493. Woodcut, 1′ 2″ × 9″. Printed by ANTON KOBERGER.

The *Nuremberg Chronicle* is an early example of woodcut illustrations in printed books. The more than 650 pictures include detailed views of towns, but they are generic rather than specific portrayals.

15-22 Martin Schongauer, *Saint Anthony Tormented by Demons*, ca. 1480–1490. Engraving, $1' \frac{1}{4}'' \times 9''$. Fondazione Magnani Rocca, Corte di Mamiano.

Martin Schongauer was the most skilled of the early masters of metal engraving. By using a burin to incise lines in a copper plate, he was able to create a marvelous variety of tonal values and textures.

1 in.

castle on the hill. Despite the numerous architectural structures, historians cannot determine whether this illustration represents the artist's accurate depiction of the city or his fanciful imagination. Artists often reprinted the same image as illustrations of different cities, and this depiction of Tarvisium is very likely a generic view. Regardless, the work is a monument to a new craft, which expanded in concert with the art of the printed book.

MARTIN SCHONGAUER The woodcut medium hardly had matured when the technique of *engraving* (inscribing on a hard surface), begun in the 1430s and well developed by 1450, proved much more flexible. Predictably, in the second half of the century, engraving began to replace the woodcut process, for making both book illustrations and widely popular single prints. Metal engraving produces an *intaglio* (incised) surface for printing. The incised lines (hollows) of the design, rather than the ridges, take the ink. It is the reverse of the woodcut technique.

MARTIN SCHONGAUER (ca. 1430–1491) was the most skilled and subtle Northern European master of metal engraving. His *Saint Anthony Tormented by Demons* (FIG. **15-22**) shows both the versatility of the medium and the artist's mastery of it. The stoic saint is caught in a revolving thornbush of spiky demons, who claw and tear at him

furiously. With unsurpassed skill and subtlety, Schongauer created marvelous distinctions of tonal values and textures—from smooth skin to rough cloth, from the furry and feathery to the hairy and scaly. The use of *cross-hatching* to describe forms, which Schongauer probably developed, became standard among German graphic artists. The Italians preferred *parallel hatching* (FIG. **16-29**) and rarely adopted cross-hatching, which, in keeping with the general Northern European approach to art, tends to describe the surfaces of things rather than their underlying structures.

Schongauer probably engraved *Saint Anthony* between 1480 and 1490. By then, the political geography of Europe had changed dramatically. Charles the Bold, who had assumed the title of duke of Burgundy in 1467, died in 1477, bringing to an end the Burgundian dream of forming a strong middle kingdom between France and the Holy Roman Empire. After Charles's death at the battle of Nancy, the French monarchy reabsorbed the southern Burgundian lands, and the Netherlands passed to the Holy Roman Empire by virtue of the dynastic marriage of Charles's daughter, Mary of Burgundy, to Maximilian of Habsburg. Thus was inaugurated a new political and artistic era in Northern Europe (see Chapter 18). The next two chapters, however, explore Italian developments in painting, sculpture, and architecture during the 15th and 16th centuries.

NORTHERN EUROPE, 1400 TO 1500

BURGUNDY AND FLANDERS

▮ The most powerful rulers north of the Alps during the first three-quarters of the 15th century were the dukes of Burgundy. They controlled Flanders, which derived its wealth from wool and banking.

▮ Duke Philip the Bold (r. 1363–1404) was the great patron of the Carthusian monastery at Champmol, near Dijon. He employed Claus Sluter, whose *Well of Moses* features innovative statues of prophets with portraitlike features and realistic costumes.

▮ Flemish painters popularized the use of oil paints on wooden panels. By superimposing translucent glazes, they created richer colors than possible using tempera or fresco. One of the earliest examples of oil paintng is Melchior Broederlam's *Retable de Champmol* (1399).

▮ A major art form in churches and private homes alike was the altarpiece with folding wings. Robert Campin's *Mérode Altarpiece* is an early example painted in oils, in which the *Annunciation* takes place in a Flemish home. The work's donors are present as witnesses to the sacred event. Typical of "Northern Renaissance" painting, the everyday objects depicted often have symbolic significance.

▮ Jan van Eyck, Rogier van der Weyden, and others established portraiture as an important art form in 15th-century Flanders. Van Eyck's self-portrait, *Man in a Red Turban,* and Rogier's *Saint Luke Drawing the Virgin* reveal the growing self-awareness of Renaissance artists.

▮ Among the other major Flemish painters were Petrus Christus, Dirk Bouts, Hans Memling, and Hugo van der Goes. Hugo achieved such renown that he won a commission to paint an altarpiece for a church in Florence. The Italians marveled at the Flemish painter's masterful technique and extraordinary realism.

Sluter, *Well of Moses,* 1395–1406

Campin, *Mérode Altarpiece,* ca. 1425–1428

van Eyck, *Man in a Red Turban,* 1433

FRANCE

▮ During the 15th century, the Hundred Years' War crippled the French economy, but dukes and members of the royal court still commissioned some notable artworks.

▮ The Limbourg brothers expanded the illusionistic capabilities of manuscript illumination in the Book of Hours they produced for Jean, duke of Berry (r. 1360–1416) and brother of King Charles V (r. 1364–1380). Their full-page calendar pictures alternately represent the nobility and the peasantry, always in naturalistic settings with realistically painted figures.

▮ French court art—for example, Jean Fouquet's *Melun Diptych*—owes a large debt to Flemish painting in style and technique as well as in the integration of sacred and secular themes.

Limbourg brothers, *Les Très Riches Heures du Duc de Berry,* 1413–1416

HOLY ROMAN EMPIRE

▮ The Late Gothic style remained popular in 15th-century Germany for large carved wooden retables featuring highly emotive figures amid Gothic tracery.

▮ The major German innovation of the 15th century was the development of the printing press, which soon was used to produce books with woodcut illustrations. Woodcuts are relief prints in which the artist carves out the areas around the printed lines, a method that requires the images to be conceptualized negatively.

▮ German artists such as Martin Schongauer were also the earliest masters of engraving. This intaglio technique allows for a wider variety of linear effects because the artist incises the image directly onto a metal plate.

Schongauer, *Saint Anthony Tormented by Demons,* ca. 1480–1490

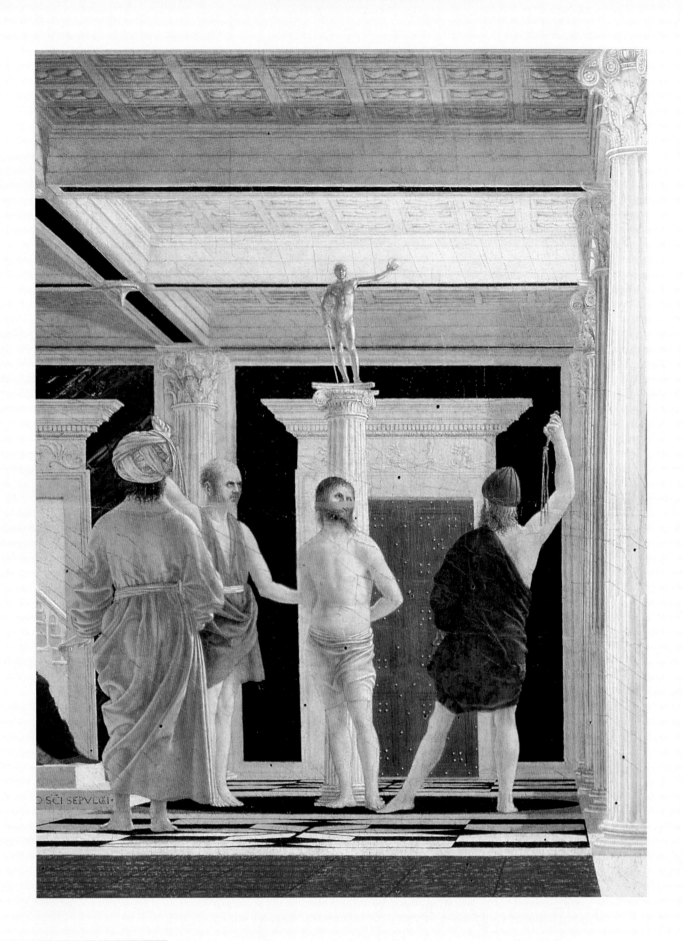

16-1 PIERO DELLA FRANCESCA, detail of *Flagellation of Christ* (FIG. 16-43), ca. 1455–1465. Galleria Nazionale delle Marche, Urbino.

One hallmark of Italian Renaissance painting is the representation of architecture using the new mathematically based science of linear perspective. Piero della Francesca was a master of perspective painting.

16

ITALY, 1400 TO 1500

The humanism that Petrarch and Boccaccio promoted during the 14th century (see Chapter 14) fully blossomed in the 15th century. Increasingly, Italians in elite circles embraced the tenets underlying humanism—an emphasis on education and on expanding knowledge (especially of classical antiquity), the exploration of individual potential and a desire to excel, and a commitment to civic responsibility and moral duty. Italy in the 1400s also enjoyed an abundance of artistic talent. The fortunate congruence of artistic genius, the spread of humanism, and economic prosperity nourished a significantly new and expanded artistic culture—the Renaissance. Artistic developments in 15th-century Italy forever changed the direction and perception of art in the Western world.

For the Italian humanists, the quest for knowledge began with the legacy of the Greeks and Romans—the writings of Socrates, Plato, Aristotle, Ovid, and others. The development of a literature based on the commonly spoken Tuscan dialect expanded the audience for humanist writings. Further, the invention of movable metal type in Germany around 1450 (see Chapter 15) facilitated the printing and widespread distribution of books. Italians enthusiastically embraced this new printing process. By 1464 Subiaco (near Rome) boasted a press, and by 1469 Venice had established one as well. Among the first books printed in Italy using this new press was Dante's vernacular epic about Heaven, Purgatory, and Hell, *Divine Comedy*. The production of editions in Foligno (1472), Mantua (1472), Venice (1472), Naples (1477 and 1478–1479), and Milan (1478) testifies to the extensive popularity of Dante's work.

The humanists also avidly acquired information in a wide range of subjects, including botany, geology, geography, optics, medicine, and engineering. Leonardo da Vinci's phenomenal expertise in many fields—from art and architecture to geology, aerodynamics, hydraulics, botany, and military science, among others—still defines the modern notion of a "Renaissance man." Humanism also fostered a belief in individual potential and encouraged individual achievement as well as civic responsibility. Whereas people in medieval society accorded great power to divine will in determining the events that affected lives, those in Renaissance Italy adopted a more secular stance. Humanists not only encouraged individual improvement but also rewarded excellence with fame and honor. Achieving and excelling through hard work became moral imperatives.

Fifteenth-century Italy witnessed constant fluctuations in its political and economic spheres, including shifting power relations among the numerous city-states and the rise of princely courts (see "Italian Princely Courts and Artistic Patronage," page 447). *Condottieri* (military leaders) with large numbers of mercenary

MAP 16-1
Renaissance Florence.

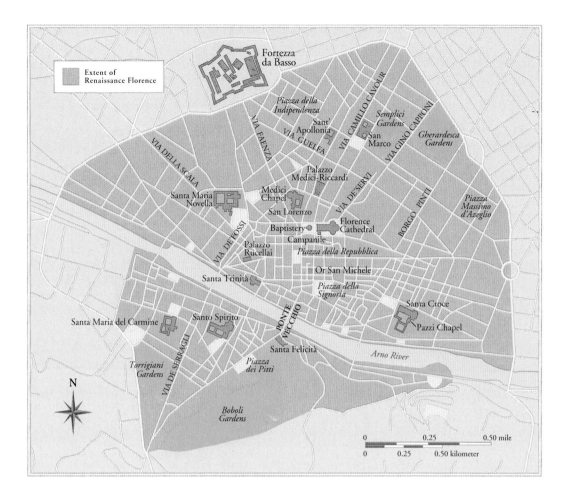

troops at their disposal played a major role in the ongoing struggle for power. Princely courts, such as those in Urbino and Mantua, emerged as cultural and artistic centers alongside the great art centers of the 14th century, especially the Republic of Florence. The association of humanism with education and culture appealed to accomplished individuals of high status, and humanism had its greatest impact among the elite and powerful, whether in the republics or the princely courts. These individuals were in the best position to commission art. As a result, humanist ideas permeate Italian Renaissance art. The intersection of art with humanist doctrines during the Renaissance is evident in the popularity of subjects selected from classical history or mythology; the increased concern with developing perspectival systems and depicting anatomy accurately; the revival of portraiture and other self-aggrandizing forms of patronage; and citizens' extensive participation in civic and religious art commissions.

FLORENCE

Because high-level patronage required significant accumulated wealth, the individuals and families who had managed to prosper economically, whether princes or merchants, came to the fore in artistic circles. The best-known Italian Renaissance art patrons were the Medici of the Republic of Florence (MAP 16-1). Early in the 15th century, the banker Giovanni de' Medici (ca. 1360–1429) had established the family fortune. His son Cosimo (1389–1464) expanded his family's dominance in financial circles, which led to considerable political power as well. This consolidation of power in a city that prided itself on its republicanism did not go unchallenged. In the early 1430s, a power struggle with other elite families led to the family's expulsion from Florence. In 1434 the Medici returned and used their tremendous wealth to commission art and architecture on a scale rarely seen.

The Medici were avid humanists. Cosimo began the first public library since the ancient world, and historians estimate that in some 30 years he and his descendants expended the equivalent of more than $20 million for manuscripts and books. Scarcely a great architect, painter, sculptor, philosopher, or humanist scholar escaped the family's notice. Cosimo was the very model of the cultivated humanist. His grandson Lorenzo (1449–1492), called "the Magnificent," was a talented poet himself and gathered about him a galaxy of artists and gifted men in all fields, extending the library Cosimo had begun and revitalizing his academy for instructing artists. Lorenzo also participated in what some have called the Platonic Academy of Philosophy (most likely an informal reading group), and lavished funds (often the city's own) on splendid buildings, festivals, and pageants. The Medici were such grand patrons of art and learning that, to this day, a generous benefactor of the fine arts is often called "a Medici."

Sculpture

The earliest important artistic commission in 15th-century Florence was not, however, a Medici project, but a guild-sponsored competition in 1401 for a design for the east doors of the city's baptistery (FIG. 12-26). Artists and public alike considered this commission particularly prestigious because of the intended placement of the doors on the building's east side, facing Florence Cathedral (FIG. 14-18). Several traits associated with mature Renaissance art already characterized the baptistery competition: patronage as both a civic imperative and a form of self-promotion, the esteem accorded to individual artists, and the development of a new pictorial illusionism.

SACRIFICE OF ISAAC Andrea Pisano (ca. 1290–1348), unrelated to the two 13th-century Pisan sculptors Nicola and Giovanni discussed in Chapter 14, had designed the south doors of Florence's baptistery between 1330 and 1335. The wool merchants' guild sponsored the 1401 competition for the second set of doors, requiring each entrant to submit a relief panel depicting the sacrifice of Isaac. This biblical event centers on God's order to Abraham that he sacrifice his son Isaac as a demonstration of Abraham's devotion to God (see "Jewish Subjects in Christian Art," Chapter 8, page 213). Just as Abraham is about to comply, an angel intervenes and stops him from plunging the knife into his son's throat. Because of the parallel between Abraham's willingness to sacrifice Isaac and God's sacrifice of his son Jesus to redeem mankind, the sacrifice of Isaac was often linked to the Crucifixion. Both refer to covenants, and given that the sacrament of baptism initiates the newborn or the convert into the possibilities of these covenants, Isaac's sacrifice was certainly appropriate for representation on a baptistery.

Contemporary events, however, may have been an important factor in the selection of this theme. In the late 1390s, Giangaleazzo Visconti, the first duke of Milan (r. 1378–1395), began a military campaign to take over the Italian peninsula. By 1401, when the cathedral's art directors initiated the baptistery competition, Visconti's troops had surrounded Florence, and its independence was in serious jeopardy. Despite dwindling water and food supplies, Florentine officials exhorted the public to defend the city's freedom. For example, the humanist chancellor Coluccio Salutati (1331–1406) urged his fellow citizens to adopt the republican ideal of civil and political liberty associated with ancient Rome and to identify themselves with its spirit. To be Florentine was to be Roman. Freedom was the distinguishing virtue of both republics. The story of Abraham and Isaac, with its theme of sacrifice, paralleled the message city officials had conveyed to inhabitants. It is certainly plausible that the wool merchants, asserting both their preeminence among Florentine guilds and their civic duty, selected the subject with this in mind. The Florentines' reward for their faith and sacrifice came in 1402 when Visconti died suddenly, ending the invasion threat.

BRUNELLESCHI AND GHIBERTI The jury selected seven semifinalists from among the many who entered the widely advertised competition for the baptistery commission. Only the panels of the two finalists, FILIPPO BRUNELLESCHI (1377–1446) and LORENZO GHIBERTI (1378–1455), have survived. As instructed, both artists used the same French Gothic *quatrefoil* frames Andrea Pisano had used for the baptistery's south doors and depicted the same moment of the narrative— the angel's halting of the action. Brunelleschi's panel (FIG. 16-2) shows a sturdy and vigorous interpretation of the theme, with something of the emotional agitation of Giovanni Pisano's relief sculptures (FIG. 14-4). Abraham seems suddenly to have summoned the dreadful courage needed to kill his son at God's command. He lunges forward, robes flying, exposing Isaac's throat to the knife. Matching Abraham's energy, the saving angel darts in from the left, grabbing Abraham's arm to stop the killing. Brunelleschi's figures demonstrate his ability to observe carefully and represent faithfully all the elements in the biblical narrative.

Whereas Brunelleschi imbued his image with dramatic emotion, Ghiberti, the youngest artist in the competition, emphasized grace and smoothness. In Ghiberti's panel (FIG. 16-3), Abraham

16-2 FILIPPO BRUNELLESCHI, *Sacrifice of Isaac,* competition panel for east doors of the baptistery, Florence, Italy, 1401–1402. Gilded bronze, 1′ 9″ × 1′ 5½″. Museo Nazionale del Bargello, Florence.

Brunelleschi's entry in the competition to create new bronze doors for the Florentine baptistery shows a frantic angel about to halt an emotional, lunging Abraham clothed in swirling Gothic robes.

16-3 LORENZO GHIBERTI, *Sacrifice of Isaac,* competition panel for east doors of the baptistery, Florence, Italy, 1401–1402. Gilded bronze, 1′ 9″ × 1′ 5½″. Museo Nazionale del Bargello, Florence.

In contrast to Brunelleschi's panel (FIG. 16-2), Ghiberti's entry in the baptistery competition features gracefully posed figures that recall classical statuary. Even Isaac's altar has a Roman acanthus frieze.

appears in a typically Gothic pose with outthrust hip (compare FIG. 13-26) and seems to contemplate the act he is about to perform, even as he draws his arm back to strike. The figure of Isaac, beautifully posed and rendered, recalls Greco-Roman statuary and could be regarded as the first classical nude since antiquity. (Compare, for example, the torsion of Isaac's body and the dramatic turn of his head with those of the Hellenistic statue of a Gaul plunging a sword into his own chest, FIG. 5-80). Unlike his medieval predecessors, Ghiberti revealed a genuine appreciation of the nude male form and a deep interest in how the muscular system and skeletal structure move the human body. Even the altar on which Isaac kneels displays Ghiberti's emulation of antique models. Decorating it are acanthus scrolls of a type that commonly adorned Roman temple friezes in Italy and throughout the former Roman Empire (for example, FIG. 7-32). These classical references reflect the increasing influence of humanism in the 15th century. Ghiberti's entry in the baptistery competition is also noteworthy for the artist's interest in spatial illusion. The rocky landscape seems to emerge from the blank panel toward the viewer, as does the strongly foreshortened angel. Brunelleschi's image, in contrast, emphasizes the planar orientation of the surface.

Ghiberti's training included both painting and metalwork. His careful treatment of the gilded bronze surfaces, with their sharply and accurately incised detail, proves his skill as a goldsmith. That Ghiberti cast his panel in only two pieces (thereby reducing the amount of bronze needed) no doubt impressed the selection committee. Brunelleschi's panel consists of several cast pieces. Thus, not only would Ghiberti's doors, as proposed, be lighter and more impervious to the elements, but they also represented a significant cost savings. The younger artist's submission clearly had much to recommend it, both stylistically and technically, and the judges awarded the commission to him. Ghiberti's pride in winning is evident in his description of the award, which also reveals the fame and glory increasingly accorded to individual achievement during the Early Renaissance:

> To me was conceded the palm of the victory by all the experts and by all who had competed with me. To me the honor was conceded universally and with no exception. To all it seemed that I had at that time surpassed the others without exception, as was recognized by a great council and an investigation of learned men. . . . There were thirty-four judges from the city and the other surrounding countries. The testimonial of the victory was given in my favor by all.[1]

OR SAN MICHELE A second major Florentine sculptural project of the early 1400s was the decoration of Or San Michele, an early-14th-century building prominently located on the main street connecting the Palazzo della Signoria (seat of the *signoria*, Florence's governing body) and the cathedral (MAP 16-1). At various times Or San Michele housed a church, a granary, and the headquarters of Florence's guilds. After construction of the building, city officials assigned each of the niches on the exterior to a specific guild for decoration with a sculpture of its patron saint. By 1406 the guilds had placed statues in only 5 of the 14 niches, so the officials issued a dictum requiring the guilds to comply with the original plan and fill their assigned niches. A few years later, Florence was once again under siege, this time by King Ladislaus (r. 1399–1414) of Naples. Ladislaus had marched north, occupied Rome and the Papal States (MAP 14-1) by 1409, and threatened to overrun Florence. As they had previously, Florentine officials urged citizens to stand firm and defend their city-state from tyranny. Once again,

16-4 NANNI DI BANCO, *Four Crowned Saints,* Or San Michele, Florence, Italy, ca. 1410–1416. Marble, figures 6′ high. Modern copy in exterior niche. Original sculpture in museum on second floor of Or San Michele, Florence.

Nanni's group representing the four martyred patron saints of Florence's sculptors' guild is an early example of Renaissance artists' attempt to liberate statuary from its architectural setting.

Florence escaped unscathed. Ladislaus, on the verge of military success in 1414, fortuitously died. The guilds may well have viewed this new threat as an opportunity to perform their civic duty by rallying their fellow Florentines while also promoting their own importance and position in Florentine society. By 1423 statues by Ghiberti and other leading Florentine artists filled the nine remaining niches of Or San Michele.

NANNI DI BANCO Among the niches filled during the Neapolitan king's attempted siege was that assigned to the Florentine guild

16-5 DONATELLO, *Saint Mark,* Or San Michele, Florence, Italy, ca. 1411–1413. Marble, 7′ 9″ high. Modern copy in exterior niche. Original sculpture in museum on second floor of Or San Michele, Florence.

In this statue carved for the guild of linen drapers, Donatello introduced the classical principle of contrapposto into Early Renaissance sculpture. The drapery falls naturally and moves with the body.

them put to death. Because they placed their faith above all else, these saints were perfect role models for the 15th-century Florentines whom city leaders exhorted to stand fast in the face of the armies of Ladislaus.

Nanni's sculptural group, *Four Crowned Saints* (FIG. 16-4), is an early attempt to solve the problem of integrating figures and space on a monumental scale. The artist's positioning of the figures, which stand in a niche that is *in* but confers some separation *from* the architecture, furthered the gradual emergence of sculpture from its architectural setting. This process began with works such as the 13th-century jamb statues (FIG. 13-24) on the west front of Reims Cathedral. At Or San Michele, the niche's spatial recess permitted a new and dramatic possibility for the interrelationship of the figures. By placing them in a semicircle within their deep niche and relating them to one another by their postures and gestures, as well as by the arrangement of robes, Nanni arrived at a unified spatial composition. A remarkable psychological unity also connects these unyielding figures, whose bearing expresses the discipline and integrity necessary to face adversity. As the figure on the right speaks, pointing to his right, the two men opposite listen, and the one next to him looks out into space, pondering the meaning of the words and reinforcing the formal unity of the figural group with psychological cross-references.

In *Four Crowned Saints,* Nanni also displayed a deep respect for and close study of Roman portrait statues. The emotional intensity of the faces of the two inner saints owes much to the extraordinarily moving portrayals in stone of third-century Roman emperors (FIG. 7-68), and the bearded heads of the outer saints reveal a familiarity with second-century imperial portraiture (FIG. 7-59). Often, when Renaissance artists sought to portray individual personalities, they turned to ancient Roman models for inspiration, but they did not simply copy them. Rather, they strove to interpret or offer commentary on their classical models in the manner of humanist scholars dealing with classical texts.

DONATELLO Another sculptor who carved statues for Or San Michele's facade was Donato di Niccolo Bardi, or DONATELLO (ca. 1386–1466), who incorporated Greco-Roman sculptural principles in his *Saint Mark* (FIG. 16-5), executed for the guild of linen drapers. In this sculpture, Donatello took a fundamental step toward depicting motion in the human figure by recognizing the principle of weight shift, or *contrapposto*. Greek sculptors of the fifth century BCE were the first to grasp that the act of standing requires balancing the position and weight of the different parts of the human body, as they demonstrated in works such as the *Kritios Boy* (FIG. 5-34) and the *Doryphoros* (FIG. 5-40). In contrast to earlier sculptors, they recognized that the human body is not a rigid mass but a flexible structure that moves by continuously shifting its weight from one supporting leg to the other, its constituent parts moving in consonance. Donatello reintroduced this concept into Renaissance statuary. As the saint's body "moves," his garment "moves" with it, hanging and folding naturally from and around different body parts so that the viewer senses the figure as a clothed nude human, not a stone statue with arbitrarily incised drapery. Donatello's *Saint Mark* is the first Renaissance statue whose voluminous cloth garment (the pride of the Florentine guild that paid for the statue) does not conceal but accentuates the movement of the arms, legs, shoulders, and hips. This development further contributed to the sculpted figure's independence from its architectural setting. Saint Mark's stirring limbs, shifting weight, and mobile drapery suggest impending movement out of the niche.

of stone- and woodworkers. They chose one of their members, NANNI DI BANCO (ca. 1380–1421), to create four life-size marble statues of the guild's martyred patron saints. These four Christian sculptors had defied an order from the Roman emperor Diocletian to carve a statue of a pagan deity. In response, the emperor ordered

16-6 Donatello, *Saint George,* Or San Michele, Florence, Italy, ca. 1410–1415. Marble, 6′ 10″ high. Museo Nazionale del Bargello, Florence.

Donatello's statue for the armorers' guild once had a bronze sword and helmet. The warrior saint stands defiantly, ready to spring from his niche to defend Florence, his sword pointed at the spectator.

SAINT GEORGE

For the Or San Michele niche of the armorers' and swordmakers' guild, Donatello made a statue of *Saint George* (FIG. 16-6). The saintly knight stands proudly with his shield in front of him. He once held a bronze sword in his right hand and wore a bronze helmet on his head, both fashioned by the sponsoring guild. The statue continues the Gothic tradition of depicting warrior saints on church facades, as seen in the statue of Saint Theodore (FIG. 13-18) on the south-transept portal of Chartres Cathedral, but here it has a civic role to play. Saint George stands in a defiant manner—ready to spring out of his niche to defend Florence against attack from another Visconti or Ladislaus, his sword jutting out threateningly at all passersby. The saint's body is taut, and Donatello has given him a face filled with nervous energy.

Directly below the statue's base is Donatello's marble relief representing *Saint George and the Dragon* (FIG. 16-7). Commissioned about two years after he installed the statue in its niche, the relief marks a turning point in Renaissance sculpture. Even the landscapes

16-8 Donatello, *Feast of Herod,* panel on the baptismal font of Siena Cathedral, Siena, Italy, 1423–1427. Gilded bronze, 1′ 11½″ × 1′ 11½″.

Donatello's *Feast of Herod* marked the advent of rationalized perspective space in Renaissance relief sculpture. Two arched courtyards of diminishing size open the space of the action well into the distance.

in the baptistery competition reliefs (FIGS. 16-2 and 16-3) are modeled forms seen against a blank background. In *Saint George and the Dragon,* Donatello took a painterly approach to representation, creating an atmospheric effect by using incised lines. It is impossible to talk about a background plane in this work. The landscape recedes into distant space. The depth of that space cannot be measured. The relief is a window onto an infinite vista.

FEAST OF HEROD

Donatello's mastery of relief sculpture is also evident in *Feast of Herod* (FIG. 16-8), a bronze relief on the baptismal font in Siena Cathedral. Some of the figures, especially the dancing Salome (to the right), derive from classical reliefs, but nothing in Greco-Roman art can match the illusionism of Donatello's rendition of this New Testament scene. In Donatello's relief, Salome has already delivered the severed head of John the Baptist, which the kneeling executioner offers to King Herod. The other figures recoil in horror in two groups. At the right, one man covers his face with his

16-7 Donatello, *Saint George and the Dragon,* relief below the statue of Saint George (FIG. 16-6), Or San Michele, Florence, Italy, ca. 1417. Marble, 1′ 3¼″ × 3′ 11¼″. Museo Nazionale del Bargello, Florence.

Donatello's relief marked a turning point in Renaissance sculpture. He took a painterly approach, creating an atmospheric effect by using incised lines. The depth of the background cannot be measured.

Renaissance Perspectival Systems

Scholars long have noted the Renaissance fascination with perspective. In essence, portraying perspective involves constructing a convincing illusion of space in two-dimensional imagery while unifying all objects within a single spatial system. Renaissance artists were not the first to focus on depicting illusionistic space. Both the Greeks and the Romans were well versed in perspective rendering. Many frescoes of buildings and colonnades (for example, FIG. 7-19, *right*) using a Renaissance-like system of converging lines survive on the walls of Roman houses. However, the Renaissance rediscovery of and interest in perspective contrasted sharply with the portrayal of space during the Middle Ages, when spiritual concerns superseded the desire to depict objects illusionistically.

Renaissance perspectival systems included both linear perspective and atmospheric perspective. Developed by Filippo Brunelleschi, *linear perspective* allows artists to determine mathematically the relative size of rendered objects to correlate them with the visual recession into space. Linear perspective can be either one-point or two-point.

▐ In one-point linear perspective (FIG. 16-9*a*), the artist first must identify a horizontal line that marks, in the image, the horizon in the distance (hence the term *horizon line*). The artist then selects a *vanishing point* on that horizon line (often located at the exact center of the line). By drawing *orthogonals* (diagonal lines) from the edges of the picture to the vanishing point, the artist creates a structural grid that organizes the image and determines the size of objects within the image's illusionistic space. Among the works that provide clear examples of one-point linear perspective are Masaccio's *Holy Trinity* (FIG. 16-20), Leonardo da Vinci's *Last Supper* (FIG. 17-4), and Raphael's *School of Athens* (FIG. 17-9). All of these are representations of figures in architectural settings, but linear perspective can also be applied to single figures. An especially dramatic example of the use of one-point perspective to depict a body receding into the background is Andrea Mantegna's *Foreshortened Christ* (FIG. 16-49).

▐ Two-point linear perspective (FIG. 16-9*b*) also involves the establishment of a horizon line. Rather than using a single vanishing point along this horizon line, the artist identifies two of them. The orthogonals that result from drawing lines from an object to each of the vanishing points create, as in one-point perspective, a grid that indicates the relative size of objects receding into space. An example of two-point perspective is Titian's *Madonna of the Pesaro Family* (FIG. 17-38).

▐ Unlike linear perspective, which relies on a structured mathematical system, *atmospheric perspective* involves optical phenomena. Artists using atmospheric (sometimes called *aerial*) perspective exploit the principle that the farther back the object is in space, the blurrier, less detailed, and bluer it appears. Further, color saturation and value contrast diminish as the image recedes into the distance. Leonardo da Vinci used atmospheric perspective to great effect, as seen in works such as *Madonna of the Rocks* (FIG. 17-2) and *Mona Lisa* (FIG. 17-5).

These two methods of creating the illusion of space in pictures are not exclusive, and Renaissance artists often used both linear and atmospheric perspective in the same work to heighten the sensation of three-dimensional space, as in Raphael's *Marriage of the Virgin* (FIG. 17-7).

16-9 One-point (a) and two-point (b) linear perspective.

Linear perspective reflected the emergence of modern science itself. With its mathematical certitude, perspective also elevated the stature of painting by making pictures rational and measurable.

hand. At the left, Herod and two terrified children shrink back in dismay. The psychic explosion drives the human elements apart, leaving a gap across which the emotional electricity crackles. This masterful stagecraft obscures another drama Donatello was playing out on the stage itself. His *Feast of Herod* marks the advent of rationalized perspective space, long prepared for in 14th-century Italian art. As in *Saint George and the Dragon* (FIG. 16-7), Donatello opened the space of the action well into the distance. But here he employed the new mathematically based science of linear perspective to depict two arched courtyards and the groups of attendants in the background.

RENAISSANCE PERSPECTIVE In the 14th century, Italian artists, such as Duccio and the Lorenzetti brothers, had used several devices to indicate distance, but with the development of *linear perspective* (FIG. 16-9), Early Renaissance artists acquired a way to make the illusion of distance certain and consistent (see "Renaissance Perspectival Systems," above). In effect, they conceived the picture plane as a transparent window through which the observer looks to see the constructed pictorial world. This discovery was enormously important, for it made possible what has been called the "rationalization of sight." It brought all random and infinitely various visual

16-10 LORENZO GHIBERTI, east doors (*Gates of Paradise*), baptistery, Florence, Italy, 1425–1452. Gilded bronze, 17′ high. Modern copy, ca. 1980. Original panels in Museo dell'Opera del Duomo, Florence.

In Ghiberti's later doors for the Florentine baptistery, the sculptor abandoned the Gothic quatrefoil frames for the biblical scenes (compare FIG. 16-3) and employed painterly illusionistic devices.

16-11 LORENZO GHIBERTI, *Isaac and His Sons* (detail of FIG. 16-10), east doors (*Gates of Paradise*), baptistery, Florence, Italy, 1425–1452. Gilded bronze, 2′ 7½″ × 2′ 7½″. Museo dell'Opera del Duomo, Florence.

In this relief, Ghiberti employed linear perspective to create the illusion of distance, but he also used sculptural aerial perspective, with forms appearing less distinct the deeper they are in space.

sensations under a simple rule that could be expressed mathematically. Indeed, Renaissance artists' interest in perspective reflects the emergence at this time of modern science itself. Of course, 15th-century artists were not primarily scientists. They simply found perspective an effective way to order and clarify their compositions. Nonetheless, there can be little doubt that perspective, with its new mathematical certitude, conferred a kind of aesthetic legitimacy on painting by making the picture measurable and exact. According to Plato, measure is the basis of beauty, and Classical Greek art reflects this belief (see "Polykleitos," Chapter 5, page 110). In the Renaissance, when humanists rediscovered Plato and eagerly read his works, artists once again exalted the principle of measure as the foundation of the beautiful in the fine arts. The projection of measurable objects on flat surfaces influenced the character of Renaissance paintings and made possible scale drawings, maps, charts, graphs, and diagrams—means of exact representation that laid the foundation for modern science and technology. Mathematical truth and formal beauty united in the minds of Renaissance artists.

GATES OF PARADISE Ghiberti was among the first Italian artists in the 15th century to embrace a unified system for representing space. His enthusiasm for perspectival illusion is particularly evident in the famous east doors (FIG. 16-10) that in 1425 church officials commissioned him to make for the Florentine baptistery (FIG. 12-26). Michelangelo later declared these as "so beautiful that they would do well for the gates of Paradise."[2] Three sets of doors provide access to the building. Andrea Pisano created the first set, on the south side, between 1330 and 1335. Ghiberti made his first pair of doors (1403–1424), the result of the competition, for the east portal, but church officials moved those doors to the north entrance so that his second pair of doors (1425–1452) could be placed on the east side. In the *Gates of Paradise*, Ghiberti abandoned the quatrefoil pattern that frames the reliefs on the south and north doors and reduced the number of panels from 28 to 10. Each panel contains a relief set in plain moldings and depicts a scene from the Old Testament. The complete gilding of the reliefs creates an effect of great splendor and elegance.

The individual panels, such as *Isaac and His Sons* (FIG. 16-11), clearly recall painting techniques in their depiction of space as well as in their treatment of the narrative. Some exemplify more fully than painting many of the principles the architect and theorist Leon Battista Alberti formulated in his 1435 treatise, *On Painting*. In his relief, Ghiberti created the illusion of space partly through the use of pictorial perspective and partly by sculptural means. He represented buildings according to a painter's one-point perspective construction, but the figures (in the bottom section of the relief, which actually projects slightly toward the viewer) appear almost fully in the round, some of their heads standing completely free. As the eye progresses upward, the relief increasingly flattens, concluding with the architecture in the background, which Ghiberti depicted in barely raised lines. In this manner, the artist created a sort of sculptor's aerial perspective, with forms appearing less distinct the deeper they are in space. Ghiberti described the east doors as follows:

> I strove to imitate nature as closely as I could, and with all the perspective I could produce [to have] excellent compositions rich with many figures. In some scenes I placed about a hundred figures, in some less, and in some more. . . . There were ten stories, all [sunk] in frames because the eye from a distance measures and interprets the scenes in such a way that they appear round. The scenes are in the lowest relief and the figures are seen in the planes; those that are near appear large, those in the distance small, as they do in reality. I executed this entire work with these principles.[3]

In these panels, Ghiberti achieved a greater sense of depth than had previously seemed possible in a relief. His principal figures do not occupy the architectural space he created for them. Rather, the artist arranged them along a parallel plane in front of the grandiose architecture. (According to Leon Battista Alberti, in his *On the Art of Building*, the grandeur of the architecture reflects the dignity of the events shown in the foreground.) Ghiberti's figure style mixes a Gothic patterning of rhythmic line, classical poses and motifs, and a new realism in characterization, movement, and surface detail. Ghiberti retained the medieval narrative method of presenting several episodes within a single frame. In *Isaac and His Sons*, the women in the left foreground attend the birth of Esau and Jacob in the left background. In the central foreground, Isaac sends Esau and his dogs to hunt game. In the right foreground, Isaac blesses the kneeling Jacob as Rebecca looks on. Yet viewers experience little confusion because of Ghiberti's careful and subtle placement of each scene. The figures, in varying degrees of projection, gracefully twist and turn, appearing to occupy and move through a convincing stage space, which Ghiberti deepened by showing some figures from behind. The classicism derives from the artist's close study of ancient art. Ghiberti admired and collected classical sculpture, bronzes, and coins. Their influence appears throughout the panel, particularly in the figure of Rebecca, which Ghiberti based on a popular Greco-Roman statuary type. The emerging practice of collecting classical art in the 15th century had much to do with the incorporation of classical motifs and the emulation of classical style in Renaissance art.

DONATELLO, *DAVID* The use of perspectival systems in relief sculpture and painting represents only one aspect of the Renaissance revival of classical principles and values in the arts. Another was the revival of the freestanding nude statue. The first Renaissance sculptor to portray the nude male figure in statuary was Donatello. The date of his bronze *David* (FIG. **16-12**) is unknown, but he probably cast it sometime between 1440 and 1460 for display in the courtyard (FIG. **16-37**) of the Medici palace in Florence. In the Middle Ages, the clergy regarded nude statues as both indecent and idolatrous, and nudity in general appeared only rarely in art—and then only in biblical or moralizing contexts, such as the story of Adam and Eve or depictions of sinners in Hell. With *David*, Donatello reinvented the classical nude. His subject, however, was not a pagan god, hero, or athlete but the youthful biblical slayer of Goliath who had become the symbol of the independent Florentine republic—and therefore an ideal choice of subject for the residence of the most powerful family in Florence. The Medici were aware of Donatello's earlier *David* in the Palazzo della Signoria, Florence's town hall. The artist had pro-

duced it during the threat of invasion by King Ladislaus. Their selection of the same subject suggests that the Medici identified themselves with Florence or, at the very least, saw themselves as responsible for Florence's prosperity and freedom. The invoking of classical poses and formats also appealed to the humanist Medici. Donatello's *David* possesses both the relaxed classical contrapposto stance and the proportions and sensuous beauty of the gods (FIG. **5-63**) of Praxiteles, a famous Greek sculptor. These qualities were, not surprisingly, absent from medieval figures.

VERROCCHIO Another *David* (FIG. **16-13**), by ANDREA DEL VERROCCHIO (1435–1488), one of the most important sculptors during the second half of the century, reaffirms the Medici family's identification with Florence. A painter as well as a sculptor, Verrocchio

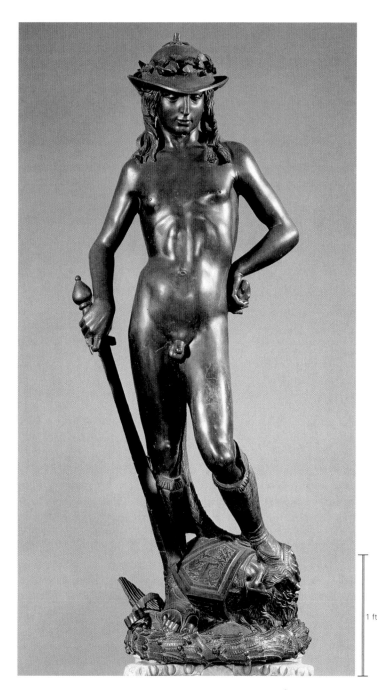

16-12 DONATELLO, *David,* ca. 1440–1460. Bronze, 5′ 2¼″ high. Museo Nazionale del Bargello, Florence.

Donatello's *David* possesses both the relaxed contrapposto and the sensuous beauty of nude Greek gods (FIG. 5-60). The revival of classical statuary style appealed to the sculptor's patrons, the Medici.

1 ft.

1 in.

16-13 Andrea del Verrocchio, *David,* ca. 1465–1470. Bronze, 4′ 1½″ high. Museo Nazionale del Bargello, Florence.

Verrocchio's *David,* also made for the Medici, displays a brash confidence. The statue's narrative realism contrasts strongly with the quiet classicism of Donatello's *David* (FIG. **16-12**).

16-14 Antonio del Pollaiuolo, *Hercules and Antaeus,* ca. 1470–1475. Bronze, 1′ 6″ high with base. Museo Nazionale del Bargello, Florence.

The Renaissance interest in classical culture led to the revival of Greco-Roman mythological themes in art. *Hercules and Antaeus* exhibits the stress and strain of the human figure in violent action.

directed a flourishing *bottega* (studio-shop) in Florence that attracted many students, among them Leonardo da Vinci. Verrocchio, like Donatello, also had a broad repertoire. His *David* contrasts strongly in its narrative realism with the quiet classicism of Donatello's *David.* Verrocchio's *David* is a sturdy, wiry, young apprentice clad in a leathern doublet who stands with a jaunty pride. As in Donatello's version, Goliath's head lies at David's feet. He poses like a hunter with his kill. The easy balance of the weight and the lithe, still thinly adolescent musculature, with prominent veins, show how closely Verrocchio read the biblical text and how clearly he knew the psychology of brash young men. The Medici eventually sold Verrocchio's bronze *David* to the Florentine government for placement in the Palazzo della Signoria. After the expulsion of the Medici from Florence, officials appropriated Donatello's *David* for civic use and moved it to the city hall as well.

POLLAIUOLO The Renaissance interest in classical culture naturally also led to the revival of Greco-Roman mythological themes in art. The Medici were leading patrons in this sphere as well. Around 1470, Antonio del Pollaiuolo (ca. 1431–1498), who was also important as a painter and engraver (FIG. **16-29**), received a Medici com-

mission to produce a small-scale sculpture, *Hercules and Antaeus* (FIG. **16-14**). The subject matter, derived from Greek mythology, and the emphasis on human anatomy reflect the Medici preference for humanist imagery. Even more specifically, the state seal of Florence had featured Hercules since the end of the 13th century. As commissions such as the two *David* sculptures demonstrate, the Medici clearly embraced every opportunity to associate themselves with the glory of the Florentine Republic, surely claiming much of the credit for it.

In contrast to the placid presentation of Donatello's *David* (FIG. **16-12**), Pollaiuolo's *Hercules and Antaeus* exhibits the stress and strain of the human figure in violent action. This sculpture departs dramatically from the convention of frontality that had dominated statuary during the Middle Ages and the Early Renaissance. Only 18 inches high, *Hercules and Antaeus* embodies the ferocity and vitality of elemental physical conflict. The group illustrates the wrestling match between Antaeus (Antaios), a giant and son of the goddess Earth, and Hercules (Herakles), a theme the Greek painter Euphronios had represented on an ancient Greek vase (FIG. **5-23**) 2,000 years before. According to the Greek myth, each time Hercules threw him down, Antaeus sprang up again, his strength renewed by contact with the earth. Finally, Hercules held him aloft so that he could not touch the ground, and strangled him around the waist. Pollaiuolo strove to convey the final excruciating moments of the struggle—the straining and cracking of sinews, the clenched teeth of Hercules, and the kicking and screaming of Antaeus. The figures intertwine and interlock as they fight, and the flickering reflections of light on the dark gouged bronze surface contribute to a fluid play of planes and the effect of agitated movement.

GATTAMELATA Given the increased emphasis on individual achievement and recognition that humanism fostered, it is not surprising that portraiture enjoyed a revival in the 15th century. Commemorative portraits of the deceased were common, and patrons also commissioned portraits of themselves. In 1443, Donatello left Florence for northern Italy to accept a rewarding commission from the Republic of Venice to create a commemorative monument in honor of the recently deceased Venetian condottiere Erasmo da Narni (1370–1443), nicknamed Gattamelata ("honeyed cat," a wordplay on his mother's name, Melania Gattelli). Although Gattamelata's family paid for the general's portrait (FIG. 16-15), the Venetian senate formally authorized its erection in the square in front of the church of Sant'Antonio in Padua, the condottiere's birthplace. Equestrian statues occasionally had been set up in Italy in the late Middle Ages, but Donatello's *Gattamelata* was the first to rival the grandeur of the mounted portraits of antiquity, such as that of Marcus Aurelius (FIG. 7-59), which the artist must have

seen in Rome. Donatello's contemporaries, one of whom described Gattamelata as sitting "there with great magnificence like a triumphant Caesar,"[4] recognized this reference to antiquity. The statue stands on a lofty elliptical base, set apart from its surroundings, and almost celebrates sculpture's liberation from architecture. Massive and majestic, the great horse bears the armored general easily, for, unlike the sculptor of Marcus Aurelius, Donatello did not represent the Venetian commander as superhuman and more than life-size. Gattamelata dominates his mighty steed by force of character rather than sheer size. The Italian rider, his face set in a mask of dauntless resolution and unshakable will, is the very portrait of the Renaissance individualist. Such a man—intelligent, courageous, ambitious, and frequently of humble origin—could, by his own resourcefulness and on his own merits, rise to a commanding position in the world. Together, man and horse convey an overwhelming image of irresistible strength and unlimited power—an impression Donatello reinforced visually by placing the left forehoof of the horse on an orb, reviving a venerable ancient symbol for hegemony over the earth (compare FIG. 11-12). The imperial imagery is all the more remarkable because Erasmo da Narni was not a head of state.

BARTOLOMMEO COLLEONI Verrocchio also received a commission to make an equestrian statue of a Venetian condottiere, Bartolommeo Colleoni (1400–1475). His portrait (FIG. 16-16) provides a counterpoint to Donatello's statue. Eager to garner the same fame

16-15 DONATELLO, *Gattamelata* (equestrian statue of Erasmo da Narni), Piazza del Santo, Padua, Italy, ca. 1445–1453. Bronze, 12′ 2″ high.

Donatello based his giant portrait of a Venetian general on equestrian statues of ancient Roman emperors (FIG. 7-59). Together, man and horse convey an overwhelming image of irresistible strength.

16-16 ANDREA DEL VERROCCHIO, *Bartolommeo Colleoni* (equestrian statue), Campo dei Santi Giovanni e Paolo, Venice, Italy, ca. 1481–1496. Bronze, 13′ high.

Eager to compete with Donatello's *Gattamelata* (FIG. 16-15), Colleoni provided the funds for his own equestrian statue in his will. The statue stands on a pedestal even taller than Gattamelata's.

16-17 Gentile da Fabriano, *Adoration of the Magi,* altarpiece from Strozzi Chapel, Santa Trinità, Florence, Italy, 1423. Tempera on wood, 9′ 11″ × 9′ 3″. Galleria degli Uffizi, Florence.

Gentile was the leading Florentine painter working in the International Style, but he successfully blended naturalistic details with Late Gothic splendor in color, costume, and framing ornament.

the *Gattamelata* portrait achieved, Colleoni provided funds in his will for his own statue. Since both Donatello and Verrocchio executed their statues after the deaths of their subjects, neither artist knew personally the individual he portrayed. The result is a fascinating difference of interpretation (like that between their two *Davids*) as to the demeanor of a professional captain of armies. Verrocchio placed the statue of the bold equestrian general on a pedestal even higher than that Donatello used for *Gattamelata* so that viewers could see the dominating, aggressive figure from all major approaches to the piazza (the Campo dei Santi Giovanni e Paolo). In contrast to the near repose of the *Gattamelata* steed and rider, the *Colleoni* horse moves in a prancing stride, arching and curving its powerful neck, while the commander seems suddenly to shift his whole weight to the stirrups and rise from the saddle with a violent twist of his body. The artist depicted the figures with an exaggerated tautness—the animal's bulging muscles and the man's fiercely erect and rigid body together convey brute strength. In *Gattamelata,* Donatello created a portrait of grim sagacity. Verroc-

chio's *Bartolommeo Colleoni* is a portrait of merciless might. Niccolò Machiavelli wrote in his famous political treatise of 1513, *The Prince,* that the successful ruler must combine the traits of the lion and the fox. Donatello's *Gattamelata* approaches the latter, whereas Verrocchio's *Bartolommeo Colleoni* tilts toward the former.

Painting

In 15th-century Italy, humanism and the celebration of classical artistic values also characterized panel and mural painting. The new Renaissance style did not, however, immediately displace all vestiges of the Late Gothic style. In particular, the International Style, the dominant mode in painting around 1400 (see Chapter 14) persisted well into the century.

GENTILE DA FABRIANO The leading Florentine master of the International Style was GENTILE DA FABRIANO (ca. 1370–1427), who in 1423 painted *Adoration of the Magi* (FIG. **16-17**) as the

Cennino Cennini on Imitation and Emulation in Renaissance Art

The familiar premium that contemporary Western society places on artistic originality is actually a fairly recent phenomenon. Among the concepts Renaissance artists most valued were imitation and emulation. Although many Renaissance artists did develop unique, recognizable styles, convention, in terms of both subject matter and representational practices, predominated. In a review of Italian Renaissance art, certain themes, motifs, and compositions surface with great regularity, and the traditional training practices reveal the importance of imitation and emulation to aspiring Renaissance artists.

▌ *Imitation* Imitation was the starting point in a young artist's training (see "Artistic Training in Renaissance Italy," Chapter 19, page 510). Italian Renaissance artists believed that the best way to learn was to copy the works of masters. Accordingly, much of an apprentice's training consisted of copying exemplary artworks. Leonardo da Vinci filled his sketchbooks with drawings of well-known sculptures and frescoes, and Michelangelo spent days sketching artworks in churches around Florence and Rome.

▌ *Emulation* The next step was emulation, which involved modeling one's art after that of another artist. Although imitation still provided the foundation for this practice, an artist used features of another's art only as a springboard for improvements or innovations. Thus, developing artists went beyond previous artists and attempted to prove their own competence and skill by improving on established and recognized masters. Comparison and a degree of competition were integral to emulation. To evaluate the "improved" artwork, viewers had to know the original "model."

Renaissance artists believed that developing artists would ultimately arrive at their own unique style through this process of imitation and emulation. Cennino Cennini (ca. 1370–1440) explained the value of this training procedure in a book he published in 1400, *Il Libro dell'Arte* (*The Artist's Handbook*), which served as a practical guide to producing art:

> Having first practiced drawing for a while, . . . take pains and pleasure in constantly copying the best things which you can find done by the hand of great masters. And if you are in a place where many good masters have been, so much the better for you. But I give you this advice: take care to select the best one every time, and the one who has the greatest reputation. And, as you go on from day to day, it will be against nature if you do not get some grasp of his style and of his spirit. For if you undertake to copy after one master today and after another one tomorrow, you will not acquire the style of either one or the other, and you will inevitably, through enthusiasm, become capricious, because each style will be distracting your mind. You will try to work in this man's way today, and in the other's tomorrow, and so you will not get either of them right. If you follow the course of one man through constant practice, your intelligence would have to be crude indeed for you not to get some nourishment from it. Then you will find, if nature has granted you any imagination at all, that you will eventually acquire a style individual to yourself, and it cannot help being good; because your hand and your mind, being always accustomed to gather flowers, would ill know how to pluck thorns.*

* Translated by Daniel V. Thompson Jr., *Cennino Cennini, The Artist's Handbook* (*Il Libro dell'Arte*), (New York: Dover Publications, 1960; reprint of 1933 ed.), 14–15.

altarpiece for the family chapel of Palla Strozzi (1372–1462) in the church of Santa Trinità in Florence. At the beginning of the 15th century, the Strozzi family was the wealthiest in Florence. The altarpiece, with its elaborate gilded Gothic frame, is testimony to Strozzi's lavish tastes. So too is the painting itself, with its gorgeous surface and sumptuously costumed kings, courtiers, captains, and retainers accompanied by a menagerie of exotic animals. Gentile portrayed all these elements in a rainbow of color with extensive use of gold. The painting presents all the pomp and ceremony of chivalric etiquette in a scene that sanctifies the aristocracy in the presence of the Madonna and Child. Although the style is fundamentally Late Gothic, Gentile inserted striking naturalistic details. For example, the artist depicted animals from a variety of angles and foreshortened the forms convincingly, most notably the horse at the far right seen in a three-quarter rear view. Gentile did the same with human figures, such as the kneeling man removing the spurs from the standing *magus* in the center foreground. In the left panel of the predella, Gentile painted what may have been the very first nighttime Nativity with the central light source—the radiant Christ Child—introduced into the picture itself. Although predominantly conservative, Gentile demonstrated that he was not oblivious to contemporary experimental trends and that he could blend naturalistic and

inventive elements skillfully and subtly into a traditional composition without sacrificing Late Gothic splendor in color, costume, and framing ornament.

MASACCIO The artist who epitomizes the innovative spirit of early-15th-century Florentine painting was Tommaso di ser Giovanni di Mone Cassai, known as MASACCIO (1401–1428). Although his presumed teacher, Masolino da Panicale (see "Italian Artists' Names," Chapter 14, page 376), had worked in the International Style, Masaccio broke sharply from the normal practice of imitating his master's style (see "Imitation and Emulation in Renaissance Italy," above). He moved suddenly, within the short span of six years, into unexplored territory. Most art historians recognize no other painter in history to have contributed so much to the development of a new style in so short a time as Masaccio, whose untimely death at age 27 cut short his brilliant career. Masaccio was the artistic descendant of Giotto (see Chapter 14), whose calm, monumental style he revolutionized with a whole new repertoire of representational devices that generations of Renaissance painters later studied and developed. Masaccio also knew and understood the innovations of his great contemporaries, Ghiberti, Brunelleschi, and Donatello, and he introduced new possibilities for both form and content.

16-18 Masaccio, *Tribute Money,* Brancacci Chapel, Santa Maria del Carmine, Florence, Italy, ca. 1424–1427. Fresco, 8′ 4$\frac{1}{8}$″ × 19′ 7$\frac{1}{8}$″.

Masaccio's figures recall Giotto's in their simple grandeur, but they convey a greater psychological and physical credibility. He modeled his figures with light coming from a source outside the picture.

BRANCACCI CHAPEL The frescoes Masaccio painted in the Brancacci family chapel of Santa Maria del Carmine in Florence provide excellent examples of his innovations. In *Tribute Money* (FIG. 16-18), painted shortly before his death, Masaccio depicted a seldom-represented narrative from the Gospel of Matthew (17:24–27). As the tax collector confronts Christ at the entrance to the Roman town of Capernaum, Christ directs Saint Peter to the shore of Lake Galilee. There, as Christ foresaw, Peter finds the tribute coin in the mouth of a fish and returns to pay the tax. Art historians have debated why Felice Brancacci (1382–1447), the chapel's patron, selected this obscure biblical narrative. Some scholars have suggested that *Tribute Money,* in which Christ condones taxation, served as a commentary on the income tax the Florentine republic was considering implementing at the time. However, Brancacci's considerable wealth makes it unlikely he would have supported a tax on income. Moreover, this fresco's placement in a private family chapel meant that the public had only limited access. Therefore, because this fresco lacked the general audience enjoyed by, for example, the Or San Michele niche sculptures, it seems ill-suited for public statements.

Whatever the reason for the choice of subject, Masaccio decided to divide the story into three episodes within the fresco. In the center, Christ, surrounded by his disciples, tells Saint Peter to retrieve the coin from the fish, while the tax collector stands in the foreground, his back to spectators and hand extended, awaiting payment. At the left, in the middle distance, Saint Peter extracts the coin from the fish's mouth, and, at the right, he thrusts the coin into the tax collector's hand. Masaccio's figures recall Giotto's in their simple grandeur, but they convey a greater psychological and physical credibility. Masaccio created the bulk of the figures by modeling not with a flat, neutral light lacking an identifiable source but with a light coming from a specific source outside the picture. The light comes from the right and strikes the figures at an angle, illuminating the parts of the solids that obstruct its path and leaving the rest in shadow, producing the illusion of deep sculptural relief. Between the extremes of light and dark, the light appears as a constantly active but fluctuating force highlighting the

scene in varying degrees, almost a tangible substance independent of the figures. In his frescoes, Giotto used light only to model the masses. In Masaccio's works, light has its own nature, and the masses are visible only because of its direction and intensity. The viewer can imagine the light as playing over forms—revealing some and concealing others, as the artist directs it. The individual figures in *Tribute Money* are solemn and weighty, but they also move freely and reveal body structure, as do Donatello's statues. Masaccio's representations adeptly suggest bones, muscles, and the pressures and tensions of joints. Each figure conveys a maximum of contained energy. *Tribute Money* helps the viewer understand Giorgio Vasari's comment: "[T]he works made before his [Masaccio's] day can be said to be painted, while his are living, real, and natural."[5]

Masaccio's arrangement of the figures is equally inventive. They do not appear as a stiff screen in the foreground. Instead, the artist grouped them in circular depth around Christ, and he placed the whole group in a spacious landscape, rather than in the confined stage space of earlier frescoes. The group itself generates the foreground space that the architecture on the right amplifies. Masaccio depicted the building in one-point perspective, locating the vanishing point, where all the orthogonals converge, at Christ's head. Atmospheric perspective—the diminishing of light and the blurring of outlines as the distance increases (see "Renaissance Perspectival Systems," page 425)—unites the foreground with the background. Although ancient Roman painters used atmospheric perspective (FIG. 7-20), medieval artists had abandoned it. Thus, it virtually disappeared from art until Masaccio and his contemporaries rediscovered it. They came to realize that the light and air interposed between viewers and what they see are two parts of the visual experience called "distance."

In an awkwardly narrow space at the entrance to the Brancacci Chapel, Masaccio painted *Expulsion of Adam and Eve from Eden* (FIG. 16-19), another fresco displaying the representational innovations of *Tribute Money.* For example, the sharply slanted light from an outside source creates deep relief, with lights placed alongside darks, and acts as a strong unifying agent. Masaccio also presented the figures

16-19 MASACCIO, *Expulsion of Adam and Eve from Eden,* Brancacci Chapel, Santa Maria del Carmine, Florence, Italy, ca. 1424–1427. Fresco, 7′ × 2′ 11″.

Adam and Eve, expelled from Eden, stumble on blindly, driven by the angel's will and their own despair. The hazy background specifies no locale but suggests a space around and beyond the figures.

16-20 MASACCIO, *Holy Trinity,* Santa Maria Novella, Florence, Italy, ca. 1424–1427. Fresco, 21′ 10$\frac{5}{8}$″ × 10′ 4$\frac{3}{4}$″.

Masaccio's *Holy Trinity* is the premier early-15th-century example of the application of mathematics to pictorial organization in Brunelleschi's new science of perspective. The illusionism is breathtaking.

the cry issuing from Eve's mouth voices her anguish. The angel does not force them physically from Eden. Rather, they stumble on blindly, the angel's will and their own despair driving them. The composition is starkly simple, its message incomparably eloquent.

HOLY TRINITY Masaccio's *Holy Trinity* fresco (FIG. 16-20) in Santa Maria Novella is another of the young artist's masterworks and the premier early-15th-century example of the application of mathematics to the depiction of space. Masaccio painted the composition on two levels of unequal height. Above, in a *coffered* barrel-vaulted chapel reminiscent of a Roman *triumphal arch*

16-21 FRA ANGELICO, *Annunciation*, San Marco, Florence, Italy, ca. 1438–1447. Fresco, 7′ 1″ × 10′ 6″.

Painted for the Dominican monks of San Marco, Fra Angelico's fresco is simple and direct. Its figures and architecture have a pristine clarity that befits the fresco's function as a devotional image.

1 ft.

(FIG. 7-39), the Virgin Mary and Saint John appear on either side of the crucified Christ. God the Father emerges from behind Christ, supporting the arms of the cross and presenting his Son to the worshiper as a devotional object. The dove of the Holy Spirit hovers between God's head and Christ's head. Masaccio also included portraits of the donors of the painting, Lorenzo Lenzi and his wife, who kneel just in front of the *pilasters* that frame the chapel's entrance. Below, the artist painted a tomb containing a skeleton. An inscription in Italian painted above the skeleton reminds the spectator that "I was once what you are, and what I am you will become."

The illusionism of *Holy Trinity* is breathtaking. In this fresco, Masaccio brilliantly demonstrated the principles and potential of Brunelleschi's new science of perspective. Indeed, some historians have suggested Brunelleschi may have collaborated with Masaccio. The vanishing point of the composition is at the foot of the cross. With this point at eye level, spectators look up at the Trinity and down at the tomb. About five feet above the floor level, the vanishing point pulls the two views together, creating the illusion of an actual structure that transects the wall's vertical plane. Whereas the tomb appears to project forward into the church, the chapel recedes visually behind the wall and appears as an extension of the spectator's space. This adjustment of the pictured space to the viewer's position was an important innovation in illusionistic painting that other artists of the Renaissance and the later Baroque period would develop further. Masaccio was so exact in his metrical proportions that it is possible to calculate the dimensions of the chapel (for example, the span of the painted vault is seven feet and the depth of the chapel is nine feet). Thus, he achieved not only a successful illusion but also a rational measured coherence that is responsible for the unity and harmony of the fresco. *Holy Trinity* is, however, much more than a demonstration of Brunelleschi's perspective or of the painter's ability to represent fully modeled figures bathed in light. In this painting, Masaccio also powerfully conveyed one of the central tenets of Christian faith. The ascending pyramid of figures leads viewers from the despair of death to the hope of resurrection and eternal life through Christ's crucifixion.

FRA ANGELICO As Masaccio's *Holy Trinity* clearly demonstrates, humanism and religion were not mutually exclusive, but for many 15th-century Italian artists, humanist concerns were not a primary consideration. The art of FRA ANGELICO (ca. 1400–1455) focused on serving the Roman Catholic Church. In the late 1430s, the abbot of the Dominican monastery of San Marco (Saint Mark) in Florence asked Fra Angelico to produce a series of frescoes for the monastery. The Dominicans (see "The Great Schism," Chapter 14, page 379) of San Marco had dedicated themselves to lives of prayer

and work, and the religious compound was mostly spare and austere to encourage the monks to immerse themselves in their devotional lives. Fra Angelico's *Annunciation* (FIG. 16-21) appears at the top of the stairs leading to the friars' cells. Appropriately, Fra Angelico presented the scene of the Virgin Mary and the Archangel Gabriel with simplicity and serenity. The two figures appear in a plain *loggia* resembling San Marco's *portico,* and the artist painted all the fresco elements with a pristine clarity. As an admonition to heed the devotional function of the images, Fra Angelico included a small inscription at the base of the image: "As you venerate, while passing before it, this figure of the intact Virgin, beware lest you omit to say a Hail Mary." Like most of Fra Angelico's paintings, *Annunciation*'s simplicity and directness still have an almost universal appeal and fully reflect the artist's simple, humble character.

ANDREA DEL CASTAGNO Like Fra Angelico, ANDREA DEL CASTAGNO (ca. 1421–1457) accepted a commission to produce a series of frescoes for a religious establishment. His *Last Supper* (FIG. 16-22) in the *refectory* (dining hall) of Sant'Apollonia in Florence, a convent for Benedictine nuns, manifests both a commitment to the biblical narrative and an interest in perspective. The lavishly painted room that Christ and his 12 disciples occupy suggests Castagno's absorption with creating the illusion of three-dimensional space. However, close scrutiny reveals inconsistencies, such as the fact that Renaissance perspectival systems make it impossible to see both the ceiling from inside and the roof from outside, as Castagno depicted. The two side walls also do not appear parallel. The artist chose a conventional compositional format, with the figures seated at a horizontally placed table. Castagno derived the apparent self-absorption of most of the disciples and the malevolent features of Judas (who sits alone on the outside of the table) from the Gospel of Saint John, rather than the more familiar version of the Last Supper recounted in the Gospel of Saint Luke. Castagno's dramatic and spatially convincing depiction of the event no doubt was a powerful presence for the nuns during their daily meals.

FRA FILIPPO LIPPI A younger contemporary of Fra Angelico, FRA FILIPPO LIPPI (ca. 1406–1469), was also a friar—but there all resemblance ends. Fra Filippo seems to have been unsuited for

16-22 ANDREA DEL CASTAGNO, *Last Supper,* the refectory, convent of Sant'Apollonia, Florence, Italy, 1447. Fresco, 15′ 5″ × 32′.

Judas sits isolated in this *Last Supper* fresco based on the Gospel of Saint John. The figures are small compared to the setting, reflecting Castagno's preoccupation with the new science of perspective.

monastic life. He indulged in misdemeanors ranging from forgery and embezzlement to the abduction of a pretty nun, Lucretia, who became his mistress and the mother of his son, the painter Filippino Lippi (1457–1504). Only the intervention of the Medici on his behalf at the papal court saved Fra Filippo from severe punishment and total disgrace. An orphan, Fra Filippo spent his youth in a monastery adjacent to the church of Santa Maria del Carmine. When he was still in his teens, he must have met Masaccio there and witnessed the decoration of the Brancacci Chapel. Fra Filippo's early work survives only in fragments, but these show that he tried to work with Masaccio's massive forms. Later, probably under the influence of Ghiberti's and Donatello's relief sculptures, he developed a linear style that emphasized the contours of his figures and permitted him to suggest movement through flying and swirling draperies.

A painting from Fra Filippo's later years, *Madonna and Child with Angels* (FIG. 16-23), shows his skill in employing a wonderfully fluid line, which unifies the composition and contributes to the precise and smooth delineation of forms. Fra Filippo interpreted his subject in a surprisingly worldly manner. The Madonna, a beautiful young mother, is not at all spiritual or fragile, and neither is the Christ Child, whom two angels hold up. One of the angels turns with the mischievous, puckish grin of a boy refusing to behave for the pious occasion. Significantly, all figures reflect the use of live models (perhaps even Lucretia for the Madonna). Fra Filippo plainly relished the charm of youth and beauty as he found it in this world. He

16-23 FRA FILIPPO LIPPI, *Madonna and Child with Angels,* ca. 1455. Tempera on wood, 2′ 11½″ × 2′ 1″. Galleria degli Uffizi, Florence.

Fra Filippo, a monk guilty of many misdemeanors, represented the Virgin and Christ Child in a distinctly worldly manner, carrying the humanization of the holy family further than ever before.

16-24 DOMENICO GHIRLANDAIO, *Birth of the Virgin,* Cappella Maggiore, Santa Maria Novella, Florence, Italy, ca. 1485–1490. Fresco, 24′ 4″ × 14′ 9″.

Ludovica Tornabuoni holds as prominent a place in Ghirlandaio's fresco as she must have held in Florentine society—evidence of the secularization of sacred themes in 15th-century Italian painting.

preferred the real in landscape also. The background, seen through the window, incorporates recognizable features of the Arno River valley. Compared with the earlier Madonnas by Giotto (FIG. **14-8**) and Duccio (FIG. **14-10**), this work shows how far artists had carried the humanization of the religious theme. Whatever the ideals of spiritual perfection may have meant to artists in past centuries, Renaissance artists realized those ideals in terms of the sensuous beauty of this world.

DOMENICO GHIRLANDAIO Toward the end of the 15th century, DOMENICO GHIRLANDAIO (1449–1494) received an important commission from Giovanni Tornabuoni, one of the wealthiest Florentines of his day. Tornabuoni asked Ghirlandaio to paint a cycle of frescoes depicting scenes from the lives of the Virgin and Saint John the Baptist for the choir of Santa Maria Novella, the Dominican church where Masaccio had earlier painted his revolutionary *Holy Trinity* (FIG. **16-20**). In *Birth of the Virgin* (FIG. **16-24**), Mary's mother, Saint Anne, reclines in a palatial Renaissance room embellished with fine wood inlay and sculpture, while midwives prepare the infant's bath. From the left comes a grave procession of women led by a young Tornabuoni family member, probably Ludovica, Giovanni's daughter. Ghirlandaio's composition epitomizes the achievements of 15th-century Florentine painting: clear spatial representation, statuesque figures, and rational order and logical relations among all figures and objects. If anything of earlier artistic traits remains here, it is the arrangement of the figures, who still cling somewhat rigidly to layers parallel to the picture plane. New, however, and in striking contrast to the dignity and austerity of Fra Angelico's frescoes (FIG. **16-21**) for the Dominican monastery of San Marco, is the dominating presence of the donor's family in the religious tableau. Ludovica holds as prominent a place in the composition (close to the central axis) as she must have held in Florentine society.

16-25 DOMENICO GHIRLANDAIO, *Giovanna Tornabuoni*(?), 1488. Oil and tempera on wood, 2′ 6″ × 1′ 8″. Museo Thyssen-Bornemisza, Madrid.

Renaissance artists revived the ancient art of portraiture. This portrait reveals the great wealth, courtly manners, and humanistic interest in classical literature that lie behind much 15th-century Florentine art.

16-26 PAOLO UCCELLO, *Battle of San Romano*, ca. 1455 (?). Tempera on wood, 6′ × 10′ 5″. National Gallery, London.

In this panel once in the bedchamber of Lorenzo de' Medici, Niccolò da Tolentino leads the charge against the Sienese. The foreshortened spears and figures reveal Uccello's fascination with perspective.

1 ft.

Her appearance in the painting (a different female member of the house appears in each fresco) is conspicuous evidence of the secularization of sacred themes. Artists depicted living persons of high rank not only as being present at biblical dramas (as Masaccio did in *Holy Trinity*) but also as even stealing the show—as here, where the Florentine women upstage the Virgin and Child. The display of patrician elegance tempers the biblical narrative and subordinates the fresco's devotional nature.

Ghirlandaio also painted individual portraits of wealthy Florentines. His 1488 panel painting (FIG. 16-25) of an aristocratic young woman is probably a portrait of Giovanna Tornabuoni (1468–1488), a member of the powerful Albizzi family and wife of Lorenzo Tornabuoni. Although artists at this time were beginning to employ three-quarter and full-face views for portraits in place of the more traditional profile pose, Ghirlandaio used the conventional format. This did not prevent him from conveying a character reading of the sitter. His portrait reveals the proud bearing of a sensitive and beautiful young woman. It also tells viewers much about the advanced state of culture in Florence, the value and careful cultivation of beauty in life and art, the breeding of courtly manners, and the great wealth behind it all. In addition, the painting shows the powerful attraction classical literature held for Italian humanists. In the background, an epitaph (Giovanna Tornabuoni died in childbirth) quotes the ancient Roman poet Martial.

PAOLO UCCELLO   This secular side of Florentine art is on display in *Battle of San Romano* (FIG. 16-26) by PAOLO UCCELLO (1397–1475), a Florentine painter trained in the International Style. The panel painting is one of a series of three that Lorenzo de' Medici acquired for his bedchamber in the palatial family residence (FIGS. 16-36 and 16-37) in Florence. There is some controversy about the date of the painting because recently discovered documents suggest that Lorenzo may have purchased at least two of the paintings from a previous owner instead of commissioning the full series himself. The scenes commemorate the Florentine victory over the Sienese in 1432 and must have been painted no earlier than the mid-1430s if

not around 1455, the traditional date assigned to the commission. In the panel illustrated, Niccolò da Tolentino (ca. 1350–1435), a friend and supporter of Cosimo de' Medici, leads the charge against the Sienese. Although the painting focuses on Tolentino's military exploits, it also acknowledges the Medici, albeit in symbolic form. The bright orange fruit (appropriately placed) behind the unbroken and sturdy lances on the left were known as "mela medica" (Italian, "medicinal apples"). Given that the name Medici means "doctors," this fruit was a fitting symbol (one of many) of the family. It also suggests that at least this panel was a Medici commission.

Uccello was one of many 15th-century painters (and patrons) obsessed with the new science of perspective. The development of perspectival systems intrigued the humanists, because perspective represented the rationalization of vision. As staunch humanists, the Medici pursued all facets of expanding knowledge. In *Battle of San Romano,* Uccello created a composition that recalls the International Style processional splendor of Gentile's *Adoration of the Magi* (FIG. 16-17). But in contrast with Gentile, who emphasized surface decoration, Uccello painted immobilized solid forms. He foreshortened broken spears, lances, and a fallen soldier and carefully placed them along the converging orthogonals of the perspective system to create a base plane like a checkerboard, on which he then placed the larger volumes in measured intervals. This diligently created space recedes to a landscape that resembles the low cultivated hillsides between Florence and Lucca. The rendering of three-dimensional form, used by other painters for representational or expressive purposes, became for Uccello a preoccupation. For him, it had a magic of its own, which he exploited to satisfy his inventive and original imagination.

SANDRO BOTTICELLI   Of all the Florentine painters the Medici employed, perhaps the most famous today is SANDRO BOTTICELLI (1444–1510), a pupil of Fra Filippo Lippi (FIG. 16-23), who must have taught him the method of using firm, pure outlines with light shading within the contours. Art historians universally recognize Botticelli as one of the great masters of line. He was, however, a

16-27 Sandro Botticelli, *Primavera,* ca. 1482. Tempera on wood, 6′ 8″ × 10′ 4″. Galleria degli Uffizi, Florence.

Probably intended to commemorate the May 1482 wedding of Lorenzo di Pierfrancesco de' Medici, Botticelli's lyrical painting celebrates love in spring, with Venus and Cupid at the center of the composition.

1 ft.

brilliant colorist as well, as is evident in *Primavera* (*Spring;* FIG. **16-27**), one of the most popular paintings among a host of other extraordinary works in the collection of the Uffizi Gallery in Florence. The precise meaning of this painting continues to elude scholars. Created for Lorenzo di Pierfrancesco de' Medici, one of Lorenzo the Magnificent's cousins, it features a friezelike series of classically inspired figures in the foreground and a lush backdrop of orange trees in honor of the patron (compare FIG. **16-26**). Venus stands just to the right of center with her son Cupid hovering above her head. Botticelli drew attention to the goddess of love by opening the landscape behind her to reveal a portion of sky that forms a kind of halo around her head. To Venus's right, seemingly the target of Cupid's arrow, are the dancing Three Graces, based closely on ancient prototypes but clothed, albeit in thin, transparent garments. At the right, the blue ice-cold Zephyrus, the west wind, is about to carry off and then marry the nymph Chloris, whom he transforms into Flora, goddess of spring, appropriately shown wearing a rich floral gown. At the far left, the enigmatic figure of Mercury turns away from all the others and reaches up with his distinctive staff, the *caduceus,* perhaps to dispel storm clouds. The sensuality of the representation, the appearance of Venus in springtime, and the abduction and marriage of Chloris all suggest that the painting was commissioned on the occasion of young Lorenzo's May 1482 wedding.

BIRTH OF VENUS Rivaling *Primavera* in fame is Botticelli's tempera on canvas *Birth of Venus* (FIG. **16-28**), which the painter also created for the Medici family. The theme was the subject of a poem by Angelo Poliziano (1454–1494), a leading humanist of the day. In Botticelli's lyrical painting of the poet's retelling of the Greek myth, Zephyrus, carrying Chloris, blows Venus, born of sea foam and carried on a cockle shell, to her sacred island, Cyprus. There, the nymph Pomona runs to meet her with a brocaded mantle. The lightness and bodilessness of the winds propel all the figures without effort. Draperies undulate easily in the gentle gusts, perfumed by rose petals that fall on the whitecaps. In this painting, unlike *Primavera*, Botticelli depicted Venus as nude. As noted earlier, the nude, especially the female nude, was exceedingly rare during the Middle Ages. The artist's

use (particularly on such a large scale) of an ancient Venus statue (a Hellenistic variant of Praxiteles' famous *Aphrodite of Knidos,* FIG. **5-62**) as a model could have drawn the charge of paganism. But in the more accommodating Renaissance culture and under the protection of the powerful Medici, the depiction went unchallenged.

Botticelli's style is clearly distinct from the earnest search many other artists pursued to comprehend humanity and the natural world through a rational, empirical order. Indeed, Botticelli's elegant and beautiful style seems to have ignored all of the scientific knowledge 15th-century artists had gained in the areas of perspective and anatomy. For example, the seascape in *Birth of Venus* is a flat backdrop devoid of atmospheric perspective. Botticelli's style paralleled the Florentine allegorical pageants that were chivalric tournaments structured around allusions to classical mythology. The same trend is evident in the poetry of the 1470s and 1480s. Artists and poets at this time did not directly imitate classical antiquity but used the myths, with delicate perception of their charm, in a way still tinged with medieval romance. Ultimately, Botticelli created a style of visual poetry parallel to the love poetry of Lorenzo de' Medici. His paintings possess a lyricism and courtliness that appealed to cultured Florentine patrons.

MEDICI PATRONAGE The wide range of Medici commissions illustrated in this chapter makes clear that the Florentine banking family did not restrict its collecting to any specific style or artist. Medici acquisitions ranged from mythological to biblical to contemporary historical subject matter and included both paintings and sculptures. Collectively, the art of the Medici reveals their wide and eclectic tastes and sincere love of art and learning and makes a statement about the patrons themselves as well. Careful businessmen that they were, the Medici were not sentimental about their endowment of art and scholarship. Cosimo acknowledged that his good works were not only for the honor of God but also to construct his own legacy. Fortunately, the Medici desired to promote their own fame, and this led to the creation of many of the most cherished masterpieces in the history of Western art.

16-28 Sandro Botticelli, *Birth of Venus,* ca. 1484–1486. Tempera on canvas, 5′ 9″ × 9′ 2″. Galleria degli Uffizi, Florence.

Inspired by an Angelo Poliziano poem and classical statues of Aphrodite (FIG. 5-62), Botticelli revived the theme of the female nude in this elegant and romantic representation of Venus born of sea foam.

1 ft.

ENGRAVING Although the most prestigious commissions in 15th-century Florence were for large-scale panel paintings and frescoes and for monumental statues and reliefs, some artists also produced important small-scale works, such as Pollaiuolo's *Hercules and Antaeus* (FIG. 16-14). Pollaiuolo also experimented with the new medium of engraving, which Northern European artists had pioneered around the middle of the century. But whereas German graphic artists, such as Martin Schongauer (FIG. 15-22), used cross hatching that followed the forms, Italian engravers, such as Pollaiuolo, preferred parallel hatching. The former method was in keeping with the general Northern European approach to art, which tended to describe surfaces of forms rather than their underlying structures, whereas the latter better suited the anatomical studies that preoccupied Pollaiuolo and his Italian contemporaries.

Pollaiuolo's *Battle of the Ten Nudes* (FIG. 16-29), like his *Hercules and Antaeus,* reveals the artist's interest in the realistic presentation of human figures in action. Earlier artists, such as Donatello and Masaccio, had dealt effectively with the problem of rendering human anatomy, but they usually depicted their figures at rest or in restrained motion. As is evident in his engraving as well as in his sculpture, Pollaiuolo took delight in showing violent action. He conceived the body as a powerful machine and liked to display its mechanisms, such as knotted muscles and taut sinews that activate the skeleton as ropes pull levers. To show this to best effect, Pollaiuolo developed a figure so lean and muscular that it appears *écorché* (as if without skin), with strongly accentuated delineations at the wrists, elbows, shoulders, and knees. *Battle of the Ten Nudes* shows this figure type in a variety of poses and from numerous

16-29 Antonio del Pollaiuolo, *Battle of the Ten Nudes,* ca. 1465. Engraving, 1′ 3$\frac{1}{8}$″ × 1′ 11$\frac{1}{4}$″. Metropolitan Museum of Art, New York (bequest of Joseph Pulitzer, 1917).

Pollaiuolo was fascinated by how muscles and sinews activate the human skeleton. He delighted in showing nude figures in violent action and from numerous foreshortened viewpoints.

1 in.

viewpoints, allowing Pollaiuolo to demonstrate his prowess in rendering the nude male figure. In this, he was a kindred spirit of late-sixth-century Greek vase painters, such as Euthymides (FIG. 5-24), who had experimented with foreshortening for the first time in history. Even though Pollaiuolo's figures hack and slash at each other without mercy, they nevertheless seem somewhat stiff and frozen, because Pollaiuolo depicted *all* the muscle groups at maximum tension. Not until several decades later did an even greater anatomist, Leonardo da Vinci, observe that only part of the body's muscle groups participate in any one action, while the others remain relaxed.

Architecture

Filippo Brunelleschi's ability to codify a system of linear perspective derived in part from his skill as an architect. Although in a biography of him written around 1480, Antonio Manetti (1423–1497) reported that Brunelleschi turned to architecture out of disappointment over the loss of the commission for Florence's baptistery doors, he continued to work as a sculptor for several years and received commissions for sculpture as late as 1416. It is true, however, that as the 15th century progressed, Brunelleschi's interest turned increasingly toward architecture. Several trips to Rome (the first in 1402, probably with his friend Donatello), where the ruins of the ancient city captivated him, heightened his fascination with architecture. His close study of Roman monuments and his effort to make an accurate record of what he saw may well have been the catalyst that led Brunelleschi to develop his revolutionary system of geometric linear perspective.

FLORENCE CATHEDRAL Brunelleschi's broad knowledge of Roman construction principles, combined with an analytical and inventive mind, permitted him to solve an engineering problem that no other 15th-century architect could tackle. The challenge was the design and construction of a *dome* for the huge *crossing* of the unfinished Florence Cathedral (FIG. 14-18). The problem was staggering. The space to be spanned (140 feet) was much too wide to permit construction with the aid of traditional wooden centering. Nor was it possible (because of the crossing plan) to support the dome with *buttressed* walls. Brunelleschi began work on the problem about 1417. In 1420 the officials overseeing cathedral projects awarded Brunelleschi and Ghiberti a joint commission. The latter, however, soon retired from the project.

With exceptional ingenuity, Brunelleschi not only discarded traditional building methods and devised new ones but also invented much of the machinery necessary for the job. Although he might have preferred the hemispheric shape of Roman domes, Brunelleschi raised the center of his dome and designed it around an *ogival* (pointed arch) section (FIG. 16-30), which is inherently more stable because it reduces the outward *thrust* around the dome's base. To minimize the structure's weight, he designed a relatively thin double shell (the first in history) around a skeleton of 24 *ribs*. The eight most important are visible on the exterior. Finally, in almost paradoxical fashion, Brunelleschi anchored the structure at the top with a heavy lantern, built after his death but from his design. Despite Brunelleschi's knowledge of and admiration for Roman building techniques, and even though Florence Cathedral's dome was his most outstanding engineering achievement, he solved this critical structural problem through what were essentially Gothic building principles. Thus, the dome, which also had to harmonize in formal terms with the century-old building, does not express Brunelleschi's Renaissance architectural style.

SANTO SPIRITO Santo Spirito (FIGS. 16-31 and 16-32), begun around 1436 and completed, with some changes, after Brunel-

16-30 FILIPPO BRUNELLESCHI, cutaway view of the dome of Florence Cathedral, Florence, Italy, 1420–1436 (after Piero Sanpaolesi).

Brunelleschi solved the problem of placing a dome over the 140-foot-wide crossing of Florence Cathedral by designing a thin double shell that was ogival in section. A heavy lantern anchors the dome at the top.

leschi's death, is one of two *basilican* churches the architect built in Florence. It showcases the clarity and classically inspired rationality that characterize Brunelleschi's mature designs. Brunelleschi laid out this *cruciform* building in either multiples or segments of the dome-covered *crossing square*. The aisles, subdivided into small squares covered by shallow, saucer-shaped vaults, run all the way around the flat-roofed central space. They have the visual effect of compressing the longitudinal design into one comparable to a *central plan*, because the various aspects of the interior resemble one another, no matter where an observer stands. Originally, this centralization effect would have been even stronger. Brunelleschi had planned to extend the aisles across the front of the nave as well, as shown on the plan (FIG. 16-32, *left*). However, adherence to that design would have required four entrances in the facade, instead of the traditional and symbolic three, a feature hotly debated during Brunelleschi's lifetime and changed after his death. Successor builders later also modified the appearance of the exterior walls (compare the two plans in FIG. 16-32) by filling in the recesses between the projecting semicircular chapels to convert the original highly sculpted wall surface into a flat one.

The major features of Santo Spirito's interior (FIG. 16-31), however, are much as Brunelleschi designed them. In this *modular* scheme, a mathematical unit served to determine the dimensions of every aspect of the church. This unit, repeated throughout the interior, creates a rhythmic harmony. For example, the nave is twice as high as it is wide, and the arcade and clerestory are of equal height, which means that the height of the arcade equals the nave's width.

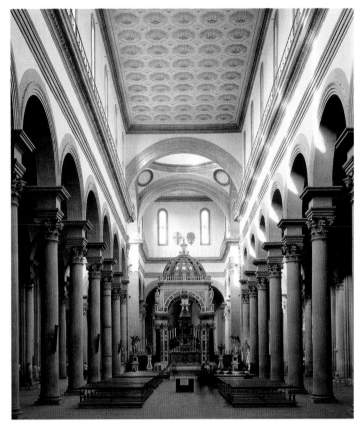

16-31 FILIPPO BRUNELLESCHI, interior of Santo Spirito (looking northeast), Florence, Italy, designed 1434–1436; begun 1446.

The austerity of the decor and the mathematical clarity of the interior of Santo Spirito contrast sharply with the soaring drama and spirituality of the nave arcades and vaults of Gothic churches.

16-32 FILIPPO BRUNELLESCHI, early plan (*left*) and plan as constructed (*right*) of Santo Spirito, Florence, Italy, designed 1434–1436; begun 1446.

Santo Spirito displays the classically inspired rationality of Brunelleschi's mature architectural style in its all-encompassing modular scheme based on the dimensions of the dome-covered crossing square.

16-33 FILIPPO BRUNELLESCHI, facade of the Pazzi Chapel, Santa Croce, Florence, Italy, designed ca. 1423, begun 1442.

The Pazzi family erected this chapel as a gift to the Franciscan church of Santa Croce. One of the first independent Renaissance central-plan buildings, it served as the monks' chapter house.

Astute observers can read the proportional relationships among the interior's parts as a series of mathematical equations. The austerity of the decor enhances the rationality of the design and produces a restful and tranquil atmosphere. Brunelleschi left no space for expansive wall frescoes that only would interrupt the clarity of his architectural scheme. The calculated logic of the design echoes that of ancient Roman buildings, such as the Pantheon (FIG. 7-50, *right*). The rationality of Santo Spirito contrasts sharply, however, with the soaring drama and spirituality of the nave arcades and vaults of Gothic churches (for example, FIGS. 13-19 and 13-20). It even deviates from the design of Florence Cathedral's nave (FIG. 14-19), whose verticality is restrained compared with its Northern European counterparts. Santo Spirito fully expresses the new Renaissance spirit that placed its faith in reason rather than in the emotions.

PAZZI CHAPEL Brunelleschi's apparent effort to impart a centralized effect to the interior of Santo Spirito suggests that the compact and self-contained qualities of earlier central-plan buildings, such as the Roman Pantheon (FIGS. 7-49 to 7-51), intrigued him. The Pazzi Chapel (FIG. 16-33) presented Brunelleschi with the opportunity to explore this interest, in a structure much better suited to a centralized design than a basilican church. The chapel was the Pazzi family's gift to the Franciscan church of Santa Croce in Florence (see "Renaissance Family Chapel Endowments," page 442) and served as

Renaissance Family Chapel Endowments

During the 14th through 16th centuries in Italy, wealthy families regularly endowed chapels in or adjacent to major churches. These family chapels were usually on either side of the choir near the altar at the church's east end. Particularly wealthy families endowed chapels in the form of separate buildings constructed adjacent to churches. For example, the Medici Chapel (Old Sacristy) abuts San Lorenzo in Florence. Powerful banking families, such as the Baroncelli, Bardi, and Peruzzi, each sponsored chapels in the Florentine church of Santa Croce. The Pazzi commissioned a chapel (FIGS. 16-33 to 16-35) adjacent to Santa Croce, and the Brancacci family sponsored the decorative program (FIGS. 16-18 and 16-19) of their chapel in Santa Maria del Carmine.

These families endowed chapels to ensure the well-being of the souls of individual family members and ancestors. The chapels served as burial sites and as spaces for liturgical celebrations and commemorative services. Chapel owners sponsored Masses for the dead, praying to the Virgin Mary and the saints for intercession on behalf of their deceased loved ones. Changes in Christian doctrine prompted these concerted efforts to improve donors' chances for eternal salvation. Until the 13th century, Christians believed that after death, souls went either to Heaven or to Hell. After that time, the concept of Purgatory—a way station between Heaven and Hell where souls could atone for sins before Judgment Day—increasingly won favor. Pope Innocent III (1198–1216) recognized the existence of such a place in 1215. Because Purgatory represented an opportunity for the faithful to improve their chances of eventually gaining admission to Heaven, they eagerly embraced this opportunity. When they extended this idea to improving their chances while alive, charitable work, good deeds, and devotional practices proliferated. Family chapels provided the space necessary for the performance of devotional rituals. Most chapels included altars as well as chalices, vestments, candlesticks, and other objects used in the Mass. Most patrons also commissioned decorations, such as painted altarpieces, frescoes on the walls, and sculptural objects. The chapels were therefore expressions of piety and devotion but also opportunities for the donors to burnish their images in the larger community.

the monk's *chapter house* (meeting hall). Brunelleschi began to design the Pazzi Chapel around 1423, but work continued until the 1460s, long after his death. The exterior (FIG. 16-33) probably does not reflect Brunelleschi's original design. The loggia, admirable as it is, seems to have been added as an afterthought, perhaps by the sculptor-architect Giuliano da Maiano (1432–1490). Historians have

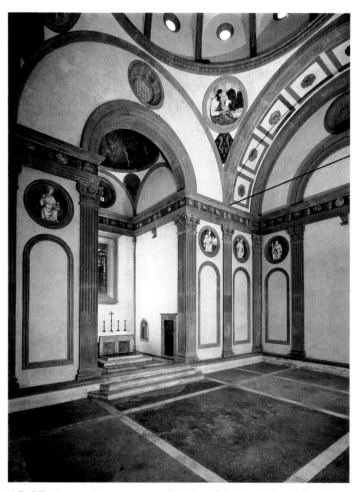

16-34 FILIPPO BRUNELLESCHI, plan of the Pazzi Chapel, Santa Croce, Florence, Italy, designed ca. 1423, begun 1442.

Although the Pazzi Chapel is rectangular, rather than square or round, Brunelleschi created a central plan by placing all emphasis on the dome-covered space at the heart of the building.

16-35 FILIPPO BRUNELLESCHI, interior of the Pazzi Chapel (looking northeast), Santa Croce, Florence, Italy, designed ca. 1423, begun 1442, with glazed terracotta roundels by LUCA DELLA ROBBIA.

The interior trim of the Pazzi Chapel is gray pietra serena, which stands out against the white stuccoed walls and crisply defines the modular relationships of Brunelleschi's plan and elevation.

The Medici palace, with its combination of dressed and rusticated masonry and classical moldings, draws heavily on ancient Roman architecture, but Michelozzo creatively reinterpreted his models.

suggested that the local chapter of Franciscan monks who held meetings in the chapel needed the expansion. Behind the loggia stands one of the first independent Renaissance buildings conceived basically as a central-plan structure. Although the plan (FIG. 16-34) is rectangular, rather than square or round, the architect placed all emphasis on the central dome-covered space. The short barrel-vaulted sections that brace the dome on two sides appear to be incidental appendages. The interior trim (FIG. 16-35) is gray *pietra serena* ("serene stone"), which stands out against the white stuccoed walls and crisply defines the modular relationships of plan and elevation. As he did in his design for Santo Spirito, Brunelleschi used a basic unit that allowed him to construct a balanced, harmonious, and regularly proportioned space.

Circular medallions, or *tondi*, in the dome's *pendentives* (see "Pendentives and Squinches," Chapter 9, page 235) consist of *glazed terracotta* reliefs representing the four evangelists. The technique for manufacturing these baked clay reliefs was of recent invention. Around 1430, LUCA DELLA ROBBIA (1400–1482) perfected the application of vitrified (heat-fused) colored potters' glazes to sculpture. Inexpensive and durable, these colorful sculptures became extremely popular and provided the basis for a flourishing family business. Luca's nephew Andrea della Robbia (1435–1525) and Andrea's sons, Giovanni della Robbia (1469–1529) and Girolamo della Robbia (1488–1566), carried on this tradition well into the 16th century. Most of the *roundels* in the Pazzi Chapel are the work of Luca della Robbia himself. Together with the images of the 12 apostles on the pilaster-framed wall panels, they add striking color accents to the tranquil interior.

PALAZZO MEDICI It seems curious that Brunelleschi, the most renowned architect of his time, did not participate in the upsurge of palace building that Florence experienced in the 1430s and 1440s. This proliferation of palazzi testified to the stability of the Florentine economy and to the affluence and confidence of the city's leading citizens. Brunelleschi, however, confined his efforts in this field to work on the Palazzo di Parte Guelfa (headquarters of Florence's then-ruling "party") and to a rejected model for a new palace that Cosimo de' Medici intended to build. When the Medici returned to Florence in 1434 after their short-lived exile, Cosimo, aware of the importance of public perception, attempted to maintain a lower profile and to wield his power from behind the scenes. In all probability, this attitude accounted for his rejection of Brunelleschi's design for the Medici residence, which he evidently found too imposing and ostentatious to be politically wise. Cosimo eventually awarded the commission to MICHELOZZO DI BARTOLOMMEO (1396–1472), a young architect who had collaborated with Donatello in several sculptural enterprises. Although Cosimo passed over Brunelleschi, his architectural style in fact deeply influenced Michelozzo. To a limited extent, the Palazzo Medici (FIG. 16-36) reflects Brunelleschian principles.

Later bought by the Riccardi family (hence the name Palazzo Medici-Riccardi), who almost doubled the facade's length in the 18th century, the palace, both in its original and extended form, is a simple, massive structure. Heavy *rustication* (rough unfinished masonry) on the ground floor accentuates its strength. Michelozzo divided the building block into stories of decreasing height by using long, unbroken *stringcourses* (horizontal bands), which give it coherence. *Dressed* (smooth, finished) *masonry* on the second level and an even smoother surface on the top story modify the severity of the ground floor and make the building appear progressively lighter as the eye moves upward. The extremely heavy *cornice*, which Michelozzo related not to the top story but to the building as a whole, dramatically reverses this effect. Like the ancient Roman cornices that served as

Michelozzo's models (compare FIGS. 7-32, 7-39, and 7-47), the Palazzo Medici-Riccardi cornice is an effective lid for the structure, clearly and emphatically defining its proportions. Michelozzo also may have drawn inspiration from the many extant examples of Roman rusticated masonry, and Roman precedents even existed for the juxtaposition of rusticated and dressed stone masonry on the same facade (FIG. 7-34). However, nothing in the ancient world precisely compares to Michelozzo's design. The Palazzo Medici exemplifies the simultaneous respect for and independence from the antique that characterize the Early Renaissance in Italy.

The heart of the Palazzo Medici is an open colonnaded court (FIG. 16-37) that clearly shows Michelozzo's debt to Brunelleschi. The round-arched colonnade, although more massive in its proportions, closely resembles other buildings Brunelleschi designed. This internal court surrounded by an arcade was the first of its kind and influenced a long line of descendants in Renaissance domestic architecture.

LEON BATTISTA ALBERTI Although he entered the profession of architecture rather late in life, LEON BATTISTA ALBERTI (1404–1472) nevertheless made a remarkable contribution to architectural design. He was the first to study seriously the ancient Roman architectural treatise of Vitruvius, and his knowledge of it, combined with his own archaeological investigations, made him the first Renaissance architect to understand classical architecture in depth. Alberti's most influential theoretical work, *On the Art of Building* (written about 1450, published 1486), although inspired by Vitruvius, contains much original material. Alberti advocated a system of ideal proportions and believed that the central plan was the ideal form for a Christian church. He also considered incongruous the combination of column and arch, which had persisted since Roman times and throughout the Middle Ages. He argued that the arch is a wall opening that should be supported only by a section of wall (a pier), not by an independent sculptural element (a column) as in Brunelleschi's and Michelozzo's buildings (FIGS. 16-31, 16-33, and 16-37).

PALAZZO RUCELLAI Alberti's own architectural style represents a scholarly application of classical elements to contemporary buildings. He designed the Palazzo Rucellai (FIG. 16-38) in Flor-

16-38 Leon Battista Alberti and Bernardo Rossellino, Palazzo Rucellai, Florence, Italy, ca. 1452–1470.

Alberti was an ardent student of classical architecture. He created the illusion that the Palazzo Rucellai becomes lighter toward its top by adapting the Roman manner of using different capitals for each story.

16-39 Leon Battista Alberti, west facade of Santa Maria Novella, Florence, Italy, 1456–1470.

Alberti's design for the facade of this Gothic church features a pediment-capped temple front and pilaster-framed arcades. Numerical ratios are the basis of the proportions of all parts of the facade.

his cue from a *Romanesque* design—that of the Florentine church of San Miniato al Monte (FIG. 12-27). Following his medieval model, he designed a small, pseudoclassical, *pediment*-capped temple front for the facade's upper part and supported it with a pilaster-framed arcade that incorporates the six tombs and three doorways of the Gothic building. But in the organization of these elements, Alberti applied Renaissance principles. The height of Santa Maria Novella (to the pediment tip) equals its width so that the entire facade can be inscribed in a square. Throughout the facade, Alberti defined areas and related them to one another in terms of proportions that can be expressed in simple numerical ratios. For example, the upper structure can be encased in a square one-fourth the size of the main square. The cornice separating the two levels divides the major square in half so that the lower portion of the building is a rectangle twice as wide as it is high. In his treatise, Alberti wrote at length about the necessity of employing harmonic proportions to achieve beautiful buildings. Alberti shared this conviction with Brunelleschi, and this fundamental dependence on classically derived mathematics distinguished their architectural work from that of their medieval predecessors. They believed in the eternal and universal validity of numerical ratios as the source of beauty. In this respect, Alberti and Brunelleschi revived the true spirit of the High Classical age of ancient Greece, as epitomized by the sculptor Polykleitos and the architect Iktinos, who produced canons of proportions for the perfect statue and the perfect temple (see Chapter 5). But it was not only a desire to emulate Vitruvius and the Greek masters that motivated Alberti to turn to mathematics in his quest for beauty. His contemporary, the Florentine humanist Giannozzo Manetti (1396–1459), had argued that Christianity itself possessed the order and logic of mathematics. In his 1452 treatise, *On the Dignity and Excellence of Man,* Manetti stated that Christian religious truths were as self-evident as mathematical axioms.

The Santa Maria Novella facade was an ingenious solution to a difficult design problem. On the one hand, it adequately expressed the organization of the structure attached to it. On the other hand, it subjected preexisting and quintessentially medieval features, such as the large round window on the second level, to a rigid geometrical order that instilled a quality of classical calm and reason. This facade also introduced a feature of great historical consequence—the scrolls that simultaneously unite the broad lower and narrow upper level and screen the sloping roofs over the aisles. With variations, similar spirals appeared in literally hundreds of church facades throughout the Renaissance and Baroque periods.

ence, although his pupil and collaborator, Bernardo Rossellino (1409–1464), actually constructed the building using Alberti's plans and sketches. The facade of the palace is much more severe than that of the Palazzo Medici-Riccardi (FIG. 16-36). Pilasters define each story, and a classical cornice crowns the whole. Between the smooth pilasters are subdued and uniform wall surfaces. Alberti created the sense that the structure becomes lighter in weight toward its top by adapting the ancient Roman manner of using different capitals for each story. He chose *Tuscan* (the Etruscan variant of the Greek *Doric order;* FIG. 5-14 or in the "Before 1300" section) for the ground floor, *Composite* (the Roman combination of *Ionic volutes* with the acanthus leaves of the *Corinthian;* FIG. 5-73 or in the "Before 1300" section) for the second story, and Corinthian for the third floor. Alberti modeled his facade on the most imposing Roman ruin of all, the Colosseum (FIG. 7-1), but he was no slavish copyist. On the Colosseum's facade, the capitals employed are, from the bottom up, Tuscan, Ionic, and Corinthian. Moreover, Alberti adapted the Colosseum's varied surface to a flat facade, which does not allow the deep penetration of the building's mass that is so effective in the Roman structure. By converting his ancient model's *engaged columns* (half-round columns attached to a wall) into shallow pilasters that barely project from the wall, Alberti created a large-meshed linear net. Stretched tightly across the front of his building, it not only unifies the three levels but also emphasizes the wall's flat, two-dimensional qualities.

SANTA MARIA NOVELLA The Rucellai family also commissioned Alberti to design the facade (FIG. 16-39) of the 13th-century Gothic church of Santa Maria Novella in Florence. Here, Alberti took

GIROLAMO SAVONAROLA In the 1490s, Florence underwent a political, cultural, and religious upheaval. Florentine artists and their fellow citizens responded then not only to humanist ideas but also to the incursion of French armies and especially to the preaching of the Dominican monk Girolamo Savonarola (1452–1498), the reforming priest-dictator who denounced the paganism of the Medici and their artists, philosophers, and poets. Savonarola exhorted the people of Florence to repent their sins, and when Lorenzo de' Medici died in 1492, he prophesied the downfall of the city and of Italy and assumed absolute control of the state. Together with a large number of citizens, Savonarola believed that the Medici's political, social, and religious power had corrupted Florence and had invited the scourge of foreign invasion. Savonarola denounced humanism and encouraged citizens to burn their classical texts, scientific treatises, and philosophical publications. The Medici fled in 1494. Scholars still debate the significance of Savonarola's brief span of power. Apologists for the undoubtedly sincere monk deny that his actions played a role in the decline of Florentine culture at the end of the 15th century. But the puritanical spirit that moved Savonarola must have dampened considerably the neopagan enthusiasm of the Florentine Early Renaissance. Certainly, his condemnation of humanism as heretical nonsense, and his banishing of the Medici, Tornabuoni, and other wealthy families from Florence, deprived local artists of some of their major patrons. There were, however, abundant commissions for artists elsewhere in Italy.

THE PRINCELY COURTS

Although Florentine artists led the way in creating the Renaissance in art and architecture, art production flourished throughout Italy in the 15th century. The papacy in Rome and the princely courts in Urbino, Mantua, and elsewhere also deserve credit for nurturing Renaissance art (see "Italian Princely Courts and Artistic Patronage," page 447). These princely courts consisted of the prince (whose title varied from city to city), his consort and children, courtiers, household staff, and administrators. The considerable wealth these princes possessed, coupled with their desire for recognition, fame, and power, resulted in major art commissions.

Rome and the Papal States

Although not a secular ruler, the pope in Rome was the head of a court with enormous wealth at his disposal. In the 16th and 17th centuries, the popes became the major patrons of art and architecture in Italy (see Chapters 17 and 19), but even in the 15th century, the papacy was the source of some significant artistic commissions.

PERUGINO Between 1481 and 1483, Pope Sixtus IV (r. 1414–1484) summoned a group of artists, including Botticelli and Ghirlandaio, to Rome to decorate the walls of the newly completed Sistine Chapel (MAP 19-1). Pietro Vannucci of Perugia in Umbria, who was known as PERUGINO (ca. 1450–1523), was among the painters the pope em-

16-40 PERUGINO, *Christ Delivering the Keys of the Kingdom to Saint Peter,* Sistine Chapel, Vatican, Rome, Italy, 1481–1483. Fresco, 11′ 5½″ × 18′ 8½″.

Painted for the Vatican, this fresco depicts the event on which the papacy bases its authority. The converging lines of the pavement connect the action in the foreground with the background.

Italian Princely Courts
and Artistic Patronage

The absence of a single sovereign ruling all of Italy and the fragmented nature of the independent city-states (MAP 14-1) provided a fertile breeding ground for the ambitions of the power-hungry. In the 15th century, Italian society witnessed the expansion of princely courts throughout the peninsula. A prince was in essence the lord of a territory, and despite this generic title, he could have been a duke, marquis, tyrant, cardinal, pope, or papal vicar. At this time, major princely courts emerged in papal Rome, Milan, Naples, Ferrara, Savoy, Urbino, and Mantua. Rather than denoting a specific organizational structure or physical entity, the term "princely court" refers to a power relationship between the prince and the territory's inhabitants based on imperial models. Each prince worked tirelessly to preserve and extend his control and authority, seeking to establish a societal framework of people who looked to him for jobs, favors, protection, prestige, and leadership. The importance of these princely courts derived from their role as centers of power and culture.

The efficient functioning of a princely court required a sophisticated administrative structure. Each prince employed an extensive household staff, ranging from counts, nobles, cooks, waiters, stewards, footmen, stable hands, and ladies-in-waiting to dog handlers, leopard keepers, pages, and runners. The duke of Milan had more than 40 chamberlains to attend to his personal needs alone. Each prince also needed an elaborate bureaucracy to oversee political, economic, and military operations and to ensure his continued control. These officials included secretaries, lawyers, captains, ambassadors, and condottieri. Burgeoning international diplomacy and trade made each prince the center of an active and privileged sphere. The princes' domains extended to the realm of culture, for they saw themselves as more than political, military, and economic leaders. They felt responsible for the vitality of cultural life in their territories, and art was a major component for developing a cultured populace. Visual imagery also appealed to them as effective propaganda for reinforcing their control. As the wealthiest individuals in their regions, princes possessed the means to commission numerous artworks and buildings. Thus, art functioned in several

capacities—as evidence of princely sophistication and culture, as a form of prestige or commemoration, as public education and propaganda, as a demonstration of wealth, and as a source of visual pleasure.

Princes often researched in advance the reputations and styles of the artists and architects they commissioned. Such assurances of excellence were necessary, because the quality of the work reflected not just on the artist but on the patron as well. Yet despite the importance of individual style, princes sought artists who also were willing, at times, to subordinate their personal styles to work collaboratively on large-scale projects.

Princes bestowed on selected individuals the title of "court artist." Serving as a court artist had its benefits, among them a guaranteed salary (not always forthcoming), living quarters in the palace, liberation from guild restrictions, and, on occasion, status as a member of the prince's inner circle, perhaps even a knighthood. For artists struggling to elevate their profession from the ranks of craftspeople, working for a prince presented a marvelous opportunity. Until the 16th century, artists had limited status and were in the same class as small shopkeepers and petty merchants. Indeed, at court dinners, artists most often sat with the other members of the salaried household: tailors, cobblers, barbers, and upholsterers. Thus, the possibility of advancement was a powerful and constant incentive.

Princes demanded a great deal from court artists. Artists not only created the frescoes, portraits, and sculptures that have become their legacies but also designed tapestries, seat covers, costumes, masks, and decorations for various court festivities. Because princes constantly entertained, received ambassadors and dignitaries, and needed to maintain a high profile to reinforce their authority, lavish social functions were the norm. Artists often created gifts for visiting nobles and potentates. Recipients judged such gifts on the quality of both the work and the materials. By using expensive materials—gold leaf, silver leaf, lapis lazuli (a rich azure-blue stone imported from Afghanistan), silk, and velvet brocade—princes could impress others with their wealth and good taste.

ployed. His contribution to the fresco cycle of the Sistine Chapel was *Christ Delivering the Keys of the Kingdom to Saint Peter* (FIG. 16-40). The papacy had, from the beginning, based its claim to infallible and total authority over the Roman Catholic Church on this biblical event, and therefore the subject was one of obvious appeal to Sixtus IV. In Perugino's version, Christ hands the keys to Saint Peter, who stands amid an imaginary gathering of the 12 apostles and Renaissance contemporaries. These figures occupy the apron of a great stage space that extends into the distance to a point of convergence in the doorway of a central-plan temple. (Perugino used parallel and converging lines in the pavement to mark off the intervening space.) Figures in the middle distance complement the near group, emphasizing its density and order by their scattered arrangement. At the corners of the great piazza, duplicate triumphal arches serve as the base angles of a distant compositional triangle whose apex is in the central building. Perugino modeled the arches very closely on the Arch of Constantine (FIG. 7-75) in Rome. Although an anachronism in a painting depicting a scene from Christ's life, the arches served to underscore the close ties between

Saint Peter and Constantine, the first Christian emperor and the builder of the great basilica (FIG. 8-9) over Saint Peter's tomb in Rome. Christ and Peter flank the triangle's central axis, which runs through the temple's doorway, the perspective's vanishing point. Thus, the composition interlocks both two-dimensional and three-dimensional space, and the placement of central actors emphasizes the axial center. This spatial science allowed the artist to organize the action systematically. Perugino, in this single picture, incorporated the learning of generations.

LUCA SIGNORELLI Another Umbrian artist that Sixtus IV employed for the decoration of the Sistine Chapel was LUCA SIGNORELLI (ca. 1445–1523), in whose work the fiery passion of the sermons of Savonarola found its pictorial equal. Signorelli further developed Pollaiuolo's interest in the depiction of muscular bodies in violent action in a wide variety of poses and foreshortenings. In the San Brizio Chapel in the cathedral of the papal state of Orvieto (MAP 14-1), Signorelli painted for Pope Alexander VI (r. 1492–1503)

16-41 Luca Signorelli, *Damned Cast into Hell,* San Brizio Chapel, Orvieto Cathedral, Orvieto, Italy, 1499–1504. Fresco, 23′ wide.

Few figure compositions of the 15th century have the same psychic impact as Luca Signorelli's Orvieto Cathedral fresco of writhing, foreshortened muscular bodies tortured by demons in Hell.

scenes depicting the end of the world, including *Damned Cast into Hell* (FIG. 16-41). Few figure compositions of the 15th century have the same psychic impact. Saint Michael and the hosts of Heaven hurl the damned into Hell, where, in a dense, writhing mass, they are vigorously tortured by demons. The horrible consequences of a sinful life had not been so graphically depicted since Gislebertus carved his vision of the Last Judgment (FIGS. I-6 and 12-12) in the west *tympanum* of Saint-Lazare at Autun around 1130. The figures—nude, lean, and muscular—assume every conceivable posture of anguish. Signorelli's skill at foreshortening the human figure was equaled by his mastery of its action, and although each figure is clearly a study from a model, he fit his theme to the figures in an entirely convincing manner. Terror and rage explode like storms through the wrenched and twisted bodies. The fiends, their hair flaming and their bodies the color of putrefying flesh, lunge at their victims in ferocious frenzy.

Urbino

Under the patronage of Federico da Montefeltro (1422–1482), Urbino, southeast of Florence across the Appennines (MAP 14-1), became an important center of Renaissance art and culture. In fact, the humanist writer Paolo Cortese (1465–1540) described Federico as one of the two greatest artistic patrons of the 15th century (the other was Cosimo de' Medici). Federico was a condottiere so renowned for his military expertise that he was in demand by popes and kings, and soldiers came from across Europe to study under his direction.

PIERO DELLA FRANCESCA One artist who received several commissions from Federico was PIERO DELLA FRANCESCA (ca. 1420–1492) of San Sepolcro in Tuscany, who had earlier painted for the Medici, among others. One of Piero's major works at the Urbino court was *Enthroned Madonna and Saints Adored by Federico da Montefeltro,* also called the *Brera Altarpiece* (FIG. 16-42). Federico, clad in armor, kneels piously at the Virgin's feet. Directly behind him stands Saint John the Evangelist, his patron saint. Where the viewer would expect to see Federico's wife, Battista Sforza (on the lower left, kneeling and facing her husband), no figure is present. Battista had died in 1472, shortly before Federico commissioned this painting. Thus, her absence clearly announces his loss. Piero further called attention to it by depicting Saint John the Baptist, Battista's patron saint, at the far left. The ostrich egg that hangs suspended from a shell over the Virgin's head was common over altars dedicated to Mary. The figures appear in an illusionistically painted, coffered barrel vault, which may have resembled part of the interior of the church of

16-42 Piero della Francesca, *Enthroned Madonna and Saints Adored by Federico da Montefeltro* (*Brera Altarpiece*), ca. 1472–1474. Oil on wood, 8′ 2″ × 5′ 7″. Pinacoteca di Brera, Milan.

The illusionism of Piero's *Brera Altarpiece* is so convincing that the viewer is compelled to believe in Federico da Montefeltro's presence before the Virgin Mary, Christ Child, and saints.

1 ft.

San Bernadino degli Zoccolanti near Urbino, the painting's intended location. If so, the viewer would be compelled to believe in Federico's presence in the church before the Virgin, Christ Child, and saints. That Piero depicted Federico in left profile was undoubtedly a concession to his patron. The right side of Federico's face had sustained severe injury in a tournament, and the resulting deformity made him reluctant to show that side.

The *Brera Altarpiece* reveals Piero's deep interest in the properties of light and color. In his effort to make the clearest possible dis-tinction among forms, he flooded his pictures with light, imparting a silver-blue tonality. To avoid heavy shadows, he illuminated the dark sides of his forms with reflected light. By moving the darkest tones of his modeling toward the centers of his volumes, he separated them from their backgrounds. Because of this technique, Piero's paintings lack some of Masaccio's relieflike qualities but gain in spatial clarity, as each shape forms an independent unit surrounded by an atmospheric envelope and movable to any desired position, like a figure on a chessboard.

16-43 Piero della Francesca, *Flagellation of Christ,* ca. 1455–1465. Oil and tempera on wood, 1′ 11$\frac{1}{8}$″ × 2′ 8$\frac{1}{4}$″. Galleria Nazionale delle Marche, Urbino.

The identification of the foreground figures continues to elude scholars. They appear to discuss the biblical tragedy that takes place in Pilate's palace (FIG. 16-1), which Piero rendered in perfect perspective.

FLAGELLATION Piero's most enigmatic painting is *Flagellation of Christ* (FIG. 16-43), a small panel painting perhaps also produced for Federico da Montefeltro. The setting for the New Testament drama is the portico of Pontius Pilate's palace in Jerusalem. Curiously, the focus of the composition is not Christ but the group of three large figures in the foreground, whose identity scholars still debate. Some have identified the bearded figure as a Turk and interpreted the painting as a commentary on the capture in 1453 of Christian Constantinople by the Muslims (see Chapter 9). Other scholars, however, identify the three men as biblical figures, including the Old Testament's King David, one of whose psalms theologians believed predicted the conspiracy against Christ. In any case, the three men appear to discuss the event in the background. As Pilate, the seated judge, watches, Christ, bound to a column topped by a classical statue, is about to be whipped (FIG. 16-1). Piero's perspective is so meticulous that the floor pattern can be reconstructed perfectly as a central porphyry (purple marble) circle with surrounding squares composed of various geometric shapes. Whatever the solution is to the iconographical puzzle of Piero's *Flagellation,* the panel reveals a mind cultivated by mathematics. The careful delineation of the setting suggests an architect's vision, certainly that of a man entirely familiar with compass and straightedge.

Piero planned his compositions almost entirely by his sense of the exact and lucid structures defined by mathematics. He believed that the highest beauty resides in forms that have the clarity and purity of geometric figures. Toward the end of his long career, Piero, a skilled geometrician, wrote the first theoretical treatise on systematic perspective, after having practiced the art with supreme mastery for almost a lifetime. His association with the architect Alberti at Ferrara and at Rimini around 1450–1451 probably turned his attention fully to perspective (a science in which Alberti was an influential pioneer) and helped determine his later, characteristically architectonic compositions. This approach appealed to Federico, a patron fascinated by architectural space and its depiction.

Mantua

Marquis Ludovico Gonzaga (1412–1478) ruled the court of Mantua in northeastern Italy (MAP 14-1). A famed condottiere like Federico da Montefeltro, Gonzaga established his reputation as a fierce military general while commanding the Milanese armies. The visit of Pope Pius II (r. 1458–1464) to Mantua in 1459 stimulated the marquis's determination to transform Mantua into a city that all Italy would envy.

16-44 Leon Battista Alberti, west facade of Sant'Andrea, Mantua, Italy, designed 1470, begun 1472.

Alberti's design for Sant'Andrea reflects his study of ancient Roman architecture. Employing a colossal order, the architect locked together a triumphal arch and a Roman temple front with pediment.

SANT'ANDREA One of the major projects Gonzaga instituted was the redesigning of the church of Sant'Andrea to replace an 11th-century church. Gonzaga turned to the renowned architect Leon Battista Alberti for this important commission. The facade (FIG. 16-44) Alberti designed locked together two complete ancient Roman architectural motifs—the temple front and the triumphal arch. The combination was already a familiar feature of Roman buildings still standing in Italy. For example, many triumphal arches incorporated a pediment over the arcuated passageway and engaged columns, but there is no close parallel in antiquity for Alberti's eclectic and

ingenious design. The Renaissance architect's concern for proportion led him to equalize the vertical and horizontal dimensions of the facade, which left it considerably shorter than the church behind it. Because of the primary importance of visual appeal, many Renaissance architects made this concession not only to the demands of a purely visual proportionality in the facade but also to the facade's relation to the small square in front of it, even at the expense of continuity with the body of the building. Yet structural correspondences to the building do exist in Sant'Andrea's facade. The pilasters are the same height as those on the nave's interior walls, and the central barrel vault over the main exterior entrance, with smaller barrel vaults branching off at right angles, introduces on a smaller scale the arrangement of the nave and aisles (FIG. 16-45). The facade pilasters, as part of the wall, run uninterrupted through three stories in an early application of the *colossal* or *giant order* that became a favorite motif of Michelangelo.

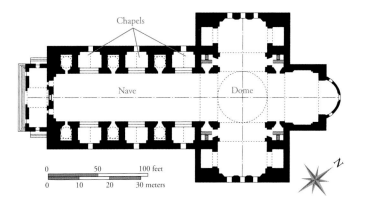

16-45 Leon Battista Alberti, plan of Sant'Andrea, Mantua, Italy, designed 1470, begun 1472.

In his architectural treatise, Alberti criticized the traditional basilican plan as impractical and designed Sant'Andrea as a single huge hall with independent chapels branching off at right angles.

16-46 Leon Battista Alberti, interior of Sant'Andrea (looking northeast), Mantua, Italy, designed 1470, begun 1472.

Alberti abandoned the medieval columnar arcade for the nave of Sant'Andrea. The tremendous vaults suggest that he may have been inspired by Constantine's Basilica Nova (FIG. 7-78) in Rome.

The tremendous vaults in the interior of Sant'Andrea suggest that Alberti's model may have been Constantine's Basilica Nova (FIG. 7-78) in Rome—erroneously thought in the Middle Ages and Renaissance to be a Roman temple. Consistent with his belief that arches should not be used with freestanding columns, Alberti abandoned the medieval columned arcade Brunelleschi still used in Santo Spirito (FIG. 16-31). Thick walls alternating with vaulted chapels, interrupted by a massive dome over the crossing, support the huge coffered barrel vault. Because Filippo Juvara (1678–1736) added the present dome in the 18th century, the effect may be somewhat different from what Alberti planned. Regardless, the vault calls to mind the vast interior spaces and dense enclosing masses of Roman architecture. In his treatise, Alberti criticized the traditional basilican plan (with continuous aisles flanking the central nave) as impractical because the colonnades conceal the ceremonies from the faithful in the aisles. For this reason, he designed a single huge hall (FIG. 16-46) with independent chapels branching off at right angles. This break with a Christian building tradition that had endured for a thousand years was extremely influential in later Renaissance and Baroque church planning.

ANDREA MANTEGNA Like other princes, Ludovico Gonzaga believed an impressive palace was an important visual expression of his authority. One of the most spectacular rooms in the Palazzo Ducale (Ducal Palace) is the duke's bedchamber and audience hall, the so-called Camera degli Sposi (Room of the Newlyweds), originally the Camera Picta (Painted Room; FIGS. 16-47 and 16-48). Andrea Mantegna (ca. 1431–1506) of Padua, near Venice, took almost nine years to complete the extensive fresco program in which he sought to aggrandize Ludovico Gonzaga and his family. The particulars of each scene are still a matter of scholarly debate, but any viewer standing in the Camera Picta surrounded by the spectacle and majesty of courtly life cannot help but be thoroughly impressed by both the commanding presence and elevated status of the patron and the dazzling artistic skills of Mantegna.

In the Camera Picta, Mantegna performed a triumphant feat by producing the first completely consistent illusionistic decoration of an entire room. By integrating real and painted architectural elements, Mantegna dissolved the room's walls in a manner that foretold later Baroque decoration (see Chapter 19). It recalls the efforts of Italian painters more than 15 centuries earlier at Pompeii and elsewhere to merge mural painting and architecture in frescoes of the so-called Second Style of Roman painting (FIGS. 7-18 and 7-19). Mantegna's *trompe l'oeil* (French, "deceives the eye") design, however, went far beyond anything preserved from ancient Italy.

16-47 ANDREA MANTEGNA, interior of the Camera Picta (Painted Chamber), Palazzo Ducale, Mantua, Italy, 1465–1474.

Working for Ludovico Gonzaga, who established Mantua as a great art city, Mantegna produced for the duke's palace the first completely consistent illusionistic fresco decoration of an entire room.

1 ft.

The Renaissance painter's daring experimentalism led him to complete the room's decoration with the first perspective of a ceiling (FIG. **16-48**) seen from below (called, in Italian, *di sotto in sù*, "from below upward"). Baroque ceiling decorators later broadly developed this technique. Inside the Camera Picta, the viewer becomes the viewed as figures look down into the room from the painted *oculus* ("eye"). Seen against the convincing illusion of a cloud-filled blue sky, several *putti* (cupids), strongly foreshortened, set the amorous mood of the Room of the Newlyweds, as the painted spectators (who are not identified) smile down on the scene. The prominent peacock is an attribute of Juno, Jupiter's bride, who oversees lawful marriages. This brilliant feat of illusionism climaxes almost a century of experimentation with perspective.

16-48 ANDREA MANTEGNA, ceiling of the Camera Picta (Painted Chamber), Palazzo Ducale, Mantua, Italy, 1465–1474. Fresco, 8′ 9″ in diameter.

Inside the Camera Picta, the viewer becomes the viewed as figures look down into the room from a painted oculus opening onto a blue sky. This is the first perspectival view of a ceiling from below.

16-49 Andrea Mantegna, *Foreshortened Christ,* ca. 1500. Tempera on canvas, 2' 2¾" × 2' 7⅞". Pinacoteca di Brera, Milan.

In this work of overwhelming emotional power, Mantegna presented both a harrowing study of a strongly foreshortened cadaver and an intensely poignant depiction of a biblical tragedy.

FORESHORTENED CHRIST One of Mantegna's later paintings (FIG. 16-49) is another example of the artist's mastery of perspective. In fact, Mantegna seems to have set up for himself difficult problems in perspective simply for the joy in solving them. The painting popularly known as *Dead Christ,* but recorded under the name *Foreshortened Christ* at the time of Mantegna's death, is a work of overwhelming power. At first glance, as its 16th-century title implies, this painting seems to be a strikingly realistic study in foreshortening. Careful scrutiny, however, reveals that Mantegna reduced the size of the figure's feet, which, as he must have known, would cover much of the body if properly represented. Thus, tempering naturalism with artistic license, Mantegna presented both a harrowing study of a strongly foreshortened cadaver and an intensely poignant depiction of a biblical tragedy. The painter's harsh, sharp line seems to cut the surface as if it were metal and conveys, by its grinding edge, the theme's corrosive emotion. Remarkably, in the hands of Andrea Mantegna all the scientific learning of the 15th century serves the purpose of devotion.

ITALY, 1400 TO 1500

FLORENCE

■ The fortunate congruence of artistic genius, the spread of humanism, and economic prosperity nourished the flowering of the new artistic culture that historians call the Renaissance—the rebirth of classical values in art and life. The greatest center of Renaissance art in the 15th century was Florence, home of the powerful Medici, who were among the most ambitious art patrons in history.

■ Some of the earliest examples of the new Renaissance style in sculpture are the statues Nanni di Banco and Donatello made for the facade niches of Or San Michele. Donatello's *Saint Mark* reintroduced the classical concept of contrapposto into Renaissance statuary. His later *David* was the first nude male statue since antiquity. Donatello was also a pioneer in relief sculpture, the first to incorporate the principles of linear and atmospheric perspective, devices also employed brilliantly by Lorenzo Ghiberti in his *Gates of Paradise* for the Florence baptistery.

Donatello, *Saint Mark*, ca. 1411–1413

■ The Renaissance interest in classical culture naturally also led to the revival of Greco-Roman mythological themes in art, for example, Antonio del Pollaiuolo's *Hercules and Antaeus,* and to the revival of equestrian portraits, such as Donatello's *Gattamelata* and Andrea del Verrocchio's *Bartolommeo Colleoni.*

■ Although some painters continued to work in the Late Gothic International Style, others broke fresh ground by exploring new modes of representation. Masaccio's figures recall Giotto's but have a greater psychological and physical credibility, and the light shining on Masaccio's figures comes from a source outside the picture. His *Holy Trinity* epitomizes Early Renaissance painting in its convincing illusionism, achieved through Filippo Brunelleschi's new science of linear perspective, yet it remains effective as a devotional painting in a church setting.

Masaccio, *Holy Trinity*, ca. 1424–1427

■ The secular side of 15th-century Italian painting is on display in historical works, such as Paolo Uccello's *Battle of San Romano* and Domenico Ghirlandaio's portrait *Giovanna Tornabuoni.* The humanist love of classical themes comes to the fore in the works of Sandro Botticelli, whose lyrical *Primavera* and *Birth of Venus* were inspired by contemporaneous poetry and scholarship.

■ Italian architects also revived the classical style. Brunelleschi's Santo Spirito showcases the clarity and Roman-inspired rationality of 15th-century Florentine architecture. The model for Leon Battista Alberti's influential treatise *On the Art of Building* was a similar work by the ancient Roman architect Vitruvius.

Brunelleschi, Santo Spirito, Florence, designed 1434–1436

THE PRINCELY COURTS

■ Although Florentine artists led the way in creating the Renaissance in art and architecture, the papacy in Rome and the princely courts in Urbino, Mantua, and elsewhere also were major art patrons.

■ Among the important papal commissions of the 15th century was the decoration of the walls of the Sistine Chapel with frescoes, including Perugino's *Christ Delivering the Keys of the Kingdom to Saint Peter,* a prime example of linear perspective.

Perugino, *Christ Delivering the Keys to Saint Peter*, 1481–1483

■ Under the patronage of Federico da Montefeltro, Urbino became a major center of Renaissance art and culture. The leading painter in Federico's employ was Piero della Francesca, a master of color and light and the author of the first theoretical treatise on perspective.

■ Mantua became an important art center under Marquis Ludovico Gonzaga, who brought in Alberti to rebuild the church of Sant'Andrea. Alberti applied the principles he developed in his architectural treatise to the project and freely adapted forms from Roman religious, triumphal, and civic architecture.

■ Gonzaga hired Andrea Mantegna to decorate the Camera Picta of his Ducal Palace, in which the painter produced the first completely consistent illusionistic decoration of an entire room.

Alberti, Sant'Andrea, Mantua, designed 1470

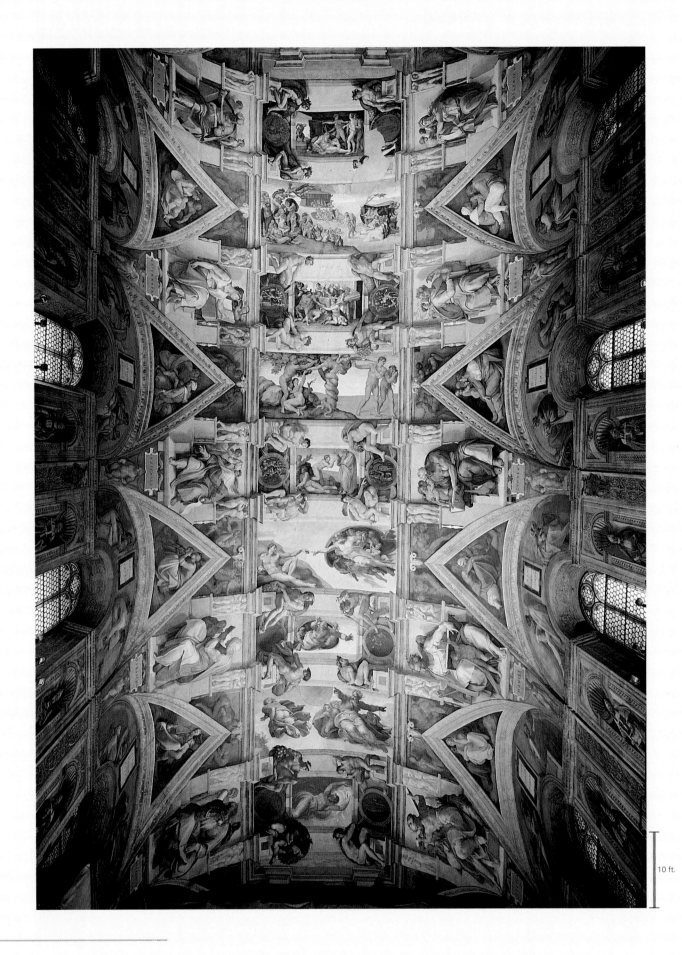

10 ft.

17-1 MICHELANGELO BUONARROTI, ceiling of the Sistine Chapel, Vatican City, Rome, Italy, 1508–1512. Fresco, 128′ × 45′.

Michelangelo, the Renaissance genius who was also a sculptor and architect, labored almost four years in the Sistine Chapel painting more than 300 biblical figures illustrating the creation and fall of humankind.

17

ITALY, 1500 TO 1600

The 15th-century artistic developments in Italy (for example, the interest in perspective, anatomy, and classical cultures) matured during the early 16th century in the brief era that art historians call the High Renaissance—the period between 1495 and the deaths of Leonardo da Vinci in 1519 and Raphael in 1520. The Renaissance style, however, dominated the remainder of the 16th century (the Late Renaissance), although a new style, called Mannerism, challenged it almost as soon as Raphael had been laid to rest (in the ancient Roman Pantheon, FIG. 7-51). Thus, no singular artistic style characterizes 16th-century Italy. Nonetheless, Italian art of this period uniformly exhibits an astounding mastery, both technical and aesthetic.

HIGH AND LATE RENAISSANCE

The High Renaissance produced a cluster of extraordinary geniuses and found in divine inspiration the rationale for the exaltation of the artist-genius. The Neo-Platonists read in Plato's *Ion* his famous praise of the poet: "All good poets . . . compose their beautiful poems not by art, but because they are inspired and possessed. . . . For not by art does the poet sing, but by power divine."[1] And what the poet could claim, the Renaissance claimed also, raising visual art to the status formerly held only by poetry. Thus, painters, sculptors, and architects came into their own, successfully advocating for their work a high place among the fine arts. During the High Renaissance, the masters in essence created a new profession, one having its own rights of expression, its own venerable character, and its own claims to recognition by the great. The "fine" artist today lives, often without realizing it, on the accumulated prestige won by preceding artists, beginning with those who made the first great gains of the High Renaissance.

As in many other artistic eras, regional differences abounded in the 16th century, not only between Northern Europe (discussed in Chapter 18) and Italy but within Italy itself. The leading artistic centers of Central Italy were Florence and Rome, where three of the greatest artists who ever lived—Leonardo da Vinci, Raphael, and Michelangelo—created works whose appeal has endured for 500 years.

Leonardo da Vinci

Born in the small town of Vinci, near Florence, LEONARDO DA VINCI (1452–1519) trained in the studio of Andrea del Verrocchio (FIG. 16-13). The quintessential "Renaissance man," Leonardo had prodigious talent and an unbridled imagination. Art was but one of his innumerable interests. The scope and depth of these interests were without precedent—so great as to frustrate any hopes Leonardo might have had of realizing all that his extraordinarily inventive mind could conceive. Still, he succeeded in mapping the routes that both art and science were to take for generations. Although the discussion here focuses on Leonardo as an artist, exploring his art in conjunction with his other pursuits considerably enhances an understanding of his artistic production. Leonardo revealed his unquenchable curiosity in his voluminous notes, liberally interspersed with sketches dealing with botany, geology, geography, cartography, zoology, military engineering, animal lore, anatomy, and aspects of physical science, including hydraulics and mechanics. These studies informed his art. In his notes, he stated repeatedly that all his scientific investigations made him a better painter. For example, Leonardo's in-depth exploration of optics gave him an understanding of perspective, light, and color. His scientific drawings (FIG. 17-6) are themselves artworks.

Leonardo's great ambition in his painting, as well as in his scientific endeavors, was to discover the laws underlying the processes and flux of nature. With this end in mind, he also studied the human body and contributed immeasurably to the fields of physiology and psychology. Leonardo believed that reality in an absolute sense was inaccessible and that humans could know it only through its changing images. He considered the eyes the most vital organs and sight the most essential function. Better to be deaf than blind, he argued, because through the eyes individuals could grasp reality most directly and profoundly.

Around 1481, Leonardo left Florence after offering his services to Ludovico Sforza (1451–1508), the son and heir apparent of the ruler of Milan. The political situation in Florence was uncertain, and Leonardo may have felt that his particular skills would be in greater demand in Milan, providing him with the opportunity for increased financial security. He devoted most of a letter to Ludovico to advertising his competence and his qualifications as a military engineer, mentioning only at the end his abilities as a painter and sculptor. The letter illustrates the relationship between Renaissance artists and their patrons, as well as Leonardo's breadth of competence. That he should select expertise in military engineering as his primary attraction to the Sforzas is an index of the period's instability.

> And in short, according to the variety of cases, I can contrive various and endless means of offence and defence. . . . In time of peace I believe I can give perfect satisfaction and to the equal of any other in architecture and the composition of buildings, public and private; and in guiding water from one place to another. . . . I can carry out sculpture in marble, bronze, or clay, and also I can do in painting whatever may be done, as well as any other, be he whom he may.[2]

Ludovico accepted Leonardo's offer, and the Florentine artist remained in Milan for almost 20 years.

MADONNA OF THE ROCKS Shortly after settling in Milan, Leonardo painted *Madonna of the Rocks* (FIG. 17-2) as the central panel of an altarpiece for the chapel of the Confraternity of the Immaculate Conception in San Francesco Grande. The painting builds on Masaccio's understanding and usage of chiaroscuro, the subtle play of light and dark. Modeling with light and shadow and expressing emotional states were, for Leonardo, the heart of painting:

17-2 LEONARDO DA VINCI, *Madonna of the Rocks,* from San Francesco Grande, Milan, Italy, begun 1483. Oil on wood (transferred to canvas), 6′ 6½″ × 4′. Louvre, Paris.

In this groundbreaking work, Leonardo used gestures and a pyramidal composition to unite the Virgin, Saint John the Baptist, the Christ Child, and an angel. The figures share the same light-infused environment.

> A good painter has two chief objects to paint—man and the intention of his soul. The former is easy, the latter hard, for it must be expressed by gestures and the movement of the limbs. . . . A painting will only be wonderful for the beholder by making that which is not so appear raised and detached from the wall.[3]

Leonardo presented the figures in *Madonna of the Rocks* in a pyramidal grouping and, more notably, as sharing the same environment. This groundbreaking achievement—the unified representation of objects in an atmospheric setting—was a manifestation of his scientific curiosity about the invisible substance surrounding things. The Madonna, Christ Child, infant John the Baptist, and angel emerge through nuances of light and shade from the half-light of the cavernous visionary landscape. Light simultaneously veils and reveals the forms, immersing them in a layer of atmosphere. Leonardo's

Renaissance Drawings

In the 16th century in Italy, drawing (or *disegno*) assumed a position of greater prominence than ever before in artistic production. Until the late 15th century, the expense of drawing surfaces and their lack of availability limited the production of preparatory sketches. Most artists drew on *parchment* (prepared from the skins of calves, sheep, and goats) or on *vellum* (made from the skins of young animals and therefore very expensive). Because of the cost of these materials, drawings in the 14th and 15th centuries tended to be extremely detailed and meticulously executed. Artists often drew using *silverpoint* (a *stylus* made of silver) because of the fine line it produced and the sharp point it maintained. The introduction in the late 15th century of less expensive paper made of fibrous pulp produced for the developing printing industry (see "Woodcuts, Engravings, and Etchings," Chapter 15, page 415) allowed artists to experiment more and to draw with greater freedom. As a result, sketches abounded. Artists executed these drawings in pen and ink (FIG. 17-6), chalk, charcoal (FIG. 17-3), brush, and graphite or lead.

The importance of drawing transcended the mechanical or technical possibilities it afforded artists, however. The term *disegno* referred also to design, an integral component of good art. Design was the foundation of art, and drawing was the fundamental element of design. The painter Federico Zuccaro (1542–1609) summed up this philosophy when he stated that drawing is the external physical manifestation (*disegno esterno*) of an internal intellectual idea or design (*disegno interno*).

The design dimension of art production became increasingly important as artists cultivated their own styles. The early stages of artistic training largely focused on imitation and emulation (see "Cennino Cennini on Imitation and Emulation," Chapter 16, page 431), but to achieve widespread recognition, artists had to develop their own styles. Although the artistic community and public at large acknowledged technical skill, the conceptualization of the artwork—its theoretical and formal development—was paramount. Disegno—or design in this case—represented an artist's conception and intention. In the literature of the period, the terms writers and critics often invoked to praise esteemed artists included *invenzione* (invention), *ingegno* (innate talent), *fantasia* (imagination), and *capriccio* (originality).

1 ft.

17-3 LEONARDO DA VINCI, cartoon for *Madonna and Child with Saint Anne and the Infant Saint John*, ca. 1505–1507. Charcoal heightened with white on brown paper, 4′ 6″ × 3′ 3″. National Gallery, London.

The introduction of less expensive paper in the late 15th century allowed artists to draw more frequently. In this cartoon, Leonardo depicted monumental figures in a scene of tranquil grandeur and balance.

effective use of atmospheric perspective is the result in large part of his mastery of the relatively new medium of oil painting, which had previously been used mostly by Northern European painters (see "Tempera and Oil Painting," Chapter 15, page 401). The figures pray, point, and bless, and these acts and gestures, although their meanings are not certain, visually unite the individuals portrayed. The angel points to the infant John and, through his outward glance, involves the viewer in the tableau. John prays to the Christ Child, who blesses him in return. The Virgin herself completes the series of interlocking gestures, her left hand reaching toward the Christ Child and her right hand resting protectively on John's shoulder. The melting mood of tenderness, which the caressing light enhances, suffuses the entire composition. By creating an emotionally compelling, visually unified, and spatially convincing image, Leonardo succeeded in expressing "the intention of his soul."

MADONNA AND CHILD CARTOON Leonardo's style fully emerges in *Madonna and Child with Saint Anne and the Infant Saint John* (FIG. 17-3), a preliminary drawing for a painting (see "Renaissance Drawings," above) he made in 1505 or shortly thereafter. Here, the glowing light falls gently on the majestic forms in a scene of tranquil grandeur and balance. Leonardo ordered every part of his cartoon with an intellectual pictorial logic that results in an appealing visual unity. The figures are robust and monumental, the stately grace of their movements reminiscent of the Greek statues of goddesses (FIG. 5-49) in the pediments of the Parthenon. Leonardo's infusion of the principles of classical art into his designs, however, cannot be attributed to specific knowledge of Greek monuments. He and his contemporaries never visited Greece. Their acquaintance with classical art extended only to Etruscan and Roman monuments and Roman copies of Greek statues in Italy.

17-4 Leonardo da Vinci, *Last Supper*, ca. 1495–1498. Oil and tempera on plaster, 13′ 9″ × 29′ 10″. Refectory, Santa Maria delle Grazie, Milan.

Christ has just announced that one of his disciples will betray him, and each one reacts. Christ is both the psychological focus of Leonardo's fresco and the focal point of all the converging perspective lines.

LAST SUPPER For the refectory of the church of Santa Maria delle Grazie in Milan, Leonardo painted *Last Supper* (FIG. **17-4**). Cleaned and restored in 1999, the mural is still in a poor state, in part because of the painter's unfortunate experiments with his materials (see "Restoring Renaissance Paintings," page 473). Nonetheless, the painting is both formally and emotionally Leonardo's most impressive work. Christ and his 12 disciples sit at a long table placed parallel to the picture plane in a simple, spacious room. The austere setting amplifies the painting's highly dramatic action. Christ, with outstretched hands, has just said, "One of you is about to betray me" (Matt. 26:21). A wave of intense excitement passes through the group as each disciple asks himself and, in some cases, his neighbor, "Is it I?" (Matt. 26:22). Leonardo visualized a sophisticated conjunction of the dramatic "One of you is about to betray me" with the initiation of the ancient liturgical ceremony of the Eucharist, when Christ, blessing bread and wine, said, "This is my body, which is given for you. Do this for a commemoration of me. . . . This is the chalice, the new testament in my blood, which shall be shed for you" (Luke 22:19–20).

In the center, Christ appears isolated from the disciples and in perfect repose, the calm eye of the stormy emotion swirling around him. The central window at the back, whose curved pediment arches above his head, frames his figure. The pediment is the only curve in the architectural framework, and it serves here, along with the diffused light, as a halo. Christ's head is the focal point of all converging perspective lines in the composition. Thus, the still, psychological

focus and cause of the action is also the perspectival focus, as well as the center of the two-dimensional surface. The two-dimensional, the three-dimensional, and the psychodimensional focuses are the same.

Leonardo presented the agitated disciples in four groups of three, united among and within themselves by the figures' gestures and postures. The artist sacrificed traditional iconography to pictorial and dramatic consistency by placing Judas on the same side of the table as Jesus and the other disciples (compare FIG. **16-22**). The light source in the painting corresponds to the windows in the Milanese refectory. Judas's face is in shadow and he clutches a money bag in his right hand as he reaches his left forward to fulfill the Master's declaration: "But yet behold, the hand of him that betrayeth me is with me on the table" (Luke 22:21). The two disciples at the table ends are quieter than the others, as if to bracket the energy of the composition, which is more intense closer to Christ, whose serenity both halts and intensifies it. The disciples register a broad range of emotional responses, including fear, doubt, protestation, rage, and love. Leonardo's numerous preparatory studies—using live models—suggest that he thought of each figure as carrying a particular charge and type of emotion. Like a stage director, he read the Gospel story carefully, and scrupulously cast his actors as the New Testament described their roles. In this work, as in his other religious paintings, Leonardo revealed his extraordinary ability to apply his voluminous knowledge about the observable world to the pictorial representation of a religious scene, resulting in a psychologically complex and compelling painting.

17-5 LEONARDO DA VINCI, *Mona Lisa,* ca. 1503–1505. Oil on wood, 2′ 6¼″ × 1′ 9″. Louvre, Paris.

Leonardo's skill with chiaroscuro and atmospheric perspective is on display in this new kind of portrait depicting the sitter as an individual personality who engages the viewer psychologically.

MONA LISA Leonardo's *Mona Lisa* (FIG. **17-5**) is probably the world's most famous portrait. The sitter's identity is still the subject of scholarly debate, but in his biography of Leonardo, Giorgio Vasari asserted she was Lisa di Antonio Maria Gherardini, the wife of Francesco del Giocondo, a wealthy Florentine—hence, "Mona (an Italian contraction of *ma donna,* "my lady") Lisa." Despite the uncertainty of this identification, Leonardo's portrait is a convincing representation of an individual. Unlike earlier portraits, it does not serve solely as an icon of status. Indeed, Mona Lisa neither wears jewelry nor holds any attribute associated with wealth. She sits quietly, her hands folded, her mouth forming a gentle smile, and her gaze directed at the viewer. Renaissance etiquette dictated that a woman should not look directly into a man's eyes. Leonardo's portrayal of this self-assured young woman without the trappings of power but engaging the audience psychologically is thus quite remarkable. The painting is darker today than 500 years ago, and the colors are less vivid, but *Mona Lisa* still reveals the artist's fascination and skill with chiaroscuro and atmospheric perspective. *Mona Lisa* is a prime example of Leonardo's famous smoky *sfumato* (misty haziness)—his subtle adjustment of light and blurring of precise planes.

The lingering appeal of *Mona Lisa* derives in large part from Leonardo's decision to set his subject against the backdrop of a mysterious uninhabited landscape. This landscape, with roads and bridges that seem to lead nowhere, recalls his *Madonna of the Rocks* (FIG. 17-2). The composition also resembles Fra Filippo Lippi's *Madonna and Child with Angels* (FIG. 16-23) with figures seated in front of a window through which the viewer sees a distant landscape. Originally, the artist represented Mona Lisa in a *loggia* (columnar gallery). When the painting was trimmed (not by Leonardo), these columns were eliminated, but the remains of the column bases may still be seen to the left and right of Mona Lisa's shoulders.

ANATOMICAL STUDIES Leonardo completed very few paintings. His perfectionism, relentless experimentation, and far-ranging curiosity diffused his efforts. However, the drawings in his notebooks preserve an extensive record of his ideas. His interests focused increasingly on science in his later years, and he embraced knowledge of all facets of the natural world. His investigations in anatomy yielded drawings of great precision and beauty of execution. *The Fetus and Lining of the Uterus* (FIG. **17-6**), although it does not meet 21st-century standards for accuracy (for example, Leonardo regularized the uterus's shape to a sphere, and his characterization of the

17-6 LEONARDO DA VINCI, *The Fetus and Lining of the Uterus,* ca. 1511–1513. Pen and ink with wash, over red chalk and traces of black chalk on paper, 1′ × 8⅝″. Royal Library, Windsor Castle.

Leonardo's analytical anatomical studies epitomize the scientific spirit of the Renaissance, establishing that era as a prelude to the modern world and setting it in sharp contrast to the preceding Middle Ages.

17-7 RAPHAEL, *Marriage of the Virgin,* from the Chapel of Saint Joseph, San Francesco, Città di Castello, Italy, 1504. Oil on wood, 5′ 7″ × 3′ 10½″. Pinacoteca di Brera, Milan.

In this early work depicting the marriage of the Virgin to Saint Joseph, Raphael demonstrated his mastery of foreshortening and of the perspective system he learned from his teacher, Perugino (FIG. 16-40).

neer for Cesare Borgia (1476–1507), who, with the support of his father, Pope Alexander VI (r. 1492–1503), tried to conquer the cities of the Romagna region in north-central Italy and create a Borgia duchy. Leonardo eventually returned to Milan in the service of the French. At the invitation of King Francis I (FIG. 18-10), he then went to France, where he died at the château of Cloux in 1519.

Raphael

Alexander VI's successor was Julius II (r. 1503–1513). In addition to his responsibility as the spiritual leader of Christendom, the new pope extended his quest for authority to the temporal realm, as other medieval and Renaissance popes had done. An immensely ambitious man, Julius II indulged his enthusiasm for engaging in battle, which earned him a designation as the "warrior-pope." Further, his selection of the name Julius, after Julius Caesar, reinforced the perception that the Roman Empire served as his governmental model. Julius II's 10-year papacy, however, was most notable for his contributions to the arts. He was an avid art patron and understood well the propagandistic value of visual imagery. After his election, he immediately commissioned artworks that would present an authoritative image of his rule and reinforce the primacy of the Catholic Church. Among the many projects he commissioned were a new design for Saint Peter's basilica (FIGS. 17-23 and 17-24), the painting of the Sistine Chapel ceiling (FIG. 17-1), the decoration of the papal apartments (FIG. 17-9), and the construction of his tomb (FIGS. 17-15 and 17-16).

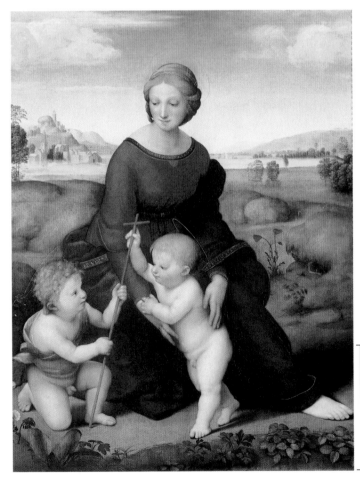

17-8 RAPHAEL, *Madonna in the Meadow,* 1505–1506. Oil on wood, 3′ 8½″ × 2′ 10¼″. Kunsthistorisches Museum, Vienna.

Emulating Leonardo's pyramidal composition (FIG. 17-2) but rejecting his dusky modeling and mystery, Raphael set his Madonna in a well-lit landscape and imbued her with grace, dignity, and beauty.

lining is incorrect), was an astounding achievement in its day. Analytical anatomical studies such as this epitomize the scientific spirit of the Renaissance, establishing that era as a prelude to the modern world and setting it in sharp contrast to the preceding Middle Ages. Although Leonardo may not have been the first scientist of the modern world (at least not in the modern sense of the term), he certainly originated a method of scientific illustration, especially *cutaway* views. Scholars have long recognized the importance of these drawings for the development of anatomy as a science, especially in an age predating photographic methods such as X-rays.

Leonardo also won renown in his time as both architect and sculptor, although no surviving buildings or sculptures can be definitively attributed to him. From his many drawings of central-plan buildings, it appears he shared the interest of other Renaissance architects in this building type. As for sculpture, Leonardo left numerous drawings of monumental equestrian statues, and also made a full-scale model for a monument to Francesco Sforza (1401–1466; Ludovico's father). The French used the statue as a target and shot it to pieces when they occupied Milan in 1499. Due to the French presence, Leonardo left Milan and served for a while as a military engi-

17-9 RAPHAEL, *Philosophy* (*School of Athens*), Stanza della Segnatura, Vatican Palace, Rome, Italy, 1509–1511. Fresco, 19′ × 27′.

Raphael included himself in this gathering of great philosophers and scientists whose self-assurance conveys calm reason. The setting resembles the interior of the new Saint Peter's (FIG. 19-5).

In 1508, Julius II called Raffaello Santi (or Sanzio), known as RAPHAEL (1483–1520) in English, to the papal court in Rome. Born in a small town in Umbria near Urbino, Raphael probably learned the rudiments of his art from his father, Giovanni Santi, a painter connected with the ducal court of Federico da Montefeltro (see Chapter 16), before entering the studio of Perugino in Perugia. Although strongly influenced by Perugino, Leonardo, and others, Raphael developed an individual style that exemplifies the ideals of High Renaissance art.

MARRIAGE OF THE VIRGIN Among Raphael's early works is *Marriage of the Virgin* (FIG. **17-7**), which he painted for the Chapel of Saint Joseph in the church of San Francesco in Città di Castello, southeast of Florence. The subject is a fitting one for a chapel dedicated to Saint Joseph. According to the *Golden Legend* (a 13th-century collection of stories about the lives of the saints), Joseph competed with other suitors for Mary's hand. The high priest was to give the Virgin to whichever suitor presented to him a rod that had miraculously bloomed. Raphael depicted Joseph with his flowering rod in his left hand. In his right hand Joseph holds the wedding ring he is about to place on Mary's finger. Other virgins congregate at the left, and the unsuccessful suitors stand on the right. One of them breaks his rod in half over his knee in frustration, giving Raphael an opportunity to demonstrate his mastery of foreshortening. The perspective system he used is the one he learned from Perugino (FIG. **16-40**). The temple in the background is Raphael's version of a centrally planned building (FIG. **17-22**), featuring Brunelleschian arcades (FIG. **16-31**).

MADONNA IN THE MEADOW Raphael spent the four years from 1504 to 1508 in Florence. There, still in his early 20s, he discovered that the painting style he had learned so painstakingly from Perugino was already outmoded (as was Brunelleschi's architectural style). Florentine crowds flocked to the church of Santissima Annunziata to see Leonardo's recently unveiled cartoon of the Virgin, Christ Child, Saint Anne, and Saint John (probably an earlier version of FIG. 17-3). Under Leonardo's influence, Raphael began to modify the Madonna compositions he had learned in Umbria. In *Madonna in the Meadow* (FIG. **17-8**) of 1505–1506, Raphael adopted Leonardo's pyramidal composition and modeling of faces and figures in subtle chiaroscuro. Yet the Umbrian artist placed the large, substantial figures in a Peruginesque landscape, with his former master's typical feathery trees in the middle ground. Although Raphael experimented with Leonardo's dusky modeling, he tended to return to Perugino's lighter tonalities and blue skies. Raphael preferred clarity to obscurity, not fascinated, as Leonardo was, with mystery.

SCHOOL OF ATHENS Three years after completing *Madonna in the Meadow,* Raphael received one of the most important painting commissions (FIG. **17-9**) Julius II awarded—the decoration of

17-10 RAPHAEL, *Galatea,* Sala di Galatea, Villa Farnesina, Rome, Italy, ca. 1513. Fresco, 9′ 8″ × 7′ 5″.

Based on a poem by Poliziano, Raphael's fresco depicts Galatea fleeing from Polyphemus. The painting, made for the banker Agostino Chigi's private palace, celebrates human beauty and zestful love.

1 ft.

the papal apartments in the Apostolic Palace of the Vatican (MAP 19-1). Of the suite's several rooms (*stanze*), Raphael painted the Stanza della Segnatura (Room of the Signature—the papal library, where Julius II signed official documents) and the Stanza d'Eliodoro (Room of Heliodorus—the pope's private audience room, named for one of the paintings). His pupils completed the others, following his sketches. On the four walls of the Stanza della Segnatura, under the headings *Theology, Law (Justice), Poetry,* and *Philosophy,* Raphael presented images that symbolized and summed up Western learning as Renaissance society understood it. The frescoes refer to the four branches of human knowledge and wisdom while pointing out the virtues and the learning appropriate to a pope. Given Julius II's desire for recognition as both a spiritual and temporal leader, it is appropriate that the *Theology* and *Philosophy* frescoes face each other. The two images present a balanced picture of the pope—as a cultured, knowledgeable individual and as a wise, divinely ordained religious authority.

In Raphael's *Philosophy* mural (commonly known as *School of Athens,* FIG. 17-9) the setting is not a "school" but a congregation of the great philosophers and scientists of the ancient world. Raphael depicted these luminaries, revered by Renaissance humanists, conversing and explaining their various theories and ideas. The setting is a vast hall covered by massive vaults that recall ancient Roman architecture—and approximate the appearance of the new Saint Peter's (FIG. 19-5) in 1509, when Raphael began the fresco. Colossal statues of Apollo and Athena, patron deities of the arts and of wisdom, oversee the interactions. Plato and Aristotle serve as the central figures around whom Raphael carefully arranged the others. Plato holds his book *Timaeus* and points to Heaven, the source of his inspiration, while Aristotle carries his book *Nicomachean Ethics* and gestures toward the earth, from which his observations of reality sprang. Appropriately, ancient philosophers, men concerned with the ultimate mysteries that transcend this world, stand on Plato's side. On Aristotle's side are the philosophers and scientists interested in nature and human affairs. At the lower left, Pythagoras writes as a servant holds up the harmonic scale. In the foreground, Heraclitus (probably a portrait of Raphael's great contemporary, Michelangelo) broods alone. Diogenes sprawls on the steps. At the right, students surround Euclid, who demonstrates a theorem. Euclid may be a portrait of the architect Bramante, whom Julius II had recently commissioned to design a new Saint Peter's (FIGS. 17-23 and 17-24) to replace the Constantinian basilica (FIG. 8-9). At the extreme right, just to the right of the astronomers Zoroaster and Ptolemy, both holding globes, Raphael included his own portrait.

The groups appear to move easily and clearly, with eloquent poses and gestures that symbolize their doctrines and present an engaging variety of figural positions. Their self-assurance and natural dignity convey the very nature of calm reason, that balance and measure the great Renaissance minds so admired as the heart of philosophy. Significantly, in this work Raphael placed himself among the mathematicians and scientists rather than the humanists. Certainly the evolution of pictorial science came to its perfection in *School of Athens*. Raphael's convincing depiction of a vast perspectival space on a two-dimensional surface was the consequence of the union of mathematics with pictorial science, here mastered completely.

The artist's psychological insight matured along with his mastery of the problems of physical representation. All the characters in Raphael's *School of Athens,* like those in Leonardo's *Last Supper* (FIG. 17-4), communicate moods that reflect their beliefs, and the artist's placement of each figure tied these moods together. Raphael carefully considered his design devices for relating individuals and groups to one another and to the whole. These compositional elements demand close study. From the center, where Plato and Aristotle stand, Raphael arranged the groups of figures in an ellipse with a wide opening in the foreground. Moving along the floor's perspectival pattern, the viewer's eye penetrates the assembly of philosophers and continues, by way of the reclining Diogenes, up to the here-reconciled leaders of the two great opposing camps of Renaissance philosophy. The perspective vanishing point falls on Plato's left hand, drawing attention to *Timaeus*. In the Stanza della Segnatura, Raphael reconciled and harmonized not only the Platonists and Aristotelians but also paganism and Christianity, surely a major factor in his appeal to Julius II.

GALATEA Pope Leo X (r. 1513–1521), the second son of Lorenzo de' Medici, succeeded Julius II as Raphael's patron. Leo was a worldly, pleasure-loving prince who, as a true Medici, spent huge sums on the arts. Raphael moved in the highest circles of the papal court, the star of a brilliant society. He was young, handsome, wealthy, and admired, not only by his followers but also by Rome and all of Italy. Genial, even-tempered, generous, and high-minded, Raphael had a personality that contrasted strikingly with that of the aloof, mysterious Leonardo or the tormented and obstinate Michelangelo (so depicted in *School of Athens*).

The pope was not Raphael's sole patron. Agostino Chigi (1465–1520), an immensely wealthy banker who managed the papal state's financial affairs, commissioned Raphael to decorate his palace on the Tiber River with scenes from classical mythology. Outstanding among the frescoes Raphael painted in the small but splendid Villa Farnesina is *Galatea* (FIG. 17-10), which Raphael based on *Stanzas for the Joust of Giuliano de' Medici* by the poet Angelo Poliziano (1454–1494). In Raphael's fresco, Galatea flees on a shell drawn by leaping dolphins as she escapes from her uncouth lover, the Cyclops Polyphemus (painted on another wall by a different artist). Sea creatures and playful cupids surround her. The painting erupts in unrestrained pagan joy and exuberance, an exultant song in praise of human beauty and zestful love. Compositionally, Raphael enhanced the liveliness of the image by arranging the sturdy figures around Galatea in bounding and dashing movements that always return to her as the energetic center. The cupids, skillfully foreshortened, repeat the circling motion. Raphael conceived his figures sculpturally, and Galatea's body—supple, strong, and vigorously in motion—contrasts with Botticelli's delicate, hovering, almost dematerialized Venus (FIG. 16-28) while suggesting the spiraling compositions of Hellenistic statuary (FIG. 5-80). In *Galatea*, pagan myth—presented here in monumental form, in vivacious movement, and

in a spirit of passionate delight—resurrects the naturalistic art and poetry of the classical world.

BALDASSARE CASTIGLIONE Raphael also excelled at portraiture. His subjects were the illustrious scholars and courtiers who surrounded Leo X, among them the pope's close friend Count Baldassare Castiglione (1478–1529), the author of a handbook on genteel behavior. In *Book of the Courtier,* Castiglione enumerated the attributes of the perfect Renaissance courtier: impeccable character, noble birth, military achievement, classical education, and knowledge of the arts. Castiglione then described a way of life based on cultivated rationality in imitation of the ancients. In Raphael's portrait of the count (FIG. 17-11), Castiglione, splendidly yet soberly garbed, looks directly at the viewer with a philosopher's grave and benign expression, clear-eyed and thoughtful. The figure is in half-length (the lower part with the hands was later cut off) and three-quarter view, a pose Leonardo made popular with *Mona Lisa* (FIG. 17-5). Both portraits exhibit the increasing attention High Renaissance artists paid to the subject's personality and psychic state. The muted and low-keyed tones befit the temper and mood of this reflective middle-aged man—the background is entirely neutral, without the usual landscape or architecture. The head and the hands wonderfully reveal the man, who himself had written so eloquently in *Courtier* of enlightenment through the love of beauty. This kind of love animated Raphael, Castiglione, and other artists and writers of their age, and Michelangelo's poetry suggests he shared in the widespread appreciation for the beauty found in the natural world.

1 in.

17-11 RAPHAEL, *Baldassare Castiglione,* ca. 1514. Oil on canvas, 2′ 6¼″ × 2′ 2½″. Louvre, Paris.

Raphael's painting of the famed courtier Count Baldassare Castiglione typifies High Renaissance portraiture in the increasing attention the artist paid to the subject's personality and psychic state.

Leonardo and Michelangelo
on Painting versus Sculpture

Leonardo da Vinci and Michelangelo each produced work in a variety of artistic media, earning enviable reputations not just as painters and sculptors but as architects and draftsmen as well. The two disagreed, however, on the relative merits of the different media. In particular, Leonardo, with his intellectual and analytical mind, preferred painting to sculpture, which he denigrated as manual labor. In contrast, Michelangelo, who worked in a more intuitive manner, regarded himself primarily as a sculptor. Two excerpts from their writings reveal their positions on the relationship between the two media.

Leonardo da Vinci wrote the following in his so-called *Treatise on Painting:*

> Painting is a matter of greater mental analysis, of greater skill, and more marvelous than sculpture, since necessity compels the mind of the painter to transform itself into the very mind of nature, to become an interpreter between nature and art. Painting justifies by reference to nature the reasons of the pictures which follow its laws: in what ways the images of objects before the eye come together in the pupil of the eye; which, among objects equal in size, looks larger to the eye; which, among equal colors, will look more or less dark or more or less bright; which, among things at the same depth, looks more or less low; which, among those objects placed at equal height, will look more or less high, and why, among objects placed at various distances, one will appear less clear than the other.

> This art comprises and includes within itself all visible things such as colors and their diminution which the poverty of sculpture cannot include. Painting represents transparent objects but the sculptor will show you the shapes of natural objects without artifice. The painter will show you things at different distances with variation of color due to the air lying between the objects and the eye; he shows you mists through which visual images penetrate with difficulty; he shows you rain which discloses within it clouds with mountains

and valleys; he shows the dust which discloses within it and beyond it the combatants who stirred it up; he shows streams of greater or lesser density; he shows fish playing between the surface of the water and its bottom; he shows the polished pebbles of various colors lying on the washed sand at the bottom of rivers, surrounded by green plants; he shows the stars at various heights above us, and thus he achieves innumerable effects which sculpture cannot attain.*

In response, although decades later, Michelangelo wrote these excerpts in a letter to Benedetto Varchi (1502–1565), a Florentine poet best known for his 16-volume history of Florence:

> I believe that painting is considered excellent in proportion as it approaches the effect of relief, while relief is considered bad in proportion as it approaches the effect of painting.

> I used to consider that sculpture was the lantern of painting and that between the two things there was the same difference as that between the sun and the moon. But . . . I now consider that painting and sculpture are one and the same thing.

> Suffice that, since one and the other (that is to say, both painting and sculpture) proceed from the same faculty, it would be an easy matter to establish harmony between them and to let such disputes alone, for they occupy more time than the execution of the figures themselves. As to that man [Leonardo] who wrote saying that painting was more noble than sculpture, if he had known as much about the other subjects on which he has written, why, my serving-maid would have written better!†

---

* Leonardo da Vinci, *Treatise on Painting,* 51, in Robert Klein and Henri Zerner, *Italian Art 1500–1600: Sources and Documents* (Evanston, Ill.: Northwestern University Press, 1966), 7–8.
† Michelangelo to Benedetto Varchi, Rome, 1549; in Klein and Zerner, 13–14.

Michelangelo

Pope Julius II had a keen eye for talent and during his decade-long papacy also entrusted highly coveted commissions to MICHELANGELO BUONARROTI (1475–1564). Although Michelangelo was an architect, sculptor, painter, poet, and engineer, he thought of himself first as a sculptor, regarding that calling as superior to that of a painter because the sculptor shares in something like the divine power to "make man" (see "Leonardo and Michelangelo on Painting versus Sculpture," above). Drawing a conceptual parallel to Plato's ideas, Michelangelo believed that the image the artist's hand produces must come from the idea in the artist's mind. The idea, then, is the reality that the artist's genius has to bring forth. But artists are not the creators of the ideas they conceive. Rather, they find their ideas in the natural world, reflecting the absolute idea, which, for the artist, is beauty. One of Michelangelo's best-known observations about sculpture is that the artist must proceed by finding the idea—the image locked in the stone. By removing the excess stone, the sculptor extricates the idea from the block (FIG. I-16), bringing forth the living form. The artist, Michelangelo felt, works many years at this unceasing process of revelation and "arrives late at novel and lofty things."[4]

Michelangelo did indeed arrive "at novel and lofty things," for he broke sharply from the lessons of his predecessors and contemporaries in one important respect. He mistrusted the application of mathematical methods as guarantees of beauty in proportion. Measure and proportion, he believed, should be "kept in the eyes." Vasari quoted Michelangelo as declaring that "it was necessary to have the compasses in the eyes and not in the hand, because the hands work and the eye judges."[5] Thus, Michelangelo set aside the ancient Roman architect Vitruvius, Alberti, Leonardo, and others who tirelessly sought the perfect measure, asserting that the artist's inspired judgment could identify other pleasing proportions. In addition, Michelangelo argued that the artist must not be bound, except by the demands made by realizing the idea. This insistence on the artist's own authority was typical of Michelangelo and anticipated the modern concept of the right to a self-expression of talent limited only by the artist's judgment. The artistic license to aspire far beyond the "rules" was, in part, a manifestation of the pursuit of fame and success that humanism fostered. In this context, Michelangelo created works in architecture, sculpture, and painting that departed from High Renaissance regularity. He put in its stead a style of vast, expressive

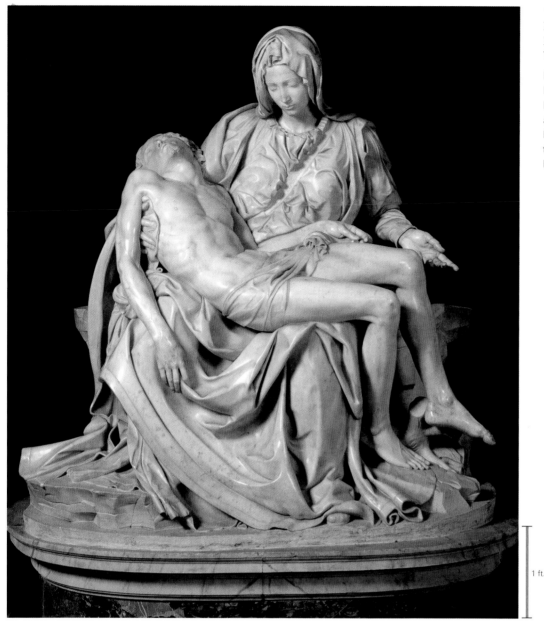

17-12 MICHELANGELO BUONARROTI, *Pietà*, ca. 1498–1500. Marble, 5′ 8½″ high. Saint Peter's, Vatican City, Rome.

Michelangelo's representation of Mary cradling Christ's corpse brilliantly captures the sadness and beauty of the young Virgin but was controversial because the Madonna seems younger than her son.

1 ft.

strength conveyed through complex, eccentric, and often titanic forms that loom before the viewer in tragic grandeur. Michelangelo's self-imposed isolation, creative furies, proud independence, and daring innovations led Italians to speak of the dominating quality of the man and his works in one word—*terribilità*, the sublime shadowed by the awesome and the fearful.

As a youth, Michelangelo was an apprentice in the studio of the painter Domenico Ghirlandaio, whom he left before completing his training. Although Michelangelo later claimed that in his art he owed nothing to anyone, he made detailed drawings in the manner of the great Florentines Giotto and Masaccio. Early on, he came to the attention of Lorenzo the Magnificent and studied sculpture under one of Lorenzo's favorite artists, Bertoldo di Giovanni (ca. 1420–1491), a former collaborator of Donatello. When the Medici fell in 1494, Michelangelo fled from Florence to Bologna, where the sculptures of the Sienese artist Jacopo della Quercia (1367–1438) impressed him.

PIETÀ Michelangelo's wanderings took him to Rome, where, around 1498, still in his early 20s, he produced his first masterpiece, a *Pietà* (FIG. 17-12), for the French cardinal Jean de Bilhères La-

graulas (1439–1499). The cardinal commissioned the statue to adorn the chapel in Old Saint Peter's (FIG. 8-9) in which he was to be buried. (The work is now on view in the new church that replaced the fourth-century basilica.) The theme—Mary cradling the dead body of Christ in her lap—was a staple in the repertoire of French and German artists (FIG. 13-51), and Michelangelo's French patron doubtless chose the subject. The Italian, however, rendered the Northern theme in an unforgettable manner. Michelangelo transformed marble into flesh, hair, and fabric with a sensitivity for texture that is almost without parallel. The polish and luminosity of the exquisite marble surface cannot be captured fully in photographs and can be appreciated only in the presence of the original. Breathtaking too is the tender sadness of the beautiful and youthful Mary as she mourns the death of her son. In fact, her age—seemingly less than that of Christ—was a subject of controversy from the moment of the unveiling of the statue. Michelangelo explained Mary's ageless beauty as an integral part of her purity and virginity. Beautiful too is the son whom she holds. Christ seems less to have died than to have drifted off into peaceful sleep in Mary's maternal arms. His wounds are barely visible.

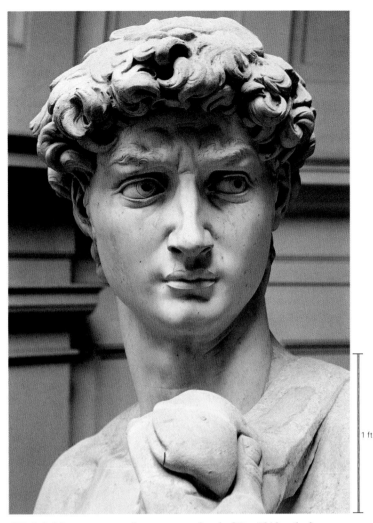

17-14 MICHELANGELO BUONARROTI, head of *David* (detail of FIG. 17-13), 1501–1504. Galleria dell'Accademia, Florence.

In contrast to earlier Renaissance depictions (FIGS. 16-12 and 16-13) of this Old Testament drama, Michelangelo portrayed David *before* the battle with Goliath, as he sternly watches his gigantic foe.

17-13 MICHELANGELO BUONARROTI, *David,* from Piazza della Signoria, Florence, Italy, 1501–1504. Marble, 17′ high. Galleria dell'Accademia, Florence.

In this colossal statue, Michelangelo represented David in heroic classical nudity, capturing the tension of Lysippan athletes (FIG. 5-65) and the emotionalism of Hellenistic statuary (FIGS. 5-80 and 5-81).

DAVID Michelangelo returned to Florence in 1501, seven years after the exile of the Medici (see Chapter 16). In 1495 the Florentine Republic had ordered the transfer of Donatello's *David* (FIG. 16-12) from the Medici palace to the Palazzo della Signoria to join Verrocchio's *David* (FIG. 16-13) there. The importance of David as a civic symbol led the Florence Cathedral building committee to invite Michelangelo to work a great block of marble left over from an earlier aborted commission into still another statue of *David* (FIG. 17-13). The colossal statue—Florentines referred to it as "the Giant"— Michelangelo created from that block assured his reputation then and now as an extraordinary talent. Only 40 years after *David*'s completion, Vasari extolled the work, which had been set up near the

west door of the Palazzo della Signoria, and claimed that "without any doubt the figure has put in the shade every other statue, ancient or modern, Greek or Roman—this was intended as a symbol of liberty for the Palace, signifying that just as David had protected his people and governed them justly, so whoever ruled Florence should vigorously defend the city and govern it with justice."[6]

Despite the traditional association of David with heroism, Michelangelo chose to represent the young biblical warrior not after his victory, with Goliath's head at his feet, but turning his head (FIG. 17-14) to his left, sternly watchful of the approaching foe. *David* exhibits the characteristic representation of energy in reserve that imbues Michelangelo's later figures with the tension of a coiled spring. The anatomy of David's body plays an important part in this prelude to action. His rugged torso, sturdy limbs, and large hands and feet alert viewers to the strength to come. The swelling veins and tightening sinews amplify the psychological energy of David's pose.

Michelangelo doubtless had the classical nude in mind when he conceived his *David*. Like many of his colleagues, he greatly admired Greco-Roman statues, in particular the skillful and precise rendering of heroic physique. Without strictly imitating the antique style, the Renaissance sculptor captured in his portrayal of the biblical hero the tension of Lysippan athletes (FIG. 5-65) and the psychological

17-15 MICHELANGELO BUONARROTI, *Moses,* from the tomb of Pope Julius II, Rome, Italy, ca. 1513–1515. Marble, 7′ 8½″ high. San Pietro in Vincoli, Rome.

Not since Hellenistic times had a sculptor captured as much pent-up energy, both emotional and physical, in a seated statue as Michelangelo did in the over-life-size *Moses* he carved for Julius II's tomb.

17-16 MICHELANGELO BUONARROTI, *Bound Slave* (*Rebellious Captive*), from the tomb of Pope Julius II, Rome, Italy, ca. 1513–1516. Marble, 7′ ⅝″ high. Louvre, Paris.

For Pope Julius II's grandiose tomb, Michelangelo planned a series of statues of captives or slaves in various attitudes of revolt and exhaustion. This defiant figure exhibits a violent contrapposto.

insight and emotionalism of Hellenistic statuary (FIGS. **5-80** and **5-81**). His *David* differs from those of Donatello and Verrocchio in much the same way later Hellenistic statues departed from their Classical predecessors (see Chapter 5). Michelangelo abandoned the self-contained compositions of the 15th-century *David* statues by abruptly turning the hero's head (FIG. **17-14**) toward his gigantic adversary. This *David* is compositionally and emotionally connected to an unseen presence beyond the statue, a feature also of Hellenistic sculpture (FIG. **5-85**). As early as 1501, then, Michelangelo invested his efforts in presenting towering, pent-up emotion rather than calm, ideal beauty. He transferred his own doubts, frustrations, and passions into the great figures he created or planned.

TOMB OF JULIUS II The formal references to classical antiquity in *David* surely appealed to Julius II, who associated himself with

the humanists and with Roman emperors. Thus, this sculpture and the fame that accrued to Michelangelo on its completion called the artist to the pope's attention, leading shortly thereafter to major papal commissions. The first project Julius II commissioned from Michelangelo was the pontiff's own tomb, to be placed in Old Saint Peter's. The original 1505 design called for a freestanding two-story structure with some 28 statues (FIGS. **17-15** and **17-16**). This colossal monument would have given Michelangelo the latitude to sculpt numerous human figures while providing Julius II with a grandiose memorial that would associate the 16th-century pope with the first pope, Peter himself. Shortly after Michelangelo began work on this project, the pope, for unknown reasons, interrupted the commission, possibly because funds had to be diverted to the rebuilding of Saint Peter's. After Julius II's death in 1513, Michelangelo reluctantly reduced the scale of the project step-by-step until, in 1542, a final contract specified a simple wall tomb with fewer than one-third of the originally planned figures. Michelangelo completed the tomb in

1545 and saw it placed in San Pietro in Vincoli, Rome, where Julius II had served as a cardinal before his accession to the papacy. Given Julius's ambitions, it is safe to say that had he seen the final design of his tomb, or known where it would eventually be located, he would have been bitterly disappointed.

The spirit of the tomb may be summed up in *Moses* (FIG. 17-15), which Michelangelo completed during one of his sporadic resumptions of the work. Meant to be seen from below and to be balanced with seven other massive forms related to it in spirit, *Moses* in its final comparatively paltry setting does not convey the impact originally intended. Michelangelo depicted the Old Testament prophet seated, the Tablets of the Law under one arm and his hands gathering his voluminous beard. The horns that appear on Moses's head were a convention in Christian art (based on a mistranslation of the Hebrew word for "rays") and helped Renaissance viewers identify the prophet (compare FIGS. 12-36 and 15-2). Here again, Michelangelo used the turned head, which concentrates the expression of awful wrath that stirs in the mighty frame and eyes. The muscles bulge, the veins swell, and the great legs seem to begin slowly to move. Not since Hellenistic times had a sculptor captured so much pent-up energy—both emotional and physical—in a seated statue (FIG. 5-85).

Originally, Michelangelo intended the tomb to have some 20 statues of captives, popularly known as slaves, in various attitudes of revolt and exhaustion. One is *Bound Slave,* or *Rebellious Captive* (FIG. 17-16). Another is shown in FIG. I-16. Considerable scholarly uncertainty exists about these statues. Although art historians have traditionally connected them with Julius's tomb, some now doubt the association. Some scholars even reject their identification as "slaves" or "captives." Despite these unanswered questions, the statues, like *David* and *Moses,* represent definitive statements. Michelangelo created figures that do not so much represent an abstract concept, as in medieval allegory, as they embody powerful emotional states associated with oppression. Indeed, Michelangelo communicated his expansive imagination through every plane and hollow of the stone. In *Bound Slave,* the defiant figure's violent contrapposto is the image of frantic but impotent struggle. Michelangelo based his whole art on his conviction that whatever can be said greatly through sculpture and painting must be said through the human figure.

TOMB OF GIULIANO DE' MEDICI Following the death of Julius II, Michelangelo, like Raphael, went into the service of the Medici popes, Leo X and his successor Clement VII (r. 1523–1534). These Medici chose not to perpetuate their predecessor's fame by let-

ting Michelangelo complete Julius's tomb. Instead, they (Pope Leo X and the then-cardinal Giulio de' Medici) commissioned him in 1519 to build a funerary chapel, the New Sacristy, in San Lorenzo in Florence. At opposite sides of the New Sacristy stand Michelangelo's sculpted tombs of Giuliano (1478–1516), duke of Nemours (south of Paris), and Lorenzo (1492–1519), duke of Urbino, son and grandson of Lorenzo the Magnificent. Giuliano's tomb (FIG. 17-17) is compositionally the twin of Lorenzo's. Michelangelo finished neither tomb. Most scholars believe he intended to place pairs of recumbent river gods at the bottom of the sarcophagi, balancing the pairs of figures that rest on the sloping sides, but Michelangelo's grand design for the tombs remains a puzzle.

The traditional interpretation is that the arrangement Michelangelo planned, but never completed, mirrors the soul's ascent through the levels of the Neo-Platonic universe. Neo-Platonism, a school of thought based on Plato's idealistic, spiritualistic philosophy, experienced a renewed popularity in the 16th-century humanist community. The lowest level of the tomb, which the river gods represent, would have signified the Underworld of brute matter, the source of evil. The two statues on the sarcophagi would symbolize the realm of time—the specifically human world of the cycles of dawn, day, evening, and night. Humanity's state in this world of time was one of pain and anxiety, of frustration and exhaustion. At left, the female figure of Night and, at right, the male figure of Day ap-

17-17 MICHELANGELO BUONARROTI, tomb of Giuliano de' Medici, New Sacristy (Medici Chapel), San Lorenzo, Florence, Italy, 1519–1534. Marble, central figure 5′ 11″ high.

Michelangelo's portrait of Giuliano de' Medici clad in ancient Roman armor depicts the deceased as the model of the active and decisive man. Below are the anguished and twisting figures of Night and Day.

1 ft.

pear to be chained into never-relaxing tensions. Both exhibit that anguished twisting of the body's masses in contrary directions, seen also in Michelangelo's *Bound Slave* (FIG. 17-16) and in his Sistine Chapel paintings (FIG. 17-19). This contortion is a staple of Michelangelo's figural art. Day, with a body the thickness of a great tree and the anatomy of Hercules (or of a reclining Greco-Roman river god that may have inspired Michelangelo's statue), strains his huge limbs against each other, his unfinished visage rising menacingly above his shoulder. Night, the symbol of rest, twists as if in troubled sleep, her posture wrenched and feverish. The artist surrounded her with an owl, poppies, and a hideous mask symbolic of nightmares. Some scholars argue, however, that the personifications Night and Day allude not to humanity's pain but to the life cycle and the passage of time leading ultimately to death.

On their respective tombs, sculptures of Lorenzo and Giuliano appear in niches at the apex of the structures. Transcending worldly existence, they represent the two ideal human types—the contemplative man (Lorenzo) and the active man (Giuliano). Giuliano (FIG. 17-17) sits clad in the armor of a Roman emperor and holds a commander's baton, his head turned alertly as if in council (he looks toward the statue of the Virgin at one end of the chapel). Across the room, Lorenzo appears wrapped in thought, his face in deep shadow. Together, they symbolize the two ways human beings might achieve union with God—through meditation or through the active

life fashioned after that of Christ. In this sense, they are not individual portraits. Indeed, Michelangelo declined to make likenesses of Lorenzo and Giuliano. Who, he asked, would care what the two dukes looked like in a thousand years? This attitude is consistent with Michelangelo's interests. Throughout his career he demonstrated less concern for facial features and expressions than for the overall human form. The rather generic visages of the two Medici captains of the Church attest to this. For the artist, more important was the contemplation of what lies beyond the corrosion of time.

SISTINE CHAPEL CEILING When Julius II suspended work on his tomb, the pope gave the bitter Michelangelo the commission to paint the ceiling (FIG. 17-1) of the Sistine Chapel (FIG. 17-18) in 1508. The artist, insisting that painting was not his profession (a protest that rings hollow after the fact, but Michelangelo's major works until then had been in sculpture, and painting was of secondary interest to him), assented in the hope that the tomb project could be revived. Michelangelo faced enormous difficulties in painting the Sistine ceiling. He had to address the ceiling's dimensions (some 5,800 square feet), its height above the pavement (almost 70 feet), and the complicated perspective problems the vault's height and curve presented, as well as his inexperience in the fresco technique. (The first section Michelangelo completed had to be redone because of faulty preparation of the intonaco; see "Fresco Painting," Chapter 14, page 382.) Yet, in less than four years, Michelangelo produced an unprecedented work—a monumental fresco incorporating his patron's agenda, Church doctrine, and the artist's interests. Depicting the most august and solemn themes of all, the creation, fall, and redemption of humanity—themes most likely selected by Julius II with input from Michelangelo and a theological adviser, probably Cardinal Marco Vigerio della Rovere (1446–1516)—Michelangelo spread a colossal decorative scheme across the vast surface. He succeeded in weaving together more than 300 figures in an ultimate grand drama of the human race.

A long sequence of narrative panels describing the creation, as recorded in Genesis, runs along the crown of the vault, from *God's Separation of Light and Darkness* (above the altar) to *Drunkenness of Noah* (nearest the entrance to the chapel). Thus, as viewers enter the chapel, look up, and walk toward the altar, they review, in reverse order, the history of the fall of humankind. The Hebrew prophets and pagan sibyls who foretold the coming of Christ appear seated in large thrones on both sides of the central row of scenes

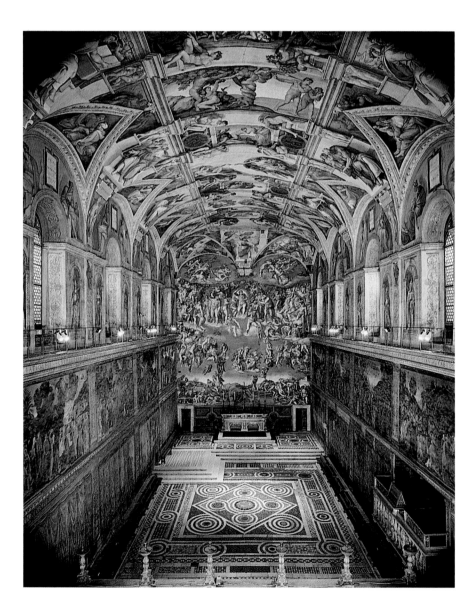

17-18 Interior of the Sistine Chapel (looking east), Vatican City, Rome, Italy, built 1473.

Michelangelo reluctantly agreed to paint the ceiling (FIG. 17-1) of the Sistine Chapel for Pope Julius II. He had to overcome the complicated perspective problems that the height and curve of the vault presented.

17-19 Michelangelo Buonarroti, *Creation of Adam,* detail of the ceiling (FIG. 17-1) of the Sistine Chapel, Vatican City, Rome, Italy, 1511–1512. Fresco, 9′ 2″ × 18′ 8″.

Life leaps to Adam like a spark from the extended hand of God in this fresco, which recalls the communication between gods and heroes in the classical myths Renaissance humanists admired so much.

from Genesis, where the vault curves down. In the four corner *pendentives,* Michelangelo placed four Old Testament scenes with David, Judith, Haman, and Moses and the Brazen Serpent. Scores of lesser figures also appear. The ancestors of Christ fill the triangular compartments above the windows, nude youths punctuate the corners of the central panels, and small pairs of putti in *grisaille* (monochrome painting using shades of gray to imitate sculpture) support the painted cornice surrounding the entire central corridor. The overall conceptualization of the ceiling's design and narrative structure not only presents a sweeping chronology of Christianity but also is in keeping with Renaissance ideas about Christian history. These ideas included interest in the conflict between good and evil and between the energy of youth and the wisdom of age. The conception of the entire ceiling was astounding in itself, and the articulation of it in its thousands of details was a superhuman achievement.

Unlike Andrea Mantegna's decoration of the Camera Picta (FIGS. 16-47 and 16-48) in Mantua, the strongly marked unifying architectural framework in the Sistine Chapel does not produce "picture windows" enframing illusions just within. Rather, the viewer focuses on figure after figure, each sharply outlined against the neutral tone of the architectural setting or the plain background of the panels. Here, as in his sculpture, Michelangelo relentlessly concentrated his expressive purpose on the human figure. To him, the body was beautiful not only in its natural form but also in its spiritual and philosophical significance. The body was the manifestation of the soul or of a state of mind and character. Michelangelo represented the body in its most simple, elemental aspect—in the nude or simply draped, with no background and no ornamental embellishment. He always painted with a sculptor's eye for how light and shadow communicate volume and surface. It is no coincidence that many of the figures seem to be tinted reliefs or freestanding statues.

CREATION OF ADAM One of the ceiling's central panels is *Creation of Adam* (FIG. 17-19). Michelangelo did not paint the traditional representation but instead produced a bold humanistic interpretation of the momentous event. God and Adam confront each other in a primordial unformed landscape of which Adam is still a material part, heavy as earth. The Lord transcends the earth, wrapped in a billowing cloud of drapery and borne up by his powers. Life leaps to Adam as if a spark flashed from the extended, mighty hand of God. The communication between gods and heroes, so familiar in classical myth, is here concrete. This blunt depiction of the Lord as ruler of Heaven in the Olympian pagan sense indicates how easily High Renaissance thought joined classical and Christian traditions. Yet the classical trappings do not obscure the essential Christian message.

Beneath the Lord's sheltering left arm is a female figure, apprehensively curious but as yet uncreated. Scholars traditionally believed her to represent Eve, but many now think she is the Virgin Mary (with the Christ Child at her knee). If the second identification is correct, it suggests that Michelangelo incorporated into his fresco one of the essential tenets of Christian faith—the belief that Adam's Original Sin eventually led to the sacrifice of Christ, which in turn made possible the redemption of all humankind.

As God reaches out to Adam, the viewer's eye follows the motion from right to left, but Adam's extended left arm leads the eye back to the right, along the Lord's right arm, shoulders, and left arm to his left forefinger, which points to the Christ Child's face. The focal point of this right-to-left-to-right movement—the fingertips of Adam and the Lord—is dramatically off-center. Michelangelo replaced the straight architectural axes found in Leonardo's compositions with curves and diagonals. For example, the bodies of the two great figures are complementary—the concave body of Adam fitting the convex body and billowing "cloak" of God. Thus, motion directs

Restoring Renaissance Paintings

The year 1989 marked the culmination of a 12-year project to clean the Sistine Chapel ceiling (FIG. 17-1). Cleaning of Michelangelo's *Last Judgment* (FIG. 17-21) behind the altar followed during the next five years. Restorers removed centuries of accumulated grime, overpainting, and protective glue, uncovering much of Michelangelo's original form, color, style, and procedure.

The before-and-after details (FIG. 17-20) of one of the lunettes over the windows reveal the stark contrast in the appearance of the frescoes in 1977 and today. In these semicircular spaces, Michelangelo painted figures representing the ancestors of Christ (Matt. 1:1–17). After computer assessment of the damage (including use of infrared and ultraviolet lights), the restorers worked carefully and slowly to clean the fresco of soot, dirt, dissolved salts, and various types of gums and varnishes made of animal glues. Over the centuries, restorers had used various varnishes to brighten the darkening fresco. Unfortunately, over time the varnishes deteriorated, darkening the painting even more. For the latest cleaning effort, the restorers first wet a small section of the fresco with distilled, deionized water. The application of a cleaning solution made of bicarbonates of sodium and ammonium and supplemented with an antibacterial, antifungal agent followed. Adding carboxymethyl cellulose and water to this solution created a gel that clung to the ceiling fresco. After three minutes, restorers removed the gel.

Michelangelo's figures, once thought purposefully dark, now show brilliant colors of high intensity, brushed on with an astonishing freedom and verve. The fresh, luminous hues, boldly joined in unexpected harmonies, seemed uncharacteristically dissonant to some experts when first revealed and aroused brisk controversy. Some scholars believed that the restorers removed Michelangelo's

work along with the accumulated layers and that the apparently strident coloration could not possibly be his. Most art historians, however, now agree that the restoration effort has revealed to modern eyes the artist's real intentions and effects—and that in the Sistine Chapel, Michelangelo already had paved the way for the Mannerist reaction to the High Renaissance, examined later in this chapter.

The restoration of Leonardo's *Last Supper* (FIG. 17-4), which took more than two decades, presented conservators with an even greater challenge. Leonardo had mixed oil and tempera, applying much of it *a secco* (to dried, rather than wet, plaster) in order to create a mural that more closely approximated oil painting on canvas or wood instead of fresco. But because the wall did not absorb the pigment as in the *buon fresco* technique, the paint quickly began to flake (see "Fresco Painting," Chapter 14, page 382). Milan's humidity further accelerated the deterioration. Restoration efforts, completed in May 1999, were painstaking and slow, as were those in the Sistine Chapel, and involved extensive scholarly, chemical, and computer analysis. Like other restorations, this one was not without controversy. One scholar has claimed that 80 percent of what is visible today is the work of the modern restorers, not Leonardo. The controversies surrounding the cleanings of the Sistine Chapel ceiling and Santa Maria delle Grazie have not put a damper on other restoration projects. After the cleaning of *Last Judgment*, the Vatican continued the restoration of the remaining frescoes in the Sistine Chapel (FIG. 17-18), including Perugino's *Christ Delivering the Keys of the Kingdom to Saint Peter* (FIG. 16-40), completing the project in December 1999. Restorers have also cleaned the frescoes in the Stanza della Segnatura in the Vatican Apartments in Rome, including Raphael's *School of Athens* (FIG. 17-9).

17-20 Detail of the Azor-Sadoch lunette over one of the Sistine Chapel windows (FIG. 17-18) at the beginning (*left*) and final stage (*right*) of the restoration process.

The 1977–1989 restoration of the frescoes on the Sistine Chapel ceiling removed centuries of accumulated grime and revealed the original bright and luminous colors of Michelangelo's figures.

not only the figures but also the whole composition. The reclining positions of the figures, the heavy musculature, and the twisting poses are all intrinsic parts of Michelangelo's style.

The photographs of the Sistine Chapel reproduced here record the appearance of Michelangelo's frescoes after the completion of a 12-year cleaning project (1977–1989). The painstaking restoration

(FIG. 17-20) elicited considerable controversy because it revealed vivid colors that initially shocked art historians, producing accusations that the restorers were destroying Michelangelo's masterpieces (see "Restoring Renaissance Paintings," above). That reaction, however, was largely attributable to the fact that for centuries no one had ever seen Michelangelo's frescoes except covered with soot and grime.

Religious Art in Counter-Reformation Italy

Both Catholics and Protestants took seriously the role of devotional imagery in religious life. However, their views differed dramatically. Whereas Catholics deemed art as valuable for cultivating piety, Protestants believed visual imagery could produce idolatry and could distract the faithful from their goal—developing a personal relationship with God (see "Protestantism and Iconoclasm," Chapter 18, page 510). As part of the Counter-Reformation effort, Pope Paul III convened the Council of Trent in 1545 to review controversial Church doctrines. At its conclusion in 1563, the Council issued the following edict:

> The holy council commands all bishops and others who hold the office of teaching and have charge of the *cura animarum* [literally, "cure of souls"—the responsibility of laboring for the salvation of souls], that in accordance with the usage of the Catholic and Apostolic Church, received from the primitive times of the Christian religion, and with the unanimous teaching of the holy Fathers and the decrees of sacred councils, they above all instruct the faithful diligently in matters relating to intercession and invocation of the saints, the veneration of relics, and the legitimate use of images. . . . Moreover, that the images of Christ, of the Virgin Mother of God, and of the other saints are to be placed and retained especially in the churches, and that due honor and veneration is to be given them; . . . because the honor which is shown them is referred to the prototypes which they represent, so that by means of the images which we kiss and before which we uncover the head and prostrate ourselves, we adore Christ and venerate the saints whose likeness they bear. That is what was defined by the decrees of the councils, especially of the Second Council of Nicaea, against the opponents of images.
>
> Moreover, let the bishops diligently teach that by means of the stories of the mysteries of our redemption portrayed in paintings and other representations the people are instructed and confirmed in the articles of faith, which ought to be borne in mind and constantly reflected upon; also that great profit is derived from all holy images, not only because the people are thereby reminded of the benefits and gifts bestowed on them by Christ, but also because through the saints the miracles of God and salutary examples are set before the eyes of the faithful, so that they may give God thanks for those things, may fashion their own life and conduct in imitation of the saints and be moved to adore and love God and cultivate piety. . . .
>
> That these things may be the more faithfully observed, the holy council decrees that no one is permitted to erect or cause to be erected in any place or church, howsoever exempt, any unusual image unless it has been approved by the bishop.*

* *Canons and Decrees of the Council of Trent,* December 3–4, 1563, in Robert Klein and Henri Zerner, *Italian Art 1500–1600: Sources and Documents* (Evanston, Ill.: Northwestern University Press, 1966), 120–121.

THE COUNTER-REFORMATION Paul III (r. 1534–1549) succeeded Clement VII as pope in 1534 at a time of widespread dissatisfaction with the leadership and policies of the Roman Catholic Church. Led by clerics such as Martin Luther (1483–1546) and John Calvin (1509–1564) in the Holy Roman Empire, early-16th-century reformers directly challenged papal authority, especially regarding secular issues. Disgruntled Catholics voiced concerns about the sale of *indulgences* (pardons for sins, reducing the time a soul spent in Purgatory), about nepotism (the appointment of relatives to important positions), and about how high Church officials were pursuing personal wealth. This Reformation movement resulted in the establishment of Protestantism, with sects such as Lutheranism and Calvinism (see Chapter 18). Central to Protestantism was a belief in personal faith rather than adherence to decreed Church practices and doctrines. Because the Protestants believed that the only true religious relationship was the personal relationship between an individual and God, they were, in essence, eliminating the need for Church intercession, which is central to Catholicism.

The Catholic Church, in response, mounted a full-fledged campaign to counteract the defection of its members to Protestantism. Led by Paul III, this response, the Counter-Reformation, consisted of numerous initiatives. The Council of Trent, which met intermittently from 1545 through 1563, was a major element of this effort. Composed of cardinals, archbishops, bishops, abbots, and theologians, the Council of Trent dealt with issues of Church doctrine, including many the Protestants contested. Many papal commissions during this period can be viewed as an integral part of the Counter-Reformation effort. Popes long had been aware of the power of visual imagery to construct and reinforce ideological claims, and 16th-century popes exploited this capability (see "Religious Art in Counter-Reformation Italy," above).

LAST JUDGMENT Among Paul III's first papal commissions was an enormous (48 feet tall) fresco for the Sistine Chapel. Michelangelo agreed to paint the *Last Judgment* fresco (FIG. **17-21**) on the chapel's altar wall. Here, the artist depicted Christ as the stern judge of the world—a giant who raises his mighty right arm in a gesture of damnation so broad and universal as to suggest he will destroy all creation. The choirs of Heaven surrounding him pulse with anxiety and awe. Crowded into the space below are trumpeting angels, the ascending figures of the just, and the downward-hurtling figures of the damned. On the left, the dead awake and assume flesh. On the right, demons, whose gargoyle masks and burning eyes revive the demons of Romanesque tympana (FIG. I-6), torment the damned.

Michelangelo's terrifying vision of the fate that awaits sinners goes far beyond even Signorelli's gruesome images (FIG. **16-41**). Martyrs who suffered especially agonizing deaths crouch below the Judge. One of them, Saint Bartholomew, who was skinned alive, holds the flaying knife and the skin, its face a grotesque self-portrait of Michelangelo. The figures are huge and violently twisted, with small heads and contorted features. Although this immense fresco impresses on viewers Christ's wrath on Judgment Day, it also holds out hope. A group of saved souls—the elect—crowd around Christ, and on the far right appears a figure with a cross, most likely the Good Thief (crucified with Christ) or a saint martyred by crucifixion, such as Saint Andrew.

17-21 Michelangelo Buonarroti, *Last Judgment*, altar wall of the Sistine Chapel (FIG. 17-18), Vatican City, Rome, Italy, 1536–1541. Fresco, 48′ × 44′.

Michelangelo completed his fresco cycle in the Sistine Chapel with this terrifying vision of the fate that awaits sinners. Near the center, he placed his own portrait on the flayed skin Saint Bartholomew holds.

10 ft.

Architecture: Rome

The Sistine Chapel was but a small part of the vast Vatican palace complex on the west side of the Tiber River (MAPS **17-1** and **19-1**), construction of which began under Constantine with the erection of a church over the site of Saint Peter's burial place (Old Saint Peter's, FIG. 8-9). By the 15th century, it was obvious that the millennium-old basilica was insufficient for the needs and aspirations of the Renaissance papacy. Rebuilding the fourth-century church would occupy some of the leading architects of Italy for more than a century.

BRAMANTE The first in the distinguished line of architects of the new Saint Peter's was DONATO D'ANGELO BRAMANTE (1444–1514). Born in Urbino and trained as a painter (perhaps by Piero della Francesca), Bramante went to Milan in 1481 and, like Leonardo, stayed there until the French arrived in 1499. In Milan, he abandoned painting to become one of his generation's most renowned architects. Under the influence of Filippo Brunelleschi, Leon Battista Alberti, and perhaps Leonardo, all of whom strongly favored the art and architecture of classical antiquity, Bramante developed the High Renaissance form of the central-plan church.

TEMPIETTO The architectural style Bramante championed was, consistent with the humanistic values of the day, based on ancient Roman models. This style is on display in the small architectural gem known as the Tempietto (FIG. **17-22**) on the Janiculum hill overlooking the Vatican. The building received its name because, to contemporaries, it had the look of a small ancient temple. "Little Temple" is, in fact, a perfect nickname for the structure, because the round temples of Roman Italy (FIG. 7-4) directly inspired Bramante's design. King Ferdinand and Queen Isabella of Spain commissioned the Tempietto to mark the presumed location of Saint Peter's crucifixion. The patrons asked Bramante to undertake the project in 1502, but work may not have commenced until the end of the decade. Today the Tempietto stands inside the rectangular cloister alongside the church of San Pietro in Montorio, but Bramante planned, although never executed, a circular colonnaded courtyard

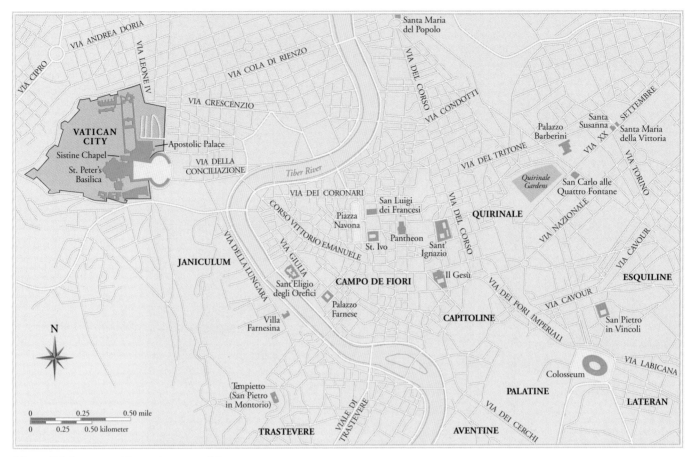

MAP 17-1 Rome with Renaissance and Baroque monuments.

to frame the "temple." His intent was to coordinate the Tempietto and its surrounding portico by aligning the columns of the two structures.

At first glance, the Tempietto (FIG. 17-22) may seem severely rational with its sober circular *stylobate* (stepped temple platform) and the austere *Tuscan* style of the *colonnade*, neither feature giving any indication of the placement of an interior altar or of the entrance. However, Bramante achieved a truly wonderful balance and harmony in the relationship of the parts (dome, drum, and base) to one another and to the whole. Conceived as a tall, domed cylinder projecting from the lower, wider cylinder of its colonnade, this small building incorporates all the qualities of a sculptured monument. Bramante's sculptural eye is most evident in the rhythmical play of light and shadow seen around the columns and balustrade and across the deep-set rectangular windows alternating with shallow shell-capped niches in the *cella* (central room of a temple), walls, and drum. Although the Tempietto, superficially at least, may resemble a Greek *tholos* (a circular shrine; FIG. 5-72), and although antique models provided the inspiration for all its details, the combination of parts and details was new and original. (Classical tholoi, for instance, had neither drum nor balustrade.)

17-22 DONATO D'ANGELO BRAMANTE, Tempietto, San Pietro in Montorio, Rome, Italy, 1502(?).

Contemporaries celebrated Bramante as the first to revive the classical style in architecture. Roman round temples (FIG. 7-4) inspired this "little temple," but Bramante combined the classical parts in new ways.

One of the main differences between the Early and High Renaissance styles of architecture is the former's emphasis on detailing flat wall surfaces versus the latter's sculptural handling of architectural masses. Bramante's Tempietto initiated the High Renaissance era. Andrea Palladio, a brilliant theorist as well as a major later 16th-century architect (FIGS. 17-29 and 17-32), included the Tempietto in his survey of ancient temples because Bramante was "the first to bring back to light the good and beautiful architecture that from antiquity to that time had been hidden."[7] Round in plan and elevated on a base that isolates it from its surroundings, the Tempietto conforms to Alberti's and Palladio's strictest demands for an ideal church.

NEW SAINT PETER'S As noted, Bramante was the architect Julius II selected to design a replacement for the Constantinian basilican church of Old Saint Peter's (FIG. 8-9). The earlier building had fallen into considerable disrepair and, in any event, did not suit this ambitious pope's taste for the colossal. Julius wanted to gain control over the whole of Italy and to make the Rome of the popes reminiscent of (if not more splendid than) the Rome of the caesars. As the symbolic seat of the papacy, Saint Peter's represented the history of the Church.

Bramante originally designed the new Saint Peter's (FIG. 17-23) to consist of a cross with arms of equal length, each terminating in an apse. Julius II intended the new building to serve as a *martyrium* to mark Saint Peter's grave and also hoped to have his own tomb in it. A large dome would have covered the crossing, and smaller domes over subsidiary chapels would have covered the diagonal axes of the roughly square plan. Thus, Bramante's ambitious design called for a boldly sculptural treatment of the walls and piers under the dome. His organization of the interior space was complex in the extreme, with the intricate symmetries of a crystal. It is possible to detect in the plan some nine interlocking crosses, five of them supporting domes. The scale was titanic. According to sources, Bramante boasted he would place the dome of the Pantheon (FIGS. 7-49 to 7-51) over the Basilica Nova (FIG. 7-78).

A commemorative medal (FIG. 17-24) by CRISTOFORO FOPPA CARADOSSO (ca. 1452–1526) shows how Bramante's scheme would have attempted to do just that. The dome is hemispherical, as is that of the Pantheon, but the massive unity of that building is broken up here by two towers and a medley of domes and porticos. In light of Julius II's interest in the Roman Empire, using the Pantheon as a model was entirely appropriate. That Bramante's design for the new Saint Peter's was commemorated on a medal is in itself significant. Such medals proliferated in the 15th century, reviving the ancient Roman practice of placing images of important imperial building projects on the reverses of Roman coins and portraits of the emperors who commissioned them on the coins' fronts. Julius II appears on the front of the Caradosso medal.

During Bramante's lifetime, the actual construction of the new Saint Peter's did not advance beyond the building of the crossing piers and the lower choir walls. After his death, the work passed from one architect to another and, in 1546, to Michelangelo. With the Church facing challenges to its supremacy, Pope Paul III surely felt a sense of urgency about the completion of this project. Michelangelo's work on Saint Peter's became a long-term show of dedication, thankless and without pay. Among Michelangelo's difficulties was his struggle to preserve and carry through Bramante's original plan

0   50   100 feet
0   15   30 meters
N

17-23 DONATO D'ANGELO BRAMANTE, plan for the new Saint Peter's, the Vatican, Rome, Italy, 1505. (1) dome, (2) apse.

Bramante's design for the new church to replace the Constantinian basilica of Saint Peter's (FIG. 8-9) featured a central plan consisting of a cross with arms of equal length, each terminating in an apse.

1 in.

17-24 CRISTOFORO FOPPA CARADOSSO, medal showing Bramante's design for the new Saint Peter's, 1506. Bronze, $2\frac{1}{4}''$ diameter. British Museum, London.

Bramante's unexecuted 1506 design for Saint Peter's called for a large dome over the crossing, smaller domes over the subsidiary chapels, and a boldly sculptural treatment of the walls and piers.

17-25 Michelangelo Buonarroti, plan for Saint Peter's, Vatican City, Rome, Italy, 1546. (1) dome, (2) apse, (3) portico.

In his modification of Bramante's plan (FIG. 17-23), Michelangelo reduced the central component from a number of interlocking crosses to a compact domed Greek cross inscribed in a square.

(FIG. 17-23), which he praised and chose to retain as the basis for his own design (FIG. 17-25). Michelangelo shared Bramante's conviction that a central plan was the ideal form for a church. Always a sculptor first and foremost, Michelangelo carried his obsession with human form over to architecture and reasoned that buildings should follow the form of the human body. This meant organizing their units symmetrically around a central and unique axis, as the arms relate to the body or the eyes to the nose. "For it is an established fact," he wrote, "that the members of architecture resemble the members of man. Whoever neither has been nor is a master at figures, and especially at anatomy, cannot really understand architecture."[8]

In his modification of Bramante's plan, Michelangelo reduced the central component from a number of interlocking crosses to a compact domed *Greek cross* inscribed in a square and fronted with a double-columned portico. Without destroying the centralizing features of Bramante's plan, Michelangelo, with a few strokes of the pen, converted its snowflake complexity into massive, cohesive unity. His treatment of the building's exterior further reveals his interest in creating a unified and cohesive design. Because of later changes to the front of the church, the west (apse) end (FIG. 17-26) offers the best view of his style and intention. Michelangelo's design incorporated the colossal order, the two-story pilasters first seen in more reserved fashion in Alberti's Mantuan church of Sant'Andrea (FIG. 16-44). The giant pilasters seem to march around the undulating wall surfaces, confining the movement without interrupting it. The architectural sculpturing here extends up from the ground through the attic stories and into the *drum* and the dome (FIG. 19-4), unifying the whole building from base to summit. Baroque architects later learned much from this kind of integral design, which Michelangelo based on his conviction that architecture is one with the organic beauty of the human form.

The domed west end—as majestic as it is today and as influential as it has been on architecture throughout the centuries—is not quite as Michelangelo intended it. Originally, he had planned a dome with an ogival section, like that of Florence Cathedral (FIG. 14-18). But in his final version he decided on a hemispherical dome to temper the verticality of the design of the lower stories and to establish a balance between dynamic and static elements. However, when Giacomo della Porta (ca. 1533–1602) executed the dome (FIG. 19-4) after Michelangelo's death, he restored the earlier high design, ignoring Michelangelo's later version. Giacomo's reasons were probably the same ones that had impelled Brunelleschi to use an ogival section for his Florentine dome—greater stability and ease of construction. The result is that the dome seems to rise from its base, rather than rest firmly on it—an effect Michelangelo might not have approved. Nevertheless, Saint Peter's dome is probably the most impressive in the world.

17-26 Michelangelo Buonarroti, Saint Peter's (looking northeast), Vatican City, Rome, Italy, 1546–1564. Dome completed by Giacomo della Porta, 1590.

The west end of Saint Peter's offers the best view of Michelangelo's intentions. The giant pilasters of his colossal order march around the undulating wall surfaces of the central-plan building.

PALAZZO FARNESE Another architectural project Michelangelo took over at the request of Paul III was the construction of the lavish private palace the pope had commissioned when he was still Cardinal Alessandro Farnese. The future pope had selected Antonio da Sangallo the Younger (1483–1546) to design the Palazzo Farnese (FIG. 17-27) in Rome. (At Antonio's death in 1546, Michelangelo assumed control of the building's completion.) Antonio, the youngest of a family of architects, went to Rome around 1503 and became Bramante's draftsman and assistant. He is the perfect example of the professional architect. Indeed, his family constituted an architectural firm, often planning and drafting for other architects.

The broad, majestic front of the Palazzo Farnese asserts to the public the exalted station of a great family. This impressive facade encapsulates the aristocratic epoch that followed the stifling of the nascent middle-class democracy of European cities (especially the Italian cities) by powerful rulers heading centralized states. It is thus significant that Paul chose to enlarge greatly the original rather modest palace to its present form after his accession to the papacy in 1534, reflecting his ambitions both for his family and for the papacy. Facing a spacious paved square, the facade is the very essence of princely dignity in architecture. The *quoins* (rusticated building corners) and cornice firmly anchor the rectangle of the smooth front,

and lines of windows (the central row with alternating triangular and segmental pediments, in Bramante's fashion) mark a majestic beat across it. The window frames are not flush with the wall, as in the Palazzo Medici-Riccardi (FIG. 16-36), but project from its surface, so instead of being a flat, thin plane, the facade is a spatially active three-dimensional mass. The rusticated doorway and second-story balcony, surmounted by the Farnese coat of arms, emphasize the central axis and bring the design's horizontal and vertical forces into harmony. This centralizing feature, absent from the palaces of Michelozzo (FIG. 16-36) and Alberti (FIG. 16-38), is the external opening of a central corridor axis that runs through the entire building and continues in the garden beyond. Around this axis, Antonio arranged the rooms with strict regularity.

The interior courtyard (FIG. 17-28) displays stately column-enframed arches on the first two levels, as in the Roman Colosseum (FIG. 7-1). On the third level, Michelangelo incorporated his sophisticated variation on that theme (based in part on the Colosseum's fourth-story Corinthian pilasters), with overlapping pilasters replacing the weighty columns of Antonio's design. The Palazzo Farnese set the standard for Italian Renaissance palaces and fully expresses the classical order, regularity, simplicity, and dignity of the High Renaissance.

17-29 Andrea Palladio, Villa Rotonda (formerly Villa Capra), near Vicenza, Italy, ca. 1550–1570.

Andrea Palladio's Villa Rotonda has four identical facades, each one resembling a Roman temple with a columnar porch. In the center is a great dome-covered rotunda modeled on the Pantheon (FIG. 7-49).

Architecture: Venice

Venice long had been a major Mediterranean coastal port and served as the gateway to the Orient. Reaching the height of its commercial and political power during the 15th century, the city saw its fortunes decline in the 16th century. Even so, Venice and the Papal States were the only Italian sovereignties to retain their independence during the century of strife. Either France or Spain dominated all others. Although the discoveries in the New World and the economic shift from Italy to areas such as the Netherlands were largely responsible for the decline of Venice, even more immediate and pressing events drained its wealth and power. After their conquest of Constantinople, the Turks began to vie with the Venetians for control of the eastern Mediterranean. The Ottoman Empire evolved into a constant threat to Venice. Early in the century, the European powers of the League of Cambrai also attacked the Italian port city. Formed and led by Pope Julius II, who coveted Venetian holdings on Italy's mainland, the league included Spain, France, and the Holy Roman Empire, in addition to the Papal States. Despite these challenges, Venice developed a flourishing, independent, and influential school of artists.

ANDREA PALLADIO The chief architect of the Venetian Republic from 1570 until his death a decade later was Andrea di Pietro, known as ANDREA PALLADIO (1508–1580). (The surname derives from Pallas Athena, Greek goddess of wisdom, an appropriate reference for an architect schooled in the classical tradition of Alberti and Bramante.) Palladio began his career as a stonemason and decorative sculptor in Vicenza, but at age 30 he turned to architecture, the ancient literature on architecture, engineering, topography, and military science. In order to study the ancient buildings firsthand, Palladio made several trips to Rome. In 1556 he illustrated Daniele Barbaro's edition of Vitruvius's *De architectura* and later wrote his own treatise on architecture, *I quattro libri dell'architettura* (*The Four Books of Architecture*), originally published in 1570. That work had a wide-ranging influence on succeeding generations of architects throughout Europe. Palladio's influence outside Italy, most significantly in England and in colonial America (see Chapter 21), was stronger and more lasting than that of any other architect.

Palladio accrued his significant reputation from his many designs for villas, built on the Venetian mainland. Nineteen still stand, and they especially influenced later architects. The same spirit that prompted the

17-30 Andrea Palladio, plan of the Villa Rotonda (formerly Villa Capra), near Vicenza, Italy, ca. 1550–1570. (1) dome, (2) porch.

Palladio published an influential treatise on architecture in 1570. Consistent with his design theories, all the parts of the Villa Rotonda relate to one another in terms of calculated mathematical ratios.

ancient Romans to build villas in the countryside motivated a similar villa-building boom in 16th-century Venice, which, with its very limited space, was highly congested. But a longing for the countryside was not the only motive. Declining fortunes prompted the Venetians to develop their mainland possessions with new land investment and reclamation projects. Citizens who could afford it set themselves up as aristocratic farmers and developed swamps into productive agricultural land. Wealthy families could look on their villas as providential investments. The villas were thus aristocratic farms surrounded by service outbuildings (like the much later American plantations, which emulated many aspects of Palladio's architectural style). Palladio generally arranged the outbuildings in long, low wings branching out from the main building and enclosing a large rectangular court area.

VILLA ROTONDA Palladio's most famous villa, Villa Rotonda (FIG. 17-29), near Vicenza, is exceptional because the architect did not build it for an aspiring gentleman farmer but for a retired monsignor who wanted a villa for social events. Palladio planned and designed Villa Rotonda, located on a hilltop, as a kind of *belvedere* (literally "beautiful view"; in architecture, a structure with a view of the countryside or the sea), without the usual wings of secondary buildings. It has a central plan (FIG. 17-30) with four identical facades and projecting porches oriented to the four compass points. Each facade of the Villa Rotonda resembles a Roman Ionic temple. In placing a traditional temple porch in front of a dome-covered interior, Palladio doubtless had the Pantheon (FIG. 7-49) in mind as a model. But, as Bramante did in his Tempietto (FIG. 17-22), Palladio transformed his model into a new design that has no parallel in antiquity. Each of the villa's four porches can be used as a platform for enjoying a different

view of the surrounding landscape. In this design, the central dome-covered rotunda logically functions as a kind of circular platform from which visitors may turn in any direction for the preferred view. The result is a building with functional parts systematically related to one another in terms of calculated mathematical relationships. Villa Rotonda embodies all the qualities of self-sufficiency and formal completeness most Renaissance architects sought.

SAN GIORGIO MAGGIORE One of the most dramatically placed buildings in Venice is San Giorgio Maggiore (FIG. 17-31), directly across the Grand Canal from Piazza San Marco. Dissatisfied with earlier solutions to the problem of integrating a high central nave and lower aisles into a unified facade design, Palladio solved it by superimposing a tall and narrow classical porch on a low broad one. This solution reflects the building's interior arrangement (FIG. 17-32) and in that sense is strictly logical, but the intersection of two temple facades is irrational and ambiguous, consistent with contemporaneous developments in Mannerist architecture, discussed

17-31 ANDREA PALLADIO, aerial view of San Giorgio Maggiore, Venice, Italy, begun 1566.

Dissatisfied with earlier solutions to the problem of integrating a high central nave and lower aisles into a unified facade, Palladio superimposed a tall and narrow classical porch on a low broad one.

17-32 ANDREA PALLADIO, interior of San Giorgio Maggiore, Venice, Italy, begun 1566.

In contrast to the somewhat irrational intersection of two temple facades on the exterior of San Giorgio Maggiore, Palladio's interior is strictly logical, consistent with classical architectural theory.

later. Palladio's design also created the illusion of three-dimensional depth, an effect intensified by the strong projection of the central columns and the shadows they cast. The play of shadow across the building's surfaces, its reflection in the water, and its gleaming white against sea and sky create a remarkably colorful effect. The interior of the church lacks the ambiguity of the facade and exhibits strong roots in High Renaissance architectural style. Light floods the interior and crisply defines the contours of the rich wall decorations, all beautifully and "correctly" profiled—the exemplar of what classical architectural theory meant by "rational" organization.

Venetian Painting

In the 16th century the Venetians developed a distinctive painting style. Artists in the maritime republic showed a special interest in recording the effect of Venice's soft-colored light on figures and landscapes, and Venetian paintings of the High and Late Renaissance are easy to distinguish from contemporaneous works in Florence and Rome.

GIOVANNI BELLINI One artist who contributed significantly to creating the High Renaissance painting style in Venice was GIOVANNI BELLINI (ca. 1430–1516). Trained in the International Style (see Chapter 14) by his father Jacopo, a student of Gentile da Fabriano, Bellini worked in the family shop and did not develop his own style until after his father's death in 1470. His early independent works show the dominant influence of his brother-in-law Andrea Mantegna. But in the late 1470s, he came into contact with the work of the Sicilian-born painter Antonello da Messina (ca. 1430–1479). Antonello received his early training in Naples, where he must have become familiar with Flemish painting and mastered using mixed oil (see "Tempera and Oil Painting," Chapter 15, page 401). This more flexible medium is wider in coloristic range than either tempera or fresco. Antonello arrived in Venice in 1475 and during his two-year stay introduced his Venetian colleagues to the possibilities the new oil technique offered. As a direct result of contact with Antonello, Bellini abandoned Mantegna's harsh linear style and developed a sensuous coloristic manner that was to characterize Venetian painting for a century.

SAN ZACCARIA ALTARPIECE Bellini earned great recognition for his many Madonnas, which he painted both in half-length (with or without accompanying saints) on small devotional panels and in full-length on large, monumental altarpieces of the *sacra conversazione* (holy conversation) type. In the sacra conversazione, which gained great popularity as a theme for religious paintings from the middle of the 15th century on, saints from different epochs occupy the same space and seem to converse either with each other or with the audience. (Raphael employed much the same conceit in his *School of Athens*, FIG. 17-9, where he gathered Greek philosophers of different eras.) Bellini carried on the tradition in one of his earliest major commissions, the *San Zaccaria Altarpiece* (FIG. **17-33**). As was conventional, the Virgin Mary sits enthroned, holding the Christ Child, with saints flanking her. Bellini placed the group in a carefully painted shrine. Attributes aid the identification of all the saints: Saint Lucy holding a tray with her plucked-out eyes displayed on it; Saint Peter with his key and book; Saint Catherine with the palm of martyrdom and the broken wheel; and Saint Jerome with a book (representing his translation of the Bible into Latin). At the foot of the throne sits an angel playing a viol. The painting radiates a feeling of serenity and spiritual calm. Viewers derive this sense less from the figures (no interaction occurs among them) than from Bellini's harmonious and balanced presentation of color and light. Line is not the chief agent of form, as it generally is in paintings produced in Rome and Florence. Indeed, outlines dissolve in light and shadow. Glowing color produces a soft radiance that envelops the forms with an atmospheric haze and enhances their majestic serenity.

17-33 GIOVANNI BELLINI, *San Zaccaria Altarpiece*, 1505. Oil on wood transferred to canvas, 16′ 5½″ × 7′ 9″. San Zaccaria, Venice.

In this *sacra conversazione* uniting saints from different eras, Bellini created a feeling of serenity and spiritual calm through the harmonious and balanced presentation of color and light.

1 ft.

17-34 GIOVANNI BELLINI and TITIAN, *Feast of the Gods,* from the Camerino d'Alabastro, Palazzo Ducale, Ferrara, Italy, 1529. Oil on canvas, 5′ 7″ × 6′ 2″. National Gallery of Art, Washington, D.C. (Widener Collection).

In *Feast of the Gods,* based on Ovid's *Fasti,* Bellini developed a new kind of mythological painting in which the Olympian deities appear as peasants enjoying a picnic in the soft afternoon light.

FEAST OF THE GODS In painting *Feast of the Gods* (FIG. 17-34), Bellini drew from the work of one of his students, Giorgione da Castelfranco (discussed next), who developed his master's landscape backgrounds into poetic Arcadian reveries. Derived from Arcadia, a region in southern Greece, the term *Arcadian* referred, by the time of the Renaissance, to an idyllic place of rural, rustic peace and simplicity. After Giorgione's premature death, Bellini embraced his student's interests and, in *Feast of the Gods,* developed a new kind of mythological painting. The duke of Ferrara, Alfonso d'Este, commissioned this work for a room in the Palazzo Ducale. Although Bellini drew some of the figures from the standard repertoire of Greco-Roman art—most notably, the nymph carrying a vase on her head and the sleeping nymph in the lower right corner—the Olympian gods appear as peasants enjoying a picnic in a shady glade. Bellini's source was Ovid's *Fasti,* which describes a banquet of the gods. The artist spread the figures across the foreground. Satyrs attend the gods, nymphs bring jugs of wine, a child draws from a keg, couples engage in love play, and the sleeping nymph with exposed breast receives amorous attention. The mellow light of a long afternoon glows softly around the gathering, caressing the surfaces of colorful fabrics, smooth flesh, and polished metal. Here, Bellini communicated the delight the Venetian school took in the beauty of texture revealed by the full resources of gently and subtly harmonized color. Behind the warm, lush tones of the figures, a background of cool green tree-filled glades extends into the distance. At the right, a screen of trees creates a verdant shelter. The atmosphere is idyllic, a lush countryside providing a setting for the never-ending pleasure of the immortal gods.

With Bellini, Venetian art became the great complement of the schools of Florence and Rome. The Venetians' instrument was color, that of the Florentines and Romans sculpturesque form. Scholars often distill the contrast between these two approaches down to *colorito* (colored or painted) versus *disegno* (drawing and design). Whereas most central Italian artists emphasized careful design preparation based on preliminary drawing (see "Renaissance Drawings," page 459), Venetian artists focused on color and the process of paint application. In addition, the general thematic focus of their work differed. Venetian artists painted the poetry of the senses and delighted in nature's beauty and the pleasures of humanity. Artists in Florence and

17-35 GIORGIONE DA CASTELFRANCO (and/or TITIAN), *Pastoral Symphony,* ca. 1508–1510. Oil on canvas, 3′ 7$\frac{1}{4}$″ × 4′ 6$\frac{1}{4}$″. Louvre, Paris.

Venetian art is often described as poetic. In this painting, Giorgione so eloquently evoked the pastoral mood that the uncertainty about the picture's meaning is not distressing. The mood and rich color are enough.

1 ft.

17-36 GIORGIONE DA CASTELFRANCO, *The Tempest,* ca. 1510. Oil on canvas, 2′ 8$\frac{1}{4}$″ × 2′ 4$\frac{3}{4}$″. Galleria dell'Accademia, Venice.

The subject of this painting set in a lush landscape beneath a stormy sky has never been identified. The uncertainty contributes to the painting's enigmatic quality and intriguing air and may have been intentional.

1 ft.

Rome gravitated toward more intellectual themes—the epic of humanity, the masculine virtues, the grandeur of the ideal, and the lofty conceptions of religion involving the heroic and sublime. Much of the history of later Western art involves a dialogue between these two traditions.

Describing Venetian art as "poetic" is particularly appropriate, given the development of *poesia*, or painting meant to evoke moods in a manner similar to poetry. Both classical and Renaissance poetry inspired Venetian artists, and their paintings focused on the lyrical and sensual. Thus, in many Venetian artworks, discerning concrete narratives or subjects (in the traditional sense) is virtually impossible.

GIORGIONE The Venetian artist who deserves much of the credit for developing this poetic manner of painting was GIORGIONE DA CASTELFRANCO (ca. 1477–1510). Giorgione's so-called *Pastoral Symphony* (FIG. 17-35; many scholars believe it is an early work of his student Titian) exemplifies poesia and surely inspired the late Arcadian scenes by Bellini, his teacher. Out of dense shadow emerge the soft forms of figures and landscape. Giorgione cast a mood of tranquil reverie and dreaminess over the entire scene, evoking the landscape of a lost but never-forgotten paradise. The theme is as enigmatic as the lighting. Two nude women, accompanied by two clothed young men, occupy the rich, abundant landscape through which a shepherd passes. In the distance, a villa crowns a hill. The artist so eloquently evoked the pastoral mood that the viewer does not find the uncertainty about the picture's precise meaning distressing. The mood is enough. The shepherd symbolizes the poet. The pipes and lute symbolize his poetry. The two women accompanying the young men may be thought of as their invisible inspiration, their muses. One turns to lift water from the sacred well of poetic inspiration. The voluptuous bodies of the women, softly modulated by the smoky shadow, became the standard in Venetian art. The fullness of their figures contributes to their effect as poetic personifications of nature's abundance. As a pastoral poet in the pictorial medium and one of the greatest masters in the handling of light and color, Giorgione praised the beauty of nature, music, women, and pleasure. Vasari reported that Giorgione was an accomplished lutenist and singer, and adjectives from poetry and music seem well suited for describing the pastoral air and muted chords of his painting.

The Tempest (FIG. 17-36) displays this same interest in the poetic qualities of the natural landscape inhabited by humans. Dominating the scene is a lush landscape. Stormy skies and lightning in the middle background threaten the tranquility of the pastoral setting. Pushed off to both sides are the human figures—a young woman nursing a baby in the right foreground and a man carrying a *halberd* (a combination spear and battle-ax) on the left. Although the attribution of this work to Giorgione seems secure, much scholarly debate has centered on the painting's subject, fueled by the fact that X-rays of the canvas have revealed that a nude woman originally stood where Giorgione subsequently placed the man. This flexibility in subject has led many art historians to believe that Giorgione did not intend the painting to have a definitive narrative, which is appropriate for a Venetian poetic rendering. Other scholars have suggested mythological and biblical narratives. This uncertainty about the subject contributes to the painting's enigmatic quality and intriguing air.

TITIAN Giorgione's Arcadianism passed not only to his much older yet constantly inquisitive master, Bellini, but also to Tiziano Vecelli, called TITIAN (ca. 1490–1576) in English. Titian was a supreme colorist and the most extraordinary and prolific of the great Venetian painters. His remarkable coloristic sense and ability

17-37 TITIAN, *Assumption of the Virgin*, 1516–1518. Oil on wood, 22′ 7$\frac{1}{2}$″ × 11′ 10″. Santa Maria Gloriosa dei Frari, Venice.

Titian won renown for his ability to convey light through color. In this dramatic depiction of the Virgin Mary's ascent to Heaven, the golden clouds seem to glow and radiate light into the church.

to convey light through color emerge in a major altarpiece, *Assumption of the Virgin* (FIG. 17-37), painted in oils for the main altar of Santa Maria Gloriosa dei Frari in Venice. Commissioned by the prior of this Franciscan basilica, the monumental altarpiece (close to 23 feet high) depicts the glorious ascent of the Virgin's body to Heaven on a great white cloud borne aloft by putti. Above, golden clouds, so luminous they seem to glow and radiate light into the church, envelop the Virgin. God the Father appears above, awaiting Mary with open arms. Below, apostles gesticulate wildly as they witness this momentous event. Through vibrant color, Titian infused the image with a drama and intensity that assured his lofty reputation, then and now.

17-38 TITIAN, *Madonna of the Pesaro Family,* 1519–1526. Oil on canvas, 15′ 11″ × 8′ 10″. Pesaro Chapel, Santa Maria dei Frari, Venice.

In this dynamic composition presaging a new kind of pictorial design, Titian placed the figures on a steep diagonal, positioning the Madonna, the focus of the composition, well off the central axis.

1 ft.

PESARO MADONNA Trained by both Bellini and Giorgione, Titian learned so well from them that even today scholars cannot concur about the degree of his participation in their later works. However, it is clear that Titian completed several of Bellini's and Giorgione's unfinished paintings, including the background of Bellini's *Feast of the Gods* (FIG. 17-34). On Bellini's death in 1516, the Republic of Venice appointed Titian its official painter. Shortly thereafter, Bishop Jacopo Pesaro commissioned him to paint *Madonna of the Pesaro Family* (FIG. 17-38) and presented it to the church of the Frari, which already housed Titian's *Assumption of the Virgin*. This new work, with its rich surface textures and dazzling display of color in all its nuances, furthered Titian's reputation and established his personal style.

Pesaro, bishop of Paphos in Cyprus and commander of the papal fleet, had led a successful expedition in 1502 against the Turks during the Venetian-Turkish war and commissioned this painting in gratitude. In a stately sunlit setting in what may be the Madonna's palace in Heaven, Mary receives the commander, who kneels dutifully at the foot of her throne. A soldier (Saint George?) behind the commander carries a banner with the *escutcheons* (shields with coats of arms) of the Borgia (Pope Alexander VI) and of Pesaro. Behind him is a turbaned Turk, a prisoner of war of the Christian forces. Saint Peter appears seated on the steps of the throne, and Saint Francis introduces other Pesaro family members (all male—Italian depictions of donors in this era typically excluded women and children), who kneel solemnly in the right foreground. Thus, Titian entwined the human and the heavenly, depicting the Madonna and saints honoring the achievements of a specific man in this particular world. A quite worldly transaction takes place (albeit beneath a heavenly cloud bearing angels) between a queen and her court and loyal servants. Titian constructed this tableau in terms of Renaissance protocol and courtly splendor.

A prime characteristic of High Renaissance painting is the massing of monumental figures, singly and in groups, within a weighty and majestic architecture. But here Titian did not compose a horizontal and symmetrical arrangement, as did Leonardo in *Last Supper* (FIG. 17-4) and Raphael in *School of Athens* (FIG. 17-9). Rather, he placed the figures on a steep diagonal, positioning the Madonna, the focus of the composition, well off the central axis. Titian drew attention to her with the perspective lines, the inclination of the figures, and the directional lines of gaze and gesture. The banner inclining toward the left beautifully brings the design into equilibrium, balancing the rightward and upward tendencies of its main direction. This kind of composition is more dynamic than most High Renaissance examples and presaged a new kind of pictorial design—one built on movement rather than repose.

BACCHUS AND ARIADNE In 1511 the duke of Ferrara, Alfonso d'Este (r. 1505–1534), asked Titian to produce a painting for his Camerino d'Alabastro (small room of alabaster). The patron had requested one bacchanalian scene each from Titian, Bellini, Raphael, and Fra Bartolommeo. Both Raphael and Fra Bartolommeo died before fulfilling the commission, and Bellini painted only one scene (FIG. 17-34), leaving Titian to produce three. One of these three paintings is *Meeting of Bacchus and Ariadne* (FIG. 17-39). Bacchus, accompanied by a boisterous and noisy group, arrives in a leopard-drawn chariot to save Ariadne, whom Theseus abandoned on the island of Naxos. In this scene, Titian revealed his debt to classical art. He derived one of the figures, entwined with snakes, from the recently unearthed *Laocoön* (FIG. 5-88), which also made an indelible impression on Michelangelo and many others. Titian's rich and luminous colors (see "Palma il Giovane on Titian," page 487) add greatly to the sensuous appeal of this painting, making it perfect for Alfonso's "pleasure chamber."

Palma il Giovane on Titian

An important change occurring in Titian's time was the almost universal adoption of canvas, with its rough-textured surface, in place of wood panels for paintings. Titian's works (FIGS. 17-38 to 17-41) established oil color on canvas as the typical medium of the Western pictorial tradition thereafter. One of Titian's students and collaborators was Jacopo Negretti, known as Palma il Giovane (ca. 1548–1628), or "Palma the Younger." He wrote a valuable account of his teacher's working methods and described how he used the new medium to great advantage:

> Titian [employed] a great mass of colors, which served . . . as a base for the compositions. . . . I too have seen some of these, formed with bold strokes made with brushes laden with colors, sometimes of a pure red earth, which he used, so to speak, for a middle tone, and at other times of white lead; and with the same brush tinted with red, black and yellow he formed a highlight; and observing these princi-

ples he made the promise of an exceptional figure appear in four brushstrokes. . . . Having constructed these precious foundations he used to turn his pictures to the wall and leave them there without looking at them, sometimes for several months. When he wanted to apply his brush again he would examine them with the utmost rigor . . . to see if he could find any faults. . . . In this way, working on the figures and revising them, he brought them to the most perfect symmetry that the beauty of art and nature can reveal. . . . [T]hus he gradually covered those quintessential forms with living flesh, bringing them by many stages to a state in which they lacked only the breath of life. He never painted a figure all at once and . . . in the last stages he painted more with his fingers than his brushes.*

* Quoted in Francesco Valcanover, "An Introduction to Titian," in Susanna Biadene and Mary Yakush, eds., *Titian: Prince of Painters* (Venice: Marsilio Editori, 1990), 23–24.

1 ft.

17-39 TITIAN, *Meeting of Bacchus and Ariadne,* from the Camerino d'Alabastro, Palazzo Ducale, Ferrara, Italy, 1522–1523. Oil on canvas, 5′ 9″ × 6′ 3″. National Gallery, London.

Titian's rich and luminous colors add greatly to the sensuous appeal of this mythological painting in which he based one of the figures on the recently unearthed ancient statue of *Laocoön* (FIG. 5-88).

17-40 TITIAN, *Venus of Urbino*, 1538. Oil on canvas, 3′ 11″ × 5′ 5″. Galleria degli Uffizi, Florence.

Titian established oil-based pigments on canvas as the preferred painting medium in Western art. Here, he also set the standard for representations of the reclining female nude, whether divine or mortal.

VENUS OF URBINO In 1538, at the height of his powers, Titian painted the so-called *Venus of Urbino* (FIG. **17-40**) for Guidobaldo II, who became the duke of Urbino the following year (r. 1539–1574). The title (given to the painting later) elevates to the status of classical mythology what is actually a representation of an Italian woman in her bedchamber. Indeed, no evidence suggests that Guidobaldo intended the commission as anything more than a female nude for his private enjoyment—the embodiment of womanly beauty and of the qualities he sought in a bride. Whether the subject is divine or mortal, Titian based his version on an earlier (and pioneering) painting of Venus (not illustrated) by Giorgione. Here, Titian established the compositional elements and the standard for paintings of the reclining female nude, regardless of the many variations that ensued. This "Venus" reclines on the gentle slope of her luxurious pillowed couch, the linear play of the draperies contrasting with her body's sleek continuous volume. At her feet is a pendant (balancing) figure—in this case, a slumbering lapdog. Behind her, a simple drape both places her figure emphatically in the foreground and indicates a vista into the background at the right half of the picture. Two servants bend over a chest, apparently searching for garments (Renaissance households stored clothing in carved wooden chests called *cassoni*) to clothe "Venus." Beyond them, a smaller vista opens into a landscape. Titian masterfully constructed the view backward into space and the division of the space into progressively smaller units.

As in other Venetian paintings, color plays a prominent role in *Venus of Urbino*. The red tones of the matron's skirt and the muted reds of the tapestries against the neutral whites of the matron's sleeves and the kneeling girl's gown echo the deep Venetian reds set off against the pale neutral whites of the linen and the warm ivory gold of the flesh. The viewer must study the picture carefully to realize the subtlety of color planning. For instance, the two deep reds (in the foreground cushions and in the background skirt) play a critical role in the composition as a gauge of distance and as indicators of an implied diagonal opposed to the real one of the reclining figure. Here, Titian used color not simply to record surface appearance but also to organize his placement of forms.

ISABELLA D'ESTE Titian was also a highly esteemed portraitist and in great demand. More than 50 portraits by his hand survive. Among the best is *Isabella d'Este* (FIG. **17-41**), Titian's portrait of one of the most prominent women of the Renaissance (see "Women in the Renaissance Art World," page 489). Isabella was the daughter of the duke of Ferrara. At 16, she married Francesco Gonzaga, marquis of Mantua, and through her patronage of art and music, she was instrumental in developing the Mantuan court into an important cultural center. Portraits by Titian generally emphasize his psychological reading of the subject's head and hands. Thus, Titian sharply highlighted Isabella's face, whereas her black dress fades into the undefined darkness of the background. The unseen light source also illuminates Isabella's hands, and Titian painted her sleeves with incredible detail to further draw viewers' attention to her hands. This portrait reveals not only Titian's skill but the patron's wish as well. Painted when Isabella was 60 years old, at her request it depicts her in her 20s. Titian used an earlier portrait of her as his guide, but his portrait is no copy. Rather, it is a distinctive portrayal of his poised and self-assured patron that owes little to its model.

Women in the Renaissance Art World

The Renaissance art world was decidedly male-dominated. Few women could become professional artists because of the obstacles they faced. In particular, for centuries, art-training practices mandating residence at a master's house (see "Artists' Guilds," Chapter 14, page 384) precluded women from acquiring the necessary experience. In addition, social proscriptions, such as those preventing women from drawing from nude models, further hampered an aspiring female artist's advancement through the accepted avenues of artistic training.

Still, there were determined women who surmounted these barriers and were able to develop not only considerable bodies of work but enviable reputations as well. One was Sofonisba Anguissola (FIG. 17-46), who was so accomplished that she can be considered the first Italian woman to have ascended to the level of international art celebrity. Lavinia Fontana (1552–1614) also achieved notable success, and her paintings constitute the largest surviving body of work by any woman artist before 1700. Fontana learned her craft from her father, a leading Bolognese painter. (Paternal training was the norm for aspiring women artists.) She was in demand as a portraitist and received commissions from important patrons, including members of the dominant Habsburg family. She even spent time as an official painter to the papal court in Rome.

Perhaps more challenging for women than the road to becoming a professional painter was the mastery of sculpture, made more difficult by the physical demands of the medium. Yet Properzia de' Rossi (ca. 1490–1530) established herself as a professional sculptor and was the only woman artist that Giorgio Vasari included in his comprehensive publication, *Lives of the Most Eminent Painters, Sculptors, and Architects.* Active in the early 16th century, she died of the plague in 1530, bringing her promising career to an early end.

Beyond the realm of art production, Renaissance women had a significant impact as art patrons. Scholars only recently have begun to explore systematically the role of women as patrons. As a result, current knowledge is sketchy at best but suggests that women played a much more extensive role than previously acknowledged. Among the problems researchers face in their quest to clarify women's participation as patrons is that women often wielded their influence and decision-making power behind the scenes. Many of them acquired their positions through marriage. Their power was thus indirect and provisional, based on their husbands' wealth and status. Thus, documentation of the networks within which women patrons operated and of the processes they used to exert power in a male-dominated society is less substantive than that available for male patrons.

One of the most important Renaissance patrons, male or female, was Isabella d'Este (1474–1539), marchioness of Mantua. Brought up in the cultured princely court of Ferrara (southwest of Venice), Isabella married Francesco Gonzaga (1466–1519), marquis of Mantua, in 1490. The marriage gave Isabella access to the position and wealth necessary to pursue her interest in becoming a major art patron. An avid collector, she enlisted the aid of agents who scoured Italy for appealing objects. Isabella did not limit her collection to painting and sculpture but included ceramics, glassware, gems, cameos, medals, classical texts, musical manuscripts, and musical instruments.

Isabella was undoubtedly a proud and ambitious woman well aware of how art could boost her fame and reputation. Accordingly, she commissioned several portraits of herself from the most esteemed artists of her day—Leonardo da Vinci, Andrea Mantegna, and Titian

17-41 TITIAN, *Isabella d'Este,* 1534–1536. Oil on canvas, 3′ 4⅛″ × 2′ 1³⁄₁₆″. Kunsthistorisches Museum, Vienna.

Isabella d'Este was one of the most powerful women of the Renaissance era. When, at age 60, she commissioned Titian to paint her portrait, she insisted that the artist depict her in her 20s.

(FIG. 17-41). The detail and complexity of many of her contracts with artists reveal her insistence on control over the artworks.

Other Renaissance women positioned themselves as serious art patrons. One was Caterina Sforza (1462–1509), daughter of Galeazzo Maria Sforza (heir to the duchy of Milan), who married Girolamo Riario in 1484. The death in 1488 of her husband, lord of Imola and count of Forlì, gave Caterina Sforza access to power denied most women. Another female art patron was Lucrezia Tornabuoni (married to Piero di Cosimo de' Medici), one of many Medici, both men and women, who earned reputations as unparalleled art patrons. Further archival investigation of women's roles in Renaissance Italy undoubtedly will produce more evidence of how women established themselves as patrons and artists and the extent to which they contributed to the flourishing of Renaissance art.

17-42 Jacopo da Pontormo, *Entombment of Christ,* Capponi Chapel, Santa Felicità, Florence, Italy, 1525–1528. Oil on wood, 10′ 3″ × 6′ 4″.

Mannerist paintings such as this one represent a departure from the compositions of the earlier Renaissance. Instead of concentrating masses in the center of the painting, Pontormo left a void.

17-43 Parmigianino, *Madonna with the Long Neck,* from the Baiardi Chapel, Santa Maria dei Servi, Parma, Italy, 1534–1540. Oil on wood, 7′ 1″ × 4′ 4″. Galleria degli Uffizi, Florence.

Parmigianino's Madonna displays the stylish elegance that was a principal aim of Mannerism. Mary has a small oval head, a long slender neck, attenuated hands, and a sinuous body.

MANNERISM

The Renaissance style of Rome, Florence, and Venice dominated Italian painting, sculpture, and architecture for most of the 16th century, but already in the 1520s another style—Mannerism—emerged in reaction to it. *Mannerism* is a term derived from the Italian word *maniera,* meaning "style" or "manner." In the field of art history, the term *style* usually refers to a characteristic or representative mode, especially of an artist or period (for example, Leonardo's style or Gothic style). Style also can refer to an absolute quality of fashion (for example, someone has "style"). Mannerism's style (or representative mode) is characterized by style (being stylish, cultured, elegant).

Painting

Among the features most closely associated with Mannerism is artifice. Of course, all art involves artifice, in the sense that art is not "natural"—it is a representation of a scene or idea. But many artists, including High Renaissance painters such as Leonardo and Raphael, chose to conceal that artifice by using such devices as perspective and shading to make their art look natural. In contrast, Mannerist painters consciously revealed the constructed nature of their art. In other words, Renaissance artists generally strove to create art that appeared natural, whereas Mannerist artists were less inclined to disguise the contrived nature of art production. This is why artifice is a central feature of discussions about Mannerism, and why Mannerist works can seem, appropriately, "mannered." The conscious display of artifice in Mannerism often reveals itself in imbalanced compositions and unusual complexities, both visual and conceptual. Ambiguous space, departures from expected conventions, and unique presentations of traditional themes also surface frequently in Mannerist art.

PONTORMO *Entombment of Christ* (FIG. 17-42) by Jacopo da Pontormo (1494–1557) exhibits almost all the stylistic features char-

1 ft.

tions (for example, the torso of the foreground figure bends in an anatomically impossible way), elastic elongation of the limbs, and heads rendered as uniformly small and oval. The contrasting colors, primarily light blues and pinks, add to the dynamism and complexity of the work. The painting represents a departure from the balanced, harmoniously structured compositions of the High Renaissance.

PARMIGIANINO Girolamo Francesco Maria Mazzola of Parma, known as PARMIGIANINO (1503–1540), achieved in his best-known work, *Madonna with the Long Neck* (FIG. **17-43**), the elegant stylishness that was a principal aim of Mannerism. In Parmigianino's hands, this traditional, usually sedate, religious subject became a picture of exquisite grace and precious sweetness. The Madonna's small oval head, her long and slender neck, the otherworldly attenuation and delicacy of her hand, and the sinuous, swaying elongation of her frame—all are marks of the aristocratic, sumptuously courtly taste of a later phase of Mannerism. Parmigianino amplified this elegance by expanding the Madonna's form as viewed from head to toe. On the left stands a bevy of angelic creatures, melting with emotions as soft and smooth as their limbs. On the right, the artist included a line of columns without capitals and an enigmatic figure with a scroll, whose distance from the foreground is immeasurable and ambiguous—the antithesis of rational Renaissance perspectival diminution of size with distance.

Although the elegance and sophisticated beauty of the painting are due in large part to the Madonna's attenuated limbs, that exaggeration is not solely decorative in purpose. *Madonna with the Long Neck* takes its subject from a simile in medieval hymns that compared the Virgin's neck to a great ivory tower or column, such as that which Parmigianino depicted to the right of the Madonna. Thus, the work contains religious meaning in addition to the power derived from its beauty alone.

BRONZINO *Venus, Cupid, Folly, and Time* (FIG. **17-44**), by Agnolo di Cosimo, called BRONZINO (1503–1572), also displays all the chief features of Mannerist painting. A pupil of Pontormo, Bronzino was a Florentine and painter to the first grand duke of Tuscany, Cosimo I de' Medici (r. 1537–1574). In this painting, which Cosimo I commissioned as a gift for King Francis I of France,

acteristic of Mannerism's early phase in painting. Christ's descent from the cross and subsequent entombment had frequently been depicted in art (see "The Life of Jesus in Art," Chapter 8, pages 216–217, or in the "Before 1300" section), and Pontormo exploited the familiarity that 16th-century viewers would have had by playing off their expectations. For example, he omitted from the painting both the cross and Christ's tomb, so that scholars continue to debate whether he meant to represent the *Descent from the Cross* or the *Entombment.* And instead of presenting the action as occurring across the perpendicular picture plane, as artists such as Raphael and Rogier van der Weyden (FIG. **15-8**) had done in their paintings of these episodes from Christ's Passion, Pontormo rotated the conventional figural groups along a vertical axis. As a result, the Virgin Mary falls back (away from the viewer) as she releases her dead son's hand. Unlike High Renaissance artists, who had concentrated their masses in the center of the painting, Pontormo left a void. This emptiness accentuates the grouping of hands that fill that hole, calling attention to the void—symbolic of loss and grief. The artist enhanced the painting's ambiguity with the curiously anxious glances the figures cast in all directions. (The bearded young man at the upper right who looks out at the viewer is probably a self-portrait of Pontormo.) Athletic bending and twisting characterize many of the figures, with distor-

17-45 BRONZINO, *Portrait of a Young Man*, ca. 1530–1545. Oil on wood, 3′ 1½″ × 2′ 5½″. Metropolitan Museum of Art, New York (H. O. Havemeyer Collection, bequest of Mrs. H. O. Havemeyer, 1929).

This depiction of a young intellectual with a calculated attitude of nonchalance is typical of Mannerist portraiture. Bronzino recorded the rank and station but not the personality of his subject.

Bronzino demonstrated the Mannerists' fondness for learned allegories that often had lascivious undertones, a shift from the simple and monumental statements and forms of the High Renaissance. Bronzino depicted Cupid fondling his mother Venus, while Folly prepares to shower them with rose petals. Time, who appears in the upper right corner, draws back the curtain to reveal the playful incest in progress. Other figures in the painting represent other human qualities and emotions, including Envy. The masks, a favorite device of the Mannerists, symbolize deceit. The picture seems to suggest that love—accompanied by envy and plagued by inconstancy—is foolish and that lovers will discover its folly in time. But as in many Mannerist paintings, the meaning here is ambiguous, and interpretations of the painting vary. Compositionally, Bronzino placed the figures around the front plane, and they almost entirely block the space. The contours are strong and sculptural, the surfaces of enamel smoothness. Of special interest are the heads, hands, and feet, for the Mannerists considered the extremities the carriers of grace, and the clever depiction of them as evidence of artistic skill.

Mannerist painters most often achieved in portraiture the sophisticated elegance they sought. Bronzino's *Portrait of a Young Man* (FIG. 17-45) exemplifies Mannerist portraiture. The subject is a

17-46

SOFONISBA ANGUISSOLA, *Portrait of the Artist's Sisters and Brother*, ca. 1555. Oil on panel, 2′ 5¼″ × 3′ 1½″. Methuen Collection, Corsham Court, Wiltshire.

Anguissola was the leading female artist of her time. Her contemporaries greatly admired her use of relaxed poses and expressions in intimate and informal group portraits like this one of her own family.

17-47 Tintoretto, *Last Supper*, 1594. Oil on canvas, 12′ × 18′ 8″. San Giorgio Maggiore, Venice.

Tintoretto adopted many Mannerist pictorial devices to produce oil paintings imbued with emotional power, depth of spiritual vision, glowing Venetian color schemes, and dramatic lighting.

proud youth—a man of books and intellectual society, rather than a merchant or lowly laborer. His cool demeanor seems carefully affected, a calculated attitude of nonchalance. This staid and reserved formality is a standard component of Mannerist portraits. It asserts the rank and station but not the personality of the subject. In Bronzino's portrait, the haughty poise, the graceful long-fingered hands, the book, the carved faces of the furniture, and the severe architecture all suggest the traits and environment of the highbred, disdainful patrician. The somber black of the young man's Spanish doublet and cap and the room's slightly acid, olive-green walls make for a deeply restrained color scheme. Bronzino created a muted background for the man's sharply defined, asymmetrical silhouette that contradicts his impassive pose.

SOFONISBA ANGUISSOLA The aloof formality of Bronzino's portrait is much relaxed in the portraiture of SOFONISBA ANGUISSOLA (ca. 1532–1625). A northern Italian from Cremona, Anguissola introduced a new kind of group portrait of irresistible charm, characterized by an informal intimacy and subjects that are often moving, conversing, or engaged in activities. Like many of the other works she did before moving to Spain in 1559, the portrait illustrated here (FIG. 17-46) represents members of her family. Against a neutral ground, Anguissola placed her two sisters and brother in an affectionate pose meant not for official display but for private showing. The sisters, wearing matching striped gowns, flank their brother, who caresses a lapdog. The older sister (at the left) summons the dignity required

for the occasion, while the boy looks quizzically at the portraitist with an expression of naive curiosity, and the other girl diverts her attention toward something or someone to the painter's left.

Anguissola's use of relaxed poses and expressions, her sympathetic personal presentation, and her graceful treatment of the forms did not escape the attention of her contemporaries, who praised her highly (see "Women in the Renaissance Art World," page 489). Her recognized talents allowed her to consort with esteemed individuals. She knew and learned from the aged Michelangelo, was court painter to Philip II (r. 1556–1598) of Spain, and, at the end of her life, gave advice on art to a young admirer of her work, Anthony Van Dyck, the great Flemish master (see Chapter 20).

TINTORETTO Venetian painting of the later 16th century built on established High Renaissance ideas but incorporated many elements of the Mannerist style. Jacopo Robusti, known as TINTORETTO (1518–1594), claimed to be a student of Titian and aspired to combine Titian's color with Michelangelo's drawing, but art historians consider Tintoretto the outstanding Venetian representative of Mannerism. He adopted many Mannerist pictorial devices, which he employed to produce works imbued with dramatic power, depth of spiritual vision, and glowing Venetian color schemes.

Toward the end of Tintoretto's life, his art became spiritual, even visionary, as solid forms melted away into swirling clouds of dark shot through with fitful light. In Tintoretto's *Last Supper* (FIG. 17-47), painted for the right wall next to the high altar in Andrea Palladio's

17-48 PAOLO VERONESE, *Christ in the House of Levi*, from the refectory of Santi Giovanni e Paolo, Venice, Italy, 1573. Oil on canvas, 18′ 3″ × 42′. Galleria dell'Accademia, Venice.

Veronese's paintings feature superb color and majestic classical settings. The Catholic Church accused him of impiety for including dogs and dwarfs near Christ in this work originally titled *Last Supper*.

church of San Giorgio Maggiore (FIG. **17-32**), the figures appear in a dark interior illuminated by a single light in the upper left of the image. The shimmering halos establish the biblical nature of the scene. The ability of this dramatic scene to engage viewers was well in keeping with Counter-Reformation ideals (see "Religious Art in Counter-Reformation Italy," page 474) and the Catholic Church's belief in the didactic nature of religious art.

Last Supper incorporates many Mannerist elements, including an imbalanced composition and visual complexity. In terms of design, the contrast with Leonardo's *Last Supper* (FIG. **17-4**) is both extreme and instructive. Leonardo's composition, balanced and symmetrical, parallels the picture plane in a geometrically organized and closed space. The figure of Christ is the tranquil center of the drama and the perspectival focus. In Tintoretto's painting, Christ is above and beyond the converging perspective lines that race diagonally away from the picture surface, creating disturbing effects of limitless depth and motion. The viewer locates Tintoretto's Christ via the light flaring, beaconlike, out of darkness. The contrast of the two works reflects the direction Renaissance painting took in the 16th century, as it moved away from architectonic clarity of space and neutral lighting toward the dynamic perspectives and dramatic chiaroscuro of the coming Baroque.

VERONESE Among the great Venetian masters was Paolo Caliari of Verona, called PAOLO VERONESE (1528–1588). Whereas Tintoretto gloried in monumental drama and deep perspectives, Veronese specialized in splendid pageantry painted in superb color and set within majestic classical architecture. Like Tintoretto, Veronese painted on a huge scale and often produced canvases as large as 20 by 30 feet or more for the refectories of wealthy monasteries. He painted *Christ in*

the House of Levi (FIG. **17-48**), originally called *Last Supper*, for the dining hall of Santi Giovanni e Paolo in Venice. In a great open loggia framed by three monumental arches, Christ sits at the center of the splendidly garbed elite of Venice. In the foreground, with a courtly gesture, the very image of gracious grandeur, the chief steward welcomes guests. Robed lords, their colorful retainers, dogs, and dwarfs crowd into the spacious loggia. Painted during the Counter-Reformation, this depiction prompted criticism from the Catholic Church. The Holy Office of the Inquisition accused Veronese of impiety for painting such creatures so close to the Lord, and it ordered him to make changes at his own expense. Reluctant to do so, he simply changed the painting's title, converting the subject to a less solemn one. As Palladio looked to the example of classically inspired High Renaissance architecture, so Veronese returned to High Renaissance composition, its symmetrical balance, and its ordered architectonics. His shimmering colors span the whole spectrum, although he avoided solid colors for half shades (light blues, sea greens, lemon yellows, roses, and violets), creating veritable flower beds of tone.

The Venetian Republic employed both Tintoretto and Veronese to decorate the grand chambers and council rooms of the Doge's Palace (FIG. **14-21**). A great and popular decorator, Veronese revealed himself a master of imposing illusionistic ceiling compositions, such as *Triumph of Venice* (FIG. **17-49**). Here, within an oval frame, he presented Venice, crowned by Fame, enthroned between two great twisted columns in a balustraded loggia, garlanded with clouds, and attended by figures symbolic of its glories. Unlike Mantegna's *di sotto in sù* (FIG. **16-48**) perspective, Veronese's projection is not directly up from below but at a 45-degree angle to spectators, a technique many later Baroque decorators used (see Chapter 19).

1 ft.

17-49 PAOLO VERONESE, *Triumph of Venice,* ca. 1585. Oil on canvas, 29′ 8″ × 19′. Ceiling of the Hall of the Grand Council, Doge's Palace, Venice.

Within an immense oval frame, Veronese presented an illusionistic tableau of Venice crowned by Fame amid columns, clouds, and personifications. Baroque painters adopted this 45-degree view from the ground.

17-50 CORREGGIO, *Assumption of the Virgin*, 1526–1530. Fresco, 35′ 10″ × 37′ 11″. Parma Cathedral, Parma.

Working long before Veronese, Correggio, the teacher of Parmigianino, won little fame in his day, but his illusionistic ceiling designs, like this one in Parma Cathedral, inspired many 17th-century painters.

10 ft.

CORREGGIO One painter who developed a unique personal style that is almost impossible to classify was Antonio Allegri, known as CORREGGIO (ca. 1489–1534) from his birthplace, near Parma. The teacher of Parmigianino, Correggio, working more than a half century before Veronese, pulled together many stylistic trends, including those of Leonardo, Raphael, and the Venetians. Correggio's most enduring artistic contribution was his development of illusionistic ceiling perspectives. In Parma Cathedral, he painted away the entire dome with his *Assumption of the Virgin* (FIG. **17-50**). Opening up the *cupola*, Correggio showed worshipers a view of the sky, with concentric rings of clouds where hundreds of soaring figures perform a wildly pirouetting dance in celebration of the Assumption. Versions of these angelic creatures became permanent tenants of numerous Baroque churches in later centuries. Correggio was also an influential painter of religious panels, anticipating in them many other Baroque compositional devices. Correggio's contemporaries expressed little appreciation for his art. Later, during the 17th century, Baroque painters recognized him as a kindred spirit.

Sculpture

Mannerism extended beyond painting. Artists translated its principles into sculpture and architecture as well.

BENVENUTO CELLINI Among those who made their mark as Mannerist sculptors was BENVENUTO CELLINI (1500–1571), the author of a fascinating autobiography. It is difficult to imagine a medieval artist composing an autobiography. Only in the Renaissance, with the birth of the notion of individual artistic genius, could a work such as Cellini's (or Vasari's *Lives*) have been conceived and written. Cellini's literary self-portrait presents him not only as a highly accomplished artist, but also as a statesman, soldier, and lover, among many other roles. He was, first of all, a goldsmith, but only one of his major

works in that medium survives, the saltcellar (FIG. **17-51**) he made for Francis I (FIG. **18-10**), who had hired Cellini with a retainer of an annual salary, supplemented by fees for the works he produced. The price paid for this luxurious gold-and-*enamel* item destined for the French royal table was almost 50 percent greater than Cellini's salary for the year. Neptune and Tellus (or, as Cellini named them, the Sea—the source of salt—and the Land) recline atop an ebony base decorated with relief figures of Dawn, Day, Twilight, Night, and the four winds—some based on Michelangelo's statues in the Medici Chapel (FIG. **17-17**) in San Lorenzo. The boat next to Neptune's right leg contained the salt, and the triumphal arch (compare FIG. **7-75**) next to the right leg of the earth goddess, the pepper. The elongated proportions of the figures, especially the slim, small-breasted figure of Tellus, whom ancient artists always represented as a matronly woman (FIG. **7-30**), reveal Cellini's Mannerist approach to form.

GIOVANNI DA BOLOGNA The lure of Italy drew a brilliant young Flemish sculptor, Jean de Boulogne, to Italy, where he practiced his art under the equivalent Italian name of GIOVANNI DA BOLOGNA (1529–1608). Giovanni's *Abduction of the Sabine Women*

17-51 BENVENUTO CELLINI, *Saltcellar of Francis I,* 1540–1543. Gold, enamel, and ebony, $10\frac{1}{4}'' \times 1'\ 1\frac{1}{8}''$. Kunsthistorisches Museum, Vienna.

Famed as a master goldsmith, Cellini fashioned this costly saltcellar for the table of Francis I of France. The elongated proportions of the figures clearly reveal Cellini's Mannerist approach to form.

1 in.

(FIG. **17-52**) exemplifies Mannerist principles of figure composition. Drawn from the legendary history of early Rome, the group received its present title—relating how the Romans abducted wives for themselves from the neighboring Sabines—only after its exhibition. Earlier, it was *Paris Abducting Helen,* among other mythological titles. In fact, Giovanni had no interest in depicting any particular subject. He created the group as a demonstration piece. His goal was to achieve a dynamic spiral figural composition involving an old man, a young man, and a woman, all nude in the tradition of ancient statues portraying mythological figures. Although Giovanni would have known Antonio Pollaiuolo's *Hercules and Antaeus* (FIG. **16-14**), whose Greek hero lifts his opponent off the ground, he turned directly to ancient sculpture for inspiration. *Abduction of the Sabine Women* includes references to *Laocoön* (FIG. **5-88**)—once in the crouching old man and again in the woman's up-flung arm. The three bodies interlock on a vertical axis, creating an ascending spiral movement.

To appreciate the sculpture fully, the viewer must walk around it, because the work changes radically according to the viewing point. One factor contributing to the shifting imagery is the prominence of open spaces that pass through the masses (for example, the space between an arm and a body), giving the spaces an effect equal to that of the solids. This sculpture was the first large-scale group since classical antiquity designed to be seen from multiple viewpoints, in striking contrast to Pollaiuolo's group, which the artist intended to be seen from the angle shown in FIG. **16-14**. Giovanni's figures do not break out of this spiral vortex but remain as if contained within a cylinder. Nonetheless, they display athletic flexibility and Michelangelesque potential for action.

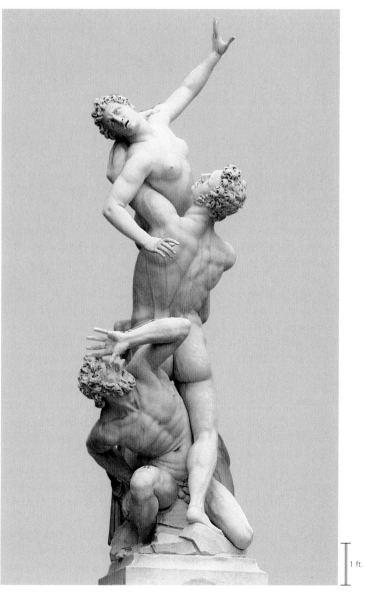

17-52 GIOVANNI DA BOLOGNA, *Abduction of the Sabine Women,* Loggia dei Lanzi, Piazza della Signoria, Florence, Italy, 1579–1583. Marble, $13'\ 5\frac{1}{2}''$ high.

This sculpture was the first large-scale group since classical antiquity designed to be seen from multiple viewpoints. The three bodies interlock to create a vertical spiral movement.

1 ft.

17-53 GIULIO ROMANO, interior courtyard facade of the Palazzo del Tè, Mantua, Italy, 1525–1535.

The Mannerist divergences from architectural convention, for example, the slipping triglyphs, are so pronounced in the Palazzo del Tè that they constitute a parody of Bramante's classical style.

Architecture

Mannerist architects used classical architectural elements in a highly personal and unorthodox manner, rejecting the balance, order, and stability that were the hallmarks of the High Renaissance style with the specific aim of revealing the contrived nature of architectural design.

GIULIO ROMANO Applying that anticlassical principle was the goal of GIULIO ROMANO (ca. 1499–1546) when he designed the Palazzo del Tè (FIG. **17-53**) in Mantua and, with it, formulated almost the entire architectural vocabulary of Mannerism. Giulio became Raphael's chief assistant in decorating the Vatican stanze. After Raphael's premature death in 1520, Giulio served as his master's artistic executor, completing Raphael's unfinished frescoes and panel paintings. In 1524, he went to Mantua, where he found a patron in Duke Federigo Gonzaga (r. 1530–1540), for whom Giulio built and decorated the Palazzo del Tè between 1525 and 1535. Gonzaga intended the Palazzo del Tè to serve as both suburban summer palace and stud farm for the duke's famous stables. Originally planned as a relatively modest country villa, Giulio's building so pleased his patron that Gonzaga soon commissioned the architect to enlarge the structure. In a second building campaign, Giulio expanded the villa to a palatial scale by adding three wings, which he placed around a square central court. This once-paved court, which functions both as a passage and as the focal point of the design, has a nearly urban character. Its surrounding buildings form a self-enclosed unit with a large garden, flanked by a stable, attached to it on the east side.

Giulio exhibited his Mannerist style in the facades that face the palace's interior courtyard (FIG. **17-53**), where the divergences from architectural convention are quite pronounced. Indeed, they consti-

tute an enormous parody of Bramante's classical style, thereby announcing the artifice of the palace design. In a building laden with structural surprises and contradictions, the design of these facades is the most unconventional of all. The *keystones* (central *voussoirs*), for example, either have not fully settled or seem to be slipping from the arches—and, more eccentric still, Giulio even placed voussoirs in the pediments over the rectangular niches, where no arches exist. The massive Tuscan columns that flank these niches carry incongruously narrow *architraves*. That these architraves break midway between the columns stresses their apparent structural insufficiency, and they seem unable to support the weight of the *triglyphs* of the *Doric frieze* above (see "Doric and Ionic Orders," Chapter 5, page 110, or in the "Before 1300" section), which threaten to crash down on the head of anyone foolish enough to stand below them. To be sure, appreciating Giulio's witticism requires a highly sophisticated audience, and recognizing some quite subtle departures from the norm presupposes a thorough familiarity with the established rules of classical architecture. It speaks well for the duke's sophistication that he accepted Giulio's form of architectural inventiveness.

LAURENTIAN LIBRARY Although he personifies the High Renaissance artist, Michelangelo, like Giulio Romano, also experimented with architectural designs that flouted most of the classical rules of order and stability. Michelangelo's restless genius is on display in the vestibule (FIG. **17-54**) he designed for the Medici library adjoining the Florentine church of San Lorenzo. The Laurentian Library had two contrasting spaces that Michelangelo had to unite: the long horizontal of the library proper and the vertical of the vestibule. The need to place the vestibule windows up high (at the level

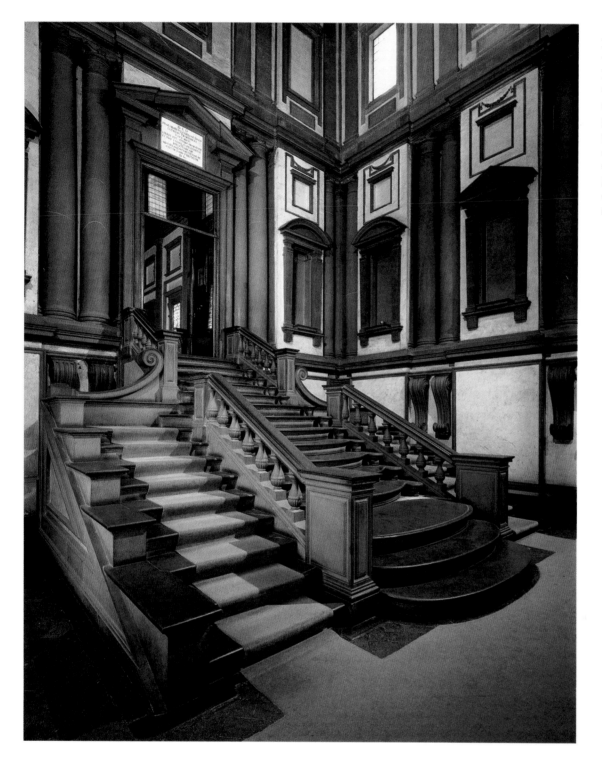

17-54 MICHELANGELO BUONARROTI, vestibule of the Laurentian Library, Florence, Italy, 1524–1534; staircase, 1558–1559.

With his customary independence of spirit, Michelangelo, working in a Mannerist mode in the vestibule of the Laurentian Library, disposed willfully of almost all the rules of classical architecture.

of the reading room) determined the narrow verticality of the vestibule's elevation and proportions. Much taller than it is wide, the vestibule gives the impression of a vertically compressed, shaftlike space. Anyone schooled exclusively in the classical architecture of Bramante and the High Renaissance would have been appalled by Michelangelo's indifference here to classical norms in the use of the orders and in proportion. He used columns in pairs and sank them into the walls, where they perform no supporting function. He also split columns in halves around corners. Elsewhere, he placed scroll corbels on the walls beneath columns. They seem to hang from the moldings, holding up nothing. He arbitrarily broke through pediments as well as through cornices and stringcourses. He sculpted pilasters that taper downward instead of upward. In short, the High

Renaissance master, working in a Mannerist mode, disposed willfully and abruptly of classical architecture. Moreover, in the vast, flowing stairway (the latest element of the vestibule) that protrudes tonguelike into the room from the "mouth" of the doorway to the library, Michelangelo foreshadowed the dramatic movement of Baroque architecture (see Chapter 19). With his customary trailblazing independence of spirit, Michelangelo created an interior space that conveyed all the strains and tensions found in his statuary and in his painted figures. Michelangelo's art began in the style of the 15th century, developed into the epitome of High Renaissance art, and, at the end, moved toward Mannerism. He was 89 when he died in 1564, still hard at work on Saint Peter's and other projects. Few artists, then or since, could escape his influence.

17-55 GIACOMO DELLA PORTA, facade of Il Gesù, Rome, Italy, ca. 1575–1584.

In Giacomo della Porta's innovative design, the march of pilasters and columns builds to a dramatic climax at the central bay. Many 17th-century Roman church facades are architectural variations of Il Gesù.

17-56 GIACOMO DA VIGNOLA, plan of Il Gesù, Rome, Italy, 1568. (1) dome, (2) nave, (3) chapel.

Giacomo da Vignola's plan for Il Gesù, with its exceptionally wide nave with side chapels instead of aisles, won wide acceptance in the Catholic world. It is an ideal space for grand processions.

IL GESÙ Probably the most influential building of the second half of the 16th century was the mother church of the Jesuit order. The activity of the Society of Jesus, known as the Jesuits, was an important component of the Counter-Reformation. Ignatius of Loyola (1491–1556), a Spanish nobleman who dedicated his life to the service of God, founded the Jesuit order. He attracted a group of followers, and in 1540 Pope Paul III formally recognized this group as a religious order. The Jesuits were the papacy's invaluable allies in its quest to reassert the supremacy of the Catholic Church. Particularly successful in the field of education, the order established numerous schools. In addition, its members were effective missionaries and carried the message of Catholicism to the Americas, Asia, and Africa.

As a major participant in the Counter-Reformation, the Jesuit order needed a church appropriate to its new prominence. Because Michelangelo was late in providing the plans for this church, called Il Gesù, or Church of Jesus, in 1568 the Jesuits turned to Giacomo della Porta, who was responsible for the facade (FIG. **17-55**)—and later designed the dome of Saint Peter's (FIG. **19-3**)—and GIACOMO DA VIGNOLA (1507–1573), who designed the ground plan (FIG. **17-56**).

The plan of Il Gesù reveals a monumental expansion of Alberti's scheme for Sant'Andrea (FIGS. **16-45** and **16-46**) in Mantua. In the new Jesuit church, the nave takes over the main volume of space, making the structure a great hall with side chapels. A dome empha-

sizes the approach to the altar. The wide acceptance of the Gesù plan in the Catholic world, even until modern times, speaks to its ritual efficacy. The opening of the church building into a single great hall provides an almost theatrical setting for large promenades and processions (which seemed to combine social with priestly functions). Above all, the space is adequate to accommodate the great crowds that gathered to hear the eloquent preaching of the Jesuits.

The facade of Il Gesù was also not entirely original, but it too had an enormous impact on later church design. The union of the lower and upper stories, effected by scroll buttresses, harks back to Alberti's Santa Maria Novella (FIG. **16-39**). Its classical pediment is familiar in Alberti's work (FIG. **16-44**) as well as in that of Palladio (FIGS. **17-29** and **17-31**). The paired pilasters appear in Michelangelo's design for Saint Peter's (FIG. **17-26**). Giacomo della Porta skillfully synthesized these existing motifs and unified the two stories. The horizontal march of the pilasters and columns builds to a dramatic climax at the central bay, and the bays of the facade snugly fit the nave-chapel system behind them. Many Roman church facades of the 17th century are architectural variations on Giacomo della Porta's design. Chronologically and stylistically, Il Gesù belongs to the Late Renaissance, but its enormous influence on later churches marks it as a significant monument for the development of Italian Baroque church architecture, discussed in Chapter 19.

ITALY, 1500 TO 1600

HIGH AND LATE RENAISSANCE, 1495–1600

▌ During the High (1500–1520) and Late (1520–1600) Renaissance periods in Italy, artists, often in the employ of the papacy, further developed the interest in perspective, anatomy, and classical cultures that had characterized 15th-century Italian art.

▌ The major regional artistic centers were Florence and Rome in central Italy and Venice in the north. Whereas most Florentine and Roman artists emphasized careful design preparation based on preliminary drawing (*disegno*), Venetian artists focused on color and the process of paint application (*colorito*).

▌ Leonardo da Vinci was a master of chiaroscuro and atmospheric perspective. He was famous for his hazy sfumato and for his psychological insight in depicting biblical narrative (*Last Supper*) and contemporary personalities (*Mona Lisa*). His anatomical drawings are the first modern scientific illustrations.

▌ Raphael favored lighter tonalities than Leonardo and clarity over obscurity. His sculpturesque figures appear in landscapes under blue skies (*Madonna of the Meadows*) or in grandiose architectural settings rendered in perfect perspective (*School of Athens*).

▌ Michelangelo, a temperamental genius, was a pioneer in several media, including architecture, but his first love was sculpture. His carved (*David, Moses*) and painted (*Creation of Adam*) figures have heroic physiques and great emotional impact. He preferred pent-up energy to Raphael's calm, ideal beauty.

▌ The leading architect of the early 16th century was Bramante, who championed the classical style of the ancients. He based his pioneering design for the Tempietto on antique models, but the combination of parts was new and original.

▌ Andrea Palladio, an important theorist as well as architect, carried on Bramante's classical style during the Late Renaissance. Famed for his villa designs, he had a lasting impact upon later European and American architecture.

▌ One of the great masters of the Venetian painting school was Giorgione, who developed the concept of *poesia,* poetical painting. The subjects of his paintings (*Pastoral Symphony, The Tempest*) are often impossible to identify. His primary goal was to evoke a pastoral mood.

▌ Titian, the official painter of the Venetian Republic, won renown for his rich surface textures and dazzling display of color in all its nuances. In paintings such as *Venus of Urbino,* he established oil color on canvas as the typical medium of the Western pictorial tradition.

MANNERISM, 1520–1600

▌ Mannerism emerged in the 1520s in reaction to the High Renaissance style. A prime feature of Mannerist art is artifice. Renaissance artists generally strove to create art that appeared natural, whereas Mannerist artists were less inclined to disguise the contrived nature of art production. Ambiguous space, departures from expected conventions, and unique presentations of traditional themes are common features of Mannerist art.

▌ Parmigianino's *Madonna with the Long Neck* epitomizes the elegant stylishness of Mannerist painting. The elongated proportions of the figures, the enigmatic line of columns without capitals, and the ambiguous position of the figure with a scroll are the antithesis of High Renaissance classical proportions, clarity of meaning, and rational perspective.

▌ Mannerism was also a sculptural style. Giovanni da Bologna's *Abduction of the Sabine Women,* which does not really have a subject, is typical. The sculptor's goal was to depict elegant nude figures in a dynamic spiral composition that presaged the movement of Baroque sculpture.

▌ The leading Mannerist architect was Giulio Romano, who rejected the balance, order, and stability that were hallmarks of the High Renaissance style. In the Palazzo del Tè in Mantua, the divergences from architectural convention parody Bramante's classical style and include triglyphs that slip out of the Doric frieze.

Michelangelo, *David,*
1501–1504

Bramante, Tempietto, Rome,
1502(?)

Titian, *Venus of Urbino,* 1538

Parmigianino, *Madonna with
the Long Neck,* 1534-1540

Giulio Romano, Palazzo del Tè,
Mantua, 1525–1535

1 in.

18-1 ALBRECHT DÜRER, *Fall of Man* (*Adam and Eve*), 1504. Engraving, $9\frac{7}{8}'' \times 7\frac{5}{8}''$. Museum of Fine Arts, Boston (centennial gift of Landon T. Clay).

Albrecht Dürer was the first Northern European artist to become an international celebrity. *Fall of Man,* with two figures based on ancient statues, reflects his studies of the Vitruvian theory of human proportions.

NORTHERN EUROPE AND SPAIN, 1500 TO 1600

The dissolution of the Burgundian Netherlands in 1477 led in the early 16th century to a realignment in the European geopolitical landscape (MAP 18-1). France and the Holy Roman Empire absorbed the former Burgundian territories and increased their power. But by the end of the century, through calculated marriages, military exploits, and ambitious territorial expansion, Spain was the dominant European state. Throughout the continent, monarchs gained additional prestige and cultivated a stronger sense of cultural and political unity among their subjects, thereby laying the foundation for today's European nations. Yet a momentous crisis in the Christian Church overshadowed these power shifts. Concerted attempts to reform the Church led to the Reformation and the establishment of Protestantism (as distinct from Catholicism), which in turn prompted the Catholic Church's response, the Counter-Reformation (see Chapter 17). Ultimately, the Reformation split Christendom in half and produced a hundred years of civil war between Protestants and Catholics.

Despite the tumultuous religious conflict engulfing 16th-century Europe, the exchange of intellectual and artistic ideas continued to thrive. Catholic Italy and the (mostly) Protestant Holy Roman Empire shared in a lively commerce—economic and cultural—and 16th-century art throughout Europe was a major beneficiary of that exchange. Humanism filtered up from Italy and spread throughout Northern Europe. Northern humanists, like their southern counterparts, cultivated a knowledge of classical cultures and literature. Because they focused more on reconciling humanism with Christianity, later scholars applied the general label "Christian humanists" to describe them.

Among the most influential Christian humanists were the Dutch-born Desiderius Erasmus (1466–1536) and the Englishman Thomas More (1478–1535). Erasmus demonstrated his interest in both Italian humanism and religion with his "philosophy of Christ," emphasizing education and scriptural knowledge. Both an ordained priest and avid scholar, Erasmus published his most famous essay, *The Praise of Folly,* in 1509. In this widely read work, he satirized not just the Church but various social classes as well. His ideas were to play an important role in the development of the Reformation, but he consistently declined to join any of the Reformation sects. Equally well educated was Thomas More, who served King Henry VIII (r. 1509–1547). Henry eventually ordered More executed because of his

MAP 18-1 Europe in the early 16th century.

opposition to England's break with the Catholic Church. In France, François Rabelais (ca. 1494–1553), a former monk who advocated rejecting stagnant religious dogmatism, disseminated the humanist spirit.

The turmoil emerging during the 16th century lasted well into the 17th century and permanently affected the face of Europe. The concerted challenges to established authority and the persistent philosophical inquiry eventually led to the rise of new political systems (for example, the nation-state) and new economic systems (such as capitalism).

HOLY ROMAN EMPIRE

Although at the opening of the 16th century many in the Holy Roman Empire were expressing dissatisfaction with the Church in Rome, Martin Luther had not yet posted the *Ninety-five Theses* that launched the Protestant Reformation. The Catholic clergy in Germany still offered artists important commissions to adorn churches and other religious institutions.

MATTHIAS GRÜNEWALD Matthias Neithardt, known conventionally as MATTHIAS GRÜNEWALD (ca. 1480–1528), worked for the archbishops of Mainz from 1511 on in several capacities, from court painter and decorator to architect, hydraulic engineer, and superintendent of works. Grünewald eventually moved to northern Germany, where he settled at Halle in Saxony. Around 1510, he began work on the *Isenheim Altarpiece* (FIG. 18-2), a complex and fascinating monument that reflects Catholic beliefs and incorporates several references to Catholic doctrines, such as the lamb (symbol of the Son of God), whose wound spurts blood into a chalice in the *Crucifixion* scene (FIG. 18-2, *top*) on the exterior of the altarpiece.

Created for the monastic hospital order Saint Anthony of Isenheim, the *Isenheim Altarpiece* consists of a wooden shrine (carved by

NIKOLAUS HAGENAUER in 1490) that includes gilded and polychromed statues of Saints Anthony Abbot, Augustine, and Jerome (FIG. 18-2, *bottom*) in addition to Grünewald's two pairs of movable wings that open at the center. Hinged together at the sides, one pair stands directly behind the other. Grünewald painted the exterior panels of the first pair (visible when the altarpiece is closed, FIG. 18-2, *top*) between 1510 and 1515: *Crucifixion* in the center, *Saint Sebastian* on the left, *Saint Anthony* on the right, and *Lamentation* in the predella. When these exterior wings are open, four additional scenes (not illustrated)—*Annunciation, Angelic Concert, Madonna and Child,* and *Resurrection*—appear. Opening this second pair of wings exposes Hagenauer's interior shrine, flanked by Grünewald's panels depicting *Meeting of Saints Anthony and Paul* and *Temptation of Saint Anthony* (FIG. 18-2, *bottom*).

The placement of this altarpiece in the choir of a church adjacent to the monastery hospital dictated much of the imagery. Saints associated with the plague and other diseases and with miraculous cures, such as Saints Anthony and Sebastian, appear prominently in the *Isenheim Altarpiece.* Grünewald's panels specifically address the themes of dire illness and miraculous healing and accordingly emphasize the suffering of the order's patron saint, Anthony. The painted images served as warnings, encouraging increased devotion from monks and hospital patients. They also functioned therapeutically by offering some hope to the afflicted. Indeed, Saint Anthony's legend encompassed his role as both vengeful dispenser of justice (by inflicting disease) and benevolent healer. Grünewald brilliantly used color to enhance the impact of the altarpiece. He intensified the contrast of horror and hope by playing subtle tones and soft harmonies against shocking dissonance of color.

One of the most memorable scenes is *Temptation of Saint Anthony* (FIG. 18-2, *bottom right*). It is a terrifying image of the five temptations, depicted as an assortment of ghoulish and bestial creatures in a dark landscape, attacking the saint. In the foreground, Grünewald

18-2 MATTHIAS GRÜNEWALD, *Isenheim Altarpiece* (closed, *top;* open, *bottom*), from the chapel of the Hospital of Saint Anthony, Isenheim, Germany, ca. 1510–1515. Oil on wood, 9′ 9½″ × 10′ 9″ (center panel), 8′ 2½″ × 3′ ½″ (each wing), 2′ 5½″ × 11′ 2″ (predella). Shrine carved by NIKOLAUS HAGENAUER in 1490. Painted and gilt limewood, 9′ 9½″ × 10′ 9″. Musée d'Unterlinden, Colmar.

Befitting its setting in a monastic hospital, Matthias Grünewald's *Isenheim Altarpiece* includes painted panels depicting suffering and disease but also miraculous healing, hope, and salvation.

painted a grotesque image of a man, whose oozing boils, withered arm, and distended stomach all suggest a horrible disease. Medical experts have connected these symptoms with ergotism (a disease caused by ergot, a fungus that grows especially on rye). Although doctors did not discover the cause of ergotism until about 1600, people lived in fear of its recognizable symptoms (convulsions and gangrene). The public referred to this illness as "Saint Anthony's Fire," and it was one of the major diseases treated at the Isenheim hospital. The gangrene often compelled amputation, and scholars have noted that the two movable halves of the altarpiece's predella (FIG. 18-2, *top*), if slid apart, make it appear as if Christ's legs have been amputated. The same observation can be made with regard to the two main exterior panels. Due to the off-center placement of the cross, opening the left panel "severs" one arm from the crucified figure.

Thus, Grünewald carefully selected and presented his altarpiece's iconography to be particularly meaningful for viewers at this hospital. In the interior shrine, the artist balanced the horrors of the disease and the punishments that awaited those who did not repent with scenes such as *Meeting of Saints Anthony and Paul,* depicting the two saints, healthy and aged, conversing peacefully. Even the exterior panels (the closed altarpiece; FIG. 18-2, *top*) convey these same concerns. *Crucifixion* emphasizes Christ's pain and suffering, but the knowledge that this act redeemed humanity tempers the misery. In addition, Saint Anthony appears in the right wing as a devout follower of Christ who, like Christ and for Christ, endured intense suffering for his faith. Saint Anthony's presence on the exterior thus reinforces the themes Grünewald intertwined throughout this entire altarpiece—themes of pain, illness, and death, as well as those of hope, comfort, and salvation.

HANS BALDUNG GRIEN Very different in size, technique, and subject, but equally dramatic, is *Witches' Sabbath* (FIG. **18-3**), a *chiaroscuro woodcut* that HANS BALDUNG GRIEN (ca. 1484–1545) produced in 1510. Chiaroscuro woodcuts were a recent German innovation. The technique requires the use of two blocks of wood instead of one. The printmaker carves and inks one block in the usual way in order to produce a traditional black-and-white print (see "Woodcuts, Engravings, and Etchings," Chapter 15, page 415). Then the artist cuts a second block consisting of broad highlights that can be inked in gray or color and printed over the first block's impression. Chiaroscuro woodcuts therefore incorporate some of the qualities of painting and feature tonal subtleties absent in traditional woodcuts.

Witchcraft was a counter-religion in the 15th and 16th centuries that involved magical rituals, secret potions, and devil worship. Witches prepared brews that they inhaled or rubbed into their skin, sending them into hallucinogenic trances in which they allegedly flew through the night sky on broomsticks or goats. The popes condemned all witches, and Church inquisitors vigorously pursued these demonic heretics and subjected them to torture to wrest confessions from them. Witchcraft fascinated Baldung, and he turned to the subject repeatedly. For him and his contemporaries, witches were evil forces in the world, threats to man—as was Eve herself, whom Baldung also frequently depicted as a temptress responsible for Original Sin.

In *Witches' Sabbath,* Baldung depicted a night scene in a forest in which a coven of nude witches—both young seductresses and old hags—gathers around a covered jar from which a fuming concoction escapes into the air. One young witch rides through the night sky on a goat. She sits backward—Baldung's way of suggesting that witchcraft is the inversion of the true religion, Christianity.

ALBRECHT DÜRER The dominant artist of the early 16th century in the Holy Roman Empire was ALBRECHT DÜRER (1471–1528) of Nuremberg. Dürer was the first artist outside Italy to become an

18-3 HANS BALDUNG GRIEN, *Witches' Sabbath,* 1510. Chiaroscuro woodcut, 1′ 2⅞″ × 10¼″. British Museum, London.

Baldung's chiaroscuro woodcut depicts witches gathered around a secret potion. One witch on a goat flies through the night sky mounted backward—suggesting witchcraft is the inversion of Christianity.

international celebrity. He traveled extensively, visiting and studying in Colmar, Basel, Strasbourg, Venice, Antwerp, and Brussels, among other locales. As a result of these travels, Dürer met many of the leading humanists and artists of his time, including Erasmus of Rotterdam and the Venetian master Giovanni Bellini (FIGS. 17-33 and 17-34). A man of exceptional talents and tremendous energy, Dürer achieved widespread fame in his own time and has enjoyed a lofty reputation ever since.

Fascinated with classical ideas as passed along by Italian Renaissance artists, Dürer was among the first Northern European artists to travel to Italy expressly to study Italian art and its underlying theories at their source. After his first journey in 1494–1495 (the second was in 1505–1506), he incorporated many Italian Renaissance developments into his art. Art historians have acclaimed Dürer as the first Northern European artist to understand fully the basic aims of the Renaissance in Italy. Like Leonardo da Vinci, Dürer wrote theoretical treatises on a variety of subjects, such as perspective, fortification, and the ideal in human proportions. Unlike Leonardo, he both finished and published his writings. Dürer also was the first Northern European artist to leave a record of his life and career through several self-portraits, through his correspondence, and through a carefully kept, quite detailed, and eminently readable diary.

18-4 ALBRECHT DÜRER, *Great Piece of Turf*, 1503. Watercolor, 1′ 3¾″ × 1′ 3⁄8″. Albertina, Vienna.

Albrecht Dürer, who visited Italy twice, shared Leonardo da Vinci's belief that sight reveals scientific truth. Botanists have been able to identify each plant and grass variety in this watercolor.

GREAT PIECE OF TURF Dürer allied himself with Leonardo's scientific studies when he painted an extremely precise watercolor study of a piece of turf (FIG. **18-4**). For both artists, observation yielded truth. Sight, sanctified by mystics such as Nicholas of Cusa (1401–1464) and artists such as Jan van Eyck (see Chapter 15), became the secularized instrument of modern knowledge. Dürer agreed with Aristotle (and Leonardo) that "sight is the noblest sense of man."[1] Nature holds the beautiful, Dürer said, for the artist who has the insight to extract it. Thus, beauty lies even in humble, perhaps ugly, things, and the ideal, which bypasses or improves on nature, may not be truly beautiful in the end. Disordered and ordinary nature might be a reasonable object of an artist's interest, quite as much as its composed and measured aspect. The remarkable *Great Piece of Turf* is as scientifically accurate as it is poetic. Botanists can distinguish each plant and grass variety—dandelions, great plantain, yarrow, meadow grass, and heath rush. "[D]epart not from nature according to your fancy," Dürer said, "imagining to find aught better by yourself; . . . For verily 'art' is embedded in nature; he who can extract it, has it."[2]

FALL OF MAN Dürer's fame in his own day, as today, rested more on his achievements as a printmaker than as a painter. Trained as a goldsmith by his father before he took up painting and printmaking, he developed an extraordinary proficiency in handling the burin, the engraving tool. This technical ability, combined with a feeling for the form-creating possibilities of line, enabled him to produce a body of graphic work in woodcut (FIG. I-8) and engraving (FIGS. 18-1 and 18-5) that few artists have rivaled for quality and number. Dürer created numerous book illustrations. He also circulated and sold prints in single sheets, which people of ordinary means could buy, expanding his audience considerably. Aggressively marketing his prints with the aid of an agent, Dürer became a wealthy man from the sale of these works. His wife, who served as his manager, and his mother also sold his prints at markets. Through his graphic works, he exerted strong influence throughout Europe (Hans Baldung Grien trained in Dürer's workshop), especially in Flanders but also in Italy. The lawsuit Dürer brought in 1506 against an Italian artist for copying his prints reveals his business acumen. Scholars generally regard this lawsuit as the first in history over artistic copyright.

An engraving, *Fall of Man* (*Adam and Eve*; FIG. **18-1**), one of Dürer's early masterpieces, represents the first distillation of his studies of the Vitruvian theory of human proportions, a theory based on arithmetic ratios. Clearly outlined against the dark background of a northern forest, the two idealized figures of Adam and Eve stand in poses reminiscent of specific classical statues probably known to Dürer through graphic representations. Preceded by numerous geometric drawings in which the artist attempted to systematize sets of ideal human proportions in balanced contrapposto poses, the final print presents Dürer's concept of the "perfect" male and female figures. Yet he tempered this idealization with naturalism, demonstrating his well-honed observational skills in his rendering of the background foliage and animals. The gnarled bark of the trees and the feathery leaves authenticate the scene, as do the various creatures skulking underfoot. The animals populating the print are symbolic. The choleric cat, the melancholic elk, the sanguine rabbit, and the phlegmatic ox represent humanity's temperaments based on the "four humors," body fluids that were the basis of theories of the human body's function developed by the ancient Greek physician Hippocrates and practiced in medieval physiology. The tension between cat and mouse in the foreground symbolizes the relation between Adam and Eve at the crucial moment in *Fall of Man*.

KNIGHT, DEATH, AND THE DEVIL Dürer's lifelong interest in both idealization and naturalism surfaces again in *Knight, Death, and the Devil* (FIG. **18-5**), in which he carried the art of engraving to the highest degree of excellence. Dürer used his burin to render differences in texture and tonal values that would be difficult to match even in the much more flexible medium of etching, which artists developed later in the century (see "Woodcuts, Engravings, and Etchings," Chapter 15, page 415). *Knight, Death, and the Devil* depicts a mounted armored knight who rides fearlessly through a foreboding landscape. Accompanied by his faithful retriever, the knight represents a Christian knight—a soldier of God. Armed with his faith, this warrior can repel the threats of Death, who appears as a crowned decaying cadaver wreathed with snakes and shaking an hourglass as a reminder of time and mortality. The knight is equally impervious to the Devil, a pathetically hideous horned creature who follows him. The knight triumphs because he has "put on the whole armor of God that [he] may be able to stand against the wiles of the devil," as urged in Saint Paul's Epistle to the Ephesians (Eph. 6:11).

The monumental knight and his mount display the strength, movement, and proportions of the Italian Renaissance equestrian statue. Dürer was familiar with Donatello's *Gattamelata* (FIG. 16-15) and Verrocchio's *Bartolommeo Colleoni* (FIG. 16-16) and had copied a number of Leonardo's sketches of horses. Dürer based the engraving on his observation of the real world, however, not other artworks, as seen in his meticulous rendering of myriad details—the knight's armor and weapons, the horse's anatomy, the textures of the

18-5 ALBRECHT DÜRER, *Knight, Death, and the Devil*, 1513. Engraving, $9\frac{5}{8}'' \times 7\frac{3}{8}''$. Metropolitan Museum of Art, New York.

Dürer's Christian knight, armed with his faith, rides fearlessly through a meticulously rendered landscape, challenging both Death and the Devil. The engraving rivals the tonal range of painting.

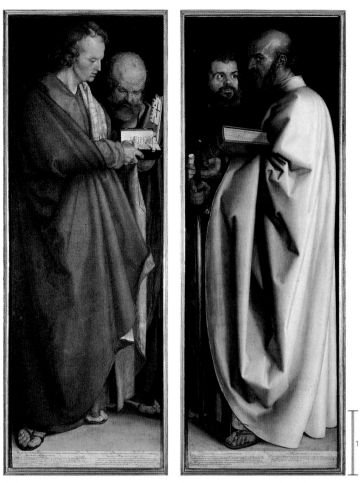

18-6 ALBRECHT DÜRER, *Four Apostles*, 1526. Oil on wood, each panel $7'\ 1'' \times 2'\ 6''$. Alte Pinakothek, Munich.

Dürer's support for Lutheranism surfaces in his portraitlike depictions of four saints on two painted panels. Peter, representative of the pope in Rome, plays a secondary role behind John the Evangelist.

loathsome features of Death and the Devil, the rock forms and rugged foliage. Dürer realized this great variety of imagery with the dense hatching of fluidly engraved lines that rival the tonal range of painting. Erasmus appropriately praised Dürer as the "Apelles [the famous ancient Greek painter] of black lines."[3]

FOUR APOSTLES Dürer was a phenomenally gifted artist. His impressive technical facility with different media extended also to oil painting. *Four Apostles* (FIG. **18-6**) is a two-panel oil painting he produced without commission and presented to the city fathers of Nuremberg in 1526 to be hung in the city hall. Saints John and Peter appear on the left panel, Mark and Paul on the right. In addition to showcasing Dürer's mastery of the oil technique, of his brilliant use of color and light and shade, and of his ability to imbue the four saints with individual personalities and portraitlike features, *Four Apostles* documents Dürer's support for the German theologian Martin Luther (1483–1546), who sparked the Protestant Reformation. Dürer conveyed his Lutheran sympathies by his positioning of the figures. He relegated Saint Peter (as representative of the pope in Rome) to a secondary role by placing him behind John the Evangelist. John assumed particular prominence for Luther because of the evangelist's focus on Christ's person in his Gospel. In addition, Peter and John both read from the Bible, the single authoritative source of religious truth, according to Luther. Dürer emphasized the Bible's centrality by depicting it open to the passage "In the beginning was the Word, and

the Word was with God, and the Word was God" (John 1:1). At the bottom of the panels, Dürer included quotations from each of the four apostles' books, using Luther's German translation. The excerpts warn against the coming of perilous times and the preaching of false prophets who will distort God's word.

LUTHER AND THE REFORMATION The Protestant Reformation, which came to fruition in the early 16th century, had its roots in long-term, growing dissatisfaction with Church leadership. The deteriorating relationship between the faithful and the Church hierarchy stood as an obstacle for the millions who sought a meaningful religious experience. Particularly damaging was the perception that the Roman popes concerned themselves more with temporal power and material wealth than with the salvation of Church members. The fact that many 15th-century popes and cardinals came from wealthy families, such as the Medici, intensified this perception. It was not only those at the highest levels who seemed to ignore their spiritual duties. Upper-level clergy (such as archbishops, bishops, and abbots) began to accumulate numerous offices, thereby increasing their revenues but also making it more difficult for them to fulfill all of their responsibilities. By 1517 dissatisfaction with the Church had grown so widespread that Luther felt free to challenge papal authority openly by posting in Wittenberg his *Ninety-five Theses,* in which he enumerated his objections to Church practices, especially the sale of indulgences. *Indulgences* were Church-sanctioned remittances (or reductions) of

Catholic and Protestant Views of Salvation

A central concern of the Protestant reformers was the question of how Christians achieve salvation. Martin Luther did not perceive salvation as something for which weak and sinful humans must constantly strive through good deeds performed under the watchful eye of a punitive God. Instead, he argued, faithful individuals attained redemption solely by God's bestowal of his grace. Therefore, people cannot earn salvation. Further, no ecclesiastical machinery with all its miraculous rites and indulgent forgivenesses could save sinners face-to-face with God. Only absolute faith in Christ could justify sinners and ensure salvation. Justification by faith alone, with the guidance of scripture, was the fundamental doctrine of Protestantism.

In *Allegory of Law and Grace* (FIG. 18-7), Lucas Cranach the Elder gave pictorial form to these doctrinal differences between Protestantism and Catholicism. Cranach was a follower and close friend of Martin Luther. (They were godfathers to each other's children.) Many scholars, in fact, call Cranach "the painter of the Reformation." Cranach produced his allegorical woodcut about a dozen years after

Luther set the Reformation in motion with his *Ninety-five Theses.* In *Allegory of Law and Grace,* Cranach depicted the differences between Catholicism (based on Old Testament law, according to Luther) and Protestantism (based on a belief in God's grace) in two images separated by a centrally placed tree. On the left half, Judgment Day has arrived, as represented by Christ's appearance at the top of the scene, hovering amid a cloud halo and accompanied by angels and saints. Christ raises his left hand in the traditional gesture of damnation, and, below, a skeleton drives off a terrified person to burn for eternity in Hell. This person tried to live a good and honorable life, but despite his efforts, he fell short. Moses stands to the side, holding the Tablets of the Law—the commandments Catholics follow in their attempt to attain salvation. In contrast to this Catholic reliance on good works and clean living, Protestants emphasized God's grace as the source of redemption. Accordingly, God showers the sinner in the right half of the print with grace, as streams of blood flow from the crucified Christ. On the far right, Christ emerges from the tomb and promises salvation to all who believe in him.

18-7 LUCAS CRANACH THE ELDER, *Allegory of Law and Grace,* ca. 1530. Woodcut, $10\frac{5}{8}''\times 1'\ \frac{3}{4}''$. British Museum, London.

Lucas Cranach was a close friend of Martin Luther, whose *Ninety-five Theses* launched the Reformation in 1517. In this woodcut Cranach contrasted Catholic and Protestant views of how to achieve salvation.

time spent in Purgatory. The increasing frequency of their sale suggested that people were buying their way into Heaven.

Luther's goal was significant reform and clarification of major spiritual issues, but his ideas ultimately led to the splitting of Christendom. According to Luther, the Catholic Church's extensive ecclesiastical structure needed to be cast out, for it had no basis in scripture. Only the Bible—nothing else—could serve as the foundation

for Christianity. Luther declared the pope the Antichrist (for which the pope excommunicated him), called the Church the "whore of Babylon," and denounced ordained priests. He also rejected most of Catholicism's sacraments, decrying them as pagan obstacles to salvation (see "Catholic and Protestant Views of Salvation," above, and FIG. 18-7). Luther maintained that for Christianity to be restored to its original purity, the Church must be cleansed of all the doctrinal

Protestantism and Iconoclasm

The Protestant concern over the role of religious imagery at times progressed to outright *iconoclasm*—the objection to and destruction of religious imagery (see "Icons and Iconoclasm," Chapter 9, page 246). In encouraging a more personal relationship with God, Protestant leaders spoke out against much of the religious art being produced. In his 1525 tract *Against the Heavenly Prophets in the Matter of Images and Sacraments,* Martin Luther explained his attitude toward religious imagery:

> I approached the task of destroying images by first tearing them out of the heart through God's Word and making them worthless and despised. . . . For when they are no longer in the heart, they can do no harm when seen with the eyes. . . . I have allowed and not forbidden the outward removal of images. . . . And I say at the outset that according to the law of Moses no other images are forbidden than an image of God which one worships. A crucifix, on the other hand, or any other holy image is not forbidden.*

Ulrich Zwingli (1484–1531), leader of the Zwinglians (a Protestant sect based in Switzerland), concurred with Luther and cautioned his followers about the potentially dangerous nature of religious imagery. Although Zwingli's ideas had much in common with those of Luther, he was more intent than Luther on simplifying religious belief and practices and rejected all sacraments (unlike Luther, who accepted both baptism and communion).

The Protestant Ten Commandments, which, although also excerpted from the Bible, differ slightly from those of the Catholic Church, further reinforced the Protestant condemnation of possibly idolatrous religious imagery. For Protestants, this is the Second Commandment:

> Thou shalt not make unto thee any graven image, or any likeness of any thing that is in heaven above, or that is in the earth beneath, or that is in the water under the earth. Thou shalt not bow down thyself to them, nor serve them, for I the Lord thy God am a jealous God, visiting the iniquity of the fathers upon the children unto the third and fourth generation of them that hate me. And showing mercy unto thousands of them that love me, and keep my commandments.

These many Protestant proscriptions against religious imagery often led to eruptions of iconoclasm. Particularly violent waves of iconoclastic fervor swept Basel, Zurich, Strasbourg, and Wittenberg in the 1520s. In an episode known as the Great Iconoclasm, bands of Calvinists visited Catholic churches in the Netherlands in 1566, shattering stained-glass windows, smashing statues, and destroying paintings and other artworks that they perceived as idolatrous. These strong reactions to art not only reflect the religious fervor of the time but also serve as dramatic demonstrations of the power of art—and of how much art mattered.

* Translated by Bernhard Erling, in Wolfgang Stechow, *Northern Renaissance Art 1400–1600: Sources and Documents* (Englewood Cliffs, N.J.: Prentice Hall, 1966), 129–130.

---

impurities that had collected through the ages. Luther advocated the Bible as the source of all religious truth. The Bible—the sole scriptural authority—was the word of God, and the Church's councils, law, and rituals carried no weight. Luther facilitated the lay public's access to biblical truths by producing the first translation of the Bible in a vernacular language. Luther's teachings found visual expression in *Allegory of Law and Grace* (FIG. 18-7) by Lucas Cranach the Elder (1472–1553).

VISUAL IMAGERY AND THE REFORMATION In addition to doctrinal differences, Catholics and Protestants took divergent stances on the role of visual imagery in religion. Catholics embraced church decoration as an aid to communicating with God, as seen in Italian ceiling frescoes (FIG. 17-1; see "Religious Art in Counter-Reformation Italy," Chapter 17, page 474) and German and Polish altarpieces (FIGS. 15-18, 15-19, and 18-2). In contrast, Protestants believed such imagery could lead to idolatry and would distract viewers from focusing on the real reason for their presence in church—to communicate directly with God (see "Protestantism and Iconoclasm," above). Because of this belief, Protestant churches were relatively austere and unadorned, and the extensive church decoration programs found especially in Italy were not as prominent in Protestant churches. This does not suggest that Protestants had no use for visual images. Art, especially prints (which were inexpensive and easily circulated), was a useful and effective teaching tool and facilitated the private devotional exercises that were fundamental to Protestantism. The popularity of prints both contributed to and received impetus from the transition from handwritten manuscripts to print media in Northern Europe during the 16th century.

ALBRECHT ALTDORFER Some 16th-century artists in the Holy Roman Empire addressed historical and political issues in their work. ALBRECHT ALTDORFER (ca. 1480–1538), for example, painted *Battle of Issus* (FIG. 18-8) in 1529, a depiction of Alexander the Great's defeat of King Darius III of Persia in 333 BCE at a town called Issus on the Pinarus River. Altdorfer announced the subject (which the Greek painter Philoxenos of Eretria [FIG. 5-70] had represented two millennia before) in the Latin inscription that hangs in the sky. The duke of Bavaria, Wilhelm IV (r. 1508–1550), commissioned *Battle of Issus* at the commencement of his military campaign against the invading Turks. The parallels between the historical and contemporary conflicts were no doubt significant to the duke. Both involved societies that deemed themselves progressive as being engaged in battles against infidels—the Persians in antiquity and the Turks in 1528. Altdorfer reinforced this connection by attiring the figures in 16th-century armor and depicting them embroiled in contemporary military alignments.

The scene also reveals Altdorfer's love of landscape. The battle takes place in an almost cosmological setting. From a bird's-eye view, the clashing armies swarm in the foreground. In the distance, craggy mountain peaks rise next to still bodies of water. Amid swirling clouds, a blazing sun descends. Although the spectacular topography may appear imaginary or invented, Altdorfer derived his depiction of the landscape from maps. Specifically, he set the scene

18-8 ALBRECHT ALTDORFER, *Battle of Issus*, 1529. Oil on wood, 5′ 2¼″ × 3′ 11¼″. Alte Pinakothek, Munich.

Interweaving history and 16th-century politics, Albrecht Altdorfer painted Alexander the Great's defeat of the Persians for a patron who had just embarked on a military campaign against the Turks.

1 ft.

in the eastern Mediterranean with a view from Greece to the Nile in Egypt. In addition, Altdorfer may have acquired his information about this battle from the German scholar Johannes Aventinus (1477–1534). In his account, Aventinus described the bloody day-long battle and Alexander's ultimate victory. Appropriately, given Alexander's designation as the "sun god," the sun sets over the victorious Greeks on the right, while a small crescent moon (a symbol of the Near East) hovers in the upper left corner over the retreating Persians.

HANS HOLBEIN Choosing less dramatic scenes, HANS HOLBEIN THE YOUNGER (ca. 1497–1543) excelled as a portraitist. Trained by his father, Holbein produced portraits reflecting the Northern European tradition of close realism that had emerged in 15th-century Flemish art (see Chapter 15). Yet he also incorporated Italian ideas about monumental composition and sculpturesque form. The surfaces of his paintings are as lustrous as enamel, his detail is exact and exquisitely drawn, and his contrasts of light and dark are never heavy.

Holbein began his artistic career in Basel, where he knew Erasmus of Rotterdam. Because of the immediate threat of a religious civil war in Basel, Erasmus suggested that Holbein leave for England and gave him a recommendation to Thomas More, chancellor of England under Henry VIII. Holbein did move and became painter to the English court. While there, he produced a superb double portrait of the French

18-9 HANS HOLBEIN THE YOUNGER, *The French Ambassadors*, 1533. Oil and tempera on wood, 6′ 8″ × 6′ 9½″. National Gallery, London.

In this double portrait, Holbein depicted two humanists with a collection of objects reflective of their worldliness and learning, but he also included an anamorphic skull, a reminder of death.

ambassadors to England, Jean de Dinteville (at *left*) and Georges de Selve. *The French Ambassadors* (FIG. **18-9**) exhibits Holbein's considerable talents—his strong sense of composition, his subtle linear patterning, his gift for portraiture, his marvelous sensitivity to color, and his faultlessly firm technique. The two men, both ardent humanists, stand at opposite ends of a side table covered with an oriental rug and a collection of objects reflective of their worldliness and their interest in learning and the arts. These include mathematical and astronomical models and implements, a lute with a broken string, compasses, a sundial, flutes, globes, and an open hymnbook with Luther's translation of *Veni, Creator Spiritus* and of the Ten Commandments.

Of particular interest is the long gray shape that slashes diagonally across the picture plane and interrupts the stable, balanced, and serene composition. This form is an *anamorphic image,* a distorted image recognizable only when viewed with a special device, such as a cylindrical mirror, or by looking at the painting at an acute angle. In this case, if the viewer stands off to the right, the gray slash becomes a skull. Although scholars do not agree on the skull's meaning, at the very least it certainly refers to death. Artists commonly incorporated skulls into paintings as reminders of mortality. Indeed, Holbein depicted a skull on the metal medallion on Jean de Dinteville's hat. Holbein may have intended the skulls, in conjunction with the cruci-

fix that appears half hidden behind the curtain in the upper left corner, to encourage viewers to ponder death and resurrection.

This painting may also allude to the growing tension between secular and religious authorities. Jean de Dinteville was a titled landowner, Georges de Selve a bishop. The inclusion of Luther's translations next to the lute with the broken string (a symbol of discord) may subtly refer to this religious strife. Despite scholars' uncertainty about the precise meaning of *The French Ambassadors,* it is a painting of supreme artistic achievement. Holbein rendered the still-life objects with the same meticulous care as the men themselves, the woven design of the deep emerald curtain behind them, and the floor tiles, constructed in faultless perspective. He surely hoped this painting's elegance and virtuosity of skill (produced shortly after Holbein arrived in England) would impress Henry VIII.

FRANCE

As *The French Ambassadors* illustrates, France in the early 16th century continued its efforts to secure widespread recognition as a political power and cultural force. The French kings were major patrons of art and architecture.

18-10 JEAN CLOUET, *Francis I,* ca. 1525–1530. Tempera and oil on wood, 3′ 2″ × 2′ 5″. Louvre, Paris.

Clouet's portrait of Francis I in elegant garb reveals the artist's attention to detail but also the flattening of features and disproportion between head and body, giving the painting a formalized quality.

1 ft.

FRANCIS I Under the rule of Francis I (r. 1515–1547), the French established a firm foothold in Milan and its environs. Francis waged a campaign (known as the Habsburg-Valois Wars) against Charles V (the Spanish king and Holy Roman Emperor; r. 1516–1558), which occupied him from 1521 to 1544. These wars involved disputed territories—southern France, the Netherlands, the Rhinelands, northern Spain, and Italy—and reflected France's central role in the shifting geopolitical landscape.

The French king also took a strong position in the religious controversies of his day. By the mid-16th century, the split between Catholics and Protestants had become so pronounced that subjects often felt compelled either to accept the religion of their sovereign or to emigrate to a territory where the sovereign's religion corresponded with their own. France was predominantly Catholic, and in 1534 Francis declared Protestantism illegal. The state persecuted its Protestants, the Huguenots, and drove them underground. The Huguenots' commitment to Protestantism eventually led to one of the bloodiest religious massacres in European history when the Protestants and Catholics clashed in Paris on August 24, 1572, with the violence quickly spreading throughout France.

Francis I also endeavored to elevate his country's cultural profile. To that end, he invited several esteemed Italian artists, including Leonardo da Vinci, to his court. Francis's attempt to glorify the state

and himself meant the religious art that dominated the Middle Ages no longer prevailed, for the king and not the Christian Church held the power.

The portrait (FIG. **18-10**) JEAN CLOUET (ca. 1485–1541) painted of Francis I about a decade after he became king shows a worldly ruler magnificently bedecked in silks and brocades, wearing a gold chain with a medallion of the Order of Saint Michael, a French order Louis XI founded in 1469. Legend has it that the "merry monarch" was a great lover and the hero of hundreds of "gallant" deeds. Appropriately, he appears suave and confident, with his hand resting on the pommel of a dagger. Despite the careful detail, the portrait also exhibits an elegantly formalized quality, the result of Clouet's suppression of modeling, which flattens features, seen particularly in Francis's neck. The disproportion between the king's small head and his broad body, swathed in heavy layers of fabric, adds to the formalized nature.

Francis and his court favored art that was at once elegant, erotic, and unorthodox. Appropriately, Mannerism appealed to them most, and Francis thus brought Benvenuto Cellini (FIG. **17-51**) to France with the promise of a lucrative retainer (see Chapter 17). He also put two prominent Florentine Mannerists—Rosso Fiorentino and Francesco Primaticcio—in charge of decorating the new royal palace at Fontainebleau.

18-11 Château de Chambord, Chambord, France, begun 1519.

French Renaissance châteaux, which developed from medieval castles, served as country houses for royalty. King Francis I's Château de Chambord reflects Italian palazzo design but features a Gothic roof.

CHÂTEAU DE CHAMBORD Francis I indulged his passion for building by commissioning several large *châteaux*, among them the Château de Chambord (FIG. **18-11**). Reflecting more peaceful times, these châteaux, developed from medieval castles, served as country houses for royalty, who usually built them near forests for use as hunting lodges. Construction of Chambord began in 1519, but Francis I never saw its completion. Chambord's plan, originally drawn by a pupil of Giuliano da Sangallo, includes a central square block with four corridors, in the shape of a cross, and a broad, central staircase that gives access to groups of rooms—ancestors of the modern suite of rooms or apartments. At each of the four corners, a round tower punctuates the square plan, and a moat surrounds the whole. From the exterior, Chambord presents a carefully contrived horizontal accent on three levels, with continuous moldings separating its floors. Windows align precisely, one exactly over another. The Italian Renaissance palazzo served as the model for this matching of horizontal and vertical features, but above the third level the structure's lines break chaotically into a jumble of high dormers, chimneys, and lanterns that recall soaring ragged Gothic silhouettes on the skyline.

LOUVRE, PARIS Chambord essentially retains French architectural characteristics. During the reign of Francis's successor, Henry II (r. 1547–1559), however, translations of Italian architectural treatises appeared, and Italian architects themselves came to work in France.

Moreover, the French turned to Italy for study and travel. These exchanges caused a more extensive revolution in style than earlier, although certain French elements derived from the Gothic tradition persisted. This incorporation of Italian architectural ideas characterizes the redesigned Louvre in Paris, originally a medieval palace and fortress (FIG. **15-16**). Since Charles V's renovation of the Louvre in the mid-14th century, the castle had languished relatively empty and fallen into a state of disrepair. Francis I initiated the project to update and expand the royal palace, but he died before the work was well under way. His architect, PIERRE LESCOT (1510–1578), continued under Henry II and produced the classical style later associated with 16th-century French architecture.

Although Chambord incorporated the formal vocabulary of the Early Renaissance, particularly from Lombardy, Lescot and his associates were familiar with the architectural style of Bramante and his school. In the west wing of the Cour Carré (Square Court; FIG. **18-12**)

18-12 PIERRE LESCOT, west wing of the Cour Carré (Square Court) of the Louvre, Paris, France, begun 1546.

Lescot's design for the Louvre palace reflects the Italian Renaissance classicism of Bramante, but the decreasing height of the stories, large scale of the windows, and steep roof are Northern European features.

of the Louvre, each of the stories forms a complete order, and the cornices project enough to furnish a strong horizontal accent. The arcading on the ground story reflects the ancient Roman use of arches and produces more shadow than in the upper stories due to its recessed placement, thereby strengthening the design's visual base. On the second story, the pilasters rising from bases and the alternating curved and angular pediments supported by consoles have direct antecedents in several High Renaissance palaces (for example, FIG. 17-27). Yet the decreasing height of the stories, the scale of the windows (proportionately much larger than in Italian Renaissance buildings), and the steep roof suggest Northern European models. Especially French are the pavilions jutting from the wall. A feature the French long favored—double columns framing a niche—punctuates the pavilions. The building's vertical lines assert themselves. Openings deeply penetrate the wall, and sculptures by Jean Goujon (ca. 1510–1565) abound. Other Northern European countries imitated this French classical manner—its double-columned pavilions, tall and wide windows, profuse statuary, and steep roofs—although with local variations. The modified classicism the French produced was the only classicism to serve as a model for Northern European architects through most of the 16th century.

THE NETHERLANDS

With the demise of the Duchy of Burgundy in 1477 and the division of that territory between France and the Holy Roman Empire, the Netherlands at the beginning of the 16th century consisted of 17 provinces (corresponding to modern Holland, Belgium, and Luxembourg). The Netherlands was among the most commercially advanced and prosperous European countries. Its extensive network of rivers and easy access to the Atlantic Ocean provided a setting conducive to overseas trade, and shipbuilding was one of the most profitable businesses. The region's commercial center shifted geographically toward the end of the 15th century, partly because of buildup of silt in the Bruges estuary. Traffic relocated to Antwerp, which became the hub of economic activity in the Netherlands after 1510. As many as 500 ships a day passed through Antwerp's harbor, and large trading companies from England, the Holy Roman Empire, Italy, Portugal, and Spain established themselves in the city.

During the second half of the 16th century, the Netherlands was under the political control of Philip II of Spain (r. 1556–1598), who had inherited the region from his father Charles V. The economic prosperity of the Netherlands served as a potent incentive for Philip II to strengthen his control over the territory. However, his heavy-handed tactics and repressive measures led in 1579 to revolt, resulting in the formation of two federations. The Union of Arras, a Catholic confederation of southern Netherlandish provinces, remained under Spanish dominion, and the Union of Utrecht, consisting of Protestant northern provinces, became the Dutch Republic (MAP 20-1).

The increasing number of Netherlandish citizens converting to Protestantism affected the arts and resulted in a corresponding decrease in large-scale altarpieces and religious works (although grand works continued to be commissioned for Catholic churches). Much of Netherlandish art of this period provides a wonderful glimpse into the lives of various strata of society, from nobility to peasantry, capturing their activities, environment, and values.

HIERONYMUS BOSCH The most famous Netherlandish painter at the turn of the 16th century was HIERONYMUS BOSCH (ca. 1450–1516), whose most famous work is *Garden of Earthly Delights* (FIG. 18-13). Bosch is one of the most fascinating and puzzling

18-13 HIERONYMUS BOSCH, *Garden of Earthly Delights*, 1505–1510. Oil on wood, center panel 7′ 2⅝″ × 6′ 4¾″, each wing 7′ 2⅝″ × 3′ 2¼″. Museo del Prado, Madrid.

Bosch was the most imaginative and enigmatic painter of his era. In this triptych, which may commemorate a wedding, he created a fantasy world filled with nude men and women and bizarre creatures and objects.

18-14 JAN GOSSAERT, *Neptune and Amphitrite*, ca. 1516. Oil on wood, 6' 2" × 4' $\frac{3}{4}$". Gemäldegalerie, Staatliche Museen, Berlin.

Dürer's *Fall of Man* (FIG. 18-1) inspired the poses of Gossaert's classical deities, but the architectural setting is probably based on sketches of ancient buildings Gossaert made during his trip to Rome.

1 ft.

painters in history. Interpretations of Bosch differ widely. Scholars debate whether he was a satirist, an irreligious mocker, or a pornographer, a heretic or an orthodox fanatic like Girolamo Savonarola, his Italian contemporary (see Chapter 16).

Garden of Earthly Delights is Bosch's most enigmatic, and no interpretation has ever won universal acceptance. This large-scale work takes the familiar form of a monumental triptych. The format suggests a religious function for Bosch's painting, but *Garden of Earthly Delights* resided in the palace of Henry III of Nassau, regent of the Netherlands, seven years after its completion. This location suggests a secular commission for private use. Some scholars have proposed that, given the work's central themes of marriage, sex, and procreation, the painting probably commemorates a wedding, a theme seen earlier in *Giovanni Arnolfini and His Bride* (FIG. 15-1) and in *A Goldsmith in His Shop* (FIG. 15-11). Any similarity to these paintings ends there, however. Whereas Jan van Eyck and Petrus Christus grounded their depictions of betrothed couples in 15th-century life and custom, Bosch's image portrays a visionary world of fantasy and intrigue.

In the left panel, God presents Eve to Adam in a landscape, presumably the Garden of Eden. Bosch placed the event in a wildly imaginative setting that includes an odd pink fountainlike structure in a body of water and an array of fanciful and unusual animals. These details may hint at an interpretation involving *alchemy*—the medieval study of seemingly magical changes, especially chemical changes. (Witchcraft also involved alchemy.) The right panel, in contrast, bombards viewers with the horrors of Hell. Beastly creatures devour people, while others are impaled or strung on musical instruments, as if on a medieval rack. A gambler is nailed to his own table. A spidery monster embraces a girl while toads bite her. A sea of inky darkness envelops all of these horrific scenes. Observers must search through the hideous enclosure of Bosch's Hell to take in its fascinating though repulsive details.

Sandwiched between Paradise and Hell is the huge central panel, in which nude people blithely cavort in a landscape dotted with bizarre creatures and unidentifiable objects. The numerous

18-15 QUINTEN MASSYS, *Money-Changer and His Wife*, 1514. Oil on wood, $2' 3\frac{3}{4}'' \times 2' 2\frac{3}{8}''$. Louvre, Paris.

Massys's painting depicting a secular financial transaction is also a commentary on 16th-century Netherlandish values. The banker's wife shows more interest in the money-weighing than in her prayer book.

fruits and birds (fertility symbols) in the scene suggest procreation, and, indeed, many of the figures are paired off as couples. The orgiastic overtones of this panel, in conjunction with the terrifying image of Hell, have led some scholars to interpret this triptych as they have other Last Judgment images—as a warning to viewers of the fate awaiting the sinful, decadent, and immoral.

JAN GOSSAERT As in the Holy Roman Empire and France, developments in Italian Renaissance art interested many Netherlandish artists. JAN GOSSAERT (ca. 1478–1535) associated with humanist scholars and visited Italy, where he became fascinated with classical antiquity and its mythological subjects. Giorgio Vasari, the Italian artist and biographer and Gossaert's contemporary, wrote about him: "Jean Gossart [*sic*] of Mabuse was almost the first who took from Italy into Flanders the true method of making scenes full of nude figures and poetical inventions,"[4] although it is obvious Gossaert derived much of his classicism from Dürer.

Indeed, Dürer's *Fall of Man* (FIG. 18-1) inspired the composition and poses in Gossaert's *Neptune and Amphitrite* (FIG. 18-14). However, unlike Dürer's exquisitely small engraving, Gossaert's painting is more than six feet tall and four feet wide. The artist executed the painting with expected Netherlandish polish, skillfully drawing and carefully modeling the figures. Gossaert depicted the sea god with his

traditional attribute, the trident, and wearing a laurel wreath and an ornate conch shell rather than Dürer's fig leaf. Amphitrite is fleshy and, like Neptune, stands in a contrapposto stance. The architectural frame, which resembles the cella of a classical temple (FIG. 5-46), is an unusual mix of Doric and Ionic elements, including *bucrania* (ox skull decorations), a common motif in ancient architectural ornament. Gossaert likely based the classical setting on sketches he had made of ancient buildings while in Rome. He had traveled to Italy with Philip, bastard of Burgundy, this painting's patron. A Burgundian admiral (hence the Neptune reference), Philip became a bishop and kept this work in the innermost room of his castle.

QUINTEN MASSYS Antwerp's growth and prosperity, along with its wealthy merchants' propensity for collecting and purchasing art, attracted artists to the city. Among them was QUINTEN MASSYS (ca. 1466–1530), who became Antwerp's leading master after 1510. Son of a Louvain blacksmith, Massys demonstrated a willingness to explore the styles and modes of a variety of models, from Jan van Eyck to Bosch and from Rogier van der Weyden to Dürer and Leonardo. Yet his eclecticism was subtle and discriminating, enriched by an inventiveness that gave a personal stamp to his paintings.

In *Money-Changer and His Wife* (FIG. 18-15), Massys presented a professional man transacting business. He holds scales,

18-16 Pieter Aertsen, *Butcher's Stall*, 1551. Oil on wood, 4′ $\frac{3}{8}$″ × 6′ 5$\frac{3}{4}$″. Uppsala University Art Collection, Uppsala.

At first glance *Butcher's Stall* appears to be a genre painting, but in the background Joseph leads a donkey carrying Mary and the Christ Child. Aertsen balanced images of gluttony with allusions to salvation.

checking the weight of coins on the table. The artist's detailed rendering of the figures, setting, and objects suggests a fidelity to observable fact. Thus, this work provides the viewer with insight into developing commercial practices. But *Money-Changer and His Wife* is also a commentary on Netherlandish values and mores. The painting highlights the financial transactions that were an increasingly prominent part of secular life in the 16th-century Netherlands and that distracted Christians from their religious duties. The banker's wife, for example, shows more interest in watching her husband weigh money than in reading her prayer book. Massys incorporated into his painting numerous references to the importance of a moral, righteous, and spiritual life, including a carafe with water and a candlestick, traditional religious symbols. The couple ignores them, focusing solely on money. On the right, through a window, an old man talks with another man, suggesting idleness and gossip. The reflected image in the convex mirror on the counter offsets this image of sloth and foolish chatter. There, a man reads what is most likely a Bible or prayer book. Behind him is a church steeple. An inscription on the original frame (now lost) read, "Let the balance be just and the weights equal" (Lev. 19:36), a caution that applies both to the money-changer's professional conduct and the eventual Last

Judgment. The couple in this painting, however, have tipped the balance in favor of the pursuit of wealth.

PIETER AERTSEN This tendency to inject reminders about spiritual well-being emerges in *Butcher's Stall* (FIG. **18-16**) by Pieter Aertsen (ca. 1507–1575), who worked in Antwerp for more than three decades. At first glance, this painting appears to be a descriptive *genre* scene (one from everyday life). On display is an array of meat products—a side of a hog, chickens, sausages, a stuffed intestine, pig's feet, meat pies, a cow's head, a hog's head, and hanging entrails. Also visible are fish, pretzels, cheese, and butter. Like Massys, Aertsen embedded strategically placed religious images in his painting. In the background, Joseph leads a donkey carrying Mary and the Christ Child. The Holy Family stops to offer alms to a beggar and his son, while the people behind the Holy Family wend their way toward a church. Furthermore, the crossed fishes on the platter and the pretzels and wine in the rafters on the upper left all refer to "spiritual food" (pretzels often served as bread during Lent). Aertsen accentuated these allusions to salvation through Christ by contrasting them to their opposite—a life of gluttony, lust, and sloth. He represented this degeneracy with the oyster and mussel shells

18-17 Caterina van Hemessen, *Self-Portrait*, 1548. Oil on panel, $1' \frac{3}{4}'' \times 9\frac{7}{8}''$. Kunstmuseum, Öffentliche Kunstsammlung Basel.

In this first known Northern European self-portrait by a woman, Caterina van Hemessen represented herself as a confident artist momentarily interrupting her work to look out at the viewer.

18-18 Attributed to Levina Teerlinc, *Elizabeth I as a Princess*, ca. 1559. Oil on wood, $3' 6\frac{3}{4}'' \times 2' 8\frac{1}{4}''$. The Royal Collection, Windsor Castle, Windsor.

Teerlinc received greater compensation for her work for the English court than did her male contemporaries. Her considerable skill is evident in this life-size portrait of Elizabeth I as a young princess.

(which Netherlanders believed possessed aphrodisiacal properties) scattered on the ground on the painting's right side, along with the people seen eating and carousing nearby under the roof.

CATERINA VAN HEMESSEN With the accumulation of wealth in the Netherlands, portraits increased in popularity. The self-portrait (FIG. **18-17**) by CATERINA VAN HEMESSEN (1528–1587) is the first known Northern European self-portrait by a woman. Here, she confidently presented herself as an artist who interrupts her work to look toward the viewer. She holds brushes, a palette, and a *maulstick* (a stick used to steady the hand while painting) in her left hand and delicately applies pigment to the canvas with her right hand. Van Hemessen's father, Jan Sanders van Hemessen, a well-known painter, trained her. Caterina ensured proper identification (and credit) through the inscription in the painting: "Caterina van Hemessen painted me / 1548 / her age 20."

LEVINA TEERLINC Another female painter, LEVINA TEERLINC (1515–1576) of Bruges, established herself as such a respected artist that Henry VIII and his successors invited her to England to paint miniatures for them. There, she was a formidable rival of some of her male contemporaries at the court, such as Hans Holbein, and received greater compensation for her work than they did for theirs. Teerlinc's considerable skill is evident in a life-size portrait (FIG. **18-18**) attributed to her, which depicts Elizabeth I (1533–1603, r. 1558–1603) as a

composed, youthful princess. Daughter of Henry VIII and Anne Boleyn, Elizabeth was probably in her late 20s when she sat for this portrait. Appropriate to her station in life, she wears an elegant brocaded gown, extravagant jewelry, and a headdress based on a style her mother popularized.

That female artists such as van Hemessen and Teerlinc were able to achieve such success is a testament to their determination and skill. Despite the difficulties for women in obtaining artistic training (see "The Artist's Profession in Flanders," Chapter 15, page 406), women contributed significantly to the lofty reputation Flemish artists enjoyed. In addition to participating as artists, women also played an important role as patrons in the 16th-century art world. Politically powerful women such as Margaret of Austria (regent of the Netherlands during the early 16th century; 1480–1530) and Mary of Hungary (queen consort of Hungary; 1505–1558) were avid collectors and patrons, and contributed substantially to the thriving state of the arts. Like other art patrons, these women collected and commissioned art not only for the aesthetic pleasure it provided but also for the status it bestowed on them and the cultural sophistication it represented.

JOACHIM PATINIR Landscape painting also flourished in the Netherlands. Particularly well known for his landscapes was JOACHIM PATINIR (d. 1524). According to one scholar, the word

18-19 JOACHIM PATINIR, *Landscape with Saint Jerome,* ca. 1520–1524. Oil on wood, 2′ 5⅛″ × 2′ 11⅞″. Museo del Prado, Madrid.

Joachim Patinir, a renowned Netherlandish landscape painter, subordinated the story of Saint Jerome to the depiction of craggy rock formations, verdant rolling fields, and expansive bodies of water.

Landschaft (landscape) first emerged in German literature as a characterization of an artistic *genre* (category of art) when Dürer described Patinir as a "good landscape painter." In *Landscape with Saint Jerome* (FIG. 18-19), Patinir subordinated the saint, who removes a thorn from a lion's paw in the foreground, to the exotic and detailed landscape. Craggy rock formations, verdant rolling fields, villages with church steeples, expansive bodies of water, and a dramatic sky fill most of the panel. Patinir amplified the sense of distance by masterfully using color to enhance the visual effect of recession and advance.

PIETER BRUEGEL THE ELDER The greatest Netherlandish painter of the mid-16th century was PIETER BRUEGEL THE ELDER (ca. 1528–1569), whose works reveal both an interest in the interrelationship of human beings and nature and Patinir's influence. But in Bruegel's paintings, no matter how huge a slice of the world the artist shows, human activities remain the dominant theme. Like many of his contemporaries, Bruegel traveled to Italy, where he seems to have spent almost two years, venturing as far south as Sicily. Unlike other artists, however, Bruegel chose not to incorporate classical elements into his paintings.

18-20 PIETER BRUEGEL THE ELDER, *Netherlandish Proverbs,* 1559. Oil on wood, 3′ 10″ × 5′ 4⅛″. Gemäldegalerie, Staatliche Museen, Berlin.

In this painting of a crowded Netherlandish village, Bruegel indulged his audience's obsession with proverbs and passion for clever imagery, and demonstrated his deep understanding of human nature.

18-21 PIETER BRUEGEL THE ELDER, *Hunters in the Snow,* 1565. Oil on wood, $3'\ 10\frac{1}{8}'' \times 5'\ 3\frac{3}{4}''$. Kunsthistorisches Museum, Vienna.

In *Hunters in the Snow,* one of a series of paintings illustrating annual seasonal changes, Bruegel draws the viewer diagonally deep into the landscape by his mastery of line, shape, and composition.

1 ft.

Bruegel's *Netherlandish Proverbs* (FIG. 18-20) depicts a Netherlandish village populated by a wide range of people (nobility, peasants, and clerics). From a bird's-eye view, the spectator encounters a mesmerizing array of activities reminiscent of the topsy-turvy scenes of Bosch (FIG. 18-13), but the purpose and meaning of Bruegel's anecdotal details are clear. By illustrating more than a hundred proverbs in this one painting, the artist indulged his Netherlandish audience's obsession with proverbs and passion for detailed and clever imagery. As the viewer scrutinizes the myriad vignettes within the painting, Bruegel's close observation and deep understanding of human nature become apparent. The proverbs depicted include, on the far left, a man in blue gnawing on a pillar ("He bites the column"—an image of hypocrisy). To his right, a man "beats his head against a wall" (an ambitious idiot). On the roof a man "shoots one arrow after the other, but hits nothing" (a shortsighted fool). In the far distance, the "blind lead the blind"—a subject to which Bruegel returned several years later in one of his most famous paintings.

In contrast to Patinir's Saint Jerome, lost in the landscape, the myriad, raucous characters of Bruegel's *Netherlandish Proverbs* fill the panel, so much so that the artist almost shut out the sky. *Hunters in the Snow* (FIG. 18-21) is very different in character and illustrates the dynamic variety of Bruegel's work. One of a series of six paintings (some scholars think there were originally 12) illustrating seasonal changes in the year, *Hunters* refers back to older traditions of depicting seasons and peasants in Books of Hours (FIGS. 15-15 and 15-16). The painting shows human figures and landscape locked in winter cold, reflecting the particularly severe winter of 1565, when Bruegel produced the painting. The weary hunters return with their hounds, women build fires, skaters skim the frozen pond, and the town and its church huddle in their mantle of snow. Bruegel rendered the landscape in an optically accurate manner. It develops

smoothly from foreground to background and draws the viewer diagonally into its depths. The painter's consummate skill in using line and shape and his subtlety in tonal harmony make this one of the great landscape paintings and an occidental counterpart of the masterworks of classical Chinese landscape.

SPAIN

Spain's ascent to power in Europe began in the mid-15th century with the marriage of Isabella of Castile (1451–1504) and Ferdinand of Aragon (1452–1516) in 1469. By the end of the 16th century, Spain had emerged as the dominant European power. Under the Habsburg rulers Charles V and Philip II, the Spanish Empire controlled a territory greater in extent than any ever known—a large part of Europe, the western Mediterranean, a strip of North Africa, and vast expanses in the New World. Spain acquired many of its New World colonies through aggressive overseas exploration. Among the most notable conquistadors sailing under the Spanish flag were Christopher Columbus (1451–1506), Vasco Nuñez de Balboa (ca. 1475–1517), Ferdinand Magellan (1480–1521), Hernán Cortés (1485–1547), and Francisco Pizarro (ca. 1470–1541). The Habsburg Empire, enriched by New World plunder, supported the most powerful military force in Europe. Spain defended and then promoted the interests of the Catholic Church in its battle against the inroads of the Protestant Reformation. Indeed, Philip II earned the title "Most Catholic King." Spain's crusading spirit, nourished by centuries of war with Islam, engaged body and soul in forming the most Catholic civilization of Europe and the Americas. In the 16th century, for good or for ill, Spain left the mark of Spanish power, religion, language, and culture on two hemispheres.

18-22 Portal, Colegio de San Gregorio, Valladolid, Spain, ca. 1498.

The Plateresque architectural style takes its name from *platero* ("silversmith" in Spanish). At the center of this Valladolid portal's Late Gothic tracery is the coat of arms of King Ferdinand and Queen Isabella.

COLEGIO DE SAN GREGORIO During the 15th century and well into the 16th, a Late Gothic style of architecture, the Plateresque, prevailed in Spain. *Plateresque* derives from the Spanish word *platero,* meaning "silversmith," and the Plateresque style in architecture is characterized by the delicate execution of its ornamentation, which resembles elegant metalwork. The Colegio de San Gregorio (Seminary of Saint Gregory; FIG. 18-22) in the Castilian city of Valladolid handsomely exemplifies the Plateresque manner. Great carved retables, like the German altarpieces that influenced them (FIGS. 15-18, 15-19, and 18-2, *bottom*), appealed to church patrons and architects in Spain. They thus made such retables a conspicuous decorative feature of their exterior architecture, dramatizing a portal set into an otherwise blank wall. The Plateresque entrance of San Gregorio is a lofty sculptured stone screen that bears no functional relation to the architecture behind it. On the entrance level, lacelike tracery reminiscent of Moorish design hems the flamboyant ogival arches. A great screen, paneled into sculptured compartments, rises above the tracery. In the center, the branches of a huge pomegranate

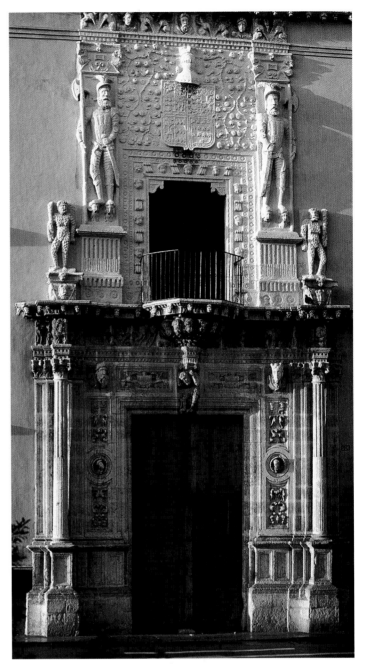

18-23 Portal, Casa de Montejo, Mérida, Mexico, 1549.

Spanish expansion brought the Plateresque style to the New World. The portal decoration of the home of the Yucatán's conqueror includes Spanish soldiers standing on the severed heads of Maya natives.

tree (symbolizing Granada, the Moorish capital of Spain the Habsburgs captured in 1492) wreathe the coat of arms of King Ferdinand and Queen Isabella. Cupids play among the tree branches, and, flanking the central panel, niches frame armed pages of the court, heraldic wild men symbolizing aggression, and armored soldiers, attesting to Spain's proud new militancy. In typical Plateresque and Late Gothic fashion, the activity of a thousand intertwined motifs unifies the whole design, which, in sum, creates an exquisitely carved panel greatly expanded in scale from the retables that inspired it.

NEW SPAIN Spanish expansion into the Western Hemisphere brought the Plateresque style to "New Spain" as well. A mid-16th-century gem of Plateresque architecture is the portal (FIG. 18-23) of the Casa de Montejo in Mérida, Mexico. The house, built in 1549,

18-24 JUAN DE HERRERA and JUAN BAUTISTA DE TOLEDO, El Escorial, near Madrid, Spain, 1563–1584 (detail of an anonymous 18th-century painting).

Conceived by Charles V and built by Philip II, El Escorial is a combined royal mausoleum, church, monastery, and palace. The complex is classical in style with severely plain walls and massive towers.

was the palatial residence of Francisco de Montejo the Younger (1508–1565), the Spanish conqueror of the Yucatán who founded Mérida in 1542. The lower story features engaged classical columns on projecting pedestals and sculptured portrait busts of Montejo and his wife in roundels. The upper story is much more fanciful and fully Plateresque in style with a central coat of arms, as at Valladolid. The four statues of the second level are of special interest. The larger pair depicts bearded and armored Spanish soldiers standing on the severed heads of the Maya natives they conquered. Smaller in scale are two sheepskin-clad wild men holding clubs (also seen at Valladolid), probably personifications of the defeated indigenous population. The triumphal imagery is, ironically, the work of Maya sculptors from nearby Maní. In fact, the very stones used to build the Montejo house were taken from dismantled Maya temples in the area.

EL ESCORIAL In Spain itself, the Plateresque style gave way under Philip II to an Italian-derived classicism. The Italian style is on display in the expansive complex called El Escorial (FIG. 18-24), which JUAN BAUTISTA DE TOLEDO (d. 1567) and JUAN DE HERRERA (ca. 1530–1597), principally the latter, constructed for Philip II. In his will, Charles V stipulated that a "dynastic pantheon" be constructed to house the remains of past and future monarchs of Spain. Philip II, obedient to his father's wishes, chose a site some 30 miles northwest of Madrid in rugged terrain with barren mountains. There he built El Escorial, not only a royal mausoleum but also a church, a monastery, and a palace. Legend has it that the gridlike plan for the enormous complex, 625 feet wide and 520 feet deep,

symbolized the gridiron on which Saint Lawrence, El Escorial's patron saint, suffered his martyrdom.

The vast structure is in keeping with Philip's austere and conscientious character, his passionate Catholic religiosity, his proud reverence for his dynasty, and his stern determination to impose his will worldwide. He insisted that in designing El Escorial, the architects focus on simplicity of form, severity in the whole, nobility without arrogance, and majesty without ostentation. The result is a classicism of Doric severity, ultimately derived from Italian architecture and with the grandeur of Saint Peter's (FIG. 19-4) implicit in the scheme, but unique in Spanish and European architecture.

Only the three entrances, with the dominant central portal framed by superimposed orders and topped by a pediment in the Italian fashion, break the long sweep of the structure's severely plain walls. Massive square towers punctuate the four corners. The stress on the central axis, with its subdued echoes in the two flanking portals, anticipates the three-part organization of later Baroque facades (see Chapter 19). The construction material for the entire complex (including the church)—granite, a difficult stone to work—conveys a feeling of starkness and gravity. The church's massive facade and the austere geometry of the interior complex, with its blocky walls and ponderous arches, produce an effect of overwhelming strength and weight. The entire complex is a monument to the collaboration of a great king and remarkably understanding architects. El Escorial stands as the overpowering architectural expression of Spain's spirit in its heroic epoch and of the character of Philip II, the extraordinary ruler who directed it.

18-25 EL GRECO, *Burial of Count Orgaz*, 1586. Oil on canvas, 16′ × 12′. Santo Tomé, Toledo.

El Greco's art is a blend of Byzantine and Italian Mannerist elements. His intense emotional content captured the fervor of Spanish Catholicism, and his dramatic use of light foreshadowed the Baroque style.

1 ft.

EL GRECO Doménikos Theotokópoulos, called EL GRECO (ca. 1547–1614), was born on Crete but emigrated to Italy as a young man. In his youth, he absorbed the traditions of Late Byzantine frescoes and mosaics. While still young, El Greco went to Venice, where he worked in Titian's studio, although Tintoretto's painting apparently made a stronger impression on him. A brief trip to Rome explains the influences of Roman and Florentine Mannerism on his work. By 1577 he had left for Spain to spend the rest of his life in Toledo.

El Greco's art is a strong personal blending of Byzantine and Mannerist elements. The intense emotionalism of his paintings, which naturally appealed to Spanish piety, and a great reliance on and mastery of color bound him to 16th-century Venetian art and to Mannerism. El Greco's art was not strictly Spanish (although it appealed to certain sectors of that society), for it had no Spanish antecedents and little effect on later Spanish painters. Nevertheless, El Greco's hybrid style captured the fervor of Spanish Catholicism.

A vivid expression of this fervor is the artist's masterpiece, *Burial of Count Orgaz* (FIG. **18-25**), painted in 1586 for the church of Santo Tomé in Toledo. El Greco based the painting on the legend that the count of Orgaz, who had died some three centuries before and who had been a great benefactor of Santo Tomé, was buried in the church by Saints Stephen and Augustine, who miraculously descended from Heaven to lower the count's body into its sepulcher. In the painting, El Greco carefully distinguished the terrestrial and celestial spheres. The brilliant Heaven that opens above irradiates the earthly scene. The painter represented the terrestrial realm with a firm realism, whereas he depicted the celestial, in his quite personal manner, with elongated undulating figures, fluttering draperies, and a visionary swirling cloud. Below, the two saints lovingly lower the count's armor-clad body, the armor and heavy robes painted with all the rich sensuousness of the Venetian school. A solemn chorus of black-clad Spanish personages fills the background. In the carefully individualized features of these figures, El Greco demonstrated that he was also a great portraitist. These men call to mind both the conquistadors of the early 16th century and the Spanish naval officers who, two years after the completion of this painting, led the Great Armada against both Protestant England and the Netherlands.

The upward glances of some of the figures below and the flight of an angel above link the painting's lower and upper spheres. The action of the angel, who carries the count's soul in his arms as Saint John and the Virgin intercede for it before the throne of Christ, reinforces this connection. El Greco's deliberate change in style to distinguish between the two levels of reality gives the viewer an opportunity to see the artist's early and late manners in the same work, one below the other. His relatively sumptuous and realistic presentation of the earthly sphere still has strong roots in Venetian art, but the abstractions and distortions El Greco used to show the immaterial nature of the heavenly realm characterized his later style. His elongated figures existing in undefined spaces, bathed in a cool light of uncertain origin, explain El Greco's usual classification as a Mannerist, but it is difficult to apply that label to him without reservations. Although he used Mannerist formal devices, El Greco's primary concerns were emotion and conveying his religious passion or arousing that of observers. The forcefulness of his paintings is the result of his unique, highly developed expressive style. His strong sense of movement and use of light prefigured the Baroque style of the 17th century, examined next in Chapter 19.

NORTHERN EUROPE AND SPAIN, 1500 TO 1600

HOLY ROMAN EMPIRE

▮ Widespread dissatisfaction with the Church in Rome led to the Protestant Reformation, splitting Christendom in half. Protestants objected to the sale of indulgences and rejected most of the sacraments of the Catholic Church. They also condemned ostentatious church decoration as a form of idolatry that distracted the faithful from communication with God.

▮ As a result, Protestant churches were relatively bare, but art, especially prints, still played a role in Protestantism. Lucas Cranach, for example, effectively used visual imagery to contrast Catholic and Protestant views of salvation in his woodcut *Allegory of Law and Grace.*

▮ The greatest printmaker of the Holy Roman Empire was Albrecht Dürer, who was also a painter. Dürer was the first artist outside Italy to become an international celebrity. His work ranged from biblical subjects to botanical studies. *Fall of Man* reflects Dürer's studies of the Vitruvian theory of human proportions and of classical statuary. Dürer's engravings rival painting in tonal quality.

▮ Other German artists, such as Albrecht Altdorfer, achieved fame as landscape painters. Hans Holbein was a renowned portraitist who became court painter in England. Holbein's *The French Ambassadors* portrays two worldly humanists and includes a masterfully rendered anamorphic skull.

Dürer, *Fall of Man,* 1504

Holbein, *The French Ambassadors,* 1533

FRANCE

▮ King Francis I fought against the Holy Roman Emperor Charles V and declared Protestantism illegal in France. An admirer of Italian art, he invited several prominent Mannerists to work at his court and decorate his palace at Fontainebleau.

▮ French architecture of the 16th century is an eclectic mix of Italian and Northern European elements, as seen in Pierre Lescot's design of the renovated Louvre palace in Paris and Francis's château at Chambord. The château combines classical motifs derived from Italian palazzi with a Gothic roof silhouette.

Château de Chambord, Chambord, begun 1519

THE NETHERLANDS

▮ The Netherlands was one of the most commercially advanced and prosperous countries in 16th-century Europe. Much of Netherlandish art of this period provides a picture of contemporary life and values.

▮ Pieter Aertsen of Antwerp, for example, painted *Butcher's Stall,* which seems to be a straightforward genre scene but includes the Holy Family offering alms to a beggar in the background. The painting provides a stark contrast between gluttony and religious piety.

▮ Landscapes were the specialty of Joachim Patinir. Pieter Bruegel's repertory also included landscape painting. His *Hunters in the Snow* is one of a series of paintings depicting the seasonal changes of the year and the activities associated with them, as in traditional Books of Hours.

▮ Prominent female artists of the period include Caterina van Hemessen, who painted the first known Northern European self-portrait of a woman, and Levina Teerlinc, who painted portraits for the English court.

Aertsen, *Butcher's Stall,* 1551

SPAIN

▮ At the end of the 16th century, Spain was the dominant power in Europe and ruled an empire greater in extent than any ever known, including vast territories in the New World.

▮ The Spanish Plateresque style of architecture takes its name from *platero* ("silversmith") and features delicate ornamentation resembling metalwork.

▮ Under Philip II the Plateresque style gave way to an Italian-derived classicism, seen at its best in El Escorial, a royal mausoleum, monastery, and palace complex near Madrid.

▮ The leading painter of 16th-century Spain was the Greek-born El Greco, who combined Byzantine style, Italian Mannerism, and the religious fervor of Catholic Spain in works such as *Burial of Count Orgaz.*

El Greco, *Burial of Count Orgaz,* 1586

19-1 Gianlorenzo Bernini, interior of the Cornaro Chapel, Santa Maria della Vittoria, Rome, Italy, 1645–1652.

Bernini was the quintessential Baroque artist. For the Cornaro Chapel, he drew on the full capabilities of architecture, sculpture, and painting to create an intensely emotional experience for worshipers.

ITALY AND SPAIN, 1600 TO 1700

Art historians traditionally describe 17th-century European art as *Baroque*, but the term is problematic because the period encompasses a broad range of styles and genres. Although its origin is unclear, "Baroque" may have come from the Portuguese word *barroco*, meaning an irregularly shaped pearl. Use of the term emerged in the late 18th and early 19th centuries, when critics disparaged the Baroque period's artistic production, in large part because of perceived deficiencies in comparison with the art of the Italian Renaissance. Over time, this negative connotation faded, but the term is still useful to describe the distinctive new style that emerged during the 17th century—a style of complexity and drama seen especially in Italian art of this period. Whereas Renaissance artists reveled in the precise, orderly rationality of classical models, Baroque artists embraced dynamism, theatricality, and elaborate ornamentation, all used to spectacular effect, often on a grandiose scale.

ITALY

Although in the 16th century the Catholic Church launched the Counter-Reformation in response to—and as a challenge to—the Protestant Reformation, the considerable appeal of Protestantism continued to preoccupy the popes throughout the 17th century. The Treaty of Westphalia (see Chapter 20) in 1648 had formally recognized the principle of religious freedom, serving to validate Protestantism (predominantly in the German states). With the Church in Rome as the leading art patron in 17th-century Italy, the aim of much of Italian Baroque art was to restore Catholicism's predominance and centrality. The Council of Trent, one 16th-century Counter-Reformation initiative, firmly resisted Protestant objections to using images in religious worship, insisting on their necessity for teaching the laity (see "Religious Art in Counter-Reformation Italy," Chapter 17, page 474). Baroque art in Italy was therefore often overtly didactic.

Architecture and Sculpture

Italian 17th-century art and architecture, especially in Rome, embodied the renewed energy of the Catholic Counter-Reformation and communicated it to the populace. At the end of the 16th century, Pope Sixtus V (r. 1585–1590) had played a key role in the Roman Catholic Church's lengthy campaign to

19-2 Carlo Maderno, facade of Santa Susanna, Rome, Italy, 1597–1603.

Maderno's facade of Santa Susanna is one of the earliest manifestations of the Baroque spirit. The rhythm of the columns and pilasters mounts dramatically toward the emphatically stressed vertical axis.

19-3 Carlo Maderno, facade of Saint Peter's, Vatican City, Rome, Italy, 1606–1612.

For the facade of Saint Peter's, Maderno elaborated on his design for Santa Susanna (FIG. 19-2), but the two outer bays with bell towers were not part of his plan and detract from the verticality he sought.

reestablish its preeminence. He augmented the papal treasury and intended to rebuild Rome as an even more magnificent showcase of Church power. Between 1606 and 1667, several strong and ambitious popes—Paul V, Urban VIII, Innocent X, and Alexander VII—brought many of Sixtus V's dreams to fruition. Rome still bears the marks of their patronage everywhere.

SANTA SUSANNA The facade (FIG. 19-2) that CARLO MADERNO (1556–1629) designed at the turn of the century for the Roman church of Santa Susanna stands as one of the earliest manifestations of the Baroque artistic spirit. In its general appearance, Maderno's facade resembles Giacomo della Porta's immensely influential design for Il Gesù (FIG. 17-55). But Maderno's later facade has a greater verticality that concentrates and dramatizes the major features of its model. The tall central section projects forward from the horizontal lower story, and the scroll buttresses that connect the two levels are narrower and set at a sharper angle. The elimination of an arch framing the pediment over the doorway further enhances the design's vertical thrust. The rhythm of Santa Susanna's vigorously projecting columns and pilasters mounts dramatically toward the emphatically stressed central axis. The recessed niches, which contain statues and create pockets of shadow, heighten the sculptural effect.

MADERNO AND SAINT PETER'S The drama inherent in Santa Susanna's facade appealed to Pope Paul V (r. 1605–1621), who commissioned Maderno in 1606 to complete Saint Peter's in Rome. As the symbolic seat of the papacy, the church Constantine originally built over the first pope's tomb (see Chapter 8) radiated enormous symbolic presence. In light of Counter-Reformation concerns, the Baroque popes wanted to conclude the already century-long rebuilding project and reestablish the force embodied in the mammoth structure. In many ways Maderno's facade (FIG. 19-3) is a gigantic expansion of the elements of Santa Susanna's first level. But the compactness and verticality of the smaller church's facade are not as prominent because Saint Peter's enormous breadth counterbalances them. Mitigating circumstances must be considered when assessing this design, however. The preexisting core of an incomplete building restricted Maderno, so he did not have the luxury of formulating a

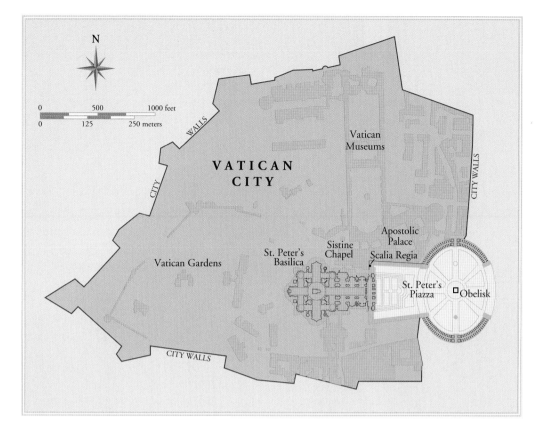

MAP 19-1 Vatican City.

longitudinal basilican plan used for the original fourth-century church (FIG. 8-9) reinforced the symbolic distinction between clergy and laity and provided a space for the processions of ever-growing assemblies. Lengthening the nave, unfortunately, pushed the dome farther back from the facade and all but destroyed the effect Michelangelo had planned—a structure pulled together and dominated by its dome. When viewed at close range, the dome barely emerges above the facade's soaring frontal plane. Seen from farther back (FIG. 19-3), it appears to have no drum. Visitors must move back quite a distance from the front (or fly over the church, FIG. 19-4) to see the dome and drum together. Today, viewers can appreciate the effect Michelangelo intended only by observing the church from the back (FIG. 17-26).

totally new concept for Saint Peter's. Moreover, the two outer bays with bell towers were not part of his original concept. Hence, had the facade been constructed according to the architect's initial design, the result would have been greater verticality and visual coherence.

Maderno's plan for Saint Peter's (MAP 19-1) also departed from the central plans designed for it during the Renaissance by Bramante (FIG. 17-23) and, later, by Michelangelo (FIG. 17-25). Paul V commissioned Maderno to add three nave bays to the earlier nucleus because Church officials had decided the central plan was too closely associated with pagan buildings, such as the Pantheon (FIG. 7-51). Moreover, the

BERNINI AND SAINT PETER'S Old Saint Peter's had a large forecourt, or *atrium* (FIG. 8-9, no. 6), in front of the church proper, and in the mid-17th century, GIANLORENZO BERNINI (1598–1680) received the prestigious commission to construct a monumental colonnade-framed *piazza* (plaza; FIG. 19-4) in front of Maderno's facade. Architect, painter, and sculptor, Bernini was one of the most important and imaginative artists of the Italian Baroque era and its most characteristic, sustaining spirit. Bernini's design had to accommodate two preexisting structures on the site—an ancient obelisk the Romans brought from Egypt (which Pope Sixtus V had moved to its present location in 1585 as part of his vision of Christian triumph in Rome) and a fountain Maderno designed. Bernini co-opted these features to define the long axis of a vast oval embraced by two colonnades joined to Maderno's facade. Four rows of huge Tuscan columns make up the two colonnades, which terminate in classical temple fronts. The colonnades extend a dramatic gesture of embrace to all who enter the piazza, symbolizing the welcome the Roman Catholic Church gave its members

19-4 Aerial view of Saint Peter's, Vatican City, Rome, Italy. Piazza designed by GIANLORENZO BERNINI, 1656–1667.

The dramatic gesture of embrace that Bernini's colonnade makes as worshipers enter Saint Peter's piazza symbolizes the welcome the Roman Catholic Church extended its members during the Counter-Reformation.

19-5 Gianlorenzo Bernini, baldacchino, Saint Peter's, Vatican City, Rome, Italy, 1624–1633. Gilded bronze, 100′ high.

Bernini's baldacchino serves both functional and symbolic purposes. It marks Saint Peter's tomb and the high altar of the church, and it visually bridges human scale to the lofty vaults and dome above.

19-6 Gianlorenzo Bernini, Scala Regia (Royal Stairway), Vatican City, Rome, Italy, 1663–1666.

By gradually reducing the distance between the columns and walls as the stairway ascends, Bernini created the illusion that the Scala Regia is of uniform width and that the aisles continue for its full length.

during the Counter-Reformation. Bernini himself referred to his colonnades as the welcoming arms of the church. Beyond their symbolic resonance, the colonnades served visually to counteract the natural perspective and bring the facade closer to the viewer. By emphasizing the facade's height in this manner, Bernini subtly and effectively compensated for its extensive width. Thus, a Baroque transformation expanded the compact central designs of Bramante and Michelangelo into a dynamic complex of axially ordered elements that reach out and enclose spaces of vast dimension. By its sheer scale and theatricality, the completed Saint Peter's fulfilled the desire of the Counter-Reformation Catholic Church to present an awe-inspiring, authoritative vision of itself.

BALDACCHINO, SAINT PETER'S Long before being invited to design the piazza, Bernini had been at work decorating the interior of Saint Peter's. His first commission, completed between 1624 and 1633, called for the design and erection of a gigantic bronze *baldacchino* (FIG. 19-5) under the great dome. The canopy-like structure (*baldacco* is Italian for "silk from Baghdad," such as for a cloth canopy) stands 100 feet high (the height of an average eight-story building). The baldacchino serves both functional and symbolic purposes. It marks the high altar and the tomb of Saint Peter, and it visually bridges human scale to the lofty vaults and dome above. Further, for worshipers entering the nave of the huge church, it provides a dramatic, compelling presence at the crossing. Its columns also create a visual frame for the elaborate sculpture representing the throne of Saint Peter (the Cathedra Petri) at the far end of Saint Peter's (FIG. 19-5,

rear). On a symbolic level, the structure's decorative elements speak to the power of the Catholic Church and of Pope Urban VIII (r. 1623–1644). Partially fluted and wreathed with vines, the baldacchino's four spiral columns recall those of the ancient baldacchino over the same spot in Old Saint Peter's, thereby invoking the past to reinforce the primacy of the Roman Catholic Church in the 17th century. At the top of the columns, four colossal angels stand guard at the upper corners of the canopy. Forming the canopy's apex are four serpentine brackets that elevate the orb and the cross. Since the time of Constantine (FIG. 7-81, *right*), the orb and the cross had served as symbols of the Church's triumph. The baldacchino also features numerous bees, symbols of Urban VIII's family, the Barberini. The structure effectively gives visual form to the triumph of Christianity and the papal claim to doctrinal supremacy.

The construction of the baldacchino was itself a remarkable feat. Each of the bronze columns consists of five sections cast from wooden models using the *lost-wax process* (see "Hollow-Casting Life-Size Bronze Statues," Chapter 5, page 108). Although Bernini did some of the hands-on work himself, for example, cleaning and repairing the wax molds and doing the final *chasing* (engraving and embossing) of the bronze casts, he contracted out much of the work for the project to experienced bronzecasters and sculptors. The superstructure is predominantly cast bronze, although some of the sculptural elements are brass or wood. The enormous scale of the baldacchino required a considerable amount of bronze. On Urban VIII's orders, workers dismantled the portico of the Pantheon (FIG. 7-49) to acquire the bronze for the baldacchino—ideologically appropriate, given the Church's rejection of paganism.

The concepts of triumph and grandeur permeate every aspect of the 17th-century design of Saint Peter's. Suggesting a great and solemn procession, the main axis of the complex traverses the piazza (marked by the central obelisk) and enters Maderno's nave. It comes to a temporary halt at the altar beneath Bernini's baldacchino, but it continues on toward its climactic destination at another great altar in the apse.

SCALA REGIA Bernini demonstrated his impressive skill at transforming space in another project he undertook for the papacy, the Scala Regia (Royal Stairway; FIG. 19-6), that connects the papal apartments to Saint Peter's. Because the original passageway was irregular, dark, and dangerous to descend, Pope Alexander VII (r. 1655–1667) commissioned Bernini to replace it. A sculptural group of trumpeting angels and the papal arms crowns the entrance to the stairway, where columns carrying a barrel vault (built in two sections) form aisles flanking the central corridor. By gradually reducing the distance between the columns and walls as the stairway ascends, Bernini eliminated the aisles on the upper levels while creating the illusion that the whole stairway is of uniform width and that the aisles continue for its entire length. Likewise, the space between the colonnades narrows with ascent, reinforcing the natural perspective and making the stairs appear longer than they are. To minimize this effect, Bernini brightened the lighting at the top of the stairs, exploiting the natural human inclination to move from darkness toward light. To make the long ascent more tolerable, he inserted an illuminated landing that provides a midway resting point. The result is a highly sophisticated design, both dynamic and dramatic, that repeats on a smaller scale, perhaps even more effectively, the processional sequence found inside Saint Peter's. The challenge of this difficult assignment must have intrigued Bernini. The biographer Filippo Baldinucci (1625–1696) reported that Bernini "said the highest merit lay not in making beautiful and commodious buildings, but in being able to make do with little, to make use of a deficit in such a way that if it had not existed one would have to invent it."[1]

BERNINI, *DAVID* Although Bernini was a great and influential Baroque architect, his fame rests primarily on his sculpture, which also energetically expresses the Italian Baroque spirit. Baldinucci asserted: "[T]here was perhaps never anyone who manipulated marble with more facility and boldness. He gave his works a marvelous softness . . . making the marble, so to say, flexible."[2] Bernini's sculpture is expansive and theatrical, and the element of time usually plays an important role in it. A sculpture that predates his work on Saint Peter's is his *David* (FIG. 19-7). Bernini surely knew the Renaissance statues by Donatello (FIG. 16-12), Verrocchio (FIG. 16-13), and Michelangelo (FIG. 17-13) portraying the young biblical hero. Bernini's *David* fundamentally differs from those earlier masterpieces, however. Donatello and Verrocchio depicted David after his triumph over Goliath. Michelangelo portrayed David before his encounter with his gigantic adversary. Bernini chose to represent the combat itself. Unlike his Renaissance predecessors, the Baroque sculptor aimed to catch the split-second of maximum action. Bernini's *David*, his muscular legs widely and firmly planted, begins the violent, pivoting motion that will launch the stone from his sling. (A bag full of stones is

19-7 GIANLORENZO BERNINI, *David*, 1623. Marble, 5′ 7″ high. Galleria Borghese, Rome.

Bernini's sculptures are expansive and theatrical, and the element of time plays an important role in them. His emotion-packed *David* seems to be moving through both time and space.

at David's left hip, suggesting that he thought the fight would be tough and long.) Unlike Myron, the fifth-century BCE Greek sculptor who froze his *Diskobolos* (FIG. 5-39) at a fleeting moment of inaction, Bernini selected the most dramatic of an implied sequence of poses, so that the viewer has to think simultaneously of the continuum and of this tiny fraction of it. The suggested continuum imparts a dynamic quality to the statue that conveys a bursting forth of the energy seen confined in Michelangelo's figures (FIGS. 17-15 and 17-16). Bernini's *David* seems to be moving through time and through space. This kind of sculpture cannot be inscribed in a cylinder or confined in a niche. Its dynamic action demands space around it. Nor is the statue self-sufficient in the Renaissance sense, as its pose and attitude direct attention beyond it to the unseen Goliath. Bernini's sculpted figure moves out into the space that surrounds it. Further, the expression of intense concentration on David's face contrasts vividly with the classically placid visages of Donatello's and

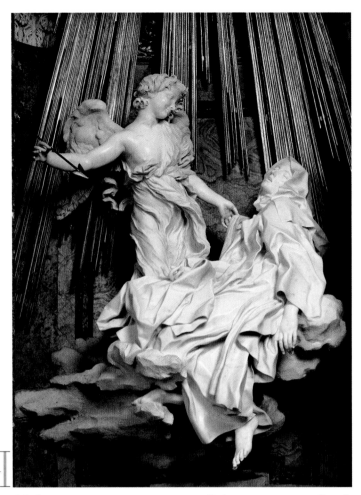

19-8 Gianlorenzo Bernini, *Ecstasy of Saint Teresa*, Cornaro Chapel, Santa Maria della Vittoria, Rome, Italy, 1645–1652. Marble, height of group 11′ 6″.

The passionate drama of Bernini's depiction of Saint Teresa correlated with the ideas of Ignatius Loyola, who argued that the re-creation of spiritual experience would do much to increase devotion and piety.

1 ft.

19-9 Francesco Borromini, facade of San Carlo alle Quattro Fontane, Rome, Italy, 1665–1667.

Borromini rejected the traditional notion that a building's facade should be a flat frontispiece. He set San Carlo's facade in undulating motion, creating a dynamic counterpoint of concave and convex elements.

Verrocchio's Davids and is more emotionally charged even than Michelangelo's (FIG. 17-14). The tension in David's face augments the dramatic impact of Bernini's sculpture.

ECSTASY OF SAINT TERESA Another work that displays the motion and emotion of Italian Baroque art and exemplifies Bernini's refusal to limit his statues to firmly defined spatial settings is *Ecstasy of Saint Teresa* in the Cornaro Chapel (FIG. 19-1) of the Roman church of Santa Maria della Vittoria. For this chapel, Bernini marshaled the full capabilities of architecture, sculpture, and painting to charge the entire area with palpable tension. He accomplished this by drawing on the considerable knowledge of the theater he absorbed from writing plays and producing stage designs. The marble sculpture (FIG. 19-8) that serves as the chapel's focus depicts Saint Teresa, a nun of the Carmelite order and one of the great mystical saints of the Spanish Counter-Reformation. Her conversion occurred after the death of her father, when she fell into a series of trances, saw visions, and heard voices. Feeling a persistent pain, she attributed it to the fire-tipped arrow of divine love that an angel had thrust repeatedly into her heart. In her writings, Saint Teresa described this experience as making her swoon in delightful anguish. In Bernini's hands, the entire Cornaro Chapel became a theater for the production of this mystical drama. The niche in which it takes place appears as a shallow

proscenium (the part of the stage in front of the curtain) crowned with a broken Baroque pediment and ornamented with polychrome marble. On either side of the chapel, sculpted portraits of the family of Cardinal Federico Cornaro (1579–1673) watch the heavenly drama unfold from choice balcony seats. Bernini depicted the saint in ecstasy, unmistakably a mingling of spiritual and physical passion, swooning back on a cloud, while the smiling angel aims his arrow. The sculptor's supreme technical virtuosity is evident in the visual differentiation in texture among the clouds, rough monk's cloth, gauzy material, smooth flesh, and feathery wings—all carved from the same white marble. Light from a hidden window of yellow glass pours down on golden rays that suggest the radiance of Heaven, whose painted representation covers the vault.

The passionate drama of Bernini's *Ecstasy of Saint Teresa* correlated with the ideas disseminated earlier by Ignatius Loyola (1491–1556), who founded the Jesuit order in 1534 and whom the Church canonized as Saint Ignatius in 1622. In his book *Spiritual Exercises,* Ignatius argued that the re-creation of spiritual experiences in artworks would do much to increase devotion and piety. Thus,

19-10 Francesco Borromini, plan of San Carlo alle Quattro Fontane, Rome, Italy, 1638–1641.

The plan of San Carlo is a hybrid of a Greek cross and an oval. The side walls pulsate in a way that reverses the facade's movement. The molded, dramatically lit space appears to flow from entrance to altar.

19-11 Francesco Borromini, San Carlo alle Quattro Fontane (view into dome), Rome, Italy, 1638–1641.

In place of a traditional round dome, Borromini capped the interior of San Carlo with a deeply coffered oval dome that seems to float on the light entering through windows hidden in its base.

theatricality and sensory impact were useful vehicles for achieving Counter-Reformation goals. Bernini was a devout Catholic, which undoubtedly contributed to his understanding of those goals. His inventiveness, technical skill, sensitivity to his patrons' needs, and energy account for his position as the quintessential Italian Baroque artist.

SAN CARLO ALLE QUATTRO FONTANE As gifted as Bernini was as an architect, FRANCESCO BORROMINI (1599–1667) took Italian Baroque architecture to even greater dramatic heights. In the little church of San Carlo alle Quattro Fontane (Saint Charles at the Four Fountains; FIG. **19-9**), Borromini went well beyond any of his predecessors or contemporaries in emphasizing a building's sculptural qualities. Although Maderno incorporated sculptural elements in his designs for the facades of Santa Susanna (FIG. **19-2**) and Saint Peter's (FIG. **19-3**), they still develop along relatively lateral planes. Borromini set his facade in undulating motion, creating a dynamic counterpoint of concave and convex elements on two levels (for example, the sway of the cornices). He emphasized the three-dimensional effect with deeply recessed niches. This facade is not the traditional flat frontispiece that defines a building's outer limits. It is a pulsating, engaging component inserted between interior and exterior space, designed not to separate but to provide a fluid transi-

tion between the two. Underscoring this functional interrelation of the building and its environment is the curious fact that the church has not one but two facades. The second, a narrow bay crowned with its own small tower, turns away from the main facade and, tracking the curve of the street, faces an intersection. (The upper facade dates seven years after Borromini's death, and it is uncertain to what degree the present design reflects his original intention.)

The interior is not only an ingenious response to an awkward site but also a provocative variation on the theme of the centrally planned church. In plan (FIG. **19-10**), San Carlo is a hybrid of a *Greek cross* (a cross with four arms of equal length) and an oval, with a long axis between entrance and apse. The side walls move in an undulating flow that reverses the facade's motion. Vigorously projecting columns define the space into which they protrude just as much as they accent the walls attached to them. Capping this molded interior space is a deeply coffered oval dome (FIG. **19-11**) that seems to float on the light entering through windows hidden in its base. Rich variations on the basic theme of the oval, dynamic relative to the static circle, create an interior that flows from entrance to altar, unimpeded by the segmentation so characteristic of Renaissance buildings.

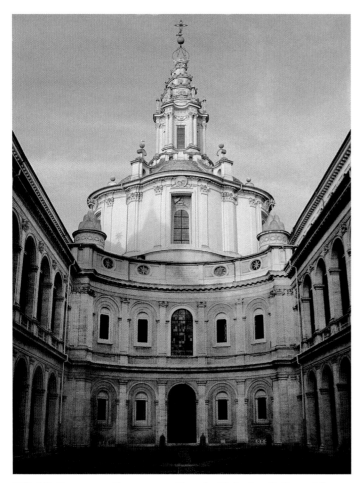

19-12 FRANCESCO BORROMINI, Chapel of Saint Ivo, College of the Sapienza, Rome, Italy, begun 1642.

In characteristic fashion, Borromini played concave against convex forms on the upper level of the Roman Chapel of Saint Ivo. Pilasters restrain the forces that seem to push the bulging forms outward.

19-13 FRANCESCO BORROMINI, plan of the Chapel of Saint Ivo, College of the Sapienza, Rome, Italy, begun 1642.

The interior elevation fully reflects all the elements of the highly complex plan of Borromini's chapel in the College of the Sapienza, which is star-shaped with rounded points and apses on all sides.

CHAPEL OF SAINT IVO Borromini carried the unification of interior space even further in the Chapel of Saint Ivo (FIG. **19-12**) in the courtyard of the College of the Sapienza (Wisdom) in Rome. In his characteristic manner, Borromini played concave against convex forms on the upper level of this chapel's exterior. The lower stories of the court, which frame the bottom facade, had already been constructed when Borromini began work. Above the facade's inward curve—its design adjusted to the earlier arcades of the court—rises a convex drumlike structure that supports the dome's lower parts.

19-14 FRANCESCO BORROMINI, Chapel of Saint Ivo (view into dome), College of the Sapienza, Rome, Italy, begun 1642.

Unlike Renaissance domes, Borromini's Saint Ivo dome is an organic part that evolves out of and shares the qualities of the supporting walls, and it cannot be separated from them.

Powerful pilasters restrain the forces that seem to push the bulging forms outward. Buttresses above the pilasters curve upward to brace a tall, ornate lantern topped by a spiral that, screwlike, seems to fasten the structure to the sky.

The centralized plan (FIG. 19-13) of the Saint Ivo chapel is that of a star having rounded points and apses on all sides. Indentations and projections along the angled curving walls create a highly complex plan, with all the elements fully reflected in the interior elevation. From floor to lantern, the wall panels rise in a continuously tapering sweep halted only momentarily by a single horizontal cornice (FIG. 19-14). Thus, the dome is not a separate unit placed on a supporting block, as in Renaissance buildings. It is an organic part that evolves out of and shares the qualities of the supporting walls, and it cannot be separated from them. This carefully designed progression up through the lantern creates a dynamic and cohesive shell that encloses and energetically molds a scalloped fragment of space. Few architects have matched Borromini's ability to translate extremely complicated designs into such masterfully unified structures as Saint Ivo.

Painting

Although architecture and sculpture provided the most obvious vehicles for manipulating space and creating theatrical effects, painting continued to be an important art form, as it was in previous centuries. Among the most noted Italian Baroque painters were Annibale Carracci and Caravaggio, whose styles, although different, were both thoroughly in accord with the period.

ANNIBALE CARRACCI A native of Bologna, ANNIBALE CARRACCI (1560–1609) received much of his training at an academy of art founded cooperatively by his family members, among them his cousin Ludovico Carracci (1555–1619) and brother Agostino Carracci (1557–1602). The Bolognese academy was the first significant institution of its kind in the history of Western art. The Carracci founded it on the premises that art can be taught—the basis of any academic philosophy of art—and that its instruction must include the classical and Renaissance traditions in addition to the study of anatomy and life drawing.

In *Flight into Egypt* (FIG. 19-15), based on the biblical narrative from Matthew 2:13–14, Annibale Carracci created the "ideal" or "classical" landscape, in which nature appears ordered by divine law and human reason. Tranquil hills and fields, quietly gliding streams, serene skies, unruffled foliage, shepherds with their flocks—all the props of the pastoral scene and mood familiar in Venetian Renaissance paintings (FIG. 17-35)—expand to fill the picture space in *Flight into Egypt* and similar paintings. Carracci regularly included screens of trees in the foreground, dark against the sky's even light. In contrast to many Renaissance artists, he did not create the sense of deep space by employing linear perspective but rather by varying light and shadow to suggest expansive atmosphere. In *Flight into Egypt*, streams or terraces, carefully placed one above the other and narrowed, zigzag through the terrain, leading the viewer's eye back to the middle ground. There, many Venetian Renaissance landscape artists depicted architectural structures (as Carracci did in *Flight into Egypt*)—walled towns or citadels, towers, temples, monumental tombs, and villas. These constructed environments captured idealized antiquity and the idyllic life. Although the artists often took the subjects for these classically rendered scenes from religious or heroic stories, they favored the pastoral landscapes over the narratives. Here, the painter greatly diminished the size of Mary, the Christ Child, and Saint Joseph, who simply become part of the landscape as they wend their way slowly to Egypt after having been ferried across a stream.

19-15 ANNIBALE CARRACCI, *Flight into Egypt,* 1603–1604. Oil on canvas, 4′ × 7′ 6″. Galleria Doria Pamphili, Rome.

Carracci's landscapes idealize antiquity and the idyllic life. Here, the pastoral setting takes precedence over the narrative of Mary, the Christ Child, and Saint Joseph wending their way slowly to Egypt.

19-16 ANNIBALE CARRACCI, *Loves of the Gods,* ceiling frescoes in the gallery, Palazzo Farnese, Rome, Italy, 1597–1601.

On the shallow curved vault of this gallery in the Palazzo Farnese, Carracci arranged the mythological scenes in a *quadro riportato* format—a fresco resembling easel paintings on a wall.

LOVES OF THE GODS Among Carracci's most notable works is his decoration of the Palazzo Farnese gallery (FIG. **19-16**) in Rome. Cardinal Odoardo Farnese (1573–1626), a wealthy descendant of Pope Paul III, commissioned this ceiling fresco to celebrate the wedding of the cardinal's brother. Appropriately, the title of its iconographic program is *Loves of the Gods*—interpretations of the varieties of earthly and divine love in classical mythology.

Carracci arranged the scenes in a format resembling framed easel paintings on a wall, but here he painted them on the surfaces of a shallow curved vault. This type of simulation of easel painting for ceiling design is called *quadro riportato* (transferred framed painting). By adapting the Northern European and Venetian tradition of oil painting to the central Italian fresco tradition, Carracci reoriented the direction of painting in Florence and Rome. His great influence made quadro riportato fashionable for more than a century.

Flanking the framed pictures are polychrome seated nude youths, who turn their heads to gaze at the scenes around them, and standing Atlas figures painted to resemble marble statues. Carracci derived these motifs from the Sistine Chapel ceiling (FIG. 17-1), but he did not copy Michelangelo's figures. Notably, the chiaroscuro of

the Farnese gallery frescoes differs for the pictures and the figures surrounding them. Carracci modeled the figures inside the quadri in an even light. In contrast, light from beneath seems to illuminate the outside figures, as if they were tangible, three-dimensional beings or statues lit by torches in the gallery below. This interest in illusion, already manifest in the Renaissance, continued in the grand ceiling compositions (FIGS. **19-21** to **19-24**) of the 17th century. In the crown of the vault, a long panel representing the *Triumph of Bacchus* is an ingenious mixture of Raphael's drawing style and lighting and Titian's more sensuous and animated figures. It reflects Carracci's adroitness in adjusting their authoritative styles to create something of his own.

CARAVAGGIO Michelangelo Merisi, known as CARAVAGGIO (1573–1610) after the northern Italian town from which he came, developed a unique style that had tremendous influence throughout Europe. His outspoken disdain for the classical masters (probably more vocal than real) drew bitter criticism from many painters, one of whom denounced him as the "anti-Christ of painting." Giovanni Pietro Bellori, the most influential critic of the age and an admirer of

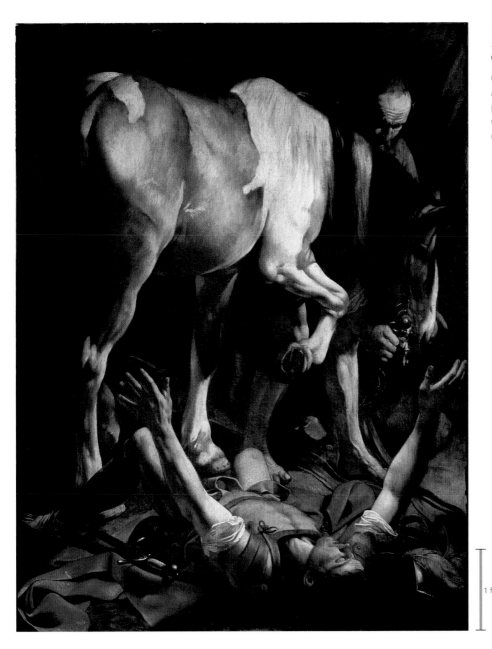

19-17 Caravaggio, *Conversion of Saint Paul,* ca. 1601. Oil on canvas, 7' 6" × 5' 9". Cerasi Chapel, Santa Maria del Popolo, Rome.

Caravaggio used perspective, chiaroscuro, and dramatic lighting to bring viewers into this painting's space and action, almost as if they were participants in Saint Paul's conversion to Christianity.

1 ft.

Annibale Carracci, felt that Caravaggio's refusal to emulate the models of his distinguished predecessors threatened the whole classical tradition of Italian painting that had reached its zenith in Raphael's work (see "Giovanni Pietro Bellori on Annibale Carracci and Caravaggio," page 538). Yet despite this criticism and the problems in Caravaggio's troubled life (reconstructed from documents such as police records), Caravaggio received many commissions, both public and private, and numerous artists paid him the supreme compliment of borrowing from his innovations. His influence on later artists, as much outside Italy as within, was immense. In his art, Caravaggio injected a naturalism into both religion and the classics, reducing them to human dramas played out in the harsh and dingy settings of his time and place. His unidealized figures selected from the fields and the streets of Italy, however, were effective precisely because of their familiarity.

CONVERSION OF SAINT PAUL Caravaggio painted *Conversion of Saint Paul* (FIG. 19-17) for the Cerasi Chapel in the Roman church of Santa Maria del Popolo. He depicted the saint-to-be at the moment of his conversion, flat on his back with his arms thrown up. In the background, an old hostler seems preoccupied with caring for the horse. At first inspection, little here suggests the momentous significance of the spiritual event in progress. The viewer of the painting could well be witnessing a mere stable accident, not a man overcome by a great miracle. Although many of his contemporaries criticized Caravaggio for departing from traditional depictions of religious scenes, the eloquence and humanity with which he imbued his paintings impressed many others.

To compel interest and involvement in Paul's conversion, Caravaggio employed a variety of formal devices. Here, as elsewhere, he used a perspective and a chiaroscuro intended to bring viewers as close as possible to the scene's space and action, almost as if they were participating in them. The low horizon line augments the sense of inclusion. Caravaggio designed *Conversion of Saint Paul* for its location on the chapel wall, positioned at the line of sight of an average-height person standing at the chapel entrance. The sharply lit figures emerge from the dark background as if lit by the light from the chapel's windows. The lighting resembles that of a stage production and is analogous to the rays in Bernini's *Ecstasy of Saint Teresa* (FIG. 19-8).

Giovanni Pietro Bellori
on Annibale Carracci and Caravaggio

The written sources to which art historians turn as aids in understanding the art of the past are invaluable, but they reflect the personal preferences and prejudices of the writers. Pliny the Elder, for example, writing in the first century CE, reported that "art ceased"* after the death of Alexander the Great—a remark usually interpreted as expressing his disapproval of Hellenistic art in contrast to Classical art (see Chapter 5). Giorgio Vasari, the biographer and champion of Italian Renaissance artists, condemned Gothic art as "monstrous and barbarous,"[†] and considered medieval art in general as a distortion of the noble art of the Greeks and Romans (see Chapter 13). Giovanni Pietro Bellori (1613–1696), the leading biographer of Baroque artists, similarly recorded his admiration for Renaissance classicism as well as his distaste for Mannerism and realism in his opposing evaluations of Annibale Carracci and Caravaggio.

In the opening lines of his *Vita* of Carracci, Bellori praised "the divine Raphael . . . [whose art] raised its beauty to the summit, restoring it to the ancient majesty of . . . the Greeks and the Romans" and lamented that soon after, "artists, abandoning the study of nature, corrupted art with the *maniera,* that is to say, with the fantastic idea based on practice and not on imitation." But fortunately, Bellori observed, just "when painting was drawing to its end," Annibale Carraccci rescued "the declining and extinguished art."[‡]

Bellori especially lauded Carracci's Palazzo Farnese frescoes (FIG. **19-16**):

No one could imagine seeing anywhere else a more noble and magnificent style of ornamentation, obtaining supreme excellence in the compartmentalization and in the figures and executed with the grandest manner in the design with the just proportion and the great strength of chiaroscuro. . . . Among modern works they have no comparison.[§]

In contrast, Bellori characterized Caravaggio as talented and widely imitated but misguided in his rejection of classicism in favor of realism.

[Caravaggio] began to paint according to his own inclinations; not only ignoring but even despising the superb statuary of antiquity and the famous paintings of Raphael, he considered nature to be the only subject fit for his brush. As a result, when he was shown the most famous statues of [the ancient Greek masters] Phidias and Glykon in order that he might use them as models, his only answer was to point toward a crowd of people, saying that nature had given him an abundance of masters. . . . [W]hen he came upon someone in town who pleased him he made no attempt to improve on the creations of nature.**

[Caravaggio] claimed that he imitated his models so closely that he never made a single brushstroke that he called his own, but said rather that it was nature's. Repudiating all other rules, he considered the highest achievement not to be bound to art. For this innovation he was greatly acclaimed, and many talented and educated artists seemed compelled to follow him. . . . Nevertheless he lacked *invenzione,* decorum, *disegno,* or any knowledge of the science of painting. The moment the model was taken from him, his hand and his mind became empty. . . . Thus, as Caravaggio suppressed the dignity of art, everybody did as he pleased, and what followed was contempt for beautiful things, the authority of antiquity and Raphael destroyed. . . . Now began the imitation of common and vulgar things, seeking out filth and deformity.[#]

---

* Pliny, *Natural History,* 25.52.
[†] Giorgio Vasari, *Introduzione alle tre arti del disegno* (1550), ch. 3.
[‡] Giovanni Pietro Bellori, *Le vite de' pittori, scultori e architetti moderni* (Rome, 1672). Translated by Catherine Enggass, *The Lives of Annibale and Agostino Carracci by Giovanni Pietro Bellori* (University Park: Pennsylvania University Press, 1968), 5–6.
[§] Ibid., 33.
** Translated by Howard Hibbard, *Caravaggio* (New York: Harper & Row, 1983), 362.
[#] Ibid., 371–372.

Caravaggio's figures are still heroic with powerful bodies and clearly delineated contours in the Renaissance tradition, but the stark and dramatic contrast of light and dark, which at first shocked and then fascinated his contemporaries, obscures the more traditional aspects of his style. Art historians call Caravaggio's use of dark settings enveloping their occupants—which profoundly influenced European art, especially in Spain and the Netherlands—*tenebrism,* from the Italian word *tenebroso,* or "shadowy" manner. In Caravaggio's work, tenebrism also contributed greatly to the essential meaning of his pictures. In *Conversion of Saint Paul,* the dramatic spotlight shining down upon the fallen Paul is the light of divine revelation converting him to Christianity.

CALLING OF SAINT MATTHEW A piercing ray of light illuminating a world of darkness and bearing a spiritual message is also a central feature of one of Caravaggio's early masterpieces, *Calling of Saint Matthew* (FIG. **19-18**). It is one of two large canvases honoring Saint Matthew that the artist painted for the side walls of the Contarelli Chapel in San Luigi dei Francesi in Rome. The commonplace setting of the painting—a tavern with unadorned walls—is typical of Caravag-

gio. Into this mundane environment, cloaked in mysterious shadow and almost unseen, Christ, identifiable initially only by his indistinct halo, enters from the right. With a commanding gesture that recalls the Lord's hand in Michelangelo's *Creation of Adam* (FIG. **17-19**), he summons Levi, the Roman tax collector, to a higher calling. The astonished Levi—his face highlighted for the viewer by the beam of light emanating from an unspecified source above Christ's head and outside the picture—points to himself in disbelief. Although Christ's extended arm is reminiscent of the Lord's in *Creation of Adam,* the position of Christ's hand and wrist is similar to that of Adam's. This reference was highly appropriate, because the Church considered Christ to be the second Adam. Whereas Adam was responsible for the Fall of Man, Christ is responsible for human redemption. The conversion of Levi (who became Matthew) brought his salvation.

ENTOMBMENT In 1603, Caravaggio produced a large-scale painting, *Entombment* (FIG. **19-19**), for the Chapel of Pietro Vittrice at Santa Maria in Vallicella in Rome. This work includes all the hallmarks of Caravaggio's distinctive style: the plebeian figure types (particularly visible in the scruffy, worn face of Nicodemus, who

19-18 CARAVAGGIO, *Calling of Saint Matthew,* ca. 1597–1601. Oil on canvas, 11′ 1″ × 11′ 5″. Contarelli Chapel, San Luigi dei Francesi, Rome.

The stark contrast of light and dark was a key feature of Caravaggio's style. Here, Christ, cloaked in mysterious shadow and almost unseen, summons Levi the tax collector (Saint Matthew) to a higher calling.

1 ft.

here holds Christ's legs in the foreground), the stark use of darks and lights, and the invitation to the viewer to participate in the scene. As in *Conversion of Saint Paul,* the action takes place in the foreground. Caravaggio positioned the figures on a stone slab the corner of which appears to extend into the viewer's space. This suggests that Christ's body will be laid directly in front of the viewer.

Beyond its ability to move its audience, Caravaggio's composition also had theological implications. In light of the ongoing Counter-Reformation efforts at that time, these implications cannot be overlooked. To viewers in the chapel, the men seem to be laying Christ's body on the altar, which stands in front of the painting. This serves to give visual form to the doctrine of *transubstantiation* (the transformation of the Eucharistic bread and wine into the body and blood of Christ)—a doctrine central to Catholicism that Protestants rejected. By depicting Christ's body as though it were physically present during the Mass, Caravaggio visually articulated an abstract theological precept. Unfortunately, because this painting is now in a museum, viewers no longer can experience this effect.

ARTEMISIA GENTILESCHI Caravaggio's combination of naturalism and drama appealed both to patrons and artists, and he had many followers. One of the most accomplished was ARTEMISIA GENTILESCHI (ca. 1593–1653), whose father Orazio (1563–1639), her teacher, was himself strongly influenced by Caravaggio. The daughter's successful career, pursued in Florence, Venice, Naples, and

19-19 CARAVAGGIO, *Entombment,* from the Chapel of Pietro Vittrice, Santa Maria in Vallicella, Rome, Italy, ca. 1603. Oil on canvas, 9′ 10$\frac{1}{8}$″ × 6′ 7$\frac{15}{16}$″. Pinacoteca, Musei Vaticani, Rome.

In *Entombment,* Caravaggio gave visual form to the doctrine of transubstantiation. The jutting painted stone slab makes it seem as if Christ's body will be laid on the actual altar of the chapel.

1 ft.

Italy **539**

The Letters of Artemisia Gentileschi

Artemisia Gentileschi (FIG. 19-20) was the most renowned woman painter in Europe during the first half of the 17th century and the first woman ever admitted to membership in Florence's Accademia del Disegno. Like other women who could not become apprentices in all-male studios (see "The Artist's Profession," Chapter 15, page 406), she learned her craft from her father. Never forgotten in subsequent centuries, Artemisia's modern fame stems from the seminal 1976 exhibition *Women Artists: 1550–1950,** which opened a new chapter in feminist art history.

In addition to scores of paintings created for wealthy patrons that included the King of England and the Grand Duke of Tuscany, Gentileschi left behind 28 letters, some of which reveal that she believed patrons treated her differently because of her gender. Three 1649 letters written in Naples to Don Antonio Ruffo (1610–1678) in Messina make her feelings explicit.

> I fear that before you saw the painting you must have thought me arrogant and presumptuous. . . . [I]f it were not for Your Most Illustrious Lordship . . . I would not have been induced to give it for one hundred and sixty, because everywhere else I have been I was paid one hundred *scudi* [Italian coins] per figure. . . . You think me pitiful, because a woman's name raises doubts until her work is seen.[†]

> I was mortified to hear that you want to deduct one third from the already very low price that I had asked. . . . It must be that in your heart Your Most Illustrious Lordship finds little merit in me.[‡]

> As for my doing a drawing and sending it, [tell the gentleman who wishes to know the price for a painting that] I have made a solemn vow never to send my drawings because people have cheated me. In particular, just today I found myself [in the situation] that, having done a drawing of souls in purgatory for the Bishop of St. Gata, he, in order to spend less, commissioned another painter to do the painting using my work. If I were a man, I can't imagine it would

19-20 ARTEMISIA GENTILESCHI, *Judith Slaying Holofernes,* ca. 1614–1620. Oil on canvas, 6′ 6$\frac{1}{3}$″ × 5′ 4″. Galleria degli Uffizi, Florence.

Narratives involving heroic women were a favorite theme of Gentileschi. In *Judith Slaying Holofernes,* the controlled highlights on the action in the foreground recall Caravaggio's paintings and heighten the drama.

1 ft.

have turned out this way, because when the concept has been realized and defined with lights and darks, and established by means of planes, the rest is a trifle.[§]

* Ann Sutherland Harris and Linda Nochlin, *Women Artists: 1550–1950* (Los Angeles, Calif.: Los Angeles County Museum of Art, 1976), 118–124.
[†] Letter dated January 30, 1649. Translated by Mary D. Garrard, *Artemisia Gentileschi: The Image of the Female Hero in Italian Baroque Art* (Princeton, N.J.: Princeton University Press, 1989), 390.
[‡] Letter dated October 23, 1649. Ibid., 395–396.
[§] Letter dated November 13, 1649. Ibid., 397–398.

Rome, helped disseminate Caravaggio's style throughout the peninsula (see "The Letters of Artemisia Gentileschi," above).

In her *Judith Slaying Holofernes* (FIG. 19-20), Gentileschi used the tenebrism and what might be called the "dark" subject matter Caravaggio favored. Significantly, she chose a narrative involving a heroic female, a favorite theme of hers. The story, from the Old Testament Book of Judith, relates the delivery of Israel from its enemy, Holofernes. Having succumbed to Judith's charms, the Assyrian general Holofernes invited her to his tent for the night. When he fell asleep, Judith cut off his head. In this version of the scene (Gentileschi produced more than one painting of the subject), Judith and her maidservant behead Holofernes. Blood spurts everywhere as the two women summon all their strength to wield the heavy sword. The tension and strain are palpable. The controlled highlights on the action in the foreground recall Caravaggio's work and heighten the drama here as well.

GUIDO RENI Caravaggio was not the only early-17th-century painter to win a devoted following. GUIDO RENI (1575–1642), known to his many admirers as "the divine Guido," trained in the Bolognese art academy founded by the Carracci family. The influence of Annibale Carracci and Raphael is evident in Reni's *Aurora* (FIG. 19-21), a ceiling fresco in the Casino Rospigliosi in Rome. Aurora (Dawn) leads Apollo's chariot, while the Hours dance about it. The artist conceived *Aurora* as a quadro riportato, like the paintings in Carracci's *Loves of the Gods* (FIG. 19-16), and painted a complex and convincing illusionistic frame. The fresco exhibits a fluid motion, soft modeling, and sure composition, although without Raphael's sculpturesque strength. It is

19-21 GUIDO RENI, *Aurora*, ceiling fresco in the Casino Rospigliosi, Rome, Italy, 1613–1614.

The "divine Guido" conceived *Aurora* as a quadro riportato, reflecting his training in the Bolognese art academy. The scene of Dawn leading Apollo's chariot derives from ancient Roman reliefs.

an intelligent interpretation of the Renaissance master's style. Reni, consistent with the precepts of the Bolognese academy, also looked to antiquity for his models. The ultimate sources for the *Aurora* composition were Roman reliefs (FIG. 7-41) and coins depicting emperors in triumphal chariots accompanied by flying Victories and other personifications.

PIETRO DA CORTONA The experience of looking up at a painting is different from simply seeing a painting hanging on a wall. The considerable height and the expansive scale of most ceiling frescoes induce a feeling of awe. Patrons who wanted to burnish their public image or control their legacy found monumental ceiling frescoes to be perfect vehicles for such statements. In 1633, Pope Urban VIII commissioned a ceiling fresco for the Gran Salone of the Palazzo Barberini in Rome. The most important decorative commission of the 1630s, the job went to PIETRO DA COR-TONA (1596–1669), a Tuscan architect and painter who had moved to Rome in about 1612. The grandiose and spectacular *Triumph of the Barberini* (FIG. 19-22) overwhelms spectators with the glory of the Barberini family (and Urban VIII

19-22 PIETRO DA CORTONA, *Triumph of the Barberini,* ceiling fresco in the Gran Salone, Palazzo Barberini, Rome, Italy, 1633–1639.

In this dramatic ceiling fresco, Divine Providence appears in a halo of radiant light directing Immortality, holding a crown of stars, to bestow eternal life on the family of Pope Urban VIII.

19-23 Giovanni Battista Gaulli, *Triumph of the Name of Jesus,* ceiling fresco with stucco figures on the nave vault of Il Gesù, Rome, Italy, 1676–1679.

In the nave of Il Gesù, gilded architecture opens up to offer the faithful a glimpse of Heaven. To heighten the illusion, Gaulli painted figures on stucco extensions that project outside the painting's frame.

in particular). The iconographic program for this fresco, designed by the poet Francesco Bracciolini (1566–1645), centered on the accomplishments of the Barberini. Divine Providence appears in a halo of radiant light directing Immortality, holding a crown of stars, to bestow eternal life on the Barberini family. The virtues Faith, Hope, and Charity hold aloft a gigantic laurel wreath (also a symbol of immortality), which frames three bees (the family's symbols, which also appeared in Bernini's baldacchino, FIG. 19-5). Also present are the papal tiara and keys announcing the personal triumphs of Urban VIII.

GIOVANNI BATTISTA GAULLI The dazzling spectacle of ceiling frescoes also proved very effective for commissions illustrating religious themes. Church authorities realized that such paintings, high above the ground, offered perfect opportunities to impress on worshipers the glory and power of the Catholic Church. In conjunction with the theatricality of Italian Baroque architecture and sculpture, frescoes spanning church ceilings contributed to creating transcendent spiritual environments well suited to the Church's needs in Counter-Reformation Rome.

19-24 FRA ANDREA POZZO, *Glorification of Saint Ignatius,* ceiling fresco in the nave of Sant'Ignazio, Rome, Italy, 1691–1694.

Pozzo created the illusion that Heaven is opening up above the viewer's head by continuing the church's architecture into the painted vault. The fresco gives the appearance that the roof has been lifted off.

Triumph of the Name of Jesus (FIG. 19-23) in the nave of Il Gesù (FIGS. 17-55 and 17-56) in Rome vividly demonstrates the dramatic impact Baroque ceiling frescoes could have. As the mother church of the Jesuit order, Il Gesù played a prominent role in Counter-Reformation efforts. In this immense fresco by GIOVANNI BATTISTA GAULLI (1639–1709), gilded architecture opens up in the center of the ceiling to offer the faithful a stunning glimpse of Heaven. Gaulli represented Jesus as a barely visible monogram (IHS) in a blinding radiant light that floats heavenward. In contrast, sinners experience a violent descent back to Earth. The painter glazed the gilded architecture to suggest shadows, thereby enhancing the scene's illusionistic quality. To further heighten the effect, Gaulli painted many of the sinners on three-dimensional stucco extensions that project outside the painting's frame.

FRA ANDREA POZZO Another master of ceiling decoration was FRA ANDREA POZZO (1642–1709), a lay brother of the Jesuit order and a master of perspective, on which he wrote an influential treatise. Pozzo designed and executed the vast ceiling fresco *Glorification of Saint Ignatius* (FIG. 19-24) for the church of Sant'Ignazio in Rome. Like Il Gesù, Sant'Ignazio was a prominent church in Baroque Rome because of its dedication to the founder of the Jesuit order. The Jesuits played a major role in Counter-Reformation education and sent legions of missionaries to the New World and the Far East. As Gaulli did in Il Gesù, Pozzo created the illusion that Heaven

is opening up above the congregation. To accomplish this, the artist painted an extension of the church's architecture into the vault so that the roof seems to be lifted off. As Heaven and Earth commingle, Christ receives Saint Ignatius in the presence of figures personifying the four corners of the world. A disk in the nave floor marks the spot the viewer should stand to gain the whole perspectival illusion. For worshipers looking up from this point, the vision is complete. They find themselves in the presence of the heavenly and spiritual.

The effectiveness of Italian Baroque religious art depended on the drama and theatricality of individual images, as well as on the interaction and fusion of architecture, sculpture, and painting. Sound enhanced this experience. Architects designed churches with acoustical effect in mind, and, in an Italian Baroque church filled with music, the power of both image and sound must have been immensely moving. Through simultaneous stimulation of both the visual and auditory senses, the faithful might well have been transported into a trancelike state that would, indeed, as the great English poet John Milton (1608–1674) eloquently stated in *Il Penseroso* (1631), "bring all Heaven before [their] eyes."[3]

SPAIN

During the 16th century, Spain had established itself as an international power. The Habsburg kings had built a dynastic state that encompassed Portugal, part of Italy, the Netherlands, and extensive

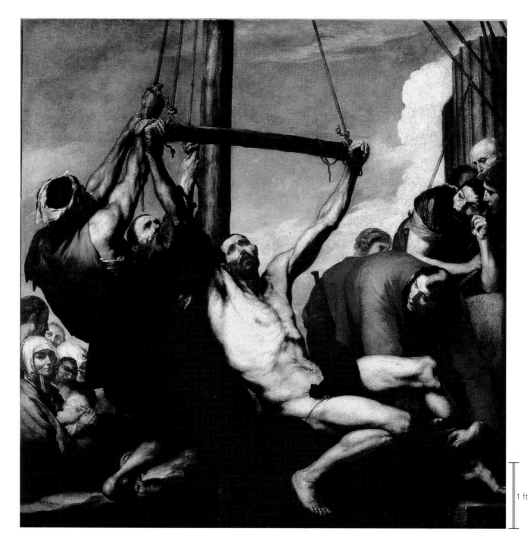

19-25 José de Ribera, *Martyrdom of Saint Philip*, ca. 1639. Oil on canvas, 7′ 8″ × 7′ 8″. Museo del Prado, Madrid.

Martyrdom scenes were popular in Counter-Reformation Spain. Scorning idealization of any kind, Ribera represented Philip's executioners hoisting him into position to die on a cross.

1 ft.

areas of the New World (see Chapter 18). By the beginning of the 17th century, however, the Habsburg Empire was struggling, and although Spain mounted an aggressive effort during the Thirty Years' War (see Chapter 20), by 1660 the imperial age of the Spanish Habsburgs was over. In part, the demise of the Spanish empire was due to economic woes. The military campaigns Philip III (r. 1598–1621) and his son Philip IV (r. 1621–1665) waged during the Thirty Years' War were costly and led to higher taxes. The increasing tax burden placed on Spanish subjects in turn incited revolts and civil war in Catalonia and Portugal in the 1640s, further straining an already fragile economy. Thus, the dawn of the Baroque period in Spain found the country's leaders struggling to maintain control of their dwindling empire. But realizing the prestige that great artworks brought and the value of visual imagery in communicating to a wide audience, both Philip III and Philip IV continued to spend lavishly on art.

Painting

In the 17th century, Spain maintained its passionate commitment to Catholic orthodoxy, and as in Counter-Reformation Italy, Spanish Baroque artists sought ways to move viewers and to encourage greater devotion and piety. Particularly appealing in this regard were scenes of death and martyrdom, which provided Spanish artists with opportunities both to depict extreme feelings and to instill those feelings in viewers. Spain prided itself on its saints—Saint Teresa of Avila (FIG. **19-8**) and Saint Ignatius Loyola (FIG. **19-24**) were both Spanish-born—and martyrdom scenes surfaced frequently in Spanish Baroque art.

JOSÉ DE RIBERA As a young man, José (Jusepe) de Ribera (ca. 1588–1652) emigrated to Naples and fell under the spell of Caravaggio, whose innovative style he introduced to Spain. Emulating

19-26 Francisco de Zurbarán, *Saint Serapion,* 1628. Oil on canvas, 3′ 11½″ × 3′ 4¾″. Wadsworth Atheneum, Hartford (The Ella Gallup Sumner and Mary Catlin Sumner Collection Fund).

The light shining on Serapion calls attention to his tragic death and increases the painting's dramatic impact. The Spanish monk's coarse features label him as common, evoking empathy from a wide audience.

1 ft.

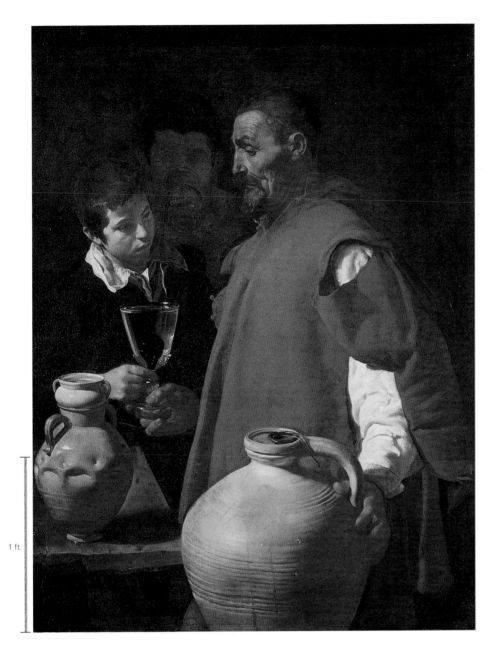

19-27 DIEGO VELÁZQUEZ, *Water Carrier of Seville,* ca. 1619. Oil on canvas, 3′ 5½″ × 2′ 7½″. Victoria & Albert Museum, London.

In this early work—a genre scene that seems to convey a deeper significance—the contrast of darks and lights and the plebeian nature of the figures reveal Velázquez's indebtedness to Caravaggio.

chapel of the monastic Order of Mercy in Seville. The saint, who participated in the Third Crusade of 1196, suffered martyrdom while preaching the Gospel to Muslims. According to one account, the monk's captors tied him to a tree and then tortured and decapitated him. The Order of Mercy dedicated itself to self-sacrifice, and Serapion's membership in this order amplified the resonance of Zurbarán's painting. In *Saint Serapion* the monk emerges from a dark background and fills the foreground. The bright light shining on him calls attention to the saint's tragic death and increases the dramatic impact of the image. In the background are two barely visible tree branches. A small note next to the saint identifies him for viewers. The coarse features of the Spanish monk label him as common, no doubt evoking empathy from a wide audience.

DIEGO VELÁZQUEZ The greatest Spanish painter of the Baroque age was DIEGO VELÁZQUEZ (1599–1660). An early work, *Water Carrier of Seville* (FIG. 19-27), painted when Velázquez was only about 20, already reveals his impressive command of the painter's craft. Velázquez rendered the figures with clarity and dignity, and his careful and convincing depiction of the water jugs in the foreground, complete with droplets of water, adds to the credibility of the scene. The plebeian nature of the figures and the contrast of darks and lights again reveal the influence of Caravaggio, whose work Velázquez had studied.

SURRENDER OF BREDA Velázquez, like many other Spanish artists, produced religious pictures as well as genre scenes, but his renown in his day rested primarily on the works he painted for his major patron, King Philip IV (see "Velázquez and Philip IV," page 546). After the king appointed Velázquez as court painter, the artist largely abandoned both religious and genre subjects in favor of royal

Caravaggio, Ribera made naturalism and compelling drama primary ingredients of his paintings, which often embraced brutal themes, reflecting the harsh times of the Counter-Reformation and the Spanish taste for stories showcasing courage and devotion. Ribera's *Martyrdom of Saint Philip* (FIG. 19-25) is grim and dark in subject and form. Scorning idealization of any kind, Ribera represented Philip's executioners hoisting him into position after tying him to a cross, the instrument of Christ's own martyrdom. The saint's rough, heavy body and swarthy, plebeian features reveal a kinship between him and his tormentors, who are similar to the types of figures found in Caravaggio's paintings. The patron of this painting is unknown, but it is possible that Philip IV commissioned the work, because Saint Philip was the king's patron saint.

FRANCISCO DE ZURBARÁN Another prominent Spanish painter of dramatic works was FRANCISCO DE ZURBARÁN (1598–1664), whose primary patrons throughout his career were rich Spanish monastic orders. Many of his paintings are quiet and contemplative, appropriate for prayer and devotional purposes. Zurbarán painted *Saint Serapion* (FIG. 19-26) as a devotional image for the funerary

Velázquez and Philip IV

Trained in Seville, Diego Velázquez was quite young when he came to the attention of Philip IV. The painter's immense talent impressed Philip, and the king named him chief court artist and palace chamberlain, a position that also involved curating the king's rapidly growing art collection and advising him regarding acquisitions and display. Among the works in Philip IV's possession were paintings by Titian, Annibale Carracci, Guido Reni, Albrecht Dürer, and Velázquez's famous Flemish contemporary, Peter Paul Rubens (see Chapter 20).

With the exception of two extended trips to Italy and a few excursions, Velázquez remained in Madrid for the rest of his life. His close relationship with Philip IV and his high office as chamberlain gave him prestige and a rare opportunity to fulfill the promise of his genius. One sign of Velázquez 's fertile imagination as well as mastery of the brush is that he was able to create timeless artworks out of routine assignments to commemorate the achievements of his patron, as he did in his record of the Spanish victory over the Dutch in 1625 (*Surrender of Breda*, FIG. 19-29).

Velázquez also painted dozens of portraits of Philip IV. One of the best is *King Philip IV of Spain* (FIG. 19-28), also known as the *Fraga Philip* because it was painted during the Aragonese campaign in the town of Fraga. Velázquez accompanied the king and his troops in their attempt to reconquer the territory, and during a three-month stay in Fraga, Philip ordered the artist to produce this portrait. In it, Philip IV appears as a military leader, arrayed in salmon and silver campaign dress but without military accoutrements except his baton of command and sword. Because the king was not a commanding presence and because he had inherited the large Habsburg jaw, Velázquez had to find creative ways to "ennoble" the monarch. He succeeded by focusing attention on the exquisite attire Philip wears, particularly the elabo-

19-28 Diego Velázquez, *King Philip IV of Spain* (*Fraga Philip*), 1644. Oil on canvas, 4′ 3⅛″ × 3′ 3⅛″. Frick Collection, New York.

Velázquez painted Philip IV during the king's campaign to reconquer Aragonese territory. The portrait is noteworthy for its faithful reproduction of the attire the king wore when reviewing troops.

1 ft.

rately embroidered cloak and *baldric* (the sashlike belt worn over one shoulder and across the chest to support a sword). Velázquez managed to make the silver needlework on these vestments shimmer. Detailed written accounts attest that this is the costume the king wore when reviewing the troops, and the artist's fidelity in depicting Philip's elegant attire no doubt added to the authority of the image.

portraits (FIG. 19-28) and canvases recording historical events. In 1635 he painted *Surrender of Breda* (FIG. 19-29) as part of an extensive program of decoration for the Hall of Realms in Philip IV's Palace of Buen Retiro in Madrid. The huge canvas (more than 12 feet long and almost as tall) was one of 10 paintings celebrating recent Spanish military successes around the globe. It commemorates the Spanish victory over the Dutch at Breda in 1625. Among the most troublesome situations for Spain was the conflict in the Netherlands. Determined to escape Spanish control, the northern Netherlands broke from the Spanish empire in the late 16th century. Skirmishes continued to flare up along the border between the northern (Dutch) and southern (Spanish) Netherlands, and in 1625 Philip IV sent General Ambrogio di Spínola to Breda to reclaim the town for Spain. Velázquez depicted the victorious Spanish troops, organized and well armed, on the right side of the painting. In sharp contrast, the defeated Dutch on the left appear bedraggled and disorganized. In the

center foreground, the mayor of Breda, Justinus of Nassau, hands the city's keys to the Spanish general—although no encounter of this kind ever occurred. Velázquez's fictional record of the event glorifies not only the strength of the Spanish military but the benevolence of Spínola as well. Velázquez portrayed the general standing and magnanimously stopping Justinus from kneeling, rather than astride his horse, lording over the vanquished Dutch. Indeed, the terms of surrender were notably lenient, and the Spaniards allowed the Dutch to retain their arms—which they used to recapture the city in 1637.

LAS MENINAS After an extended visit to Rome from 1648 to 1651, Velázquez returned to Spain and painted his greatest masterpiece, *Las Meninas* (*The Maids of Honor*; FIG. 19-30). In it, Velázquez showed his mastery of both form and content. The painter represented himself in his studio standing before a large canvas. The young Infanta (Princess) Margarita appears in the foreground with her two

19-29 DIEGO VELÁZQUEZ, *Surrender of Breda,* 1634–1635. Oil on canvas, 10′ 1″ × 12′ $\frac{1}{2}$″. Museo del Prado, Madrid.

As Philip IV's court artist, Velázquez produced many history paintings, including fictional representations like this one depicting the Dutch mayor of Breda surrendering to the Spanish general.

1 ft.

maids-in-waiting, her favorite dwarfs, and a large dog. In the middle ground are a woman in widow's attire and a male escort. In the background, a chamberlain stands in a brightly lit open doorway. Scholars have been able to identify everyone in the room, including the two *meninas* and the dwarfs. The room was the artist's studio in the palace of the Alcázar in Madrid. After the death of Prince Baltasar Carlos in 1646, Philip IV ordered part of the prince's chambers converted into a studio for Velázquez.

Las Meninas is noteworthy for its visual and narrative complexity. Indeed, art historians have yet to agree on any particular reading or interpretation. A central issue preoccupying scholars has been what, exactly, is taking place in *Las Meninas.* What is Velázquez depicting on the huge canvas in front of him? He may be painting this very picture—an informal image of the infanta and her entourage. Alternately, Velázquez may be painting a portrait of King Philip IV and Queen Mariana, whose reflections appear in the mirror on the far wall. If so, that would suggest the presence of the king and queen in the viewer's space, outside the confines of the picture. Other scholars have proposed that the mirror image reflects not the physical appearance of the royal couple in Velázquez's studio but the image that he is in the process of painting on the canvas before him. This question has never been definitively resolved.

More generally, *Las Meninas* is Velázquez's attempt to elevate both himself and his profession. As first painter to the king and as chamberlain of the palace, Velázquez was conscious not only of the importance of his court office but also of the honor and dignity belonging to his profession as a painter. Throughout his career, Velázquez hoped to be ennobled by royal appointment to membership in the ancient and illustrious Order of Santiago. Because he lacked a sufficiently noble background, he gained entrance only with difficulty at the very end of his life, and then only through the pope's dispensation. In the painting, he wears the order's red cross on his doublet, painted there, legend says, by the king himself. In all likelihood, the artist painted it. In Velázquez's mind, *Las Meninas* might have embodied the idea of the great king visiting his studio, as Alexander the Great visited the studio of the painter Apelles in ancient times. The figures in the painting all appear to acknowledge the royal presence. Placed among them in equal dignity is Velázquez, face-to-face with his sovereign. The location of the completed painting reinforced this act of looking—of seeing and being seen. *Las Meninas* hung in the personal office of Philip IV in another part of the palace. Thus, although occasional visitors admitted to the king's private quarters may have seen this painting, Philip IV was the primary audience. Each time he stood before the canvas, he again participated in the work as the probable subject of the painting within the painting and as the object of the figures' gazes. In *Las Meninas,* Velázquez elevated the art of painting, in the person of the painter, to the highest status. The king's presence enhanced this status—either in person as the viewer of *Las Meninas* or as a reflected image in the painting itself. The paintings that appear in *Las Meninas* further reinforced this celebration of the painter's craft. On the wall above the doorway and mirror, two faintly recognizable pictures have been identified as copies made by Velázquez's son-in-law, Juan del Mazo (ca. 1612–1667), of paintings by Peter Paul Rubens. The paintings depict the immortal gods as the source of art. Ultimately, Velázquez sought ennoblement not for himself alone but for his art.

19-30 Diego Velázquez, *Las Meninas* (*The Maids of Honor*), 1656. Oil on canvas, 10′ 5″ × 9′. Museo del Prado, Madrid.

Velázquez intended this huge and visually complex work, with its cunning contrasts of true spaces, mirrored spaces, and picture spaces, to elevate both himself and the profession of painting.

1 ft.

Las Meninas is extraordinarily complex visually. Velázquez's optical report of the event, authentic in every detail, pictorially summarizes the various kinds of images in their different levels and degrees of reality. He portrayed the realities of image on canvas, of mirror image, of optical image, and of the two painted images. This work—with its cunning contrasts of mirrored spaces, "real" spaces, picture spaces, and pictures within pictures—itself appears to have been taken from a large mirror reflecting the whole scene. This would mean that the artist did not paint the princess and her suite as the main subjects of *Las Meninas* but himself in the process of painting them. *Las Meninas* is a pictorial summary and a commentary on the essential mystery of the visual world, as well as on the ambiguity that results when different states or levels interact or are juxtaposed.

Velázquez achieved these results in several ways. The extension of the composition's pictorial depth in both directions is noteworthy. The open doorway and its ascending staircase lead the eye beyond the artist's studio, and the mirror device and the outward glances of several of the figures incorporate the viewer's space into the picture as well. (Compare how the mirror in Jan van Eyck's *Giovanni Arnolfini and His Bride*, FIG. **15-1**, similarly incorporates the area in front of the canvas into the picture, although less obviously and without a comparable extension of space beyond the rear wall of the room.) Velázquez also masterfully observed and represented form and shadow. Instead of putting lights abruptly beside darks, following Caravaggio, Velázquez allowed a great number of intermediate values of gray to come between the two extremes. His matching of tonal gradations approached effects that were later discovered in the photography age.

The inclusion of the copies of two Rubens paintings hanging on the wall in Velázquez's studio is the Spanish master's tribute to the great Flemish painter, one of the towering figures who made the 17th century so important in the history of art in Northern Europe. The works of Rubens, Rembrandt, and the other leading Baroque painters, sculptors, and architects of Flanders, the Dutch Republic, France, and England are the subject of Chapter 20.

ITALY AND SPAIN,
1600 TO 1700

ITALY

■ Art historians call the art of 17th-century Italy and Spain "Baroque," a term that probably derives from the Portuguese word for an irregularly shaped pearl. In contrast to the precision and orderly rationality of Italian Renaissance classicism, Baroque art and architecture are dynamic, theatrical, and highly ornate.

■ Baroque architects emphatically rejected the classical style. Francesco Borromini emphasized the sculptural qualities of buildings. The facades of his churches, for example, San Carlo alle Quattro Fontane, are not flat frontispieces but undulating surfaces that provide a fluid transition from exterior to interior space. The interiors of his buildings pulsate with energy and feature complex domes that grow organically from curving walls.

■ The greatest Italian Baroque sculptor was Gianlorenzo Bernini, who was also an important architect. In *Ecstasy of Saint Teresa,* he marshaled the full capabilities of architecture, sculpture, and painting to create an intensely emotional experience for worshipers, consistent with the Catholic Counter-Reformation principle of using artworks to inspire devotion and piety.

■ In painting, Caravaggio broke new ground by employing stark and dramatic contrasts of light and dark (tenebrism) and by setting religious scenes in everyday locales filled with rough-looking common people. An early masterpiece, *Calling of Saint Matthew,* for example, takes place in an ordinary tavern.

■ Caravaggio's combination of drama and realism attracted both loyal followers and harsh critics. The biographer Giovanni Pietro Bellori, for example, deplored Caravaggio's abandonment of the noble style of Raphael and the ancients and his "suppression of the dignity of art." He preferred the more classical style of Annibale Carracci and the Bolognese art academy.

■ Illusionistic ceiling paintings were very popular in Baroque Italy. In Sant'Ignazio in Rome, Fra Andrea Pozzo created the illusion that Heaven is opening up above the viewer's head by continuing the church's architecture into the painted nave vault.

SPAIN

■ Although the power of the Habsburg kings of Spain declined over the course of the 17th century, the royal family, which was devoutly Catholic, continued to spend lavishly on art. Spanish artists eagerly embraced the drama and emotionalism of Italian Baroque art. Scenes of death and martyrdom were popular in Spain during the Counter-Reformation. Painters such as José de Ribera and Francisco de Zurbarán produced moving images of martyred saints that incorporated the lighting and realism of Caravaggio.

■ The greatest Spanish Baroque painter was Diego Velázquez, court painter to Philip IV (r. 1621–1665). Velázquez painted a wide variety of themes ranging from religious subjects to royal portraits and historical events. His masterwork, *Las Meninas,* is extraordinarily complex visually and mixes true spaces, mirrored spaces, picture spaces, and pictures within pictures. It is a celebration of the art of painting itself.

Borromini, San Carlo alle Quattro Fontane, Rome, 1665–1667

Bernini, *Ecstasy of Saint Teresa,* 1645–1652

Caravaggio, *Calling of Saint Matthew,* ca. 1597–1601

Pozzo, *Glorification of Saint Ignatius,* 1691–1694

Velázquez, *Las Meninas,* 1656

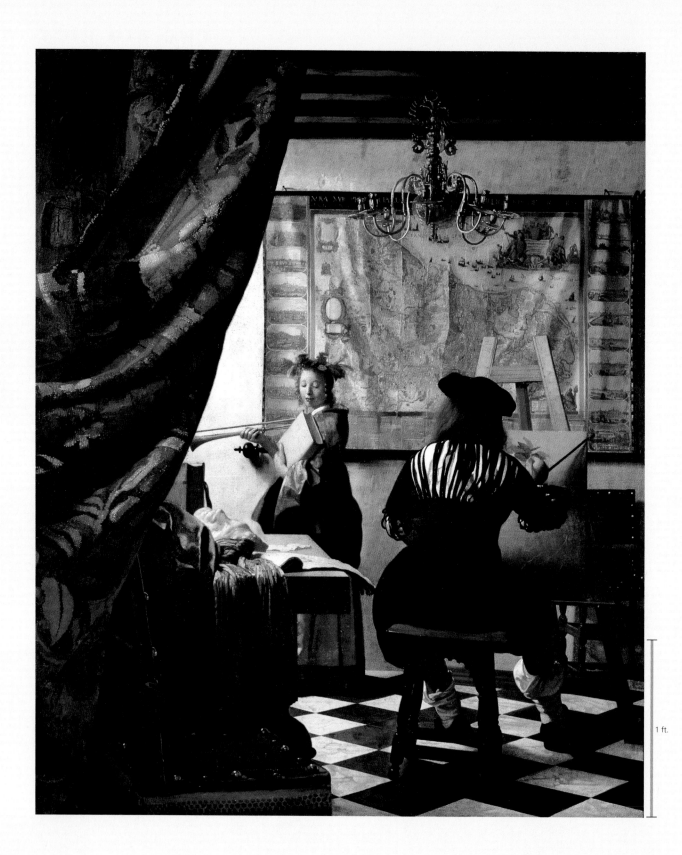

1 ft.

20-1 Jan Vermeer, *Allegory of the Art of Painting*, 1670–1675. Oil on canvas, 4′ 4″ × 3′ 8″. Kunsthistorisches Museum, Vienna.

Dutch painters often specialized in domestic scenes, but Vermeer's mother-in-law described this work as "the Art of Painting." Vermeer's tribute to his craft includes a model holding the attributes of Clio.

20

NORTHERN EUROPE, 1600 TO 1700

During the 17th and early 18th centuries, numerous geopolitical shifts occurred in Europe as the fortunes of the individual countries waxed and waned. Pronounced political and religious friction resulted in widespread unrest and warfare. Indeed, between 1562 and 1721, all of Europe was at peace for a mere four years. The major conflict of this period was the Thirty Years' War (1618–1648), which ensnared Spain, France, Sweden, Denmark, the Netherlands, Germany, Austria, Poland, the Ottoman Empire, and the Holy Roman Empire. Although the outbreak of the war had its roots in the conflict between militant Catholics and militant Protestants, the driving force quickly shifted to secular, dynastic, and nationalistic concerns. Among the major political entities vying for expanded power and authority in Europe were the Bourbon dynasty of France and the Habsburg dynasties of Spain and the Holy Roman Empire. The war, which concluded with the Treaty of Westphalia in 1648, was largely responsible for the political restructuring of Europe (MAP 20-1). As a result, the United Provinces of the Netherlands (the Dutch Republic), Sweden, and France expanded their authority. Spanish and Danish power diminished. In addition to reconfiguring territorial boundaries, the Treaty of Westphalia in essence granted freedom of religious choice throughout Europe. This treaty thus marked the abandonment of the idea of a united Christian Europe and accepted the practical realities of secular political systems. The building of today's nation-states was emphatically under way.

The 17th century also brought heightened economic competition to Europe. Much of the foundation for worldwide mercantilism—extensive voyaging and geographic exploration, improved cartography, and advances in shipbuilding—had been laid in the previous century. In the 17th century, however, changes in financial systems, lifestyles, and trading patterns, along with expanding colonialism, fueled the creation of a worldwide marketplace. The Dutch founded the Bank of Amsterdam in 1609, which eventually became the center of European transfer banking. By establishing a system in which merchant firms held money on account, the bank relieved traders of having to transport precious metals as payment. Trading practices became more complex. Rather than simple reciprocal trading, triangular trade (trade among three parties) allowed for a larger pool of desirable goods. Exposure to an ever-growing array of goods affected European diets and lifestyles. Coffee (from island colonies) and tea (from China)

MAP 20-1 Europe in 1648 after the Treaty of Westphalia.

became popular beverages during the early 17th century. Equally explosive was the growth of sugar use. Sugar, tobacco, and rice were slave crops, and the slave trade expanded to meet the demand for these goods. Traders captured and enslaved Africans and shipped them to European colonies and the Americas to provide the requisite labor force for producing these commodities.

The resulting worldwide mercantile system permanently changed the face of Europe. The prosperity international trade generated affected social and political relationships, necessitating new rules of etiquette and careful diplomacy. With increased disposable income, more of the newly wealthy spent money on art, expanding the number of possible sources of patronage.

FLANDERS

In the 16th century, the Netherlands had come under the crown of Habsburg Spain when the emperor Charles V retired, leaving the Spanish kingdoms, their Italian and American possessions, and the Netherlandish provinces to his only legitimate son, Philip II (r. 1556–1598). (Charles bestowed the imperial title and the German lands on his brother.) Philip's repressive measures against the Protestants led the northern provinces to break from Spain and to set up the Dutch Republic. The southern provinces remained under Spanish control, and they retained Catholicism as their official religion. The political distinction between modern Holland and Bel-

gium more or less reflects this original separation, which in the 17th century signaled not only religious but also artistic differences.

Painting

The leading art of 17th-century Flanders (the Spanish Netherlands) was painting. Flemish Baroque painters retained close connections to the Baroque art of Catholic Europe, whereas the Dutch schools of painting developed their own subjects and styles. This was consistent with their reformed religion and the new political, social, and economic structure of the Dutch Republic.

PETER PAUL RUBENS The renowned Flemish master PETER PAUL RUBENS (1577–1640) drew together the main contributions of the Italian Renaissance and Baroque masters to formulate the first truly pan-European painting style. Rubens's art is an original and powerful synthesis of the manners of many painters, especially Michelangelo, Titian, Carracci, and Caravaggio. His style had wide appeal, and his influence was international. Among the most learned individuals of his time, Rubens possessed an aristocratic education and a courtier's manner, diplomacy, and tact, which, with his facility for language, made him the associate of princes and scholars. He became court painter to the dukes of Mantua (descended from Mantegna's patrons), friend of King Philip IV (r. 1621–1665) of Spain and his adviser on art collecting, painter to Charles I (r. 1625–1649) of England and Marie de' Medici (1573–1642) of France, and permanent court painter to the Spanish governors of Flanders. Rubens

20-2 Peter Paul Rubens, *Elevation of the Cross,* from Saint Walburga, Antwerp, 1610. Oil on wood, 15′ 1$\frac{7}{8}$″ × 11′ 1$\frac{1}{2}$″ (center panel), 15′ 1$\frac{7}{8}$″ × 4′ 11″ (each wing). Antwerp Cathedral, Antwerp.

In this triptych, Rubens explored foreshortened anatomy and violent action. The composition seethes with a power that comes from heroic exertion. The tension is emotional as well as physical.

also won the confidence of his royal patrons in matters of state, and they often entrusted him with diplomatic missions of the highest importance. In the practice of his art, scores of associates and apprentices assisted Rubens, turning out numerous paintings for an international clientele. In addition, he functioned as an art dealer, buying and selling contemporary artworks and classical antiquities. His many enterprises made him a rich man, with a magnificent town house and a castle in the countryside. Rubens, like Raphael, was a successful and renowned artist, a consort of kings, a shrewd man of the world, and a learned philosopher.

ELEVATION OF THE CROSS Rubens became a master in 1598 and departed for Italy two years later, where he remained until 1608. During these years, he formulated the foundations of his style. Shortly after returning home, he painted *Elevation of the Cross* (FIG. 20-2) for the church of Saint Walburga in Antwerp. Later moved to the city's cathedral, the altarpiece is but one of many commissions for religious works that Rubens received at this time. By investing in sacred art, churches sought to affirm their allegiance to Catholicism and Spanish Habsburg rule after a period of Protestant iconoclastic fervor in the region.

The Saint Walburga triptych also reveals Rubens's interest in Italian art, especially the works of Michelangelo and Caravaggio. The scene brings together tremendous straining forces and counterforces

as heavily muscled men labor to lift the cross. Here, as in his *Lion Hunt* (FIG. I-13), Rubens used the subject as an opportunity to show foreshortened anatomy and the contortions of violent action reminiscent of the twisted figures that Michelangelo sculpted and painted. Rubens placed the body of Christ on the cross as a diagonal that cuts dynamically across the picture while inclining back into it. The whole composition seethes with a power that comes from genuine exertion, from elastic human sinew taut with effort. The tension is emotional as well as physical, as reflected not only in Christ's face but also in the features of his followers. Strong modeling in dark and light, which heightens the drama, marks Rubens's work at this stage of his career.

Although Rubens later developed a much subtler coloristic style, the human body in action, draped or undraped, male or female, remained the focus of his art. This interest, combined with his voracious intellect, led Rubens to copy the works of classical antiquity and of the Italian masters. When he was in Rome in 1606 to 1608, he made many black-chalk drawings of great artworks, including figures in Michelangelo's Sistine Chapel frescoes (FIG. 17-1) and the ancient marble group of Laocoön and his two sons (FIG. 5-88). In a Latin treatise he wrote titled *De imitatione statuarum* (*On the Imitation of Statues*), Rubens stated: "I am convinced that in order to achieve the highest perfection one needs a full understanding of the [ancient] statues, indeed a complete absorption in them; but one must make judicious use of them and before all avoid the effect of stone."[1]

20-3 PETER PAUL RUBENS, *Arrival of Marie de' Medici at Marseilles*, 1622–1625. Oil on canvas, 12′ 11½″ × 9′ 7″. Louvre, Paris.

Marie de' Medici asked Rubens to paint 21 large canvases glorifying her career. In this historical-allegorical picture of robust figures in an opulent setting, the sea and sky rejoice at the queen's arrival in France.

1 ft.

MARIE DE' MEDICI Rubens's interaction with royalty and aristocrats provided him with an understanding of the ostentation and spectacle of Baroque (particularly Italian) art that appealed to the wealthy and privileged. Rubens, the born courtier, reveled in the pomp and majesty of royalty. Likewise, those in power embraced the lavish spectacle that served the Catholic Church so well in Italy. The magnificence and splendor of Baroque imagery reinforced the authority and right to rule of the highborn. Among Rubens's royal patrons was Marie de' Medici, a member of the famous Florentine house and widow of Henry IV (r. 1589–1610), the first Bourbon king of France. She commissioned Rubens to paint a series memorializing and glorifying her career. Between 1622 and 1626, Rubens, working with amazing creative energy, produced 21 huge historical-allegorical pictures designed to hang in the queen's new palace, the Luxembourg, in Paris.

In *Arrival of Marie de' Medici at Marseilles* (FIG. 20-3), Marie disembarks in France after her sea voyage from Italy. An allegorical personification of France, draped in a cloak decorated with the *fleur-de-lis* (the floral symbol of French royalty), welcomes her. The sea and sky rejoice at her safe arrival. Neptune and the Nereids (daughters of the sea god Nereus) salute her, and a winged, trumpeting Fame hovers overhead. Conspicuous in the galley's opulently carved stern-castle, under the Medici coat of arms, stands the imperious commander of the vessel, the only immobile figure in the composi-

tion. In black and silver, this figure makes a sharp accent amid the swirling tonality of ivory, gold, and red. Rubens enriched the surfaces with a decorative splendor that pulls the whole composition together. The audacious vigor that customarily enlivens the artist's figures, beginning with the monumental, twisting sea creatures, vibrates through the entire design.

CONSEQUENCES OF WAR Rubens's diplomatic missions gave him great insight into European politics, and he never ceased to promote peace. Throughout most of his career, war was constant. When commissioned in 1638 to produce a painting (FIG. 20-4) for Ferdinando II de' Medici, the grand duke of Tuscany (r. 1621–1670), Rubens took the opportunity to express his attitude toward the Thirty Years' War (see "Rubens on *Consequences of War*," page 555). The fluid articulation of human forms in this work and the energy that emanates from the chaotic scene are reminiscent of Rubens's other paintings.

Rubens on *Consequences of War*

In the ancient and medieval worlds, artists rarely wrote commentaries on the works they produced. Beginning with the Renaissance, however, the increased celebrity artists enjoyed and the ready availability of paper encouraged artists to record their intentions in letters to friends and patrons.

In March 1638, Peter Paul Rubens wrote a letter to Justus Sustermans (1597–1681), court painter to Grand Duke Ferdinando II de' Medici of Tuscany, explaining his *Consequences of War* (FIG. 20-4) and his attitude toward the European military conflicts of his day.

The principal figure is Mars, who has left the open temple of Janus (which in time of peace, according to Roman custom, remained closed) and rushes forth with shield and blood-stained sword, threatening the people with great disaster. He pays little heed to Venus, his mistress, who, accompanied by Amors and Cupids, strives with caresses and embraces to hold him. From the other side, Mars is dragged forward by the Fury Alekto, with a torch in her hand. Near by are monsters personifying Pestilence and Famine, those inseparable partners of War. On the ground, turning her back, lies a woman with a broken lute, representing Harmony, which is incompatible with the discord of War. There is also a mother with her child in her arms, indicating that fecundity, procreation and charity are thwarted by War, which corrupts and destroys everything. In addition, one sees an architect thrown on his back, with his instruments in his hand, to show that which in time of peace is constructed for the use and ornamentation of the City, is hurled to the ground by the force of arms and falls to ruin. I believe, if I remember rightly, that you will find on the ground, under the feet of Mars a book and a drawing on paper, to imply that he treads underfoot all the arts and letters. There ought also to be a bundle of darts or arrows, with the band which held them together undone; these when bound form the symbol of Concord. Beside them is the caduceus and an olive branch, attribute of Peace; these are also cast aside. That grief-stricken woman clothed in black, with torn veil, robbed of all her jewels and other ornaments, is the unfortunate Europe who, for so many years now, has suffered plunder, outrage, and misery, which are so injurious to everyone that it is unnecessary to go into detail. Europe's attribute is the globe, borne by a small angel or genius, and surmounted by the cross, to symbolize the Christian world.*

* Translated by Kristin Lohse Belkin, *Rubens* (London: Phaidon, 1998), 288–289.

20-4 PETER PAUL RUBENS, *Consequences of War*, 1638–1639. Oil on canvas, 6′ 9″ × 11′ 3$\frac{7}{8}$″. Palazzo Pitti, Florence.

Beginning with the Renaissance, artists have left behind many writings shedding light on their life and work. In a 1638 letter, Rubens explained the meaning of each figure in this allegorical painting.

Van Dyck specialized in court portraiture. In this painting, he depicted the absolutist monarch Charles I at a sharp angle so that the king, a short man, appears to be looking down at the viewer.

1 ft.

ANTHONY VAN DYCK Most of Rubens's successors in Flanders were at one time his assistants. The most famous of these was ANTHONY VAN DYCK (1599–1641). Early on, the younger man, unwilling to be overshadowed by the master's undisputed stature, left his native Antwerp for Genoa and then London, where he became court portraitist to Charles I. Although Van Dyck created dramatic compositions of high quality, his specialty became the portrait. He developed a courtly manner of great elegance that was influential internationally. In one of his finest works, *Charles I Dismounted* (FIG. 20-5), the ill-fated Stuart king stands in a landscape with the Thames River in the background. An equerry and a page attend him. The portrait is a stylish image of relaxed authority, as if the king is out for a casual ride in his park, but no one can mistake the regal poise and the air of absolute authority that his Parliament resented and was soon to rise against. Here, King Charles turns his back on his attendants as he surveys his domain. The king's placement in the composition is exceedingly artful. He stands off-center but balances the picture with a single keen glance at the viewer. Van Dyck even managed to portray Charles I in a position to look down on the observer. In reality, the monarch's short stature forced him to exert his

680

1 in.

20-6 Clara Peeters, *Still Life with Flowers, Goblet, Dried Fruit, and Pretzels*, 1611. Oil on panel, 1′ 7¾″ × 2′ 1¼″. Museo del Prado, Madrid.

Clara Peeters was a pioneer of still-life painting. Although a Flemish artist, she spent time in Holland and laid the groundwork for many Dutch artists (FIGS. 20-21 to 20-23).

power in ways other than physical. Van Dyck's elegant style resounded in English portrait painting well into the 19th century.

CLARA PEETERS Some Flemish Baroque artists also explored *still-life* painting (inanimate objects artfully arranged). A pioneer of this genre was CLARA PEETERS (1594–ca. 1657), a Flemish artist who spent time in Holland and laid the groundwork for the Dutch artists Pieter Claesz (FIG. 20-21), William Kalf (FIG. 20-22), and Rachel Ruysch (FIG. 20-23). Peeters won renown for her depictions of food and flowers together, and for still lifes that included bread and fruit. Such still lifes became known as *breakfast pieces*. In the breakfast piece *Still Life with Flowers, Goblet, Dried Fruit, and Pretzels* (FIG. 20-6), Peeters's considerable skills are on full display. One of a series of four paintings, each of which depicts a typical early-17th-century meal, *Still Life* reveals Peeters's virtuosity in painting a wide variety of objects convincingly, from the smooth, reflective surfaces of the glass and silver goblets to the soft petals of the blooms in the vase. Although Peeters often depicted the objects in her still lifes against a dark background, thereby negating any sense of deep space, in this painting she presented the leaves of the flower on the stone ledge as though they were encroaching into the viewer's space.

DUTCH REPUBLIC

The Dutch succeeded in securing their independence from the Spanish in the late 16th century. Not until 1648, however, after years of continual border skirmishes with the Spanish (as depicted in Diego Velázquez's *Surrender of Breda*, FIG. 19-29), did the northern Netherlands achieve official recognition as the United Provinces of the Netherlands (the Dutch Republic; MAP 20-1). The Dutch Republic owed its ascendance during the 17th century largely to its economic prosperity. With the founding of the Bank of Amsterdam in 1609, Amsterdam emerged as the financial center of the Continent. In the 17th century, the city had the highest per capita income in Europe. The Dutch economy also benefited enormously from the country's expertise on the open seas, which facilitated establishing far-flung colonies. By 1650, Dutch trade routes extended to North America, South America, the west coast of Africa, China, Japan, Southeast Asia, and much of the Pacific. Due to this prosperity and in the absence of an absolute ruler, political power increasingly passed into the hands of an urban patrician class of merchants and manufacturers, especially in cities such as Amsterdam, Haarlem, and Delft. That all these bustling cities were located in Holland (the largest of the seven United Provinces) perhaps explains why historians informally use the name "Holland" to refer to the entire country.

Ter Brugghen, van Honthorst, Hals, Leyster

Religious differences were a major consideration during the northern Netherlands' insistent quest for independence during the 16th and early 17th centuries. Whereas Spain and the southern Netherlands were Catholic, the people of the northern Netherlands were predominantly Protestant. The prevailing Calvinism demanded a puritanical rejection of art in churches, and thus artists produced relatively little religious art in the Dutch Republic at this time (especially in comparison with that created in the wake of the Counter-Reformation in areas dominated by Catholicism; see Chapter 19).

HENDRICK TER BRUGGHEN Religious art was not unknown in the Dutch Republic, however. HENDRICK TER BRUGGHEN (1588–1629), for example, painted *Calling of Saint Matthew* (FIG. 20-7) in 1621, after returning from a trip to Italy, selecting as his subject a theme Caravaggio had painted (FIG. 19-18). The moment of the narrative depicted and the naturalistic presentation of the figures echo Caravaggio's work. But although ter Brugghen was an admirer of the Italian master, he dispensed with Caravaggio's stark contrasts of dark and light and instead presented the viewer with a more colorful palette of soft tints. Further, the Dutch painter compressed the figures into a small but well-lit space, creating an intimate effect that differs from Caravaggio's more spacious setting.

20-7 HENDRICK TER BRUGGHEN, *Calling of Saint Matthew*, 1621. Oil on canvas, 3′ 4″ × 4′ 6″. The Hague.

Although middle-class patrons in the Protestant Dutch Republic preferred genre scenes, still lifes, and portraits, some artists, including Hendrick ter Brugghen, also painted religious scenes.

1 ft.

Middle-Class Patronage and
the Art Market in the Dutch Republic

Throughout history, the wealthy have been the most avid art collectors. Indeed, the money necessary to commission major artworks from esteemed artists can be considerable. During the 17th century in the Dutch Republic, however, the widespread prosperity a large proportion of the population enjoyed significantly expanded the range of art patrons. As a result, one of the distinguishing hallmarks of Dutch art production during the Baroque period was how it catered to the tastes of a middle-class audience. The term "middle class" is used broadly here. An aristocracy and an upper class of large-ship owners, rich businesspeople, high-ranking officers, and directors of large companies still existed. These groups continued to be major patrons of the arts. But with the expansion of the Dutch economy, traders, craftspeople, bureaucrats, and soldiers also commissioned and collected art.

Although steeped in the morality and propriety central to the Calvinist ethic, members of the Dutch middle class sought ways to announce their success and newly acquired status. House furnishings, paintings, tapestries, and porcelain were among the items they collected and displayed in their homes. The Dutch disdain for excessive ostentation, however, attributable to Calvinism, led these collectors to favor small, low-key works—portraits, still lifes, genre scenes, and landscapes. This contrasted with the Italian Baroque penchant for large-scale, dazzling ceiling frescoes and opulent room decoration (see Chapter 19).

Although it is risky to generalize about the spending and collecting habits of the Dutch middle class, probate records, contracts, and archived inventories reveal some interesting facts. These records suggest that an individual earning between 1,500 and 3,000 guilders a year would have been living comfortably. This individual might have spent 1,000 guilders for a house and another 1,000 guilders on furnishings, which would have included a significant amount of art, particularly paintings. Although there was, of course, considerable variation in the prices of artworks, a great deal of art was very affordable. Prints were extremely cheap because of the quantity in which artists produced them. In terms of paintings, interior and genre scenes were relatively inexpensive, perhaps costing one or two guilders. Small landscapes fetched between three and four guilders. Commissioned portraits were the most costly. The size of the work and quality of the frame, as well as the reputation of the artist, were other factors in determining the price.

With the exception of portraits, Dutch artists produced most of their paintings for an anonymous market, hoping to appeal to a wide audience. To ensure success, artists in the United Provinces adapted to the changed conditions of art production and sales. They marketed their paintings in many ways, selling their works directly to buyers who visited their studios and through art dealers, exhibitions, fairs, auctions, and even lotteries. Because of the uncertainty of these sales mechanisms (as opposed to the certainty of an ironclad contract for a commission from a church or king), artists became more responsive to market demands. Specialization became common among Dutch artists. For example, painters might limit their practice to painting portraits, still lifes, or landscapes—the most popular genres among middle-class patrons.

Artists did not always sell their paintings. Frequently they used their work to pay off loans or debts. Tavern debts, in particular, could be settled with paintings, which may explain why many art dealers (such as Jan Vermeer and his father before him) were also innkeepers. This connection between art dealing and other businesses eventually solidified, and innkeepers, for example, often would mount art exhibitions in their taverns, hoping to make a sale. The institutions of today's open art market—dealers, galleries, auctions, and estate sales—owe their establishment to the emergence in the 17th century of a prosperous middle class in the Dutch Republic.

MERCANTILIST PATRONAGE Given the absence of an authoritative ruler and the Calvinist concern for the potential misuse of religious art, commissions from royalty or the Catholic Church, prominent in the art of other countries, were uncommon in the United Provinces. With the new prosperity, however, an expanding class of merchant patrons emerged, and this shift led to an emphasis on different pictorial content. Dutch Baroque art centered on genre scenes, landscapes, portraits, and still lifes, all of which appealed to the prosperous middle class (see "Middle-Class Patronage and the Art Market in the Dutch Republic," above).

GERRIT VAN HONTHORST Typical of 17th-century Dutch genre scenes is *Supper Party* (FIG. 20-8) by GERRIT VAN HONTHORST (1590–1656) of Utrecht. In this painting, van Honthorst presented an informal gathering of nonidealized human figures. While a musician serenades the group, his companions delight in watching a young woman feeding a piece of chicken to a man whose hands are both occupied—one holds a jug and the other a glass. Van Honthorst spent several years in Italy, and while there he carefully studied Caravaggio's work. The Italian artist's influence surfaces in the mundane tavern setting and the nocturnal lighting. Fascinated by nighttime effects, van Honthorst frequently placed a hidden light source in his pictures and used it as a pretext to work with dramatic and starkly contrasting dark and light effects. Seemingly lighthearted genre scenes such as *Supper Party* were popular in Baroque Holland, but Dutch viewers could also interpret them moralistically. For example, *Supper Party* can be read as a warning against the sins of gluttony (represented by the man on the right) and lust (the woman feeding the glutton is, in all likelihood, a prostitute with her aged procuress at her side). Or perhaps the painting represents the loose companions of the Prodigal Son (Luke 15:13)—panderers and prostitutes drinking, singing, strumming, and laughing. Strict Dutch Calvinists no doubt approved of such interpretations. Others simply took delight in the immediacy of the scenes and the skill of the artists.

FRANS HALS Dutch artists also excelled in portraiture. FRANS HALS (ca. 1581–1666), the leading painter in Haarlem, made portraits his specialty. Portrait artists traditionally had relied heavily on convention—for example, specific poses, settings, attire, and accou-

20-8 GERRIT VAN HONTHORST, *Supper Party,* 1620. Oil on canvas, 4′ 8″ × 7′. Galleria degli Uffizi, Florence.

Gerrit van Honthorst spent several years in Italy and studied the paintings of Caravaggio, whose influence is evident in the mundane tavern setting and the nocturnal light of *Supper Party.*

1 ft.

trements—to convey a sense of the sitter. Because the subject was usually someone of status or note, such as a pope, king, duchess, or wealthy banker, the artist's goal was to produce an image appropriate to the subject's station in life. With the increasing number of Dutch middle-class patrons, the tasks for portraitists became more challenging. The Calvinists shunned ostentation, instead wearing subdued and dark clothing with little variation or decoration, and the traditional conventions became inappropriate and thus unusable. Despite these difficulties, or perhaps because of them, Hals produced lively portraits that seem far more relaxed than traditional formulaic portraiture. He injected an engaging spontaneity into his images and conveyed the individuality of his sitters as well. His manner of execution intensified the casualness, immediacy, and intimacy in his paint-

ings. Because the touch of Hals's brush was as light and fleeting as the moment he captured the pose, the figure, the highlights on clothing, and the facial expression all seem instantaneously created.

ARCHERS OF SAINT HADRIAN Hals's group portraits reflect the widespread popularity in the Dutch Republic of vast canvases commemorating the participation of Dutch burghers in civic organizations. These commissions presented a far greater challenge to the painter than requests to depict a single sitter. Hals rose to the challenge and achieved great success with this new portrait genre. His *Archers of Saint Hadrian* (FIG. 20-9) is typical in that the subject is one of the many Dutch civic militia groups that claimed credit for liberating the Dutch Republic from Spain. Like other companies, the

20-9 FRANS HALS, *Archers of Saint Hadrian,* ca. 1633. Oil on canvas, 6′ 9″ × 11′. Frans Halsmuseum, Haarlem.

In this brilliant composition, Hals succeeded in solving the problem of adequately representing each individual in a group portrait while retaining action and variety in the painting as a whole.

1 ft.

20-10 FRANS HALS, *The Women Regents of the Old Men's Home at Haarlem*, 1664. Oil on canvas, 5' 7" × 8' 2". Frans Halsmuseum, Haarlem.

Dutch women played a major role in public life as regents of charitable institutions. A stern puritanical sensibility suffuses Hals's group portrait of the regents of Haarlem's old men's home.

1 ft.

Archers met on their saint's feast day in dress uniform for a grand banquet. The celebrations sometimes lasted an entire week, prompting an ordinance limiting them to three or four days. These events often involved a group portrait.

In *Archers of Saint Hadrian,* Hals attacked the problem of how to represent each militia member adequately yet retain action and variety in the composition. Whereas earlier group portraits in the Netherlands were rather ordered, regimented images, Hals sought to enliven his depictions.

In the *Archers* portrait, for example, each man is both a troop member and an individual with a distinct physiognomy. The sitters' movements and moods vary enormously. Some engage the viewer directly. Others look away or at a companion. Whereas one is stern, another is animated. Each man is equally visible and clearly recognizable. The uniformity of attire—black military dress, white ruffs, and sashes—did not deter Hals from injecting spontaneity into the work. Indeed, he used those elements to create a lively rhythm that extends throughout the composition and energizes the portrait. The impromptu effect—the preservation of every detail and fleeting facial expression—is, of course, the result of careful planning. Yet Hals's vivacious brush appears to have moved instinctively, directed by a plan in his mind but not traceable in any preparatory scheme on the canvas.

WOMEN REGENTS OF HAARLEM In *The Women Regents of the Old Men's Home at Haarlem* (FIG. **20-10**), Hals produced a group portrait of Calvinist women engaged in charitable work. Although Dutch women had primary responsibility for the welfare of the family and the orderly operation of the home, they also populated the labor force in the cities. Among the more prominent roles that educated women played in public life were regents of orphanages, hospitals, old-age homes, and houses of correction. In Hals's portrait, the regents sit quietly in a manner becoming of devout

20-11 JUDITH LEYSTER, *Self-Portrait,* ca. 1630. Oil on canvas, 2' 5 3/8" × 2' 1 5/8". National Gallery of Art, Washington, D.C. (gift of Mr. and Mrs. Robert Woods Bliss).

Although presenting herself as an artist specializing in genre scenes, Leyster wears elegant attire instead of a painter's smock, placing her socially as a member of a well-to-do family.

1 ft.

Calvinists. Unlike the more relaxed, seemingly informal character of his other group portraits, a stern, puritanical, and composed sensibility suffuses Hals's portrayal of the Haarlem regents. The women—all carefully distinguished as individuals—gaze out from the painting with expressions ranging from dour disinterest to kindly concern. The somber and virtually *monochromatic* (one-color) palette, punctuated only by the white accents of the clothing, contributes to the painting's restraint. Both the coloration and the mood of Hals's portrait are appropriate for this commission. Portraying the Haarlem regents called for a very different kind of portrait from those Hals made of men at festive militia banquets.

JUDITH LEYSTER Some of Hals's students developed thriving careers of their own as portraitists. One was JUDITH LEYSTER (1609–1660), whose *Self-Portrait* (FIG. 20-11) suggests the strong training she received. The picture is detailed, precise, and accurate but also imbued with the spontaneity found in Hals's works. In this self-portrait, Leyster succeeded at communicating a great deal about herself. She depicted herself as an artist, seated in front of a painting resting on an easel. The palette in her left hand and brush in her right announce that the painting is her creation. She thus allows the viewer to evaluate her skill, which both the fiddler on the canvas and the image of herself demonstrate as considerable. Although she produced a wide range of paintings, including still lifes and floral pieces, her specialty was genre scenes such as the comic image seen on the easel. Her self-assurance is reflected in her quick smile and her relaxed pose as she stops her work to meet the viewer's gaze. Although presenting herself as an artist, Leyster did not portray herself wearing the traditional artist's smock, as Rembrandt did in his self-portrait (FIG. 20-15). Her elegant attire distinguishes her socially as a member of a well-to-do family, another important aspect of Leyster's identity.

Rembrandt

REMBRANDT VAN RIJN (1606–1669), Hals's younger contemporary, was an artist of great versatility, a master of light and shadow, and a unique interpreter of the Protestant conception of scripture. The leading Dutch painter of his time, Rembrandt was an undisputed genius. Born in Leiden, he moved to Amsterdam around 1631, which provided him with a more extensive clientele than possible in his native city. Rembrandt had trained as a history painter in Leiden, but in Amsterdam he immediately entered the lucrative market for portrait painting and soon became renowned for that genre.

ANATOMY LESSON OF DR. TULP In a painting he created shortly after he arrived in Amsterdam, *Anatomy Lesson of Dr. Tulp* (FIG. 20-12), Rembrandt deviated even further from the traditional staid group portrait than had Hals. Despite Hals's determination to enliven his portraits, he still evenly spread his subjects across the canvas. In contrast, Rembrandt chose to portray the members of the surgeons' guild (who commissioned this group portrait) clustered together on the painting's left side. In the foreground appears the corpse that Dr. Tulp, a noted physician, is in the act of dissecting. Rembrandt diagonally placed and foreshortened the corpse, activating the space by disrupting the strict horizontal, planar orientation found in traditional portraiture. He depicted each of the "students" specifically, and although they wear virtually identical attire, their poses and facial expressions suggest the varying degrees of intensity with which they watch Dr. Tulp's demonstration—or ignore it. One, at the apex of Rembrandt's triangular composition of bodies, looks out at the viewer instead of at the operating table. Another directs his attention at the open book (a manual of anatomy) at the corpse's feet. Rembrandt produced this painting when he was 26 and just beginning his career, a fact that makes his innovative approach to group portraiture all the more remarkable.

20-12 REMBRANDT VAN RIJN, *Anatomy Lesson of Dr. Tulp*, 1632. Oil on canvas, 5' 3¾" × 7' 1¼". Mauritshuis, The Hague.

In this early work, Rembrandt used an unusual composition, portraying members of Amsterdam's surgeons' guild clustered together on one side of the painting as they watch Dr. Tulp dissect a corpse.

1 ft.

20-13 REMBRANDT VAN RIJN, *The Company of Captain Frans Banning Cocq* (*Night Watch*), 1642. Oil on canvas, 11′ 11″ × 14′ 4″ (cropped from original size). Rijksmuseum, Amsterdam.

Rembrandt's dramatic use of light contributes to the animation of this militia group portrait in which the artist showed the company rushing about as they organize themselves for a parade.

1 ft.

NIGHT WATCH Rembrandt amplified the complexity and energy of the group portrait in *The Company of Captain Frans Banning Cocq* (FIG. **20-13**), better known as *Night Watch*. This more commonly used title is a misnomer, however—the painting is not of a nocturnal scene. Rembrandt used light in a masterful way, and dramatic lighting certainly enhances the image. Still, the painting's darkness (which explains the commonly used title) is due more to the varnish the artist used, which darkened considerably over time, than to the subject depicted.

This painting was one of many civic-guard group portraits produced during this period. From the limited information available about the commission, it appears that the two officers, Captain Frans Banning Cocq and his lieutenant, Willem van Ruytenburch, along with 16 members of their militia, contributed to Rembrandt's fee. (Despite the prominence of the girl just to the left of center, scholars have yet to ascertain her identity.) *Night Watch* was one of six paintings by different artists that various groups commissioned around 1640 for the assembly and banquet room of Amsterdam's new Musketeers Hall, the largest and most prestigious interior space in the city. Unfortunately, in 1715, when city officials moved Rembrandt's painting to Amsterdam's town hall, they cropped it on all sides, leaving an incomplete record of the artist's final resolution of the challenge of portraying this group.

Even in its truncated form, *The Company of Captain Frans Banning Cocq* succeeds in capturing the excitement and frenetic activity of the men preparing for the parade. A comparison of this militia group portrait with Hals's *Archers of Saint Hadrian* (FIG. **20-9**) reveals Rembrandt's inventiveness in enlivening what was, by then, becoming a conventional portrait format. Rather than present assembled men, posed in orderly fashion, the younger artist chose to portray the company scurrying about in the act of organizing themselves, thereby animating the image considerably. At the same time, he managed to record the three most important stages of using a musket—loading, firing, and readying the weapon for reloading—details that must have pleased his patrons.

RETURN OF THE PRODIGAL SON The Calvinist injunctions against religious art did not prevent Rembrandt from making a series of religious paintings and prints. In the Dutch Republic, paintings depicting biblical themes were not objects of devotion, but they still brought great prestige, and Rembrandt and other artists vied to demonstrate their ability to narrate holy scripture in dramatic new ways. The Dutch images, however, are unlike the opulent, overwhelming art of Baroque Italy. Rather, Rembrandt's religious art is that of a committed Christian who desired to interpret biblical narratives in human (as opposed to lofty theological) terms. Rembrandt had a special interest in probing the states of the human soul. The spiritual stillness of his religious paintings is that of inward-turning contemplation, far from the choirs and trumpets and the heavenly tumult of Bernini (FIG. **19-1**) or Pozzo (FIG. **19-24**). The Dutch artist's psychological insight and his profound sympathy for human affliction produced, at the very end of his life, one of the most moving pictures in all religious art, *Return of the Prodigal Son* (FIG. **20-14**). Tenderly embraced by his forgiving father, the son crouches before him in weeping contrition, while three figures, immersed to varying degrees in the soft shadows, note the lesson of mercy. The light, everywhere mingled with shadow, directs the viewer's attention by illuminating the father and son and largely veiling the witnesses. Its focus is the beautiful, spiritual face of the old man. Secondarily, the light touches the contrasting stern face of the foremost witness. The painting demonstrates the degree to which Rembrandt developed a personal style completely in tune with the simple eloquence of the biblical passage.

REMBRANDT'S LIGHT From the few paintings by Rembrandt discussed thus far, it should be clear that the artist's use of light is among the hallmarks of his style. Rembrandt's pictorial method involved refining light and shade into finer and finer nuances until they blended with one another. Earlier painters' use of abrupt lights and darks gave way to gradation in the work of artists

1 ft.

20-14 Rembrandt van Rijn, *Return of the Prodigal Son,* ca. 1665. Oil on canvas, 8′ 8″ × 6′ 9″. Hermitage Museum, Saint Petersburg.

The spiritual stillness of Rembrandt's religious paintings is that of inward-turning contemplation, far from the choirs and trumpets and heavenly tumult of Italian Baroque Counter-Reformation works.

such as Rembrandt and Velázquez (see Chapter 19). Although these later artists may have sacrificed some of the dramatic effects of sharp chiaroscuro, a greater fidelity to actual appearances offset those sacrifices. This technique is closer to reality because the eyes perceive light and dark not as static but as always subtly changing.

In general, Renaissance artists represented forms and faces in a flat, neutral modeling light (even Leonardo's shading is of a standard kind). They represented the *idea* of light, rather than the real look of it. Artists such as Rembrandt discovered degrees of light and dark, degrees of differences in pose, in the movements of facial features, and in psychic states. They arrived at these differences optically, not conceptually or in terms of some ideal. Rembrandt found that by manipulating the direction, intensity, distance, and surface texture of light and shadow, he could render the most subtle nuances of character and mood, both in persons and in whole scenes. He discovered for the modern world that variation of light and shade, subtly modulated, can be read as emotional differences. In the visible world, light, dark, and the wide spectrum of values between the two are charged with meanings and feelings that sometimes are independent of the shapes and figures they modify. The theater and the photographic arts have used these discoveries to great dramatic effect.

REMBRANDT'S SELF-PORTRAITS Rembrandt carried over the spiritual quality of his religious works into his later portraits by the same means—what could be called the "psychology of

light." Light and dark are not in conflict in his portraits. They are reconciled, merging softly and subtly to produce the visual equivalent of quietness. Their prevailing mood is that of tranquil meditation, of philosophical resignation, of musing recollection—indeed, a whole cluster of emotional tones heard only in silence.

In a self-portrait (FIG. 20-15) produced late in Rembrandt's life, the light that shines from the upper left of the painting bathes the painter's face in soft highlights, leaving the lower part of his body in shadow. The artist depicted himself here as possessing dignity and strength, and the portrait serves as a summary of the many stylistic and professional concerns that occupied him throughout his career. Rembrandt's distinctive use of light is evident, as is the assertive brushwork that suggests a quiet confidence and self-assurance. He presented himself as a working artist holding his brushes, palette, and maulstick (compare FIG. 18-17) and wearing his studio garb—a smock and painter's turban. The circles on the wall behind him (the subject of much scholarly debate) may allude to a legendary sign of artistic virtuosity—the ability to draw a perfect circle freehand. Ultimately, Rembrandt's abiding interest in revealing the human soul emerged here in his careful focus on his expressive visage. His controlled use of light and the nonspecific setting contribute to this focus. Further, X-rays of the painting have revealed that Rembrandt originally depicted himself in the act of painting. His final resolution, with the viewer's attention drawn to his face, produced a portrait not just of the artist but of the man as well. Indeed, Rembrandt's nearly 70 self-portraits in various media have no parallel in sheer quantity. They reflect the artist's deeply personal connection to his craft.

1 ft.

20-15 Rembrandt van Rijn, *Self-Portrait,* ca. 1659–1660. Oil on canvas, 3′ 8¾″ × 3′ 1″. Kenwood House, London (Iveagh Bequest).

In this late self-portrait, Rembrandt's interest in revealing the human soul is evident in the attention given to his expressive face. The controlled use of light and the nonspecific setting contribute to this focus.

20-16 REMBRANDT VAN RIJN, *Christ with the Sick around Him, Receiving the Children* (*Hundred-Guilder Print*), ca. 1649. Etching, 11″ × 1′ 3¼″. Pierpont Morgan Library, New York.

Rembrandt's mastery of the new print-making medium of etching is evident in his expert use of light and dark to draw attention to Christ as he preaches compassionately to the blind and lame.

1 in.

REMBRANDT'S ETCHINGS

Rembrandt's virtuosity also extended to the graphic media—in particular, to etching (see "Woodcuts, Engravings, and Etchings," Chapter 15, page 415). Many artists took up etching after its perfection early in the 17th century, because etching allowed greater freedom than engraving in drawing the design. For etching, the printmaker covers a copper plate with a layer of wax or varnish. The artist incises the design into this surface with a pointed tool, exposing the metal below but not cutting into its surface. The printer then immerses the plate in acid, which etches, or eats away, the exposed parts of the metal, acting the same as the burin in engraving. The medium's softness gives etchers greater carving freedom than woodcutters and engravers have working directly in their more resistant media of wood and metal. If Rembrandt had never painted, he still would be renowned, as he principally was in his lifetime, for his prints. Prints were a major source of income for Rembrandt, as they were for Albrecht Dürer (see Chapter 18), and he often reworked the plates so that they could be used to produce a new issue or edition. This constant reworking was unusual within the context of 17th-century printmaking practices.

HUNDRED-GUILDER PRINT One of Rembrandt's most celebrated etchings is *Christ with the Sick around Him, Receiving the Children* (FIG. **20-16**). Indeed, the title by which this work has been known since the early 18th century, *Hundred-Guilder Print,* refers to the high price it brought during Rembrandt's lifetime. *Christ with the Sick* demonstrates the artist's mastery of all aspects of the printmaker's craft, for Rembrandt used both engraving and etching to depict the figures and the setting. As in his other religious works, Rembrandt suffused this print with a deep and abiding piety, presenting the viewer not the celestial triumph of the Catholic Church but the humanity and humility of Jesus. Christ appears in the center preaching compassionately to, and simultaneously blessing, the blind, the lame, and the young who are spread throughout the composition in a dazzling array of standing, kneeling, and lying positions. Also present is a young man in elegant garments with his head in his hand, lamenting Christ's insistence that the wealthy need to give their possessions to the poor in order to gain entrance to Heaven. The tonal range of the print is remarkable. At the right, the figures near the city gate are in deep shadow. At the left, the figures, some rendered almost exclusively in outline, are in bright light—not the light of day but the illumination radiating from Christ himself. A second, unseen source of light comes from the right and casts the shadow of the praying man's arms and head onto Christ's tunic. Technically and in terms of its humanity, the *Hundred-Guilder Print* is Rembrandt's supreme achievement as a printmaker.

Landscape and Interior Painting

Landscape scenes abound in 17th-century Dutch art. Due to topography and politics, the Dutch had a unique relationship to the terrain, one that differed from those of other European countries. After gaining independence from Spain, the Dutch undertook an extensive land reclamation project that lasted almost a century. Dikes and drainage systems cropped up across the countryside. Because of the effort expended on these endeavors, people developed a very direct relationship to the land. Further, the reclamation affected Dutch social and economic life. The marshy and swampy nature of much of the land made it less desirable for large-scale exploitation, so the extensive feudal landowning system that existed elsewhere in Europe never developed in the United Provinces. Most Dutch families owned and worked their own farms, cultivating a feeling of closeness to the terrain.

AELBERT CUYP One Dutch artist who established his reputation as a specialist in landscape painting was AELBERT CUYP (ca. 1620–1691). His works were the products of careful observation and a deep respect for and understanding of the Dutch terrain. *Distant View of Dordrecht, with a Milkmaid and Four Cows, and Other Figures* (FIG. **20-17**) reveals Cuyp's substantial skills. Unlike the idealized classical landscapes that appear in many Italian Renaissance paintings, this landscape is particularized. In fact, the church in the background can be identified as the Grote Kerk in Dordrecht. The dairy cows, shepherds, and milkmaid in the foreground refer to a cornerstone of Dutch agriculture—the demand for dairy products such as butter and cheese, which increased with the development of urban centers. The credibility of this and similar paintings rests on Cuyp's pristine rendering of each detail.

JACOB VAN RUISDAEL Depicting the Dutch landscape with precision and sensitivity was also a specialty of JACOB VAN RUISDAEL (ca. 1628–1682). In *View of Haarlem from the Dunes at Overveen* (FIG. **20-18**), van Ruisdael provided an overarching view of this major Dutch city. The specificity of the artist's image—the Saint Bavo church in the background, the numerous windmills that refer to the land reclamation efforts, and the figures in the foreground stretching linen

20-17 Aelbert Cuyp, *Distant View of Dordrecht, with a Milkmaid and Four Cows, and Other Figures,* late 1640s. Oil on canvas, $5' 1'' \times 6' 4\frac{7}{8}''$. National Gallery, London.

Unlike idealized Italian Renaissance classical land-scapes, Cuyp's painting portrays a particular locale. The cows, shepherds, and milkmaid refer to the Dutch Republic's important dairy industry.

1 ft.

20-18 Jacob van Ruisdael, *View of Haarlem from the Dunes at Overveen,* ca. 1670. Oil on canvas, $1' 10'' \times 2' 1''$. Mauritshuis, The Hague.

In this painting, van Ruisdael succeeded in capturing a specific view of Haarlem, its windmills, and Saint Bavo church, but he also imbued the landscape with a quiet serenity that approaches the spiritual.

1 in.

20-19 Jan Vermeer, *The Letter,* 1666. Oil on canvas, $1' \, 5\frac{1}{4}'' \times 1' \, 3\frac{1}{4}''$. Rijksmuseum, Amsterdam.

Vermeer used both mirrors and the camera obscura to depict opulent 17th-century Dutch domestic interiors so convincingly. He was also far ahead of his time in understanding the science of color.

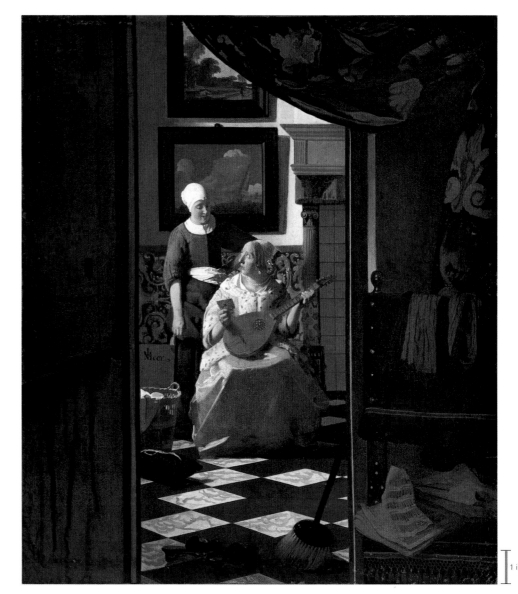

1 in.

to be bleached (a major industry in Haarlem)—reflects the pride Dutch painters took in recording their homeland and the activities of their fellow citizens. Nonetheless, in this painting the inhabitants and dwellings are so minuscule that they blend into the land itself, unlike the figures in Cuyp's view of Dordrecht (FIG. 20-17). Further, the horizon line is low, so the sky fills almost three-quarters of the picture space, and the sun illuminates the landscape only in patches, where it has broken through the clouds above. In *View of Haarlem,* as in his other landscape paintings, van Ruisdael not only captured the appearance of a specific locale but also succeeded in imbuing the work with a quiet serenity that becomes almost spiritual.

JAN VERMEER The sense of peace, familiarity, and comfort that Dutch landscape paintings exude also emerges in interior scenes, another popular subject among middle-class patrons. These paintings offer the viewer glimpses into the lives of prosperous, responsible, and cultured citizens of the United Provinces. The foremost Dutch painter of interior scenes was Jan Vermeer (1632–1675) of Delft. Vermeer derived much of his income from his work as an innkeeper and art dealer (see "Middle-Class Patronage and the Art Market," page 558), and he painted no more than 35 paintings that can be definitively attributed to him. He began his career as a painter of biblical and historical themes but soon abandoned those traditional subjects in favor of domestic scenes. Flemish artists of the 15th century also had painted domestic interiors, but persons of sacred significance often occupied those scenes (FIG. 15-4). In contrast, Vermeer and his contemporaries composed neat, quietly opulent interiors of Dutch middle-class dwellings with men, women, and children engaging in household tasks or some little recreation. Women are the primary occupants of Vermeer's homes, and his paintings are highly idealized depictions of the social values of Dutch burghers.

THE LETTER A room of a well-appointed Dutch house is the scene of Vermeer's *The Letter* (FIG. 20-19). The drawn curtain and open doorway through which viewers must peer reinforce their status as outsiders getting a glimpse of a private scene. The painting features two women. One wears elegant attire, suggesting that she is a woman of considerable means. A maid interrupts her lute playing to deliver a letter. The 17th-century Dutch audience would immediately recognize that it is a love letter, because the lute was a traditional symbol of the music of love, and the painting of a ship on a calm (as opposed to rough) sea on the back wall was a symbol of love requited. In Jan Harmensz Krul's book *Love Emblems,* published in Amsterdam in 1634, the author wrote, "Love may rightly be compared to the sea, considering its changeableness . . . just so does it go with a lover as with a skipper embarking on the sea, one day good weather, another day storm and howling wind."[2]

Vermeer was a master of pictorial light and used it with immense virtuosity. He could render space so convincingly through his depiction of light that in his works, the picture surface functions as an invisible glass pane through which the viewer looks into the constructed illusion. Historians are confident that Vermeer used as tools both mirrors and the *camera obscura,* an ancestor of the modern camera based on passing light through a tiny pinhole or lens to project an image on a screen or the wall of a room. (In later versions, artists projected the image on a ground-glass wall of a box whose opposite wall contained the pinhole or lens.) This does not mean that Vermeer merely copied the image. Instead, these aids helped him obtain results he reworked compositionally, placing his figures and the furniture of a room in a beautiful stability of quadrilateral shapes. His designs have a matchless classical serenity. Enhancing

20-20 JAN STEEN, *Feast of Saint Nicholas,* ca. 1660–1665. Oil on canvas, 2′ 8$\frac{1}{4}$″ × 2′ 3$\frac{3}{4}$″. Rijksmuseum, Amsterdam.

Steen's lively scene of Dutch children discovering their Christmas gifts may also have an allegorical dimension. *Feast of Saint Nicholas* probably alludes to selfishness, pettiness, and jealousy.

1 in.

in *The Letter,* the viewer is outside the space of the action, looking in through the drawn curtain that separates the artist in his studio from the rest of the house—and from the viewer. Some art historians have suggested that the light radiating from an unseen window on the left that illuminates both the model and the canvas being painted alludes to the light of artistic inspiration. Accordingly, many art historians have interpreted this painting as an allegory—a reference to painting inspired by history. Vermeer's mother-in-law confirmed this allegorical reading in 1677 when she sought to retain the painting after the artist's death, when 26 of his works were scheduled to be sold to pay his widow's debts. She listed the painting in her written claim as "the piece . . . wherein the Art of Painting is portrayed."[3]

JAN STEEN Whereas Vermeer's paintings reveal the charm and beauty of Dutch domesticity, the works of JAN STEEN (ca. 1625–1679) provide a counterpoint. In *Feast of Saint Nicholas* (FIG. **20-20**), Steen rejected painting a tidy, calm Dutch household and opted instead for a scene of chaos and disruption. Saint Nicholas has just visited this residence, and the children are in an uproar as they search their shoes for the Christmas gifts he has left. Some children are delighted. The little girl in the center clutches her gifts, clearly unwilling to share with the other children despite her mother's pleas. Others are disappointed. The boy on the left is in tears because he has received only a birch rod. An appropriately festive atmosphere reigns, which contrasts sharply with the decorum that prevails in Vermeer's works. Like the paintings of other Dutch artists, Steen's lively scenes often take on an allegorical dimension and moralistic tone. Steen frequently used children's activities as satirical comments on foolish adult behavior, and *Feast of Saint Nicholas* is not his only allusion to selfishness, pettiness, and jealousy.

Still-Life Painting

The prosperous Dutch were justifiably proud of their accomplishments, and the popularity of still-life paintings—particularly images of accumulated goods—reflected this pride. These still lifes, like Vermeer's interior scenes, are beautifully crafted images that are both scientific in their optical accuracy and poetic in their beauty and lyricism.

this quality are colors so true to the optical facts and so subtly modulated that they suggest Vermeer was far ahead of his time in color science. Close examination of his paintings shows that Vermeer realized shadows are not colorless and dark, that adjoining colors affect each other, and that light is composed of colors. Thus, he painted reflections off of surfaces in colors modified by others nearby. Some experts have suggested that Vermeer also perceived the phenomenon modern photographers call "circles of confusion," which appear on out-of-focus negatives. Vermeer could have seen them in images projected by the camera obscura's primitive lenses. He approximated these effects with light dabs that, in close view, give the impression of an image slightly "out of focus." When the observer draws back a step, however, as if adjusting the lens, the color spots cohere, giving an astonishingly accurate illusion of a third dimension.

THE ART OF PAINTING Vermeer's stylistic precision and commitment to his profession surface in *Allegory of the Art of Painting* (FIG. **20-1**). The artist himself appears in the painting, with his back to the viewer and dressed in "historical" clothing (reminiscent of Burgundian attire). He is hard at work on a painting of the model who stands before him wearing a laurel wreath and holding a trumpet and book, traditional attributes of Clio, the muse of history. The map of the provinces (an increasingly common adornment in Dutch homes) on the back wall serves as yet another reference to history. As

Vanitas still lifes reflect the pride Dutch citizens had in their material possessions, but Calvinist morality and humanity tempered that pride. The skull and timepiece remind the viewer of life's transience.

1 in.

PIETER CLAESZ Many Dutch still-life paintings, such as *Vanitas Still Life* (FIG. 20-21) by PIETER CLAESZ (1597/98–1660), celebrate material possessions, here presented as if strewn across a tabletop or dresser. The ever-present morality and humility central to the Calvinist faith tempered Dutch pride in worldly goods, however. Thus, while Claesz fostered the appreciation and enjoyment of the beauty and value of the objects he depicted, he also reminded the viewer of life's transience by incorporating references to death. Paintings with such features are called *vanitas* (vanity) *paintings*. Each feature is referred to as a *memento mori* (reminder of death). In *Vanitas Still Life*, references to mortality include the skull, timepiece, tipped glass, and cracked walnut. All suggest the passage of time or a presence that has disappeared. Something or someone was here—and now is gone. Claesz emphasized this element of time (and demonstrated his technical virtuosity) by including a self-portrait, reflected in the glass ball on the left side of the table. He appears to be painting this still life. But in an apparent challenge to the message of inevitable mortality that vanitas paintings convey, the portrait serves to immortalize the subject—in this case, the artist himself.

WILLEM KALF As Dutch prosperity increased, precious objects and luxury items made their way into still-life paintings. *Still Life with a Late Ming Ginger Jar* (FIG. 20-22) by WILLEM KALF (1619–1693) reveals both the wealth Dutch citizens had accrued and the painter's exquisite skills, both technical and aesthetic. Kalf highlighted the breadth of Dutch maritime trade through his depiction of the Indian floral carpet and the Chinese jar used to store ginger (a luxury item). He delighted in recording the lustrous sheen of fabric and the light glinting off reflective surfaces. As is evident in this image, Kalf's works present an array of ornamental objects, such as the Venetian

and Dutch glassware and the silver dish. The inclusion of the watch, Mediterranean peach, and peeled lemon suggests that this work is also a vanitas painting.

RACHEL RUYSCH As living objects that soon die, flowers, particularly cut blossoms, appeared frequently in vanitas paintings. However, floral painting as a distinct genre also flourished in the Dutch Republic. Among the leading practitioners of this art was RACHEL RUYSCH (1663–1750). Ruysch's father was a professor of botany and anatomy, which may account for her interest in and knowledge of plants and insects. She acquired an international reputation for lush paintings such as *Flower Still Life* (FIG. 20-23). In this image, the

20-22 WILLEM KALF, *Still Life with a Late Ming Ginger Jar*, 1669. Oil on canvas, 2′ 6″ × 2′ 1¾″. Indianapolis Museum of Art, Indianapolis (gift in commemoration of the 60th anniversary of the Art Association of Indianapolis, in memory of Daniel W. and Elizabeth C. Marmon).

The opulent objects, especially the Indian carpet and Chinese jar, attest to the prosperous Dutch maritime trade. Kalf's inclusion of a watch suggests that this painting may also be a vanitas still life.

1 ft.

20-23 RACHEL RUYSCH, *Flower Still Life,* after 1700. Oil on canvas, 2′ 5¾″ × 1′ 11⅞″. Toledo Museum of Art, Toledo (purchased with funds from the Libbey Endowment, gift of Edward Drummond Libbey).

Flower paintings were very popular in the Dutch Republic. Rachel Ruysch achieved international renown for her lush paintings of floral arrangements, noted also for their careful compositions.

lavish floral arrangement is so full that many of the blossoms seem to be spilling out of the vase. Ruysch carefully constructed her paintings. Here, for example, she positioned the flowers to create a diagonal that runs from the lower left of the painting to the upper right corner and that offsets the opposing diagonal of the table edge. Ruysch became famous for her floral paintings and still lifes, and from 1708 to 1716 she served as court painter to the elector Palatine (the ruler of the Palatinate, a former division of Bavaria) in Düsseldorf, Germany.

FRANCE

In France, monarchical authority had been increasing for centuries, culminating in the reign of Louis XIV (r. 1661–1715), who sought to determine the direction of French society and culture. Although its economy was not as expansive as that of the Dutch Republic, France became Europe's largest and most powerful country in the 17th century. Against this backdrop, the arts flourished.

Painting and Graphic Art

NICOLAS POUSSIN Rome's ancient and Renaissance monuments enticed many French artists to study there. Normandy-born NICOLAS POUSSIN (1594–1665), for example, spent most of his life in Rome, where he produced grandly severe paintings modeled on those of Titian and Raphael. He also carefully worked out a theoretical explanation of his method and was ultimately responsible for establishing classical painting as an important ingredient of 17th-century French art (see "Poussin's Notes for a Treatise on Painting," page 570). His classical style presents a striking contrast to the contemporaneous Baroque style of his Italian counterparts in Rome (see Chapter 19), underscoring the multifaceted character of the art of 17th-century Europe.

ET IN ARCADIA EGO Poussin's *Et in Arcadia Ego* (*I, Too, in Arcadia,* or *Even in Arcadia, I* [am present]; FIG. **20-24**) draws on the rational order and stability of Raphael's paintings and on antique

20-24 NICOLAS POUSSIN, *Et in Arcadia Ego,* ca. 1655. Oil on canvas, 2′ 10″ × 4′. Louvre, Paris.

Poussin was the leading proponent of classicism in 17th-century Rome. His works incorporate the rational order and stability of Raphael's compositions as well as figures inspired by ancient statuary.

Poussin's Notes for a Treatise on Painting

As the leading exponent of classical painting in 17th-century Rome, Nicolas Poussin (FIGS. 20-24 and 20-25) outlined the principles of classicism in notes for an intended treatise on painting, left incomplete at his death. In those notes, Poussin described the essential ingredients necessary to produce a beautiful painting in "the grand manner":

The grand manner consists of four things: subject-matter or theme, thought, structure, and style. The first thing that, as the foundation of all others, is required, is that the subject-matter shall be grand, as are battles, heroic actions, and divine things. But assuming that the subject on which the painter is laboring is grand, his next consideration is to keep away from minutiae . . . [and paint only] things magnificent and grand . . . . Those who elect mean subjects take refuge in them because of the weakness of their talents.*

The idea of beauty does not descend into matter unless [a painting] is prepared as carefully as possible. This preparation consists of three things: arrangement, measure, and aspect or form. Arrangement means the relative position of the parts; measure refers to their size; and form consists of lines and colors. Arrangement and relative position of the parts and making every limb of the body hold its natural place are not sufficient unless measure is added, which gives to each limb its correct size, proportionate to that of the whole body [compare "Polykleitos's Prescription for the Perfect Statue," Chapter 5, page 110], and unless form joins in, so that the lines will be drawn with grace and with a harmonious juxtaposition of light and shadow.†

* Translated by Robert Goldwater and Marco Treves, eds., *Artists on Art,* 3d ed. (New York: Pantheon Books, 1958), 155.
† Ibid., 156.

20-25 NICOLAS POUSSIN, *Burial of Phocion,* 1648. Oil on canvas, 3′ 11″ × 5′ 10″. Louvre, Paris.

Poussin's landscapes do not represent a particular place and time but are idealized settings for noble themes, like this one based on Plutarch's biography of the Athenian general Phocion.

statuary. Landscape, of which Poussin became increasingly fond, provides the setting for the picture. Dominating the foreground, however, are three shepherds, living in the idyllic land of Arcadia, who study an inscription on a tomb as a statuesque female figure quietly places her hand on the shoulder of one of them. She may be the spirit of death, reminding these mortals, as does the inscription, that death is found even in Arcadia, supposedly a spot of paradisiacal bliss. The countless draped female statues surviving in Italy from Roman times supplied the models for this figure, and the posture of the youth with one foot resting on a boulder derives from Greco-Roman statues of Neptune, the sea god, leaning on his trident. The classically compact and balanced grouping of the figures, the even light, and the thoughtful and reserved mood complement Poussin's classical figure types.

BURIAL OF PHOCION Among Poussin's finest works is *Burial of Phocion* (FIG. 20-25), a subject the artist characteristically chose from the literature of antiquity. Poussin's source was Plutarch's *Life of Phocion,* a biography of the distinguished Athenian general whom his compatriots unjustly put to death for treason. Eventually, the state gave Phocion a public funeral and memorialized him. In the foreground of Poussin's painting, the hero's body is being taken away, his burial on Athenian soil initially forbidden. The two massive bearers and the bier are starkly isolated in a great landscape that throws them into solitary relief, eloquently expressive of the hero abandoned in death. The landscape's interlocking planes slope upward to the lighted sky at the left. Its carefully arranged terraces bear slowly moving streams, shepherds and their flocks, and, in the dis-

20-26 CLAUDE LORRAIN, *Landscape with Cattle and Peasants,* 1629. Oil on canvas, 3′ 6″ × 4′ 10½″. Philadelphia Museum of Art, Philadelphia (George W. Elkins Collection).

Claude used atmospheric and linear perspective to transform the rustic Roman countryside filled with peasants and animals into an idealized classical landscape bathed in sunlight in infinite space.

tance, whole assemblies of solid geometric structures (temples, towers, walls, villas, and a central grand sarcophagus). The skies are untroubled, and the light is even and revealing of form. The trees are few and carefully arranged, like curtains lightly drawn back to reveal a natural setting carefully cultivated for a single human action. Unlike van Ruisdael in *View of Haarlem* (FIG. 20-18), Poussin did not intend this scene to represent a particular place and time. It was the French artist's construction of an idea of a noble landscape to frame a noble theme, much like Annibale Carracci's classical landscape (FIG. 19-15). The *Phocion* landscape is nature subordinated to a rational plan.

CLAUDE LORRAIN Claude Gellée, called CLAUDE LORRAIN (1600–1682) after his birthplace in the duchy of Lorraine, which was technically independent from the French monarchy during this period, rivaled Poussin in fame. Claude modulated in a softer style the disciplined rational art of Poussin, with its sophisticated revelation of the geometry of landscape. Unlike the figures in Poussin's pictures, those in Claude's landscapes tell no dramatic story, point out no moral, and praise no hero. Indeed, they often appear to be added as mere excuses for the radiant landscape itself. For Claude, painting

involved essentially one theme—the beauty of a broad sky suffused with the golden light of dawn or sunset glowing through a hazy atmosphere and reflecting brilliantly off rippling water.

In *Landscape with Cattle and Peasants* (FIG. 20-26), the figures in the right foreground chat in animated fashion. In the left foreground, cattle relax contentedly. In the middle ground, cattle amble slowly away. The well-defined foreground, distinct middle ground, and dim background recede in serene orderliness, until all form dissolves in a luminous mist. Atmospheric and linear perspective reinforce each other to turn a vista into a typical Claudian vision, an ideal classical world bathed in sunlight in infinite space (compare FIG. I-11).

Claude's formalizing of nature with balanced groups of architectural masses, screens of trees, and sheets of water followed the great tradition of classical landscape. It began with the backgrounds of Venetian painting (FIGS. 17-34 and 17-35) and continued in the art of Annibale Carracci (FIG. 19-15) and Poussin (FIG. 20-25). Yet Claude, like the Dutch painters, studied the light and the atmospheric nuances of nature, making a unique contribution. He recorded carefully in hundreds of sketches the look of the Roman countryside, its gentle terrain accented by stone-pines, cypresses, and poplars and by the ever-present ruins of ancient aqueducts,

1 ft.

20-27 Louis Le Nain, *Family of Country People,* ca. 1640. Oil on canvas, 3′ 8″ × 5′ 2″. Louvre, Paris.

Le Nain's painting expresses the grave dignity of a peasant family made stoic by hardship. It reflects 17th-century French social theory, which celebrated the natural virtue of those who worked the soil.

tombs, and towers. He made these the fundamental elements of his compositions. Travelers could understand the picturesque beauties of the outskirts of Rome in Claude's landscapes.

The artist achieved his marvelous effects of light by painstakingly placing tiny value gradations, which imitated, though on a very small scale, the range of values of outdoor light and shade. Avoiding the problem of high-noon sunlight overhead, Claude preferred, and convincingly represented, the sun's rays as they gradually illuminated the morning sky or, with their dying glow, set the pensive mood of evening. Thus, he matched the moods of nature with those of human subjects. Claude's infusion of nature with human feeling and his recomposition of nature in a calm equilibrium greatly appealed to the landscape painters of the 18th and early 19th centuries.

LOUIS LE NAIN Although classicism was an important presence in French art during the 17th and early 18th centuries, not all artists pursued this direction. Louis Le Nain (ca. 1593–1648) bears comparison to the Dutch. Subjects that in Dutch painting were opportunities for boisterous good humor, the French treated with somber stillness. *Family of Country People* (FIG. 20-27) reflects the thinking of 17th-century French social theorists who celebrated the natural virtue of peasants who worked the soil. Le Nain's painting expresses the grave dignity of one peasant family made stoic and resigned by hardship. These drab country folk surely had little reason for merriment. The peasant's lot, never easy, was miserable during the Thirty Years' War. The anguish and frustration of the peasantry, suffering from the cruel depredations of unruly armies living off the

countryside, often broke out in violent revolts that the same armies savagely suppressed. This family, however, is pious, docile, and calm. Because Le Nain depicted peasants as dignified and subservient despite their harsh living conditions, some scholars have suggested he intended to please wealthy urban patrons with these paintings.

JACQUES CALLOT Two other prominent artists from Lorraine were Jacques Callot and Georges de La Tour. Jacques Callot (ca. 1592–1635) conveyed a sense of military life during these troubled times in a series of etchings called *Miseries of War*. Callot confined himself almost exclusively to the art of etching and was widely influential in his own time and since. (Rembrandt was among those who knew and learned from his work.) Callot perfected the medium and the technique of etching, developing a very hard surface for the copper plate to permit fine and precise delineation with the needle. His quick, vivid touch and faultless drawing produced panoramas sparkling with sharp details of life—and death. In the *Miseries of War* series, he observed these details coolly, presenting without comment images based on events he himself must have seen in the wars in Lorraine.

In *Hanging Tree* (FIG. 20-28), Callot depicted a mass execution of thieves (identified in the text at the bottom of the etching). The event takes place in the presence of a disciplined army, drawn up on parade with banners, muskets, and lances, their tents in the background. Hanged men sway in clusters from the branches of a huge cross-shaped tree. A monk climbs a ladder, holding up a crucifix to a man while the executioner adjusts the noose around the man's neck. At the foot of the ladder, another victim kneels to receive absolution.

20-28 JACQUES CALLOT, *Hanging Tree,* from the *Miseries of War* series, 1629–1633. Etching, $3\frac{3}{4}'' \times 7\frac{1}{4}''$. Private collection.

Callot's *Miseries of War* etchings were among the first realistic pictorial records of the human disaster of military conflict. *Hanging Tree* depicts a mass execution of thieves in the presence of an army.

Under the crucifix tree, men roll dice on a drumhead for the belongings of the executed. (This may be an allusion to the soldiers who cast lots for the garments of the crucified Christ.) In the right foreground, a hooded priest consoles a bound man. Callot's *Miseries of War* etchings are among the first realistic pictorial records of the human disaster of armed conflict.

GEORGES DE LA TOUR France, unlike Flanders and the Dutch Republic, was a Catholic country, and religious themes, al-though not as common as in Italian Baroque art, occupied some 17th-century French painters. Among the artists well known for their religious imagery was GEORGES DE LA TOUR (1593–1652). His work, particularly his use of light, suggests a familiarity with Cara-vaggio's art. La Tour may have learned about Caravaggio from the Dutch school of Utrecht. Although La Tour used the devices of Caravaggio's northern followers, his effects are strikingly different from theirs. His *Adoration of the Shepherds* (FIG. **20-29**) makes use of the night setting favored by that school, much as van Honthorst

20-29 GEORGES DE LA TOUR, *Adoration of the Shepherds,* 1645–1650. Oil on canvas, 3′ 6″ × 4′ 6″. Louvre, Paris.

Without the aid of the title, Georges de la Tour's painting could be a genre piece instead of a biblical narrative. The French painter did not even paint halos around the heads of the holy figures.

20-30 Hyacinthe Rigaud, *Louis XIV*, 1701. Oil on canvas, 9′ 2″ × 6′ 3″. Louvre, Paris.

In this portrait set against a stately backdrop, Rigaud portrayed the 5′ 4″ Sun King wearing red high-heeled shoes and with his ermine-lined coronation robes thrown over his left shoulder.

1 ft.

portrayed it (FIG. 20-8). But here, the light, its source shaded by an old man's hand, falls upon a very different company in a very different mood. A group of humble men and women, coarsely clad, gather in prayerful vigil around a luminous baby Jesus. Without the aid of the title, this might be construed as a genre piece, a narrative of some event from peasant life. Nothing in the environment, placement, poses, dress, or attributes of the figures distinguishes them as the scriptural Virgin Mary, Joseph, Christ Child, or shepherds. The artist did not even paint halos. The light is not spiritual but material: It comes from a candle. La Tour's scientific scrutiny of the effects of light, as it throws precise shadows on surfaces that intercept it, nevertheless had religious intention and consequence. The light illuminates a group of ordinary people held in a mystic trance induced by their witnessing the miracle of the Incarnation. In this timeless tableau of simple people, La Tour eliminated the dogmatic significance and traditional iconography of the Incarnation. Still, these people reverently contemplate something they regard as holy. The devout of any religious persuasion can read this painting, regardless of their familiarity with the New Testament.

The supernatural calm that pervades *Adoration of the Shepherds* is characteristic of the mood of Georges de La Tour's art. He achieved this tone by eliminating motion and emotive gesture (only the light is dramatic), by suppressing surface detail, and by simplifying body volumes. These stylistic traits are among those associated with classical and Renaissance art. Thus, several apparently contradictory elements meet in the work of La Tour: classical composure, fervent spirituality, and genre realism.

LOUIS XIV The preeminent French art patron of the 17th century was King Louis XIV. Determined to consolidate and expand his power, Louis was a master of political strategy and propaganda. He established a carefully crafted and nuanced relationship with the nobility, granting them sufficient benefits to keep them pacified but simultaneously maintaining rigorous control to avoid insurrection or rebellion. He also ensured subservience by anchoring his rule in divine right (a belief in a king's absolute power as God's will), rendering Louis's authority incontestable. So convinced was Louis of his importance and centrality to the French kingdom that he eagerly adopted the title "le Roi Soleil" ("the Sun King"). Like the sun, Louis XIV was the center of the universe.

Louis's desire for control extended to all realms of French life, including art. The king and his principal adviser, Jean-Baptiste Colbert (1619–1683), strove to organize art and architecture in the service of the state. They understood well the power of art as propa-

ganda and the value of visual imagery for cultivating a public persona, and they spared no pains to raise great symbols and monuments to the king's absolute power. Louis and Colbert sought to regularize taste and establish the classical style as the preferred French manner. The founding of the Royal Academy of Painting and Sculpture in 1648 served to advance this goal.

Louis XIV maintained a workshop of artists, each with a specialization—faces, fabric, architecture, landscapes, armor, or fur. Thus, many of the king's portraits were a group effort, but the finest is the work of one artist. The portrait of Louis XIV (FIG. 20-30) by HYACINTHE RIGAUD (1659–1743) successfully conveys the image of an absolute monarch. The king, age 63 when Rigaud painted this work, looks out at the viewer with directness. He stands with his left hand on his hip and with his elegant ermine-lined fleur-de-lis coronation robes (compare FIG. 20-3) thrown over his shoulder, suggesting an air of haughtiness. Louis also draws his garment back to expose his legs. (The king was a ballet dancer in his youth and was proud of his well-toned legs.) The portrait's majesty derives in large part from the composition. The Sun King is the unmistakable focal point of the image, and Rigaud placed him so that he seems to look down on the viewer. Given that Louis XIV was very short in stature—only five feet, four inches, a fact that drove him to invent the red-heeled shoes he wears in the portrait—the artist apparently catered to his patron's wishes. The carefully detailed environment in which the king stands also contributes to the painting's stateliness and grandiosity. Indeed,

when the king was not present, Rigaud's portrait, which hung over the throne, served in his place, and courtiers were not permitted to turn their backs on the painting.

Architecture and Sculpture

THE LOUVRE The first great architectural project Louis XIV and his adviser Colbert undertook was the closing of the east side of the Louvre's Cour Carré (FIG. 18-12), left incomplete by Pierre Lescot in the 16th century. The king summoned Gianlorenzo Bernini, as the most renowned architect of his day, from Rome to submit plans, but Bernini envisioned an Italian palace on a monumental scale that would have involved the demolition of all previous work. His plan rejected, Bernini indignantly returned to Rome. Louis then turned to three French architects—CLAUDE PERRAULT (1613–1688), LOUIS LE VAU (1612–1670), and CHARLES LE BRUN (1619–1690)—for the Louvre's east facade (FIG. 20-31). The design is a brilliant synthesis of French and Italian classical elements, culminating in a new and definitive formula. The facade has a central and two corner projecting columnar pavilions. The central pavilion is in the form of a classical temple front. To either side is a giant colonnade of paired columns, resembling the columned flanks of a temple folded out like wings. The whole rests on a stately podium. The designers favored an even roofline, balustraded and broken only by the central pediment, over the traditional French pyramidal roof of the Louvre's west wing

20-31 CLAUDE PERRAULT, LOUIS LE VAU, and CHARLES LE BRUN, east facade of the Louvre, Paris, France, 1667–1670.

The design of the Louvre's east facade is a brilliant synthesis of French and Italian classical elements, including a central pavilion that resembles an ancient temple front with a pediment.

20-32 Aerial view (looking west) of the palace and gardens, Versailles, France, begun 1669.

Louis XIV ordered his architects to convert a royal hunting lodge at Versailles into a gigantic palace and park with a satellite city whose three radial avenues intersect in the king's bedroom.

(FIG. 18-12). The emphatically horizontal sweep of the 17th-century facade brushed aside all memory of Gothic verticality. Its stately proportions and monumentality were both an expression of the new official French taste and a symbol of centrally organized authority.

VERSAILLES PALACE Work on the Louvre had barely begun when Louis XIV decided to convert a royal hunting lodge at Versailles, a few miles outside Paris, into a great palace. He assembled a veritable army of architects, decorators, sculptors, painters, and landscape architects under the general management of Charles Le Brun. In their hands, the conversion of a simple lodge into the palace of Versailles (FIG. 20-32) became the greatest architectural project of the age—a defining statement of French Baroque style and an undeniable symbol of Louis XIV's power and ambition.

Planned on a gigantic scale, the project called not only for a large palace flanking a vast park but also for the construction of a satellite city to house court and government officials, military and guard detachments, courtiers, and servants (undoubtedly to keep them all under the king's close supervision). Le Brun laid out this town to the east of the palace along three radial avenues that converge on the palace structure. Their axes, in a symbolic assertion of the ruler's absolute power over his domains, intersected in the king's spacious bedroom, which served as an official audience chamber. The palace itself, more than a quarter mile long, is perpendicular to the dominant east-west axis that runs through the associated city and park.

Every detail of the extremely rich decoration of the palace's interior received careful attention. The architects and decorators designed everything from wall paintings to doorknobs in order to reinforce the splendor of Versailles and to exhibit the very finest sense of artisanship. Of the literally hundreds of rooms within the palace, the most famous is the Galerie des Glaces, or Hall of Mirrors (FIG. 20-33), designed by JULES HARDOUIN-MANSART (1646–1708) and Le Brun. This hall overlooks the park from the second floor and extends along most of the width of the central block. Although deprived of its original sumptuous furniture, which included gold and silver chairs and bejeweled trees, the Galerie des Glaces retains much of its splendor today. Hundreds of mirrors, set into the wall opposite the windows, alleviate the hall's tunnel-like quality and illusionistically extend the width of the room. The mirror, that ultimate source of illusion, was a favorite element of Baroque interior design. Here, it also enhanced the dazzling extravagance of the great festivals Louis XIV was so fond of hosting.

VERSAILLES PARK The enormous palace might appear unbearably ostentatious were it not for its extraordinary setting in the vast park that makes it almost an adjunct. From the Galerie des Glaces, the king and his guests could gaze out on a sweeping vista down the park's tree-lined central axis and across terraces, lawns, pools, and lakes to the horizon. The park of Versailles (FIG. 20-32), designed by ANDRÉ LE NÔTRE (1613–1700), must rank among the world's greatest artworks in both size and concept. Here, the French architect transformed an entire forest into a park. Although its geometric plan may appear stiff and formal, the park in fact offers an almost unlimited assortment of vistas, as Le Nôtre used not only the multiplicity of natural forms but also the terrain's slightly rolling contours with stunning effectiveness.

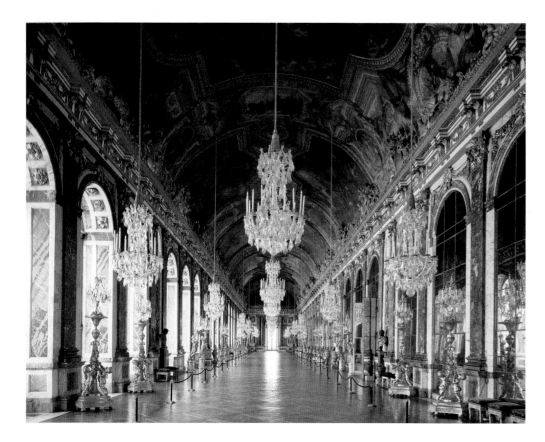

20-33 Jules Hardouin-Mansart and Charles Le Brun, Galerie des Glaces (Hall of Mirrors), palace of Louis XIV, Versailles, France, ca. 1680.

This hall overlooks the Versailles park from the second floor of Louis XIV's palace. Hundreds of mirrors illusionistically extend the room's width and once reflected gilded and jeweled furnishings.

The formal gardens near the palace provide a rational transition from the frozen architectural forms to the natural living ones. Here, the elegant shapes of trimmed shrubs and hedges define the tightly designed geometric units. Each unit is different from its neighbor and has a focal point in the form of a sculptured group, a pavilion, a reflecting pool, or perhaps a fountain. Farther away from the palace, the design loosens as trees, in shadowy masses, screen or frame views of open countryside. Le Nôtre carefully composed all vistas for maximum effect. Light and shadow, formal and informal, dense growth and open meadows—all play against one another in unending combinations and variations. No photograph or series of photographs can reveal the design's full richness. The park unfolds itself only to people who actually walk through it. In this respect, it is a temporal artwork. Its aspects change with the time of day, the seasons, and the relative position of the observer.

For the Grotto of Thetis above a dramatic waterfall in the gardens of Versailles, François Girardon (1628–1715) designed *Apollo Attended by the Nymphs* (FIG. 20-34). Both stately and graceful, the

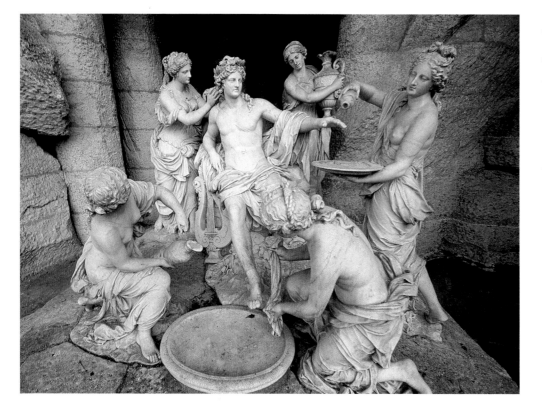

20-34 François Girardon and Thomas Regnaudin, *Apollo Attended by the Nymphs,* Grotto of Thetis, Versailles, France, ca. 1666–1672. Marble, life-size.

Girardon's study of ancient sculpture and Poussin's figure compositions influenced the design of this mythological group in a grotto above a dramatic waterfall in the gardens of Versailles.

France   **577**

20-35 JULES HARDOUIN-MANSART, Royal Chapel, with ceiling decorations by ANTOINE COYPEL, palace of Louis XIV, Versailles, France, 1698–1710.

Because the apse is as high as the nave, the central space of the Royal Chapel at Versailles has a curved Baroque quality. Louis XIV could reach the royal pew directly from his apartments.

20-36 JULES HARDOUIN-MANSART, Église du Dôme, Church of the Invalides, Paris, France, 1676–1706.

Hardouin-Mansart's church marries the Italian and French architectural styles. The grouping of the orders is similar to the Italian Baroque manner but without the dramatic play of curved surfaces.

nymphs display a compelling charm as they minister to the god Apollo at the end of the day. (The three nymphs in the background are the work of THOMAS REGNAUDIN, 1622–1706.) Girardon's close study of Greco-Roman sculpture heavily influenced his design of the figures, and Poussin's figure compositions (FIG. 20-24) inspired their arrangement. Since Apollo was often equated with the sun god, the group refers obliquely to Louis XIV as the "god of the sun." This was bound to assure the work's success at court. Girardon's classical style and mythological symbolism were well suited to France's glorification of royal majesty.

VERSAILLES CHAPEL In 1698, Jules Hardouin-Mansart received the commission to add a Royal Chapel to the Versailles palace complex. The chapel's interior (FIG. 20-35) is essentially rectangular, but because its apse is as high as the nave, the fluid central space takes on a curved Baroque quality. However, the light entering through the large clerestory windows lacks the directed dramatic effect of the Italian Baroque, instead illuminating the interior's precisely chiseled details brightly and evenly. Pier-supported arcades carry a majestic row of Corinthian columns that define the royal gallery. The royal pew occupies its rear, accessible directly from the king's apartments. Amid the restrained decoration, only the illusionistic ceiling paintings, added in 1708–1709 by ANTOINE COYPEL (1661–1722), suggest the drama and complexity of Italian Baroque art.

As a symbol of the power of absolutism, Versailles has no equal. It also expresses, in the most monumental terms of its age, the ratio-

nalistic creed—based on scientific advances, such as the physics of Sir Isaac Newton (1642–1727) and the mathematical philosophy of René Descartes (1596–1650)—that all knowledge must be systematic and all science must be the consequence of the intellect imposed on matter. The whole spectacular design of Versailles proudly proclaims the mastery of human intelligence (and the mastery of Louis XIV) over the disorderliness of nature.

ÉGLISE DU DÔME, PARIS Another of Hardouin-Mansart's masterworks, the Église du Dôme (FIG. 20-36), or Church of the Invalides, in Paris, also marries the Italian Baroque and French classical architectural styles. An intricately composed domed square of great scale, the church adjoins the veterans hospital Louis XIV established for the disabled soldiers of his many wars. Two firmly separated levels, the upper one pedimented, compose the frontispiece. The grouping of the orders and of the bays they frame is not unlike that in Italian Baroque architecture but without the dramatic play of curved surfaces characteristic of many 17th-century Italian churches (FIG. 19-9). The compact facade is low and narrow in relation to the

vast drum and dome, seeming to serve simply as a base for them. The overpowering dome, conspicuous on the Parisian skyline, is itself expressive of the Italian Baroque love for dramatic magnitude, as is the way that its designer aimed for theatrical effects of light and space. The dome consists of three shells, the lowest cut off so that a visitor to the interior looks up through it to the one above, which is filled with light from hidden windows in the third, outermost dome. Charles de La Fosse (1636–1716) painted the interior of the second dome in 1705 with an Italian-inspired representation of the heavens opening up to receive Saint Louis, patron of France.

ENGLAND

In England, in sharp distinction to France, the common law and the Parliament kept royal power in check. England also differed from France (and Europe in general) in other significant ways. Although an important part of English life, religion was not the contentious issue it was on the Continent. The religious affiliations of the English included Catholicism, Anglicanism, Protestantism, and Puritanism (the English version of Calvinism). In the economic realm, England was the one country (other than the Dutch Republic) to take advantage of the opportunities overseas trade offered. As an island country, Britain (which after 1603 consisted of England, Wales, and Scotland), like the Dutch Republic, possessed a large and powerful navy as well as excellent maritime capabilities.

Architecture

In the realm of art, the most important English achievements were in the field of architecture, much of it, as in France, incorporating classical elements.

INIGO JONES The most notable English architect of the first half of the 17th century was INIGO JONES (1573–1652), architect to Kings James I (r. 1603–1625) and Charles I (FIG. 20-5). Jones spent considerable time in Italy. He greatly admired the classical authority and restraint of Andrea Palladio's structures and studied with great care his treatise on architecture (see Chapter 17). Jones took many motifs from Palladio's villas and palaces, and he adopted Palladio's basic design principles for his own architecture. The nature of his achievement is evident in the buildings he designed for his royal patrons, among them the Banqueting House (FIG. 20-37) at Whitehall in London. For this structure, a symmetrical block of great clarity and dignity, Jones superimposed two orders, using columns in the center and pilasters near the ends. The balustraded roofline, uninterrupted in its horizontal sweep, predates the Louvre's facade (FIG. 20-31) by more than 40 years. Palladio would have recognized and approved all of the design elements, but the building as a whole is not a copy of his work. Although relying on the revered Italian's architectural vocabulary and syntax, Jones retained his own independence as a designer. For two centuries his influence was almost as authoritative in English architecture as that of Palladio.

20-37 INIGO JONES, Banqueting House at Whitehall, London, England, 1619–1622.

Jones was a great admirer of the classical architecture of Palladio, and he adopted motifs from the Italian Renaissance architect's villas and palaces for the buildings he designed for his royal patrons.

20-38 SIR CHRISTOPHER WREN, Saint Paul's Cathedral, London, England, 1675–1710.

Wren's cathedral replaced an old Gothic church. The facade design owes much to Palladio (FIG. 17-31) and Borromini (FIG. 19-12). The great dome recalls Saint Peter's in Rome (FIGS. 19-3 and 19-4).

CHRISTOPHER WREN London's majestic Saint Paul's Cathedral (FIG. 20-38) is the work of England's most renowned architect, CHRISTOPHER WREN (1632–1723). A mathematical genius and skilled engineer whose work won Isaac Newton's praise, Wren became professor of astronomy in London at age 25. Mathematics led to architecture, and Charles II (r. 1649–1685) asked Wren to prepare a plan for restoring the old Gothic church of Saint Paul. Wren proposed to remodel the building based on Roman structures. Within a few months, the Great Fire of London, which destroyed the old structure and many churches in the city in 1666, gave Wren his opportunity. Although Jones's work strongly influenced him, Wren also traveled in France, where the splendid palaces and state buildings being created in and around Paris at the time of the competition for the Louvre design must have impressed him. Wren also closely studied prints illustrating Baroque architecture in Italy. In Saint Paul's, he harmonized Palladian, French, and Italian Baroque features.

In view of its size, the cathedral was built with remarkable speed—in little more than 30 years—and Wren lived to see it com-

pleted. The building's form underwent constant refinement during construction, and Wren did not determine the final appearance of the towers until after 1700.

In the splendid skyline composition, two foreground towers act effectively as foils to the great dome. Wren must have known similar schemes that Italian architects devised for Saint Peter's (FIG. 19-4) in Rome to solve the problem of the relationship between the facade and dome. Certainly, the influence of Borromini (FIG. 19-12) appears in the upper levels and lanterns of the towers and that of Palladio (FIG. 17-31) in the lower levels. Further, the superposed paired columnar porticos recall the Louvre facade (FIG. 20-31). Wren's skillful eclecticism brought all these foreign features into a monumental unity.

Wren designed many other London churches after the Great Fire. Even today, his towers and domes punctuate the skyline of London. Saint Paul's dome is the tallest of all. Wren's legacy was significant and long-lasting, in both England and colonial America (see Chapter 21).

NORTHERN EUROPE, 1600 TO 1700

FLANDERS

▌ In the 17th century, Flanders remained Catholic and under Spanish control. Flemish Baroque art is more closely tied to the Baroque art of Italy than is the art of much of the rest of northern Europe.

▌ The leading Flemish painter of this era was Peter Paul Rubens, whose work and influence were international in scope. A diplomat as well as an artist, he counted kings and queens among his patrons and friends. His paintings of the career of Marie de' Medici exhibit Baroque splendor in color and ornament, and feature Rubens's characteristic robust and foreshortened figures in swirling motion.

Rubens, *Arrival of Marie de' Medici*, 1622–1625

DUTCH REPUBLIC

▌ The Dutch Republic received official recognition of its independence from Spain in the Treaty of Westphalia of 1648. Worldwide trade and banking brought prosperity to its predominantly Protestant citizenry, which largely rejected church art in favor of private commissions of portraits, genre scenes, landscapes, and still lifes.

▌ Frans Hals produced innovative portraits of middle-class patrons in which a lively informality replaced the formulaic patterns of traditional portraiture. Aelbert Cuyp and Jacob van Ruisdael specialized in landscapes depicting specific places, not idealized Renaissance settings. Pieter Claesz, Willem Kalf, and others painted vanitas still lifes featuring meticulous depictions of worldly goods and reminders of death.

Rembrandt, *Night Watch*, 1642

▌ Rembrandt van Rijn, the greatest Dutch artist of the age, treated a broad range of subjects, including religious themes and portraits. His oil paintings are notable for their dramatic impact and subtle gradations of light and shade as well as the artist's ability to convey human emotions. Rembrandt was also a master printmaker renowned for his etchings.

▌ Jan Vermeer specialized in painting Dutch families in serenely opulent homes. Vermeer's convincing representation of interior spaces depended in part on his employment of the camera obscura. He was also a master of light and color and understood that shadows are not colorless.

Vermeer, *The Letter*, 1666

FRANCE AND ENGLAND

▌ The major art patron in 17th-century France was the Sun King, the absolutist monarch Louis XIV, who expanded the Louvre and built a gigantic palace-and-garden complex at Versailles featuring sumptuous furnishings and sweeping vistas. Among the architects Louis employed were Charles Le Brun and Jules Hardouin-Mansart, who succeeded in marrying Italian Baroque and French classical styles.

▌ The leading French proponent of classical painting was Nicolas Poussin, who spent most of his life in Rome and championed the "grand manner" of painting, which called for heroic or divine subjects and classical compositions with figures often modeled on ancient statues.

Rigaud, *Louis XIV*, 1701

▌ Claude Lorrain, whose fame rivaled Poussin's, specialized in classical landscapes rendered in linear and atmospheric perspective. His compositions often incorporated ancient ruins.

▌ In 17th-century England, architecture was the most important art form. Two architects who achieved international fame were Inigo Jones and Christopher Wren, who harmonized the architectural principles of Andrea Palladio with the Italian Baroque and French classical styles.

Wren, Saint Paul's, London, 1675–1710

NOTES

Introduction

1. Quoted in George Heard Hamilton, *Painting and Sculpture in Europe, 1880–1940,* 6th ed. (New Haven, Conn.: Yale University Press, 1993), 345.

2. Quoted in *Josef Albers: Homage to the Square* (New York: Museum of Modern Art, 1964), n.p.

Chapter 15

1. Francisco de Hollanda, *De pintura antigua* (1548). Robert Klein and Henri Zerner, *Italian Art, 1500–1600: Sources and Documents* (Englewood Cliffs, N.J.: Prentice Hall, 1966), 33.

Chapter 16

1. Ghiberti, *I commentarii,* II. Quoted in Elizabeth Gilmore Holt, ed., *A Documentary History of Art, I: The Middle Ages and the Renaissance* (Princeton, N.J.: Princeton University Press, 1981), 157–158.

2. Giorgio Vasari, *Lives of the Painters, Sculptors, and Architects,* translated by Gaston du C. de Vere (New York: Knopf, 1996), 1: 304.

3. Ghiberti, *I commentarii,* II. Quoted in Holt, 161.

4. Quoted in H. W. Janson, *The Sculpture of Donatello* (Princeton, N.J.: Princeton University Press, 1965), 154.

5. Vasari, 1: 318.

Chapter 17

1. Plato, *Ion,* 534. Translated by Benjamin Jowett, *The Dialogues of Plato,* 4th ed., vol. 1 (Oxford: Clarendon, 1953), 107–108.

2. Leonardo to Ludovico Sforza, ca. 1480–1481. In Elizabeth Gilmore Holt, ed., *A Documentary History of Art* (Princeton, N.J.: Princeton University Press, 1981), I: 274–275.

3. Quoted in Anthony Blunt, *Artistic Theory in Italy, 1450–1600* (London: Oxford University Press, 1964), 34.

4. Quoted in James M. Saslow, *The Poetry of Michelangelo: An Annotated Translation* (New Haven, Conn.: Yale University Press, 1991), 407.

5. Giorgio Vasari, *Lives of the Painters, Sculptors, and Architects,* translated by Gaston du C. de Vere (New York: Knopf, 1996), 2: 736.

6. Quoted in A. Richard Turner, *Renaissance Florence: The Invention of a New Art* (New York: Abrams, 1997), 163.

7. Quoted in Bruce Boucher, *Andrea Palladio: The Architect in His Time* (New York: Abbeville, 1998), 229.

8. Quoted in Robert J. Clements, *Michelangelo's Theory of Art* (New York: New York University Press, 1961), 320.

Chapter 18

1. Translated by William Martin Conway, in Wolfgang Stechow, *Northern Renaissance Art, 1400–1600: Sources and Documents* (Evanston, Ill.: Northwestern University Press, 1989), 111.

2. Ibid., 118.

3. Translated by Erwin Panofsky, in Stechow, 123.

4. Giorgio Vasari, *Lives of the Painters, Sculptors, and Architects,* translated by Gaston du C. de Vere (New York: Knopf, 1996), 2: 863.

Chapter 19

1. Filippo Baldinucci, *Vita del Cavaliere Giovanni Lorenzo Bernini* (1681). Translated by Robert Enggass, in Robert Enggass and Jonathan Brown, *Italian and Spanish Art 1600–1750: Sources and Documents* (Evanston, Ill.: Northwestern University Press, 1992), 119.

2. Ibid., 116.

3. John Milton, *Il Penseroso* (1631, published 1645), 166.

Chapter 20

1. Translated by Kristin Lohse Belkin, *Rubens* (London: Phaidon, 1998), 47.

2. Jan Harmensz Krul, *Minne-beeldn* (Amsterdam 1634). Translated by Bob Haak, *The Golden Age: Dutch Painters of the Seventeenth Century* (New York: Abrams, 1984), 75.

3. Albert Blankert, *Johannes Vermeer van Delft 1632–1675* (Utrecht: Spectrum, 1975), 133, no. 51. Translated by Haak, 450.

GLOSSARY

a secco—Italian, "dried." See *fresco.*

Abstract Expressionism—The first major American avant-garde movement, Abstract Expressionism emerged in New York City in the 1940s. The artists produced abstract paintings that expressed their state of mind and that they hoped would strike emotional chords in viewers. The movement developed along two lines: *gestural abstraction* and *chromatic abstraction.*

action painting—Also called *gestural abstraction.* The kind of *Abstract Expressionism* practiced by Jackson Pollock, in which the emphasis was on the creation process, the artist's gesture in making art. Pollock poured liquid paint in linear webs on his canvases, which he laid out on the floor, thereby physically surrounding himself in the painting during its creation.

additive light—Natural light, or sunlight, the sum of all the wavelengths of the visible *spectrum.* See also *subtractive light.*

additive sculpture—A kind of sculpture *technique* in which materials (for example, clay) are built up or "added" to create form.

aerial perspective—See *perspective.*

airbrush—A tool that uses compressed air to spray paint onto a surface.

aisle—The portion of a *basilica* flanking the *nave* and separated from it by a row of *columns* or *piers.*

alchemy—The medieval study of seemingly magical changes, especially chemical changes.

altarpiece—A panel, painted or sculpted, situated above and behind an altar. See also *retable.*

Analytic Cubism—The first phase of *Cubism,* developed jointly by Pablo Picasso and Georges Braque, in which the artists analyzed form from every possible vantage point to combine the various views into one pictorial whole.

anamorphic image—A distorted image that must be viewed by some special means (such as a mirror) to be recognized.

ancien régime—French, "old order." The term used to describe the political, social, and religious order in France before the Revolution at the end of the 18th century.

apse—A recess, usually semicircular, in the wall of a building, commonly found at the east end of a church.

arcade—A series of *arches* supported by *piers* or *columns.*

Arcadian (adj.)—In Renaissance and later art, depictions of an idyllic place of rural peace and simplicity. Derived from Arcadia, an ancient district of the central Peloponnesos in southern Greece.

arch—A curved structural member that spans an opening and is generally composed of wedge-shaped blocks (*voussoirs*) that transmit the downward pressure laterally. See also *thrust.*

armature—The crossed, or diagonal, *arches* that form the skeletal framework of a *Gothic rib vault.* In sculpture, the framework for a clay form.

arriccio—In *fresco* painting, the first layer of rough lime plaster applied to the wall.

Art Deco—Descended from *Art Nouveau,* this movement of the 1920s and 1930s sought to upgrade industrial design as a "fine art" and to work new materials into decorative patterns that could be either machined or handcrafted. Characterized by streamlined, elongated, and symmetrical design.

Art Nouveau—French, "new art." A late-19th- and early-20th-century art movement whose proponents tried to synthesize all the arts in an effort to create art based on natural forms that could be mass produced by technologies of the industrial age. The movement had other names in other countries: Jugendstil in Austria and Germany, Modernismo in Spain, and Floreale in Italy.

assemblage—An artwork constructed from already existing objects.

atmospheric perspective—See *perspective.*

atrium—The central reception room of a Roman house that is partly open to the sky. Also the open, *colonnaded* court in front of and attached to a Christian *basilica.*

attribute—(n.) The distinctive identifying aspect of a person, for example, an object held, an associated animal, or a mark on the body. (v.) To make an *attribution.*

attribution—Assignment of a work to a maker or makers.

automatism—In painting, the process of yielding oneself to instinctive motions of the hands after establishing a set of conditions (such as size of paper or medium) within which a work is to be created.

avant-garde—French, "advance guard" (in a platoon). Late-19th- and 20th-century artists who emphasized innovation and challenged established convention in their work. Also used as an adjective.

baldacchino—A canopy on *columns,* frequently built over an altar. The term derives from *baldacco.*

baldacco—Italian, "silk from Baghdad." See *baldacchino.*

baldric—A sashlike belt worn over one shoulder and across the chest to support a sword.

Baroque—The traditional blanket designation for European art from 1600 to 1750. The stylistic term *Baroque,* which describes art that features dramatic theatricality and elaborate ornamentation in contrast to the simplicity and orderly rationality of Renaissance art, is most appropriately applied to Italian art of this period. The term derives from *barroco.*

barrel vault—See *vault.*

barroco—Portuguese, "irregularly shaped pearl." See *Baroque.*

base—In ancient Greek architecture, the molded projecting lowest part of *Ionic* and *Corinthian columns.* (*Doric* columns do not have bases.)

basilica—In Roman architecture, a public building for legal and other civic proceedings, rectangular in plan with an entrance usually on a long side. In Christian architecture, a church somewhat resembling the Roman basilica, usually entered from one end and with an *apse* at the other.

bas-relief—See *relief.*

battlement—A low parapet at the top of a circuit wall in a fortification.

Bauhaus—A school of architecture in Germany in the 1920s under the aegis of Walter Gropius, who emphasized the unity of art, architecture, and design.

bay—The space between two columns, or one unit in the *nave arcade* of a church; also, the passageway in an *arcuated* gate.

Beaux-Arts—An architectural style of the late 19th and early 20th centuries in France. Based on ideas taught at the École des Beaux-Arts in Paris, the Beaux-Arts style incorporated classical principles, such as symmetry in design, and included extensive exterior ornamentation.

belvedere—Italian, "beautiful view." A building or other structure with a view of a landscape or seascape.

benday dots—Named after the newspaper printer Benjamin Day, the benday dot system involves the modulation of colors through the placement and size of colored dots.

bent-axis plan—A *plan* that incorporates two or more angular changes of direction, characteristic of Sumerian architecture.

Biomorphic Surrealism—See *Surrealism.*

Book of Hours—A Christian religious book for private devotion containing prayers to be read at specified times of the day.

bottega—An artist's studio-shop.

breakfast piece—A *still life* that includes bread and fruit.

breviary—A Christian religious book of selected daily prayers and Psalms.

bucranium (pl. **bucrania**)—Latin, "bovine skull." A common motif in classical architectural ornament.

buon fresco—See *fresco.*

burgher—A middle-class citizen.

burin—A pointed tool used for *engraving* or *incising.*

buttress—An exterior masonry structure that opposes the lateral *thrust* of an *arch* or a *vault.* A pier buttress is a solid mass of masonry. A flying buttress consists typically of an inclined member carried on an arch or a series of arches and a solid buttress to which it transmits lateral *thrust.*

caduceus—In ancient Greek mythology, a magical rod entwined with serpents, the attribute of Hermes (Roman, Mercury), the messenger of the gods.

calotype—From the Greek *kalos,* "beautiful." A photographic process in which a positive image is made by shining light through a negative image onto a sheet of sensitized paper.

camera lucida—Latin, "lighted room." A device in which a small lens projects the image of an object downward onto a sheet of paper.

camera obscura—Latin, "dark room." An ancestor of the modern camera in which a tiny pinhole, acting as a lens, projects an image on a screen, the wall of a room, or the ground-glass wall of a box; used by artists in the 17th, 18th, and early 19th centuries as an aid in drawing from nature.

campanile—A bell tower of a church, usually, but not always, freestanding.

canon—A rule, for example, of proportion. The ancient Greeks considered beauty to be a matter of "correct" proportion and sought a canon of proportion, for the human figure and for buildings. The fifth-century BCE sculptor Polykleitos wrote the *Canon,* a treatise incorporating his formula for the perfectly proportioned statue.

capital—The uppermost member of a *column,* serving as a transition from the *shaft* to the *lintel.* In classical architecture, the form of the capital varies with the *order.*

capriccio—Italian, "originality." One of several terms used in Italian *Renaissance* literature to praise the originality and talent of artists.

cartoon—In painting, a full-size preliminary drawing from which a painting is made.

carving—A *technique* of sculpture in which the artist cuts away material (for example, from a stone block) in order to create a *statue* or a *relief.*

cassone (pl. **cassoni**)—A carved chest, often painted or gilded, popular in Renaissance Italy for the storing of household clothing.

casting—A sculptural *technique* in which the artist pours liquid metal, plaster, clay or another material into a *mold.* When the material dries, the sculptor removes the cast piece from the mold.

cathedral—A bishop's church. The word derives from *cathedra,* referring to the bishop's chair.

cella—The chamber at the center of an ancient temple; in a classical temple, the room (Greek, *naos*) in which the *cult statue* usually stood.

central plan—See *plan.*

chancel arch—The arch separating the chancel (the *apse* or *choir*) or the *transept* from the *nave* of a basilica or church.

chapter house—The meeting hall in a *monastery.*

chartreuse—A Carthusian *monastery.*

chasing—The engraving or embossing of metal.

château (pl. **châteaux**)—French, "castle." A luxurious country residence for French royalty, developed from medieval castles.

chiaroscuro—In drawing or painting, the treatment and use of light and dark, especially the gradations of light that produce the effect of *modeling.*

chiaroscuro woodcut—A *woodcut* technique using two blocks of wood instead of one. The printmaker carves and inks one block in the usual way in order to produce a traditional black-and-white print. Then the artist cuts a second block consisting of broad highlights that can be inked in gray or color and printed over the first block's impression.

choir—The space reserved for the clergy and singers in the church, usually east of the *transept* but, in some instances, extending into the *nave.*

chromatic abstraction—A kind of *Abstract Expressionism* that focuses on the emotional resonance of color, as exemplified by the work of Barnett Newman and Mark Rothko.

chronology—In art history, the dating of art objects and buildings.

city-state—An independent, self-governing city.

Classical—The art and culture of ancient Greece between 480 and 323 BCE. Lowercase *classical* refers more generally to Greco-Roman art and culture.

clerestory—The *fenestrated* part of a building that rises above the roofs of the other parts. The oldest known clerestories are Egyptian. In Roman *basilicas* and medieval churches, clerestories are the windows that form the *nave*'s uppermost level below the timber ceiling or the *vaults.*

cloison—French, "partition." A cell made of metal wire or a narrow metal strip soldered edge-up to a metal base to hold *enamel,* semiprecious stones, pieces of colored glass, or glass paste fired to resemble sparkling jewels.

cloisonné—A decorative metalwork technique employing *cloisons;* also, decorative brickwork in later Byzantine architecture.

coffer—A sunken panel, often ornamental, in a *vault* or a ceiling.

collage—A composition made by combining on a flat surface various materials, such as newspaper, wallpaper, printed text and illustrations, photographs, and cloth.

colonnade—A series or row of *columns,* usually spanned by *lintels.*

color—The value, or tonality, of a color is the degree of its lightness or darkness. The intensity, or saturation, of a color is its purity, its brightness or dullness. See also *primary colors, secondary colors,* and *complementary colors.*

color-field painting—A variant of *Post-Painterly Abstraction* in which artists sought to reduce painting to its physical essence by pouring diluted paint onto unprimed canvas and letting these pigments soak into the fabric, as exemplified by the work of Helen Frankenthaler and Morris Louis.

colorito—Italian, "colored" or "painted." A term used to describe the application of paint. Characteristic of the work of 16th-century Venetian artists who emphasized the application of paint as an important element of the creative process. Central Italian artists, in contrast, largely emphasized *disegno*—the careful design preparation based on preliminary drawing.

colossal order—An architectural design in which the *columns* or *pilasters* are two or more stories tall. Also called a giant order.

column—A vertical, weight-carrying architectural member, circular in cross-*section* and consisting of a *base* (sometimes omitted), a *shaft,* and a *capital.*

combines—The name American artist Robert Rauschenberg gave to his *assemblages* of painted passages and sculptural elements.

complementary colors—Those pairs of colors, such as red and green, that together embrace the entire spectrum. The complement of one of the three *primary colors* is a mixture of the other two.

compline—The last prayer of the day in a *Book of Hours.*

compose—See *composition.*

Composite capital—A capital combining *Ionic* volutes and *Corinthian* acanthus leaves, first used by the ancient Romans.

composition—The way in which an artist organizes *forms* in an artwork, either by placing shapes on a flat surface or arranging forms in space.

Conceptual Art—An American avant-garde art movement of the 1960s whose premise was that the "artfulness" of art lay in the artist's idea rather than its final expression.

condottiere (pl. **condottieri**)—An Italian mercenary general.

confraternity—In Late Antiquity, an association of Christian families pooling funds to purchase property for burial. In late medieval Europe, an organization founded by laypersons who dedicated themselves to strict religious observances.

connoisseur—An expert in *attributing* artworks to one artist rather than another. More generally, an expert on artistic *style.*

Constructivism—An early-20th-century Russian art movement formulated by Naum Gabo, who built up his sculptures piece by piece in space instead of carving or *modeling* them. In this way the sculptor worked with "volume of mass" and "volume of space" as different materials.

contour line—In art, a continuous line defining the outer shape of an object.

contrapposto—The disposition of the human figure in which one part is turned in opposition to another part (usually hips and legs one way, shoulders and chest another), creating a counterpositioning of the body about its central axis. Sometimes called "weight shift" because the weight of the body tends to be thrown to one foot, creating tension on one side and relaxation on the other.

corbel—A projecting wall member used as a support for some element in the superstructure. Also, courses of stone or brick in which each course projects beyond the one beneath it. Two such walls, meeting at the topmost course, create a corbeled *arch* or corbeled *vault.*

Corinthian capital—A more ornate form than *Doric* or *Ionic;* it consists of a double row of acanthus leaves from which tendrils and flowers grow, wrapped around a bell-shaped *echinus.* Although this *capital* form is often cited as the distinguishing feature of the Corinthian *order,* no such order exists, in strict terms, but only this style of capital used in the *Ionic* order.

cornice—The projecting, crowning member of the *entablature* framing the *pediment;* also, any crowning projection.

corona civica—Latin, "civic crown." A Roman honorary wreath worn on the head.

course—In masonry construction, a horizontal row of stone blocks.

cross-hatching—See *hatching.*

crossing square—The area in a church formed by the intersection (*crossing*) of a *nave* and a *transept* of equal width, often used as a standard *module* of interior proportion.

cruciform—Cross-shaped.

Cubism—An early-20th-century art movement that rejected naturalistic depictions, preferring compositions of shapes and forms abstracted from the conventionally perceived world. See also *Analytic Cubism* and *Synthetic Cubism.*

cupola—An exterior architectural feature composed of a *drum* with a shallow cap; a *dome.*

cutaway—An architectural drawing that combines an exterior view with an interior view of part of a building.

Dada—An early-20th-century art movement prompted by a revulsion against the horror of World War I. Dada embraced political anarchy, the irrational, and the intuitive. A disdain for convention, often enlivened by humor or whimsy, is characteristic of the art the Dadaists produced.

daguerreotype—A photograph made by an early method on a plate of chemically treated metal; developed by Louis J. M. Daguerre.

De Stijl—Dutch, "the style." An early-20th-century art movement (and magazine), founded by Piet Mondrian and Theo van Doesburg, whose members promoted utopian ideals and developed a simplified geometric style.

deconstruction—An analytical strategy developed in the late 20th century according to which all cultural "constructs" (art, architecture, literature) are "texts." People can read these texts in a variety of ways, but they cannot arrive at fixed or uniform meanings. Any interpretation can be valid, and readings differ from time to time, place to place, and person to person. For those employing this approach, deconstruction means destabilizing established meanings and interpretations while encouraging subjectivity and individual differences.

Deconstructivism—An architectural style using *deconstruction* as an analytical strategy. Deconstructivist architects attempt to disorient the observer by disrupting the conventional categories of architecture. The haphazard presentation of volumes, masses, planes, lighting, and so forth challenges the viewer's assumptions about form as it relates to function.

Der Blaue Reiter—German, "the blue rider." An early-20th-century German *Expressionist* art movement founded by Vassily Kandinsky and Franz Marc. The artists selected the whimsical name because of their mutual interest in the color blue and horses.

Die Brücke—German, "the bridge." An early-20th-century German *Expressionist* art movement under the leadership of Ernst Ludwig Kirchner. The group thought of itself as the bridge between the old age and the new.

diptych—A two-paneled painting or *altarpiece;* also, an ancient Roman, Early Christian, or Byzantine hinged writing tablet, often of ivory and carved on the external sides.

disegno—Italian, "drawing" and "design." *Renaissance* artists considered drawing to be the external physical manifestation (*disegno esterno*) of an internal intellectual idea of design (*disegno interno*).

divisionism—See *pointillism.*

documentary evidence—In art history, the examination of written sources in order to determine the date of an artwork, the circumstances of its creation, or the identity of the artist(s) who made it.

dome—A hemispherical *vault;* theoretically, an *arch* rotated on its vertical axis. In *Mycenaean* architecture, domes are beehive-shaped.

donor portrait—A portrait of the individual(s) who commissioned (donated) a religious work, for example, an *altarpiece,* as evidence of devotion.

Doric—One of the two systems (or *orders*) invented in ancient Greece for articulating the three units of the elevation of a *classical* building—the platform, the *colonnade,* and the superstructure (*entablature*). The Doric order is characterized by, among other features, *capitals* with funnel-shaped *echinuses, columns* without *bases,* and a *frieze* of *triglyphs* and *metopes.* See also *Ionic.*

dressed masonry—Stone blocks shaped to the exact dimensions required, with smooth faces for a perfect fit.

drum—One of the stacked cylindrical stones that form the *shaft* of a *column.* Also, the cylindrical wall that supports a *dome.*

drypoint—An *engraving* in which the design, instead of being cut into the plate with a *burin,* is scratched into the surface with a hard steel "pencil." See also *etching, intaglio.*

earthworks—See *Environmental Art.*

echinus—The convex element of a *capital* directly below the *abacus.*

écorché—The representation of a nude body as if without skin.

edition—A set of impressions taken from a single print surface.

elevation—In architecture, a head-on view of an external or internal wall, showing its features and often other elements that would be visible beyond or before the wall.

empiricism—The search for knowledge based on observation and direct experience.

enamel—A decorative coating, usually colored, fused onto the surface of metal, glass, or ceramics.

encaustic—A painting *technique* in which pigment is mixed with melted wax and applied to the surface while the mixture is hot.

engaged column—A half-round *column* attached to a wall. See also *pilaster.*

engraving—The process of *incising* a design in hard material, often a metal plate (usually copper); also, the *print* or impression made from such a plate.

Enlightenment—The Western philosophy based on empirical evidence that dominated the 18th century. The Enlightenment was a new way of thinking critically about the world and about humankind, independently of religion, myth, or tradition.

entablature—The part of a building above the *columns* and below the roof. The entablature has three parts: *architrave, frieze,* and *pediment.*

Environmental Art—An American art form that emerged in the 1960s. Often using the land itself as their material, Environmental artists construct monuments of great scale and minimal form. Permanent or impermanent, these works transform some section of the environment, calling attention both to the land itself and to the hand of the artist. Sometimes referred to as earthworks.

escutcheon—An emblem bearing a coat of arms.

etching—A kind of *engraving* in which the design is *incised* in a layer of wax or varnish on a metal plate. The parts of the plate left exposed are then etched (slightly eaten away) by the acid in which the plate is immersed after incising. See also *drypoint, intaglio.*

Eucharist—In Christianity, the partaking of the bread and wine, which believers hold to be either Christ himself or symbolic of him.

Events—See *Fluxus.*

exedra—Recessed area, usually semicircular.

exemplum virtutis—Latin, "example or model of virtue."

Expressionism (adj. **Expressionist**)—Twentieth-century art that is the result of the artist's unique inner or personal vision and that often has an emotional dimension. Expressionism contrasts with art focused on visually describing the empirical world.

facade—Usually, the front of a building; also, the other sides when they are emphasized architecturally.

fantasia—Italian, "imagination." One of several terms used in Italian *Renaissance* literature to praise the originality and talent of artists.

fasces—A bundle of rods with an ax attached, representing an emblem of authority in ancient Rome.

Fauves—French, "wild beasts." See *Fauvism.*

Fauvism—An early-20th-century art movement led by Henri Matisse. For the Fauves, color became the formal element most responsible for pictorial coherence and the primary conveyor of meaning.

Favrile—A type of leaded stained glass patented by Louis Comfort Tiffany in the late 19th century.

femmages—The name American artist Miriam Schapiro gave to her sewn *collages,* assembled from fabrics, quilts, buttons, sequins, lace trim, and rickrack collected at antique shows and fairs.

femme savante—French, "learned woman." The term used to describe the cultured hostesses of *Rococo* salons.

fenestrated—Having windows.

fête galante—French, "amorous festival." A type of *Rococo* painting depicting the outdoor amusements of French upper-class society.

feudalism—The medieval political, social, and economic system held together by the relationship between landholding *liege lords* and the *vassals* who were granted tenure of a portion of their land and in turn swore allegiance to the liege lord.

fin-de-siècle—French, "end of the century." A period in Western cultural history from the end of the 19th century until just before World War I, when decadence and indulgence masked anxiety about an uncertain future.

finial—A crowning ornament.

fleur-de-lis—A three-petaled iris flower; the royal flower of France.

Floreale—See *Art Nouveau.*

florin—The denomination of gold coin of Renaissance Florence that became an international currency for trade.

Fluxus—A group of American, European, and Japanese artists of the 1960s who created *Performance Art.* Their performances, or Events, often focused on single actions, such as turning a light on and off or watching falling snow, and were more theatrical than *Happenings.*

flying buttress—See *buttress.*

fons vitae—Latin, "fountain of life." A symbolic fountain of everlasting life.

foreshortening—The use of *perspective* to represent in art the apparent visual contraction of an object that extends back in space at an angle to the perpendicular plane of sight.

form—In art, an object's shape and structure, either in two dimensions (for example, a figure painted on a surface) or in three dimensions (such as a statue).

formal analysis—The visual analysis of artistic *form.*

formalism—Strict adherence to, or dependence on, stylized shapes and methods of composition. An emphasis on an artwork's visual elements rather than its subject.

freestanding sculpture—See *sculpture in the round.*

fresco—Painting on lime plaster, either dry (dry fresco, or fresco secco) or wet (true, or buon, fresco). In the latter method, the pigments are mixed with water and become chemically bound to the freshly laid lime plaster. Also, a painting executed in either method.

fresco secco—See *fresco.*

frieze—The part of the *entablature* between the *architrave* and the *cornice;* also, any sculptured or painted band in a building. See *register.*

frottage—A *technique* in which the artist rubs a crayon or another medium across a sheet of paper placed over a surface having a strong textural pattern.

Futurism—An early-20th-century Italian art movement that championed war as a cleansing agent and that celebrated the speed and dynamism of modern technology.

genre—A style or category of art; also, a kind of painting that realistically depicts scenes from everyday life.

German Expressionism—An early-20th-century regional Expressionist movement.

gesso—Plaster mixed with a binding material, used as the base coat for paintings on wood panels.

gestural abstraction—Also known as *action painting.* A kind of abstract painting in which the gesture, or act of painting, is seen as the subject of art. Its most renowned proponent was Jackson Pollock. See also *Abstract Expressionism.*

giant order—See *colossal order.*

giornata (pl. **giornate**)—Italian, "day." The section of plaster that a *fresco* painter expects to complete in one session.

glaze—A vitreous coating applied to pottery to seal and decorate the surface; it may be colored, transparent, or opaque, and glossy or *matte.* In oil painting, a thin, transparent, or semitransparent layer applied over a color to alter it slightly.

gold leaf—Gold beaten into tissue-paper-thin sheets that then can be applied to surfaces.

Gothic—Originally a derogatory term named after the Goths, used to describe the history, culture, and art of western Europe in the 12th to 14th centuries. Typically divided into periods designated Early (1140–1194), High (1194–1300), and Late (1300–1500).

Grand Manner portraiture—A type of 18th-century portrait painting designed to communicate a person's grace and class through certain standardized conventions, such as the large scale of the figure relative to the canvas, the controlled pose, the landscape setting, and the low horizon line.

Greek cross—A cross with four arms of equal length.

grisaille—A monochrome painting done mainly in neutral grays to simulate sculpture.

guild—An association of merchants, craftspersons, or scholars in medieval and Renaissance Europe.

halberd—A combination spear and battle-ax.

Happenings—A term coined by American artist Allan Kaprow in the 1960s to describe loosely structured performances, whose creators were trying to suggest the aesthetic and dynamic qualities of everyday life; as actions, rather than objects, Happenings incorporate the fourth dimension (time).

hard-edge painting—A variant of *Post-Painterly Abstraction* that rigidly excluded all reference to gesture and incorporated smooth knife-edge geometric forms to express the notion that painting should be reduced to its visual components.

hatching—A series of closely spaced drawn or *engraved* parallel lines. Cross-hatching employs sets of lines placed at right angles.

hierarchy of scale—An artistic convention in which greater size indicates greater importance.

high relief—See *relief.*

horizon line—See *perspective.*

hôtel—French, "town house."

hue—The name of a *color.* See also *primary colors, secondary colors,* and *complementary colors.*

humanism—In the *Renaissance,* an emphasis on education and on expanding knowledge (especially of *classical* antiquity), the exploration of individual potential and a desire to excel, and a commitment to civic responsibility and moral duty.

icon—A portrait or image; especially in Byzantine churches, a panel with a painting of sacred personages that are objects of veneration. In the visual arts, a painting, a piece of sculpture, or even a building regarded as an object of veneration.

iconoclasm—The destruction of religious or sacred images. In Byzantium, the period from 726 to 843 when there was an imperial ban on such images. The destroyers of images were known as iconoclasts. Those who opposed such a ban were known as iconophiles.

iconoclast—See *iconoclasm.*

iconography—Greek, the "writing of images." The term refers both to the content, or subject, of an artwork and to the study of content in art. It also includes the study of the symbolic, often religious, meaning of objects, persons, or events depicted in works of art.

illuminated manuscript—A luxurious handmade book with painted illustrations and decorations.

illusionism (adj. **illusionistic**)—The representation of the three-dimensional world on a two-dimensional surface in a manner that creates the illusion that the person, object, or place represented is three-dimensional. See also *perspective.*

impasto—A layer of thickly applied pigment.

Impressionism—A late-19th-century art movement that sought to capture a fleeting moment, thereby conveying the illusiveness and impermanence of images and conditions.

incise—To cut into a surface with a sharp instrument; also, a method of decoration, especially on metal and pottery.

incubus—A demon believed in medieval times to prey, often sexually, on sleeping women.

indulgence—A religious pardon for a sin committed.

ingegno—Italian, "innate talent." One of several terms used in Italian *Renaissance* literature to praise the originality and talent of artists.

installation—An artwork that creates an artistic environment in a room or gallery.

intaglio—A graphic technique in which the design is *incised,* or scratched, on a metal plate, either manually (*engraving, drypoint*) or chemically (*etching*). The incised lines of the design take the ink, making this the reverse of the *woodcut* technique.

intensity—See *color.*

internal evidence—In art history, the examination of what an artwork represents (people, clothing, hairstyles, and so on) in order to determine its date. Also, the examination of the *style* of an artwork to identify the artist who created it.

International Style—A *style* of 14th- and 15th-century painting begun by Simone Martini, who adapted the French *Gothic* manner to Sienese art fused with influences from Northern Europe. This style appealed to the aristocracy because of its brilliant color, lavish costumes, intricate ornamentation, and themes involving splendid processions of knights and ladies. Also, a style of 20th-century architecture associated with Le Corbusier, whose elegance of design came to influence the look of modern office buildings and skyscrapers.

intonaco—In *fresco* painting, the last layer of smooth lime plaster applied to the wall; the painting layer.

invenzione—Italian, "invention." One of several terms used in Italian *Renaissance* literature to praise the originality and talent of artists.

Ionic—One of the two systems (or *orders*) invented in ancient Greece for articulating the three units of the elevation of a *classical* building: the platform, the *colonnade,* and the superstructure (*entablature*). The Ionic order is characterized by, among other features, *volutes, capitals, columns* with *bases,* and an uninterrupted *frieze.*

Japonisme—The French fascination with all things Japanese. Japonisme emerged in the second half of the 19th century.

Jugendstil—See *Art Nouveau.*

keystone—See *voussoir.*

lancet—In *Gothic* architecture, a tall narrow window ending in a *pointed arch.*

landscape—A picture showing natural scenery, without narrative content.

Landschaft—German, "landscape."

lateral section—See *section.*

line—The extension of a point along a path, made concrete in art by drawing on or chiseling into a *plane.*

linear perspective—See *perspective.*

lintel—A horizontal *beam* used to span an opening.

lithograph—See *lithography.*

lithography—A printmaking technique in which the artist uses an oil-based crayon to draw directly on a stone plate and then wipes water onto the stone. When ink is rolled onto the plate, it adheres only to the drawing. The print produced by this method is a lithograph.

local color—An object's true color in white light.

loggia—A gallery with an open *arcade* or a *colonnade* on one or both sides.

longitudinal plan—See *plan.*

lost-wax (cire perdue) process—A bronze-casting method in which a figure is modeled in wax and covered with clay; the whole is fired, melting away the wax (French, cire perdue) and hardening the clay, which then becomes a mold for molten metal.

low relief—See *relief.*

machicolated gallery—A gallery in a defensive tower with holes in the floor to allow stones or hot liquids to be dumped on enemies below.

magus (pl. **magi**)—One of the three wise men from the East who presented gifts to the infant Jesus.

maniera—Italian, "style" or "manner." See *Mannerism.*

maniera greca—Italian, "Greek manner." The Italo-Byzantine painting style of the 13th century.

Mannerism—A style of later *Renaissance* art that emphasized "artifice," often involving contrived imagery not derived directly from nature. Such artworks showed a self-conscious stylization involving complexity, caprice, fantasy, and polish. Mannerist architecture tended to flout the classical rules of order, stability, and symmetry, sometimes to the point of parody.

Mara—A spirit in Northern European mythology that was thought to torment and suffocate sleepers.

martyrium—A shrine to a Christian martyr *saint.*

mass—The bulk, density, and weight of matter in *space.*

Mass—The Catholic and Orthodox ritual in which believers understand that Christ's redeeming sacrifice on the cross is repeated when the priest consecrates the bread and wine in the *Eucharist.*

matins—The dawn prayer in a *Book of Hours.*

matte—In painting, pottery, and photography, a dull finish.

maulstick—A stick used to steady the hand while painting.

medium (pl. **media**)—The material (for example, marble, bronze, clay, *fresco*) in which an artist works; also, in painting, the vehicle (usually liquid) that carries the pigment.

memento mori—Latin, "reminder of death." In painting, a reminder of human mortality, usually represented by a skull.

mendicants—In medieval Europe, friars belonging to the Franciscan and Dominican orders, who renounced all worldly goods, lived by contributions of laypersons (the word *mendicant* means "beggar"), and devoted themselves to preaching, teaching, and doing good works.

metamatics—The name Swiss artist Jean Tinguely gave to the motor-driven devices he constructed to produce instant abstract paintings.

miniatures—Small individual Indian paintings intended to be held in the hand and viewed by one or two individuals at one time.

Minimalism—A predominantly sculptural American trend of the 1960s characterized by works featuring a severe reduction of form, often to single, homogeneous units.

mobile—A kind of sculpture, invented by Alexander Calder, combining nonobjective organic forms and motion in balanced structures hanging from rods, wires, and colored, organically shaped plates.

modeling—The shaping or fashioning of three-dimensional forms in a soft material, such as clay; also, the gradations of light and shade reflected from the surfaces of matter in space, or the illusion of such gradations produced by alterations of value in a drawing, painting, or print.

modernism—A movement in Western art that developed in the second half of the 19th century and sought to capture the images and sensibilities of the age. Modernist art goes beyond simply dealing with the present and involves the artist's critical examination of the premises of art itself.

Modernismo—See *Art Nouveau.*

modernist formalism—See *formalism.*

module (adj. **modular**)—A basic unit of which the dimensions of the major parts of a work are multiples. The principle is used in sculpture and other art forms, but it is most often employed in architecture, where the module may be the dimensions of an important part of a building, such as the diameter of a *column.*

mold—A hollow form for *casting.*

monastery—A group of buildings in which monks live together, set apart from the secular community of a town.

monastic order—An organization of monks living according to the same rules, for example, the Benedictine, Franciscan, and Dominican orders.

monochrome (adj. **monochromatic**)—One color.

mosaic—Patterns or pictures made by embedding small pieces (*tesserae*) of stone or glass in cement on surfaces such as walls and floors; also, the technique of making such works.

mullion—A vertical member that divides a window or that separates one window from another.

mural—A wall painting.

mystery play—A dramatic enactment of the holy mysteries of the Christian faith performed at church portals and in city squares.

mystic marriage—A spiritual marriage of a woman with Christ.

Nabis—Hebrew, "prophet." A group of *Symbolist* painters influenced by Paul Gauguin.

naturalism—The style of painted or sculptured representation based on close observation of the natural world that was at the core of the *classical* tradition.

Naturalistic Surrealism—See *Surrealism.*

nave—The central area of an ancient Roman *basilica* or of a church, demarcated from *aisles* by *piers* or *columns.*

nave arcade—In *basilica* architecture, the series of *arches* supported by *piers* or *columns* separating the *nave* from the *aisles.*

Neoclassicism—A style of art and architecture that emerged in the late 18th century as part of a general revival of interest in *classical* cultures. Neoclassical artists adopted themes and styles from ancient Greece and Rome.

Neo-Expressionism—An art movement that emerged in the 1970s and that reflects artists' interest in the expressive capability of art, seen earlier in *German Expressionism* and *Abstract Expressionism.*

Neo-Gothic—The revival of the *Gothic* style in architecture, especially in the 19th century.

Neoplasticism—The Dutch artist Piet Mondrian's theory of "pure plastic art," an ideal balance between the universal and the individual using an abstract formal vocabulary.

Neue Sachlichkeit—German, "new objectivity." An art movement that grew directly out of the World War I experiences of a group of German artists who sought to show the horrors of the war and its effects.

oculus (pl. **oculi**)—Latin, "eye." The round central opening of a *dome.* Also, a small round window in a *Gothic cathedral.*

odalisque—A woman in a Turkish harem.

ogee arch—An *arch* composed of two double-curving lines meeting at a point.

ogive (adj. **ogival**)—The diagonal *rib* of a *Gothic vault;* a pointed, or Gothic, *arch.*

oil painting—A painting technique using oil-based pigments that rose to prominence in Northern Europe in the 15th century and is now the standard medium for painting on canvas.

optical mixture—The visual effect of juxtaposed *complementary colors.*

orbiculum—A disklike opening.

order—In *classical* architecture, a style represented by a characteristic design of the *columns* and *entablature.* See also *superimposed orders.*

Orphism—A form of *Cubism* developed by the French painter Robert Delaunay in which color plays an important role.

orrery—A mechanical model of the solar system demonstrating how the planets revolve around the sun.

orthogonal—A line imagined to be behind and perpendicular to the picture plane; the orthogonals in a painting appear to recede toward a vanishing point on the horizon.

palette knife—A flat tool used to scrape paint off the *palette.* Artists sometimes also use the palette knife in place of a brush to apply paint directly to the canvas.

papier collé—French, "stuck paper." See *collage.*

parallel hatching—See *hatching.*

parapet—A low, protective wall along the edge of a balcony, roof, or bastion.

parchment—Lambskin prepared as a surface for painting or writing.

pastel—A powdery paste of pigment and gum used for making crayons; also, the pastel crayons themselves.

patron—The person or entity that pays an artist to produce individual artworks or employs an artist on a continuing basis.

pediment—In *classical* architecture, the triangular space (gable) at the end of a building, formed by the ends of the sloping roof above the *colonnade;* also, an ornamental feature having this shape.

pendentive—A concave, triangular section of a hemisphere, four of which provide the transition from a square area to the circular base of a covering *dome.* Although pendentives appear to be hanging (pendant) from the dome, they in fact support it.

Performance Art—An American avant-garde art trend of the 1960s that made time an integral element of art. It produced works in which movements, gestures, and sounds of persons communicating with an audience replace physical objects. Documentary photographs are generally the only evidence remaining after these events. See also *Happenings.*

period style—See *style.*

personal style—See *style.*

personification—An abstract idea represented in bodily form.

perspective (adj. **perspectival**)—A method of presenting an illusion of the three-dimensional world on a two-dimensional surface. In linear perspective, the most common type, all parallel lines or surface edges converge on one, two, or three vanishing points located with reference to the eye level of the viewer (the horizon line of the picture), and associated objects are rendered smaller the farther from the viewer they are intended to seem. Atmospheric, or aerial, perspective creates the illusion of distance by the greater diminution of color intensity, the shift in color toward an almost neutral blue, and the blurring of contours as the intended distance between eye and object increases.

philosophe—French, "thinker, philosopher." The term applied to French intellectuals of the Enlightenment.

photomontage—A composition made by pasting together pictures or parts of pictures, especially photographs. See also *collage.*

Photorealism—See *Superrealism.*

physical evidence—In art history, the examination of the materials used to produce an artwork in order to determine its date.

piazza—Italian, "plaza."

pier—A vertical, freestanding masonry support.

Pietà—A painted or sculpted representation of the Virgin Mary mourning over the body of the dead Christ.

pilaster—A flat, rectangular, vertical member projecting from a wall of which it forms a part. It usually has a *base* and a *capital* and is often *fluted.*

pinnacle—In *Gothic* churches, a sharply pointed ornament capping the *piers* or flying *buttresses;* also used on church *facades.*

Pittura Metafisica—Italian, "metaphysical painting." An early-20th-century Italian art movement led by Giorgio de Chirico, whose work conveys an eerie mood and visionary quality.

pixels—Shortened form of "picture elements." The tiny boxes that make up digital images displayed on a computer monitor.

plan—The horizontal arrangement of the parts of a building or of the buildings and streets of a city or town, or a drawing or diagram showing such an arrangement. In an axial plan, the parts of a building are organized longitudinally, or along a given axis; in a central plan, the parts of the structure are of equal or almost equal dimensions around the center.

plane—A flat surface.

Plateresque—A style of Spanish architecture characterized by elaborate decoration based on *Gothic,* Italian *Renaissance,* and Islamic sources; derived from the Spanish word *platero,* meaning "silversmith."

platero—See *Plateresque.*

plein air—An approach to painting much popular among the *Impressionists,* in which an artist sketches outdoors to achieve a quick impression of light, air, and color. The artist then takes the sketches to the studio for reworking into more finished works of art.

poesia—A term describing "poetic" art, notably Venetian *Renaissance* painting, which emphasizes the lyrical and sensual.

pointed arch—A narrow *arch* of pointed profile, in contrast to a semicircular arch.

pointillism—A system of painting devised by the 19th-century French painter Georges Seurat. The artist separates color into its component parts and then applies the component colors to the canvas in tiny dots (points). The image becomes comprehensible only from a distance, when the viewer's eyes optically blend the pigment dots. Sometimes referred to as divisionism.

polyptych—An *altarpiece* composed of more than three sections.

Pop Art—A term coined by British art critic Lawrence Alloway to refer to art, first appearing in the 1950s, that incorporated elements from consumer culture, the mass media, and popular culture, such as images from motion pictures and advertising.

portico—A roofed *colonnade;* also an entrance porch.

positivism—A Western philosophical model that promoted science as the mind's highest achievement.

Post-Impressionism—The term used to describe the stylistically heterogeneous work of the group of late-19th-century painters in France, including van Gogh, Gauguin, Seurat, and Cézanne, who more systematically examined the properties and expressive qualities of line, pattern, form, and color than the Impressionists did.

postmodernism—A reaction against *modernist formalism,* seen as elitist. Far more encompassing and accepting than the more rigid confines of modernist practice, postmodernism offers something for everyone by accommodating a wide range of *styles,* subjects, and formats, from traditional easel painting to *installation* and from abstraction to *illusionistic* scenes. Postmodern art often includes irony or reveals a self-conscious awareness on the part of the artist of art-making processes or the workings of the art world.

Post-Painterly Abstraction—An American art movement that emerged in the 1960s and was characterized by a cool, detached rationality emphasizing tighter pictorial control. See also *colorfield painting* and *hard-edge painting.*

Poussiniste—A member of the French Royal Academy of Painting and Sculpture during the early 18th century who followed Nicolas Poussin in insisting that *form* was the most important element of painting. See also *Rubéniste.*

Precisionism—An American art movement of the 1920s and 1930s. The Precisionists concentrated on portraying man-made environments in a clear and concise manner to express the beauty of perfect and precise machine forms.

predella—The narrow ledge on which an *altarpiece* rests on an altar.

primary colors—Red, yellow, and blue—the *colors* from which all other colors may be derived.

primitivism—The incorporation in early-20th-century Western art of stylistic elements from the artifacts of Africa, Oceania, and the native peoples of the Americas.

print—An artwork on paper, usually produced in multiple impressions.

Productivism—An art movement that emerged in the Soviet Union after the Russian Revolution; its members believed that artists must direct art toward creating products for the new society.

proportion—The relationship in size of the parts of persons, buildings, or objects, often based on a *module.*

provenance—Origin or source; findspot.

psalter—A book containing the Psalms.

pulpit—A raised platform in a church on which a priest stands while leading the religious service.

punchwork—Tooled decorative work in *gold leaf.*

Purism—An early-20th-century art movement that embraced the "machine aesthetic" and sought purity of *form* in the clean functional lines of industrial machinery.

putto (pl. **putti**)—A cherubic young boy.

quadro riportato—A ceiling design in which painted scenes are arranged in panels that resemble framed pictures transferred to the surface of a shallow, curved *vault.*

quatrefoil—A shape or plan in which the parts assume the form of a cloverleaf.

quoins—The large, sometimes *rusticated,* usually slightly projecting stones that often form the corners of the exterior walls of masonry buildings.

Realism—A movement that emerged in mid-19th-century France. Realist artists represented the subject matter of everyday life (especially subjects that previously had been considered inappropriate for depiction) in a relatively naturalistic mode.

refectory—The dining hall of a Christian *monastery.*

regional style—See *style.*

Regionalism—A 20th-century American art movement that portrayed American rural life in a clearly readable, realist style. Major Regionalists include Grant Wood and Thomas Hart Benton.

register—One of a series of superimposed bands or *friezes* in a pictorial narrative, or the particular levels on which motifs are placed.

relief—In sculpture, figures projecting from a background of which they are part. The degree of relief is designated high, low (bas), or sunken. In the last, the artist cuts the design into the surface so that the highest projecting parts of the image are no higher than the surface itself. See also *repoussé.*

Renaissance—French, "rebirth." The term used to describe the history, culture, and art of 14th- through 16th-century western Europe during which artists consciously revived the *classical* style.

renovatio—Latin, "renewal." During the *Carolingian* period, Charlemagne sought to revive the culture of ancient Rome (renovatio imperi Romani).

retable—An architectural screen or wall above and behind an altar, usually containing painting, sculpture, carving, or other decorations. See also *altarpiece.*

revetment—In architecture, a wall covering or facing.

rib—A relatively slender, molded masonry *arch* that projects from a surface. In *Gothic* architecture, the ribs form the framework of the *vaulting.* A diagonal rib is one of the ribs that form the X of a *groin vault.* A transverse rib crosses the *nave* or *aisle* at a 90-degree angle.

rib vault—A *vault* in which the diagonal and transverse *ribs* compose a structural skeleton that partially supports the masonry *web* between them.

rocaille—See *Rococo.*

Rococo—A style, primarily of interior design, that appeared in France around 1700. Rococo interiors featured lavish decoration, including small sculptures, ornamental mirrors, easel paintings, *tapestries, reliefs,* wall paintings, and elegant furniture. The term Rococo derived from the French word *rocaille* ("pebble") and referred to the small stones and shells used to decorate grotto interiors.

Romanesque—"Roman-like." A term used to describe the history, culture, and art of medieval western Europe from ca. 1050 to ca. 1200.

Romanticism—A Western cultural phenomenon, beginning around 1750 and ending about 1850, that gave precedence to feeling and imagination over reason and thought. More narrowly, the art movement that flourished from about 1800 to 1840.

rose window—A circular *stained-glass* window.

rostrum—Speaker's platform.

rotunda—The circular area under a *dome;* also a domed round building.

roundel—See *tondo.*

Rubéniste—A member of the French Royal Academy of Painting and Sculpture during the early 18th century who followed Peter Paul Rubens in insisting that *color* was the most important element of painting. See also *Poussiniste.*

rusticate (n. **rustication**)—To give a rustic appearance by roughening the surfaces and beveling the edges of stone blocks to emphasize the joints between them. Rustication is a technique employed in ancient Roman architecture, and was also popular during the *Renaissance,* especially for stone *courses* at the ground-floor level.

sacra conversazione—Italian, "holy conversation." A style of *altarpiece* painting popular after the middle of the 15th century, in which *saints* from different epochs are joined in a unified space and seem to be conversing either with one another or with the audience.

sacra rappresentazione (pl. **sacre rappresentazioni**)—Italian, "holy representation." A more elaborate version of a *mystery play* performed for a lay audience by a *confraternity.*

saint—From the Latin word *sanctus,* meaning "made holy by God." Applied to persons who suffered and died for their Christian faith or who merited reverence for their Christian devotion while alive. In the Roman Catholic Church, a worthy deceased Catholic who is canonized by the pope.

Saint-Simonianism—An early-19th-century utopian movement that emphasized the education and enfranchisement of women.

sarcophagus (pl. **sarcophagi**)—Latin, "consumer of flesh." A coffin, usually of stone.

saturation—See *color.*

satyr—A Greek mythological follower of Dionysos having a man's upper body, a goat's hindquarters and horns, and a horse's ears and tail.

school—A chronological and stylistic classification of works of art with a stipulation of place.

scudi—Italian, "shields." A coin denomination in 17th-century Italy.

sculpture in the round—Freestanding figures, carved or modeled in three dimensions.

secondary colors—Orange, green, and purple, obtained by mixing pairs of *primary colors* (red, yellow, blue).

section—In architecture, a diagram or representation of a part of a structure or building along an imaginary plane that passes through it vertically. Drawings showing a theoretical slice across a structure's width are lateral sections. Those cutting through a building's length are longitudinal sections. See also *elevation* and *cutaway*.

sfumato—Italian, "smoky." A smokelike haziness that subtly softens outlines in painting; particularly applied to the paintings of Leonardo da Vinci and Correggio.

shaft—The tall, cylindrical part of a *column* between the *capital* and the *base*.

sibyl—A Greco-Roman mythological prophetess.

signoria—The governing body in the Republic of Florence.

silk-screen printing—An industrial printing *technique* that creates a sharp-edged image by pressing ink through a design on silk or a similar tightly woven porous fabric stretched tight on a frame.

silverpoint—A *stylus* made of silver, used in drawing in the 14th and 15th centuries because of the fine line it produced and the sharp point it maintained.

simultaneous contrasts—The phenomenon of juxtaposed colors affecting the eye's reception of each, as when a painter places dark green next to light green, making the former appear even darker and the latter even lighter. See also *successive contrasts*.

sinopia—A burnt-orange pigment used in *fresco* painting to transfer a *cartoon* to the *arriccio* before the artist paints the plaster.

site-specific art—Art created for a specific location. See also *Environmental Art*.

space—In art history, both the actual area an object occupies or a building encloses, and the *illusionistic* representation of space in painting and sculpture.

spectrum—The range or band of visible colors in natural light.

stained glass—In *Gothic* architecture, the colored glass used for windows.

stanza (pl. **stanze**)—Italian, "room."

statue—A three-dimensional sculpture.

stigmata—In Christian art, the wounds Christ received at his crucifixion that miraculously appear on the body of a *saint*.

still life—A picture depicting an arrangement of inanimate objects.

stretcher bar—One of a set of wooden bars used to stretch canvas to provide a taut surface for painting.

stringcourse—A raised horizontal *molding*, or band, in masonry. Its principal use is ornamental but it usually reflects interior structure.

style—A distinctive artistic manner. Period style is the characteristic style of a specific time. Regional style is the style of a particular geographical area. Personal style is an individual artist's unique manner.

stylistic evidence—In art history, the examination of the *style* of an artwork in order to determine its date or the identity of the artist.

stylobate—The uppermost course of the platform of a *classical* Greek temple, which supports the *columns*.

stylus—A needlelike tool used in *engraving* and *incising;* also, an ancient writing instrument used to inscribe clay or wax tablets.

subtractive light—The painter's light in art; the light reflected from pigments and objects. See also *additive light*.

subtractive sculpture—A kind of sculpture technique in which materials are taken away from the original mass; carving.

successive contrasts—The phenomenon of colored afterimages. When a person looks intently at a *color* (green, for example) and then shifts to a white area, the fatigued eye momentarily perceives the *complementary color* (red). See also *simultaneous contrasts*.

superimposed orders—*Orders* of architecture that are placed one above another in an *arcaded* or *colonnaded* building, usually in the following sequence: *Doric* (the first story), *Ionic,* and *Corinthian*. Superimposed orders are found in later Greek architecture and were used widely by Roman and *Renaissance* builders.

Superrealism—A *school* of painting and sculpture of the 1960s and 1970s that emphasized producing artworks based on scrupulous fidelity to optical fact. The Superrealist painters were also called Photorealists because many used photographs as sources for their imagery.

Suprematism—A type of art formulated by Kazimir Malevich to convey his belief that the supreme reality in the world is pure feeling, which attaches to no object and thus calls for new, nonobjective forms in art—shapes not related to objects in the visible world.

Surrealism—A successor to *Dada,* Surrealism incorporated the improvisational nature of its predecessor into its exploration of the ways to express in art the world of dreams and the unconscious. Biomorphic Surrealists, such as Joan Miró, produced largely abstract compositions. Naturalistic Surrealists, notably Salvador Dalí, presented recognizable scenes transformed into a dream or nightmare image.

symbol—An image that stands for another image or encapsulates an idea.

Symbolism—A late-19th-century movement based on the idea that the artist was not an imitator of nature but a creator who transformed the facts of nature into a symbol of the inner experience of that fact.

Synthetic Cubism—A later phase of *Cubism,* in which paintings and drawings were constructed from objects and shapes cut from paper or other materials to represent parts of a subject, in order to engage the viewer with pictorial issues, such as figuration, realism, and abstraction.

tapestry—A weaving technique in which the *weft* threads are packed densely over the *warp* threads so that the designs are woven directly into the fabric.

technique—The processes artists employ to create *form,* as well as the distinctive, personal ways in which they handle their materials and tools.

tempera—A *technique* of painting using pigment mixed with egg yolk, glue, or casein; also, the *medium* itself.

tenebrism—Painting in the "shadowy manner," using violent contrasts of light and dark, as in the work of Caravaggio. The term derives from *tenebroso*.

tenebroso—Italian, "shadowy." See *tenebrism*.

terracotta—Hard-baked clay, used for sculpture and as a building material. It may be *glazed* or painted.

tessera (pl. **tesserae**)—Greek, "cube." A tiny stone or piece of glass cut to the desired shape and size for use in forming a *mosaic*.

texture—The quality of a surface (rough, smooth, hard, soft, shiny, dull) as revealed by light. In represented texture, a painter depicts an object as having a certain texture even though the paint is the actual texture.

tholos (pl. **tholoi**)—A temple with a circular plan. Also, the burial chamber of a *tholos tomb*.

thrust—The outward force exerted by an *arch* or a *vault* that must be counterbalanced by a *buttress*.

tonality—See *color*.

tondo (pl. **tondi**)—A circular painting or *relief* sculpture.

tracery—Ornamental stonework for holding *stained glass* in place, characteristic of *Gothic* cathedrals. In plate tracery, the glass fills only the "punched holes" in the heavy ornamental stonework. In bar tracery, the stained-glass windows fill almost the entire opening, and the stonework is unobtrusive.

tramezzo—A screen placed across the *nave* of a church to separate the clergy from the lay audience.

transept—The part of a church with an axis that crosses the *nave* at a right angle.

transubstantiation—The transformation of the Eucharistic bread and wine into the body and blood of Christ.

trefoil—A cloverlike ornament or symbol with stylized leaves in groups of three.

triglyph—A triple projecting, grooved member of a *Doric frieze* that alternates with *metopes*.

triptych—A three-paneled painting, ivory plaque, or *altarpiece*. Also, a small, portable shrine with hinged wings used for private devotion.

triumphal arch—In Roman architecture, a freestanding *arch* commemorating an important event, such as a military victory or the opening of a new road.

trompe l'oeil—French, "fools the eye." A form of *illusionistic* painting that aims to deceive viewers into believing they are seeing real objects rather than a representation of those objects.

Tuscan column—The standard type of Etruscan *column*. It resembles ancient Greek *Doric* columns but is made of wood, is unfluted, and has a *base*. Also a popular motif in *Renaissance* and *Baroque* architecture.

tympanum (pl. **tympana**)—The space enclosed by a *lintel* and an *arch* over a doorway.

value—See *color*.

vanishing point—See *perspective*.

vanitas—Latin, "vanity." A term describing paintings (particularly 17th-century Dutch still lifes) that include references to death.

vault (adj. **vaulted**)—A masonry roof or ceiling constructed on the *arch* principle, or a concrete roof of the same shape. A barrel (or tunnel) vault, semicylindrical in cross-*section,* is in effect a deep arch or an uninterrupted series of arches, one behind the other, over an oblong space. A quadrant vault is a half-barrel vault. A groin (or cross) vault is formed at the point at which two barrel vaults intersect at right angles. In a ribbed vault, there is a framework of *ribs* or arches under the intersections of the vaulting sections. A sexpartite vault is one whose ribs divide the vault into six compartments. A fan vault is a vault characteristic of English *Perpendicular Gothic* architecture, in which radiating ribs form a fanlike pattern.

veduta (pl. **vedute**)—Italian, "scenic view."

vellum—Calfskin prepared as a surface for writing or painting.

vita—Italian, "life." Also, the title of a biography.

volume—The *space* that *mass* organizes, divides, or encloses.

volute—A spiral, scroll-like form characteristic of the ancient Greek *Ionic* and the Roman *Composite capital*.

voussoir—A wedge-shaped stone block used in the construction of a true *arch*. The central voussoir, which sets the arch, is called the keystone.

wainscoting—Paneling on the lower part of interior walls.

warp—The vertical threads of a loom or cloth.

weft—The horizontal threads of a loom or cloth.

weld—To join metal parts by heating, as in assembling the separate parts of a *statue* made by *casting*.

wet-plate photography—An early photographic process in which the photographic plate is exposed, developed, and fixed while wet.

woodcut—A wooden block on the surface of which those parts not intended to *print* are cut away to a slight depth, leaving the design raised; also, the printed impression made with such a block.

zoopraxiscope—A device invented by Eadweard Muybridge in the 19th century to project sequences of still photographic images; a predecessor of the modern motion-picture projector.

BIBLIOGRAPHY

This list of books is very selective but comprehensive enough to satisfy the reading interests of the beginning art history student and general reader. The resources listed range from works that are valuable primarily for their reproductions to those that are scholarly surveys of schools and periods or monographs on individual artists. The emphasis is on recent in-print books and on books likely to be found in college and municipal libraries. No entries for periodical articles appear, but the bibliography begins with a list of some of the major journals that publish art historical scholarship in English.

SELECTED PERIODICALS

African Arts
American Art
American Indian Art
American Journal of Archaeology
Antiquity
Archaeology
Archives of American Art
Archives of Asian Art
Ars Orientalis
Art Bulletin
Art History
Art in America
Art Journal
Artforum International
Burlington Magazine
Gesta
History of Photography
Journal of Roman Archaeology
Journal of the Society of Architectural Historians
Journal of the Warburg and Courtauld Institutes
Latin American Antiquity
Oxford Art Journal
Women's Art Journal

GENERAL STUDIES

Baxandall, Michael. *Patterns of Intention: On the Historical Explanation of Pictures.* New Haven, Conn.: Yale University Press, 1985.

Bindman, David, ed. *The Thames & Hudson Encyclopedia of British Art.* London: Thames & Hudson, 1988.

Boström, Antonia. *The Encyclopedia of Sculpture.* 3 vols. London: Routledge, 2003.

Broude, Norma, and Mary D. Garrard, eds. *The Expanding Discourse: Feminism and Art History.* New York: Harper Collins, 1992.

Bryson, Norman. *Vision and Painting: The Logic of the Gaze.* New Haven, Conn.: Yale University Press, 1983.

Bryson, Norman, Michael Ann Holly, and Keith Moxey. *Visual Theory: Painting and Interpretation.* New York: Cambridge University Press, 1991.

Büttner, Nils. *Landscape Painting: A History.* New York: Abbeville, 2006.

Chadwick, Whitney. *Women, Art, and Society.* 4th ed. New York: Thames & Hudson, 2007.

Cheetham, Mark A., Michael Ann Holly, and Keith Moxey, eds. *The Subjects of Art History: Historical Objects in Contemporary Perspective.* New York: Cambridge University Press, 1998.

Chilvers, Ian, and Harold Osborne, eds. *The Oxford Dictionary of Art.* 3d ed. New York: Oxford University Press, 2004.

Corbin, George A. *Native Arts of North America, Africa, and the South Pacific: An Introduction.* New York: Harper Collins, 1988.

Crouch, Dora P., and June G. Johnson. *Traditions in Architecture: Africa, America, Asia, and Oceania.* New York: Oxford University Press, 2000.

Curl, James Stevens. *Oxford Dictionary of Architecture and Landscape Architecture.* 2d ed. New York: Oxford University Press, 2006.

Encyclopedia of World Art. 17 vols. New York: McGraw-Hill, 1959–1987.

Fielding, Mantle. *Dictionary of American Painters, Sculptors, and Engravers.* 2d ed. Poughkeepsie, N.Y.: Apollo, 1986.

Fine, Sylvia Honig. *Women and Art: A History of Women Painters and Sculptors from the Renaissance to the 20th Century.* Rev. ed. Montclair, N.J.: Alanheld & Schram, 1978.

Fleming, John, Hugh Honour, and Nikolaus Pevsner. *The Penguin Dictionary of Architecture and Landscape Architecture.* 5th ed. New York: Penguin, 2000.

Frazier, Nancy. *The Penguin Concise Dictionary of Art History.* New York: Penguin, 2000.

Freedberg, David. *The Power of Images: Studies in the History and Theory of Response.* Chicago: University of Chicago Press, 1989.

Gaze, Delia., ed. *Dictionary of Women Artists.* 2 vols. London: Routledge, 1997.

Hall, James. *Illustrated Dictionary of Subjects and Symbols in Eastern and Western Art.* New York: Icon Editions, 1994.

Harris, Anne Sutherland, and Linda Nochlin. *Women Artists: 1550–1950.* Los Angeles: Los Angeles County Museum of Art; New York: Knopf, 1977.

Hauser, Arnold. *The Sociology of Art.* Chicago: University of Chicago Press, 1982.

Hults, Linda C. *The Print in the Western World: An Introductory History.* Madison: University of Wisconsin Press, 1996.

Kemp, Martin. *The Science of Art: Optical Themes in Western Art from Brunelleschi to Seurat.* New Haven, Conn.: Yale University Press, 1990.

Kostof, Spiro, and Gregory Castillo. *A History of Architecture: Settings and Rituals.* 2d ed. Oxford: Oxford University Press, 1995.

Kultermann, Udo. *The History of Art History.* New York: Abaris, 1993.

Lucie-Smith, Edward. *The Thames & Hudson Dictionary of Art Terms.* 2d ed. New York: Thames & Hudson, 2004.

Moffett, Marian, Michael Fazio, and Lawrence Wadehouse. *A World History of Architecture.* Boston: McGraw-Hill, 2004.

Murray, Peter, and Linda Murray. *A Dictionary of Art and Artists.* 7th ed. New York: Penguin, 1998.

Nelson, Robert S., and Richard Shiff, eds. *Critical Terms for Art History.* Chicago: University of Chicago Press, 1996.

Penny, Nicholas. *The Materials of Sculpture.* New Haven, Conn.: Yale University Press, 1993.

Pevsner, Nikolaus. *A History of Building Types.* London: Thames & Hudson, 1987. Reprint of 1979 ed.

———. *An Outline of European Architecture.* 8th ed. Baltimore: Penguin, 1974.

Pierce, James Smith. *From Abacus to Zeus: A Handbook of Art History.* 7th ed. Upper Saddle River, N.J.: Pearson Prentice Hall, 1998.

Placzek, Adolf K., ed. *Macmillan Encyclopedia of Architects.* 4 vols. New York: Macmillan, 1982.

Podro, Michael. *The Critical Historians of Art.* New Haven, Conn.: Yale University Press, 1982.

Pollock, Griselda. *Vision and Difference: Femininity, Feminism, and Histories of Art.* London: Routledge, 1988.

Preziosi, Donald, ed. *The Art of Art History: A Critical Anthology.* New York: Oxford University Press, 1998.

Read, Herbert. *The Thames & Hudson Dictionary of Art and Artists.* Rev. ed. New York: Thames & Hudson, 1994.

Reid, Jane D. *The Oxford Guide to Classical Mythology in the Arts 1300–1990s.* 2 vols. New York: Oxford University Press, 1993.

Roth, Leland M. *Understanding Architecture: Its Elements, History, and Meaning.* 2d ed. Boulder, Colo.: Westview, 2006.

Schama, Simon. *The Power of Art.* New York: Ecco, 2006.

Slatkin, Wendy. *Women Artists in History: From Antiquity to the 20th Century.* 4th ed. Upper Saddle River, N.J.: Prentice Hall, 2000.

Steer, John, and Antony White. *Atlas of Western Art History: Artists, Sites, and Monuments from Ancient Greece to the Modern Age.* New York: Facts on File, 1994.

Stratton, Arthur. *The Orders of Architecture: Greek, Roman, and Renaissance.* London: Studio, 1986.

Sutton, Ian. *Western Architecture: From Ancient Greece to the Present.* New York: Thames & Hudson, 1999.

Trachtenberg, Marvin, and Isabelle Hyman. *Architecture, from Prehistory to Post-Modernism.* 2d ed. Upper Saddle River, N.J.: Prentice Hall, 2003.

Turner, Jane, ed. *The Dictionary of Art.* 34 vols. New ed. New York: Oxford University Press, 2003.

Wittkower, Rudolf. *Sculpture Processes and Principles.* New York: Harper & Row, 1977.

Wren, Linnea H., and Janine M. Carter, eds. *Perspectives on Western Art: Source Documents and Readings from the Ancient Near East through the Middle Ages.* New York: Harper & Row, 1987.

Renaissance Art, General

Adams, Laurie Schneider. *Italian Renaissance Art.* Boulder, Colo.: Westview, 2001.

Andrés, Glenn M., John M. Hunisak, and Richard Turner. *The Art of Florence.* 2 vols. New York: Abbeville, 1988.

Campbell, Gordon. *Renaissance Art and Architecture.* New York: Oxford University Press, 2005.

Campbell, Lorne. *Renaissance Portraits: European Portrait-Painting in the Fourteenth, Fifteenth, and Sixteenth Centuries.* New Haven, Conn.: Yale University Press, 1990.

Cole, Bruce. *Italian Art, 1250–1550: The Relation of Renaissance Art to Life and Society.* New York: Harper & Row, 1987.

———. *The Renaissance Artist at Work: From Pisano to Titian.* New York: Harper Collins, 1983.

Frommel, Christoph Luitpold. *The Architecture of the Italian Renaissance.* London: Thames & Hudson, 2007.

Hall, Marcia B. *Color and Meaning: Practice and Theory in Renaissance Painting.* Cambridge: Cambridge University Press, 1992.

Hartt, Frederick, and David G. Wilkins. *History of Italian Renaissance Art.* 6th ed. Upper Saddle River, N.J.: Prentice Hall, 2006.

Haskell, Francis, and Nicholas Penny. *Taste and the Antique: The Lure of Classical Sculpture 1500–1900.* New Haven, Conn.: Yale University Press, 1981.

Kent, F. W., and Patricia Simons, eds. *Patronage, Art, and Society in Renaissance Italy.* Canberra: Humanities Research Centre and Clarendon Press, 1987.

Levey, Michael. *Florence: A Portrait.* Cambridge, Mass.: Harvard University Press, 1998.

Lubbock, Jules. *Storytelling in Christian Art from Giotto to Donatello.* New Haven, Conn.: Yale University Press, 2006.

Paoletti, John T., and Gary M. Radke. *Art, Power, and Patronage in Renaissance Italy.* Upper Saddle River, N.J.: Prentice Hall, 2005.

Pope-Hennessy, John. *Introduction to Italian Sculpture.* 3d ed. 3 vols. New York: Phaidon, 1986.

Richardson, Carol M., Kim W. Woods, and Michael W. Franklin. *Renaissance Art Reconsidered: An Anthology of Primary Sources.* Oxford: Blackwell, 2007.

Smith, Jeffrey Chipps. *The Northern Renaissance.* New York: Phaidon, 2004.

Snyder, James, Larry Silver, and Henry Luttikhuizen. *Northern Renaissance Art: Painting, Sculpture, the Graphic Arts from 1350 to 1575.* Upper Saddle River, N.J.: Prentice Hall, 2005.

Thomson, David. *Renaissance Architecture: Critics, Patrons, and Luxury.* Manchester: Manchester University Press, 1993.

Wittkower, Rudolf. *Architectural Principles in the Age of Humanism.* 4th ed. London: Academy, 1988.

Chapter 14: Italy, 1200 to 1400

Bomford, David. *Art in the Making: Italian Painting before 1400.* London: National Gallery, 1989.

Borsook, Eve, and Fiorelli Superbi Gioffredi. *Italian Altarpieces 1250–1550: Function and Design.* Oxford: Clarendon, 1994.

Cole, Bruce. *Sienese Painting: From Its Origins to the Fifteenth Century.* New York: Harper Collins, 1987.

Hills, Paul. *The Light of Early Italian Painting.* New Haven, Conn.: Yale University Press, 1987.

Maginnis, Hayden B. J. *Painting in the Age of Giotto: A Historical Reevaluation.* University Park: Pennsylvania State University Press, 1997.

———. *The World of the Early Sienese Painter.* University Park: Pennsylvania State University Press, 2001.

Meiss, Millard. *Painting in Florence and Siena after the Black Death.* Princeton, N.J.: Princeton University Press, 1976.

Moskowitz, Anita Fiderer. *Italian Gothic Sculpture, c. 1250–c. 1400.* Cambridge: Cambridge University Press, 2001.

Norman, Diana, ed. *Siena, Florence, and Padua: Art, Society, and Religion 1280–1400.* New Haven, Conn.: Yale University Press, 1995.

Pope-Hennessy, John. *Italian Gothic Sculpture.* 3d ed. Oxford: Phaidon, 1986.

Stubblebine, James H. *Duccio di Buoninsegna and His School.* Princeton, N.J.: Princeton University Press, 1979.

White, John. *Art and Architecture in Italy: 1250–1400.* 3d ed. New Haven, Conn.: Yale University Press, 1993.

———. *Duccio: Tuscan Art and the Medieval Workshop.* London: Thames & Hudson, 1979.

Chapter 15: Northern Europe, 1400 to 1500

Baxandall, Michael. *The Limewood Sculptors of Renaissance Germany.* New Haven, Conn.: Yale University Press, 1980.

Campbell, Lorne. *The Fifteenth-Century Netherlandish Schools.* London: National Gallery Publications, 1998.

Châtelet, Albert. *Early Dutch Painting.* New York: Konecky, 1988.

Friedlander, Max J. *Early Netherlandish Painting.* 14 vols. New York: Praeger/Phaidon, 1967–1976.

———. *From Van Eyck to Bruegel.* 3d ed. Ithaca, N.Y.: Cornell University Press, 1981.

Harbison, Craig. *The Mirror of the Artist: Northern Renaissance Art in Its Historical Context.* New York: Abrams, 1995.

Jacobs, Lynn F. *Early Netherlandish Carved Altarpieces, 1380–1550: Medieval Tastes and Mass Marketing.* Cambridge: Cambridge University Press, 1998.

Lane, Barbara G. *The Altar and the Altarpiece: Sacramental Themes in Early Netherlandish Painting.* New York: Harper & Row, 1984.

Meiss, Millard. *French Painting in the Time of Jean de Berry: The Limbourgs and Their Contemporaries.* New York: Braziller, 1974.

Müller, Theodor. *Sculpture in the Netherlands, Germany, France, and Spain: 1400–1500.* New Haven, Conn.: Yale University Press, 1986.

Pächt, Otto. *Early Netherlandish Painting from Rogier van der Wayden to Gerard David.* New York: Harvey Miller, 1997.

Panofsky, Erwin. *Early Netherlandish Painting: Its Origins and Character.* 2 vols. Cambridge, Mass.: Harvard University Press, 1966.

Parshall, Peter, and Rainer Schoch. *Origins of European Printmaking: Fifteenth-Century Woodcuts and Their Public.* New Haven, Conn.: Yale University Press, 2005.

Prevenier, Walter, and Wim Blockmans. *The Burgundian Netherlands.* Cambridge: Cambridge University Press, 1986.

Wolfthal, Diane. *The Beginnings of Netherlandish Canvas Painting, 1400–1530.* New York: Cambridge University Press, 1989.

Chapter 16: Italy, 1400 to 1500

Ames-Lewis, Francis. *Drawing in Early Renaissance Italy.* New Haven, Conn.: Yale University Press, 1981.

Baxandall, Michael. *Painting and Experience in Fifteenth-Century Italy: A Primer in the Social History of Pictorial Style.* 2d ed. New York: Oxford University Press, 1988.

Bober, Phyllis Pray, and Ruth Rubinstein. *Renaissance Artists and Antique Sculpture: A Handbook of Sources.* Oxford: Oxford University Press, 1986.

Borsook, Eve. *The Mural Painters of Tuscany.* New York: Oxford University Press, 1981.

Cole, Alison. *Virtue and Magnificence: Art of the Italian Renaissance Courts.* New York: Abrams, 1995.

Cole, Bruce. *Masaccio and the Art of Early Renaissance Florence.* Bloomington: Indiana University Press, 1980.

Dempsey, Charles. *The Portrayal of Love: Botticelli's* Primavera *and Humanist Culture at the Time of Lorenzo the Magnificent.* Princeton, N.J.: Princeton University Press, 1992.

Edgerton, Samuel Y., Jr. *The Heritage of Giotto's Geometry: Art and Science on the Eve of the Scientific Revolution.* Ithaca, N.Y.: Cornell University Press, 1991.

———. *The Renaissance Rediscovery of Linear Perspective.* New York: Harper & Row, 1976.

Gilbert, Creighton, ed. *Italian Art 1400–1500: Sources and Documents.* Evanston, Ill.: Northwestern University Press, 1992.

Goldthwaite, Richard A. *The Building of Renaissance Florence: An Economic and Social History.* Baltimore: Johns Hopkins University Press, 1980.

Heydenreich, Ludwig H. *Architecture in Italy, 1400–1500.* 2d ed. New Haven, Conn.: Yale University Press, 1996.

Hollingsworth, Mary. *Patronage in Renaissance Italy: From 1400 to the Early Sixteenth Century.* Baltimore: Johns Hopkins University Press, 1994.

Kemp, Martin. *Behind the Picture: Art and Evidence in the Italian Renaissance.* New Haven, Conn.: Yale University Press, 1997.

Kempers, Bram. *Painting, Power, and Patronage: The Rise of the Professional Artist in the Italian Renaissance.* London: Penguin, 1992.

Lieberman, Ralph. *Renaissance Architecture in Venice.* New York: Abbeville, 1982.

McAndrew, John. *Venetian Architecture of the Early Renaissance.* Cambridge, Mass.: MIT Press, 1980.

Murray, Peter. *Renaissance Architecture.* New York: Electa/Rizzoli, 1985.

Olson, Roberta J. M. *Italian Renaissance Sculpture.* London: Thames & Hudson, 1992.

Osborne, June. *Urbino: The Story of a Renaissance City.* Chicago: University of Chicago Press, 2003.

Seymour, Charles. *Sculpture in Italy: 1400–1500.* New Haven, Conn.: Yale University Press, 1992.

Turner, A. Richard. *Renaissance Florence: The Invention of a New Art.* New York: Abrams, 1997.

Wackernagel, Martin. *The World of the Florentine Renaissance Artist: Projects and Patrons, Workshops and Art Market.* Princeton, N.J.: Princeton University Press, 1981.

Welch, Evelyn. *Art and Society in Italy 1350–1500.* Oxford: Oxford University Press, 1997.

White, John. *The Birth and Rebirth of Pictorial Space.* 3d ed. Boston: Faber & Faber, 1987.

CHAPTER 17:
ITALY, 1500 TO 1600

Blunt, Anthony. *Artistic Theory in Italy, 1450–1600.* London: Oxford University Press, 1975.

Brown, David Alan, and Sylvia Ferino-Pagden. *Bellini, Giorgione, Titian, and the Renaissance of Venetian Painting.* New Haven, Conn.: Yale University Press, 2006.

Brown, Patricia Fortini. *Art and Life in Renaissance Venice.* New York: Abrams, 1997.

Franklin, David. *Painting in Renaissance Florence, 1500–1550.* New Haven, Conn.: Yale University Press, 2001.

Freedberg, Sydney J. *Painting in Italy: 1500–1600.* 3d ed. New Haven, Conn.: Yale University Press, 1993.

Goffen, Rona. *Piety and Patronage in Renaissance Venice: Bellini, Titian, and the Franciscans.* New Haven, Conn.: Yale University Press, 1986.

———. *Renaissance Rivals: Michelangelo, Leonardo, Raphael, Titian.* New Haven, Conn.: Yale University Press, 2002.

Hall, Marcia B. *After Raphael: Painting in Central Italy in the Sixteenth Century.* Cambridge: Cambridge University Press, 1999.

———, ed. *Rome.* Artistic Centers of the Italian Renaissance. New York: Cambridge University Press, 2005.

Holt, Elizabeth Gilmore, ed. *A Documentary History of Art. Vol. 2, Michelangelo and the Mannerists.* Rev. ed. Princeton, N.J.: Princeton University Press, 1982.

Humfry, Peter. *Painting in Renaissance Venice.* New Haven, Conn.: Yale University Press, 1995.

Huse, Norbert, and Wolfgang Wolters. *The Art of Renaissance Venice: Architecture, Sculpture, and Painting.* Chicago: University of Chicago Press, 1990.

Levey, Michael. *High Renaissance.* New York: Viking Penguin, 1978.

Lotz, Wolfgang. *Architecture in Italy, 1500–1600.* 2d ed. New Haven, Conn.: Yale University Press, 1995.

Partridge, Loren. *The Art of Renaissance Rome.* New York: Abrams, 1996.

Pietrangeli, Carlo, André Chastel, John Shearman, John O'Malley, S.J., Pierluigi de Vecchi, Michael Hirst, Fabrizio Mancinelli, Gianluigi Colalucci, and Franco Bernbei. *The Sistine Chapel: The Art, the History, and the Restoration.* New York: Harmony, 1986.

Pope-Hennessy, John. *Italian High Renaissance and Baroque Sculpture.* 3d ed. 3 vols. Oxford: Phaidon, 1986.

Rosand, David. *Painting in Cinquecento Venice: Titian, Veronese, Tintoretto.* New Haven, Conn.: Yale University Press, 1982.

Shearman, John K. G. *Mannerism.* Baltimore: Penguin, 1978.

———. *Only Connect . . . Art and the Spectator in the Italian Renaissance.* Princeton, N.J.: Princeton University Press, 1990.

Summers, David. *Michelangelo and the Language of Art.* Princeton, N.J.: Princeton University Press, 1981.

Wilde, Johannes. *Venetian Art from Bellini to Titian.* Oxford: Clarendon, 1981.

CHAPTER 18:
NORTHERN EUROPE AND SPAIN, 1500 TO 1600

Blunt, Anthony. *Art and Architecture in France, 1500–1700.* Rev. ed. New Haven, Conn.: Yale University Press, 1999.

Farago, Claire, ed. *Reframing the Renaissance: Visual Culture in Europe and Latin America, 1450–1650.* New Haven, Conn.: Yale University Press, 1995.

Gibson, W. S. *"Mirror of the Earth": The World Landscape in Sixteenth-Century Flemish Painting.* Princeton, N.J.: Princeton University Press, 1989.

Harbison, Craig. *The Mirror of the Artist: Northern Renaissance Art in Its Historical Context.* New York: Abrams, 1995.

Koerner, Joseph Leo. *The Reformation of the Image.* Chicago: University of Chicago Press, 2004.

Landau, David, and Peter Parshall. *The Renaissance Print: 1470–1550.* New Haven, Conn.: Yale University Press, 1994.

Smith, Jeffrey C. *German Sculpture of the Later Renaissance, c. 1520–1580: Art in an Age of Uncertainty.* Princeton, N.J.: Princeton University Press, 1993.

Stechow, Wolfgang. *Northern Renaissance Art, 1400–1600: Sources and Documents.* Evanston, Ill.: Northwestern University Press, 1989.

Zerner, Henri. *Renaissance Art in France: The Invention of Classicism.* Paris: Flammarion, 2003.

BAROQUE ART, GENERAL

Blunt, Anthony, ed. *Baroque and Rococo: Architecture and Decoration.* Cambridge: Harper & Row, 1982.

Harris, Ann Sutherland. *Seventeenth-Century Art & Architecture.* Upper Saddle River, N.J.: Prentice Hall, 2005.

Harrison, Charles, Paul Wood, and Jason Gaiger, eds. *Art in Theory, 1648–1815: An Anthology of Changing Ideas.* Oxford: Blackwell, 2000.

Held, Julius, and Donald Posner. *17th- and 18th-Century Art: Baroque Painting, Sculpture, Architecture.* New York: Abrams, 1971.

Minor, Vernon Hyde. *Baroque & Rococo: Art & Culture.* New York, Abrams, 1999.

Norberg-Schulz, Christian. *Baroque Architecture.* New York: Rizzoli, 1986.

———. *Late Baroque and Rococo Architecture.* New York: Electa/Rizzoli, 1985.

Toman, Rolf. *Baroque: Architecture, Sculpture, Painting.* Cologne: Könemann, 1998.

CHAPTER 19:
ITALY AND SPAIN, 1600 TO 1700

Brown, Jonathan. *The Golden Age of Painting in Spain.* New Haven, Conn.: Yale University Press, 1991.

———. *Velázquez: Painter and Courtier.* New Haven, Conn.: Yale University Press, 1988.

Enggass, Robert, and Jonathan Brown. *Italy and Spain, 1600–1750: Sources and Documents.* Upper Saddle River, N.J.: Prentice Hall, 1970.

Freedberg, Sydney J. *Circa 1600: A Revolution of Style in Italian Painting.* Cambridge, Mass.: Harvard University Press, 1983.

Haskell, Francis. *Patrons and Painters: A Study in the Relations between Italian Art and Society in the Age of the Baroque.* Rev. ed. New Haven, Conn.: Yale University Press, 1980.

Krautheimer, Richard. *The Rome of Alexander VII, 1655–1677.* Princeton, N.J.: Princeton University Press, 1985.

Lagerlöf, Margaretha R. *Ideal Landscape: Annibale Carracci, Nicolas Poussin, and Claude Lorrain.* New Haven, Conn.: Yale University Press, 1990.

Montagu, Jennifer. *Roman Baroque Sculpture: The Industry of Art.* New Haven, Conn.: Yale University Press, 1989.

Puglisi, Catherine. *Caravaggio.* London: Phaidon, 2000.

Varriano, John. *Italian Baroque and Rococo Architecture.* New York: Oxford University Press, 1986.

Wittkower, Rudolf. *Art and Architecture in Italy 1600–1750.* 6th ed. 3 vols. Revised by Joseph Connors and Jennifer Montagu. New Haven, Conn.: Yale University Press, 1999.

CHAPTER 20:
NORTHERN EUROPE, 1600 TO 1700

Alpers, Svetlana. *The Art of Describing: Dutch Art in the Seventeenth Century.* Chicago: University of Chicago Press, 1984.

———. *Rembrandt's Enterprise: The Studio and the Market.* Chicago: University of Chicago Press, 1988.

Belkin, Kristin Lohse. *Rubens.* London: Phaidon, 1998.

Blunt, Anthony. *Art and Architecture in France, 1500–1700.* Rev. ed. New Haven, Conn.: Yale University Press, 1999.

Brown, Christopher. *Scenes of Everyday Life: Dutch Genre Painting of the Seventeenth Century.* London: Faber & Faber, 1984.

Bryson, Norman. *Word and Image: French Painting of the Ancien Régime.* Cambridge: Cambridge University Press, 1981.

Chastel, André. *French Art: The Ancien Régime, 1620–1775.* New York: Flammarion, 1996.

Franits, Wayne. *Looking at Seventeenth-Century Dutch Art: Realism Reconsidered.* Cambridge: Cambridge University Press, 1997.

Haak, Bob. *The Golden Age: Dutch Painters of the Seventeenth Century.* New York: Abrams, 1984.

Mérot, Alain. *French Painting in the Seventeenth Century.* New Haven, Conn.: Yale University Press, 1995.

Muller, Sheila D., ed. *Dutch Art: An Encyclopedia.* New York: Garland, 1997.

North, Michael. *Art and Commerce in the Dutch Golden Age.* New Haven, Conn.: Yale University Press, 1997.

Rosenberg, Jakob, Seymour Slive, and E. H. ter Kuile. *Dutch Art and Architecture, 1600–1800.* New Haven, Conn.: Yale University Press, 1979.

Schama, Simon. *The Embarrassment of Riches: An Interpretation of Dutch Culture in the Golden Age.* Berkeley: University of California Press, 1988.

Stechow, Wolfgang. *Dutch Landscape Painting of the 17th Century.* 3d ed. Oxford: Phaidon, 1981.

Vlieghe, Hans. *Flemish Art and Architecture, 1585–1700.* New Haven, Conn.: Yale University Press, 1998.

Westermann, Mariët. *Rembrandt.* London: Phaidon, 2000.

———. *A Worldly Art: The Dutch Republic 1585–1718.* New Haven, Conn.: Yale University Press, 1996.

CREDITS

*The author and publisher are grateful to the proprietors and custodians of various works of art
for photographs of these works and permission to reproduce them in this book.
Sources not included in the captions are listed here.*

INDEX

Boldface names refer to artists. Page numbers in italics refer to illustrations.

THE HISTORY OF WESTERN ART . . . IN FOUR EASY-TO-CARRY PAPERBACKS.

Gardner's Art through the Ages: The Western Perspective is one of the most widely read introductions to the history of Western art in the English language. In this new *Backback Edition,* master teacher and prizewinning author Fred S. Kleiner presents a panoramic vision of Western art in a set of four easy-to-use volumes. They're more convenient for you to study from and easier to carry so you can bring just what you need to class. The *Backback Edition* includes:

- Book A: Antiquity (Chapters 1–7)
- Book B: The Middle Ages (Chapters 8–14)
- Book C: Renaissance and Baroque (Chapters 14–20)
- Book D: Modern Europe and America (Chapters 21–25)

Gardner's Art through the Ages: The Western Perspective also contains many innovative features to help you do your best in this course, including unique, new "scales" that enable you to visualize whether an image shown is a gigantic fresco or a miniature figurine.

ACCESS TO ArtStudy Online WITH EVERY NEW BACKPACK EDITION:

- **Digital flash cards** of the book's artwork—your essential study tool!
- **Google™ Map coordinates** that guide you to the famous art capitals and monuments around the world
- **Interactive maps** that help you connect the artworks to their locations
- **Compare/contrast activities** that deepen your understanding of concepts
- **Video clips** of selected monuments
- **Museum guide** with links to museum sites

WADSWORTH
CENGAGE Learning™

To learn more about Wadsworth, visit **www.cengage.com/wadsworth**

Purchase any of our products at your local college store or at our preferred online store **www.ichapters.com**

ISBN-13: 978-0-495-79456-1
ISBN-10: 0-495-79456-2

90000

9 780495 794561